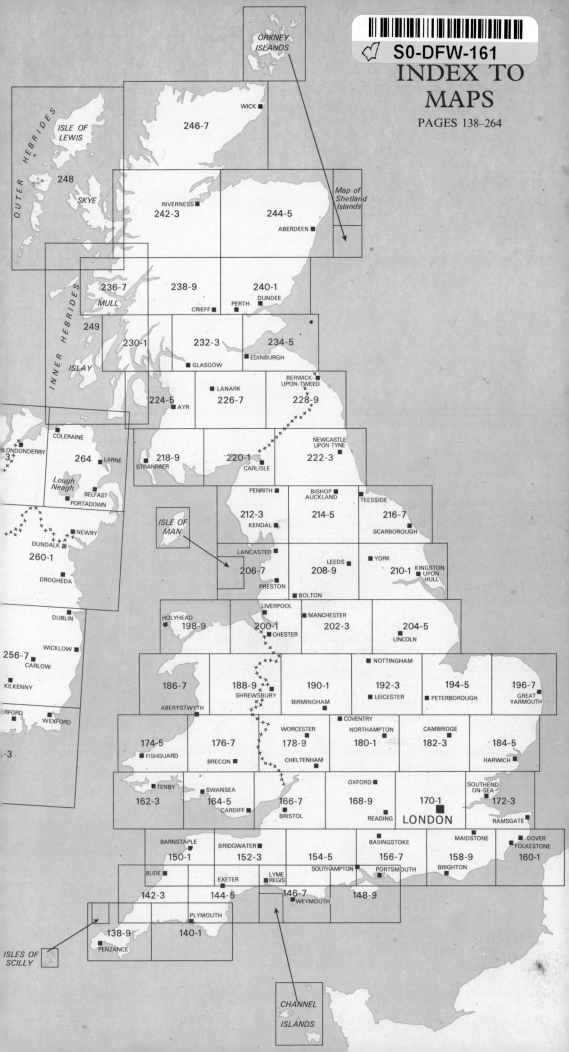

INDEX TO MAPS

PAGES 138–264

Reader's Digest

AA

NEW
BOOK
OF THE
ROAD

Published by
The Reader's Digest Association Limited
in collaboration with The Automobile Association

Contents

This book is designed for instant reference. The road maps, based on the Ordnance Survey, cover all of the British Isles. The strip maps give the motorist who is in a hurry key routes across the country. The plans of 109 cities and major towns identify the main streets and show the location of car parks, post offices, hospitals, police stations, municipal buildings and landmarks. The emergency sections – how to get yourself home after a breakdown, first aid, and law and the motorist – are grouped in the front so that they can be found quickly.

These early sections of the book advise on how to get safely by the shortest route from one place to another. The leisure pages, beginning on p. 329, give a motoring family ideas on how to get the most out of every journey – where to see some of Britain's scenic splendours, what will be found there and what to look for on the way.

BREAKDOWN

A quick guide to help you to get home

If you break down on the road this book is probably the quickest reference you have to help you to diagnose the trouble and get you home or to a garage. But it is important that you should follow the checks EXACTLY IN THE ORDER given, because only then will you find the fault and possibly be able to make running repairs. Sometimes the repair is beyond the ability of the average motorist, and the guide advises you to waste no more time but call the Automobile Association or a garage.

Contents

IMMEDIATE ACTION
As soon as the car falters get it off the road

Look behind to see if it is safe to pull on to the grass verge or hard shoulder. Give a slowing down signal.
Move the car well clear of the traffic if possible.
Do not get out of the car on the offside while traffic is overtaking – particularly on a motorway.
The rush of air created by a heavy vehicle travelling fast can drag you off your feet.
Keep your passengers, especially children, well away from the road.

Warn other drivers that you have broken down

Place a red warning triangle behind the car (see opposite) or open the boot or prop a car seat against the back of the car.
Other warnings are a torch with a flashing red light, or four-way flashing indicators.

If the driver has none of these, and the car has broken down in a dangerous place, such as just over the brow of a hill, it may be worth getting a passenger – in daylight – to walk 50 yds back along the road to flag down traffic.

Warning triangle

A warning triangle is not compulsory in the United Kingdom, but if you use one it must be prominently placed at least 50 yards (75 paces) behind the car (150 yards on a motorway). If a car breaks down just after a bend or beyond the brow of a hill, the triangle should be placed on the other side of the bend or hill, even if it means going back more than 50 yards from the vehicle.

Where to place a warning triangle.

Beware when working on the car

Do not work under the side nearest to the traffic, unless you are far enough away to be out of danger. Do not crawl under the car if it is supported only by a jack. Do not use bricks to support the car – these may crumble.

Before working under the bonnet remove your necktie or scarf – it can get caught in the engine. Remove a bracelet or a watch with a metal strap. They can cause a burn if they accidentally earth the battery.

On motorways

Posts at the back of the hard shoulder have an arrow pointing to the nearest telephone. Make a note of the number and letter on the post nearest your car, so you can be located.

The police will answer the phone and will ask where your car is, the make, model, year and registration number and what you think is wrong. So if you do not know what the fault is remember the symptoms as these may help, particularly if you want the police to call the AA.

Motorway telephones are one way only – from the motorway to control – so do not replace the receiver until the police tell you. The operator cannot call you back.

AVOID THE TROUBLE NEXT TIME

Most breakdowns occur because warning signs of trouble have been ignored.

The car's warning lights and instruments can indicate that something is going wrong. For instance, if a rise in engine temperature goes unnoticed, the coolant can boil away and the engine seize up. The engine would then have to be replaced. Once a week, or before a long journey, check the engine oil and water levels, and the tension and condition of the fan belt.

(See check lists on pp. 15 and 23.)

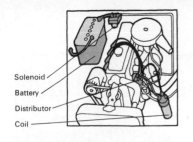

Solenoid
Battery
Distributor
Coil

Engine cuts out suddenly

> **WARNING:** No form of fault finding should be carried out on cars fitted with electronic ignition or fuel injector systems.
> When tracing a fault on other cars, do not smoke. Tuck away any dangling clothing, such as a tie, that could catch in the engine.

1 Check the power supply

Switch on headlamps or windscreen wipers to test if the battery is supplying current. The battery is usually beside the engine, although in some models it is in the boot or under the back seat.

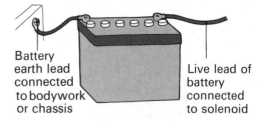

Battery earth lead connected to bodywork or chassis

Live lead of battery connected to solenoid

If no current

Inspect battery leads for loose connections. Test them with a twist and pull by hand. If loose, remove the leads, clean the terminals with emery cloth or a file and wipe with a dry cloth. Replace and tighten leads.

Post type terminal on a battery; the screw should be tight

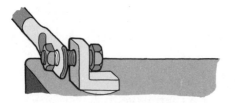

Bolt type terminal on a battery; tighten the nut and bolt with a spanner

If current is flowing

Look for loose wires, dirty connections or frayed wires around the engine compartment. Tighten loose connections (they can 'jump apart' when the starter is operated).
A nail file makes a useful screwdriver. Bind frayed wires with tape.

Lucar connector shown dismantled

Lucar connector in place

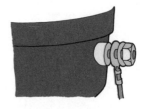

Loop and nut connector shown loose; tighten with a spanner

TRY TO START THE ENGINE

If it still fails carry out the following tests . . .

② Check the distributor

Remove the distributor cap —usually by releasing the two spring clips. If they have to be levered off, take care not to crack the distributor cap. If the contact breaker points fail to open and close when the engine is turned (see below), either the cam follower is broken and is not pressing on the cam, in which case a new set of points is needed, or adjustment has been lost.

Check that the points are clean. If they are dirty, clean them with a nail file or the striker paper from a box of safety matches. Replace the points with a new set as soon as possible.

Check the connecting wires inside the distributor. When the automatic advance mechanism operates, faulty insulation of frayed wires can cause a short circuit to the distributor body, which will stop the engine. If you cannot correct this, call the AA or a garage.

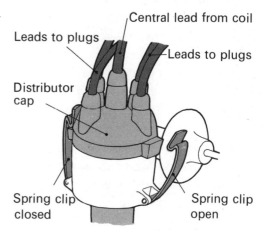

Distributor body with cap in place

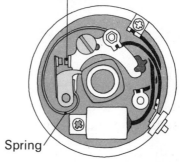

Distributor body, cap removed

THREE WAYS TO TURN THE ENGINE

The method of turning the engine depends on the model of car:

Operate the push button (where fitted) on the solenoid, a unit connected to the battery by a thick wire.

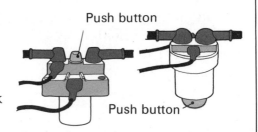

Two common types of solenoid

Or rock the car with top gear engaged. Do this by leaning on the car and gently rocking it with your body, while looking at the points in the distributor.

Or use a spanner to turn the hexagonal nut on the crankshaft pulley. Turn clockwise to avoid slackening the nut.

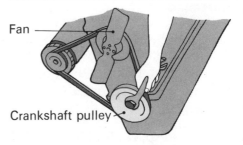

Turning the engine with a spanner

Check that the screw holding the fixed contact point is not loose. If it is, reset the points to the correct gap before tightening the screw. To do this: 1. Turn the engine until the points are fully open (see right). 2. Move the fixed point to the gap shown in the car handbook. Tighten the screw. If you have no feeler gauge for setting the gap, a piece of card gives a rough setting. Replace cap. Tighten retaining screws or line up the grooves for the spring clips. Replace clips by pushing firmly with the thumb.

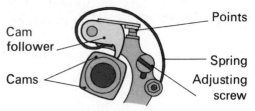

Contact points closed. The cam follower is resting on a flat side of the cam.

Contact points open. The cam follower is resting on a high point of the cam.

TRY TO START THE ENGINE

If it still fails, carry out the following tests.

③ Check for a spark from the coil

Check the spark at the plugs (p. 19). If the spark is regular, check the fuel system (p. 10). If there is no spark, the fault is in the ignition.

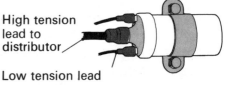

High tension lead to distributor

Low tension lead

Remove the distributor cap and turn the engine. If the contact breaker points are not opening and closing, adjust them as described above. If they are, disconnect the thick lead from the centre of the distributor cap and hold it approximately $\frac{1}{8}$ in. from a bare metal part of the car (NOT the carburettor or rocker cover). Switch on the ignition. Hold the rotor arm by its insulated body and flick open the points with its metal end.

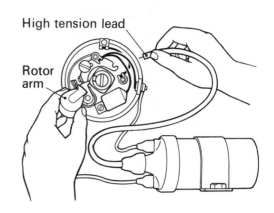

High tension lead

Rotor arm

Flicking points open to produce a spark

If a spark jumps the gap between the removed lead and the earthing point, there is a fault, usually a crack, in the distributor cap or in the rotor arm.

If there is no spark, follow the procedure outlined on p. 9.

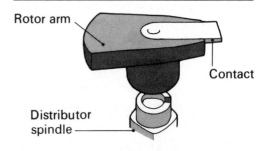

Rotor arm

Contact

Distributor spindle

Rotor arm removed from spindle

If a spark is produced

1. The rotor arm Replace the rotor arm in its normal position on the distributor drive shaft.

Hold the removed central ignition lead approximately $\frac{1}{8}$ in. from the rotor arm's central metal connector. Switch on the ignition and turn the engine over.

Large fat sparks between the lead and the rotor arm indicate a faulty rotor arm. Fit a new one.

Thin weak sparks between the lead and the rotor arm are normal and are insufficient to affect the ignition or stop the engine.

2. The distributor cap Examine the cap inside and outside for cracks, which often have the appearance of forked lightning etched in black or grey in the plastic. If there is a crack, a temporary repair can sometimes be made by carefully scraping away the plastic for at least $\frac{1}{4}$ in. across the line of the crack.

Replace the distributor cap with a new one as soon as possible.

If a replacement cannot be made

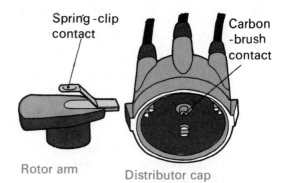

Spring-clip contact

Carbon -brush contact

Rotor arm

Distributor cap

before a long distance has to be covered, check and re-gap the plugs (p. 19). This will reduce the high tension voltage and help to prevent flash-over in the distributor cap.

Check that the carbon brush or central connector on the inside of the cap is in good condition and is making contact with the rotor arm. If the rotor arm has a spring-clip contact, the clip can be bent upwards to make better contact with a damaged distributor connector.

If there is no spring-clip contact, there should be a carbon brush and spring fitted in the centre of the distributor cap. Should that be missing, a temporary replacement can be made from rolled-up silver paper from a cigarette packet.

If no spark is produced

Check that current is passing from the ignition switch to the coil.
1. Disconnect the thin low tension wire joining the coil to the distributor from the coil.
2. Switch on the ignition.
3. Use a screwdriver to earth the now spare connector on the coil to a bare metal part of the car.

If this produces a small spark, the coil and its supply are in order.

Reconnect the low tension wire to the coil, then check the contact breaker points and the wires inside the distributor.

If there is no spark, call the AA or a garage.

NEVER TRY TO PROVIDE AN ALTERNATIVE SUPPLY TO THE COIL. IT COULD CAUSE FIRE IN SOME TYPES OF CARS.

TRY TO START THE ENGINE

There is no way of testing whether the coil and condenser are working efficiently, except by fitting new ones. But if the circuit is sound, except for these two items, assume they are faulty and call the AA or a garage.

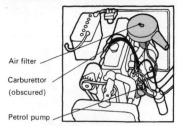

Air filter

Carburettor
(obscured)

Petrol pump

Engine splutters and dies

This is usually due to a fuel fault. Have you run out of petrol?

WARNING: No form of fault finding should be carried out on cars fitted with electronic ignition or fuel injector systems.

When tracing a fault on other cars, do not smoke. Tuck away any dangling clothing, such as a tie, that could catch in the engine.

---

① Look at the fuel gauge

Do not automatically accept the reading on the fuel gauge – it may be faulty.

Remove the petrol filler cap and rock the car. If there is no 'sloshing' sound from the petrol tank, refill the tank.

If the tank is not empty, leave the filler cap off and . . .

TRY TO START THE ENGINE

If it starts

The cause of the trouble may be a blockage in the petrol tank vent. Clear the ventilation pipe or filler cap vent.

If it fails to start

Check that petrol is reaching the carburettor. Loosen the feed pipe. Petrol should flow out if the engine is turned over a few times (mechanical pumps) or the ignition is switched on (electric pumps).

If petrol does flow, reconnect the feed pipe and . . .

TRY TO START THE ENGINE

If it still fails, carry out the following tests . . .

② Look for leaks

These can occur anywhere in the petrol line between the tank and the engine. A petrol leak will usually leave a clean patch of metal where it has washed away dirt and oil, and petrol will show clearly on the road.

Pump and carburettor Look for leaks at the connections from the pump to the carburettor.

The position of the pump varies on

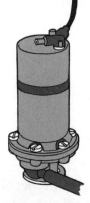

Electric
petrol pump

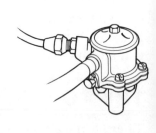

Mechanical
petrol pump

different models. It can be fitted to the engine, under the rear of the car or in the boot.

The carburettor is mounted on the side or above the engine. (It is easy to find as there is always a large air filter fitted to it.) Some cars have more than one carburettor, but they will be of the same type and are linked by a petrol pipeline. Petrol connections are either banjo unions or screwed unions, which are tightened with a spanner, or "Jubilee" clips, tightened with a screwdriver. Some cars have a fuel injection system, which means there is no carburettor.

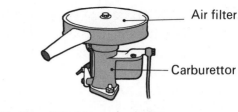

Air filter fitted to carburettor

If there is a leak

If a petrol pipeline is fractured or split, do not attempt a temporary repair with insulating tape (petrol will soon wash off the adhesive) or with chewing gum. This kind of repair can be dangerous.

Call the AA or a garage.

If any connections are loose, tighten them and . . .

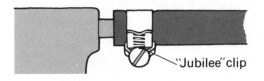

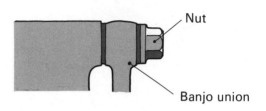

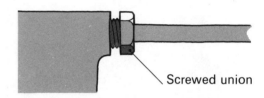

Various petrol pipe connections

TRY TO START THE ENGINE

If it still fails, check the following . . .

Vapour lock This fault is difficult to diagnose. It happens when petrol vaporises in the pipe instead of in the carburettor. This is caused in hot weather, if the pipe runs near a hot part of the engine. The cure is to wait for the engine to cool, or to wrap the fuel lines with rags soaked in cold water. Remove rags when the pipe is cool.

TRY TO START THE ENGINE

If it still fails, carry out the following tests . . .

③ Check the fuel pump

If there is petrol in the tank and there are no obvious leaks, the next step is to eliminate each component so that the fault can be isolated. Start at the petrol pump, which is either mechanical or electric.

Electric pump

This is easy to check, as it makes a ticking noise when it is working properly.

Slacken the pump outlet pipe which leads to the carburettor. Hold a rag under the loose connection and switch on the ignition.

If the pump is working correctly it will start ticking and petrol will leak out.

If petrol flows

Retighten the outlet pipe and try to start the engine. If it still fails, the fault will be in the carburettor. (See 4 on opposite page.)

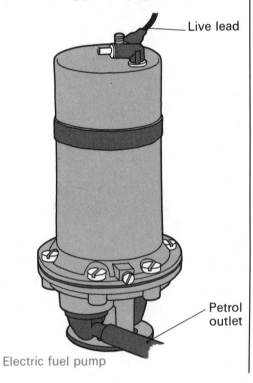

Live lead

Petrol outlet

Electric fuel pump

If no petrol flows

Make sure that electricity is reaching the pump. Slacken the terminal screw and shake the wire by hand, then retighten the connection. Check that the pump is correctly earthed. Take a screwdriver and hold the blade against the pump and mounting bracket. Turn the screwdriver to left and right to scrape away enough paint to provide a good connection.

Switch on the ignition. If the pump works, the earth connection was faulty. Clean away any dirt, remake the connection and . . .

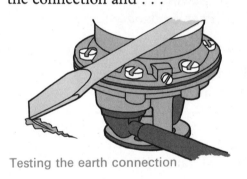

Testing the earth connection

TRY TO START THE ENGINE

If it still fails, carry out the following tests . . .

If current is reaching the pump, switch on the ignition and give the pump body a sharp slap with the flat of the hand.

If this causes the pump to operate, the points are worn and dirty and the pump should be exchanged as soon as possible.

If the pump still fails to work, call the AA or a garage.

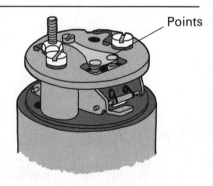

Points

If points stick slap pump body by hand to free them

Mechanical pump

Switch off the ignition. Disconnect the petrol line at the outlet to the carburettor (either at the pump or carburettor end, whichever is the easier to get at). Do not try to strip the pump. Position a clean cloth below the pipe outlet and get someone to turn the engine over. This should cause a regular spurt of petrol from the pipe end, and if that occurs the pump is working. Reconnect the petrol line to the carburettor.

If no petrol appears when the engine is turned over, the pump is faulty, the line is blocked, or the petrol tank is empty.

Call the AA or a garage.

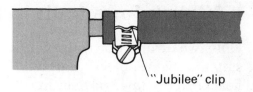

"Jubilee" clip

Petrol pipe inlet to carburettor

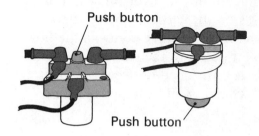

Push button

Push button

Two typical solenoids

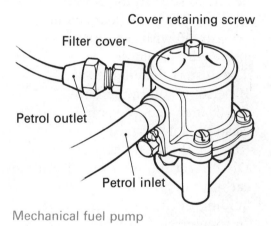

Cover retaining screw

Filter cover

Petrol outlet

Petrol inlet

Mechanical fuel pump

④ Check the air filter

A dirty air filter will rarely stop the engine, but it can seriously affect performance and increase fuel consumption.
As the filter nearly always has to be removed to work on the carburettor, this provides the opportunity to inspect it.

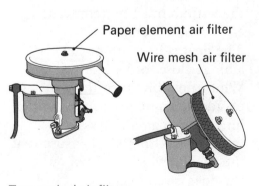

Paper element air filter

Wire mesh air filter

Two typical air filters

TRY TO START THE ENGINE

If it still fails, carry out the following tests . . .

⑥ Check for a fault in the carburettor

Only two carburettor faults will stop the engine: blockage in the float chamber inlet valve or in the main jet.

Others may prevent the engine from ticking over but will not stop the car from being driven. The inlet valve controls the flow of petrol to the carburettor and is positioned between the float chamber and the petrol pump.

The main jet controls the flow to the engine and is usually in the bottom of the float chamber. Under no circumstances should the accelerator or choke be operated when the carburettor is partly dismantled. If they are, there is a real possibility that something may fall into the inlet manifold and badly damage the engine when it is started.

The inlet valve

It is rare, but possible, for a needle to stick in the closed position. Give the float chamber a sharp tap with the knuckles or a screwdriver handle.
Try to start the engine.
If petrol is still not entering the float chamber, examine and clean the inlet valve.
Remove the air filter.
Disconnect the inlet pipe from the carburettor and undo the screws holding the lid of the chamber.
In some fixed jet carburettors the lid is part of the top. In others the float chamber drops away or the bottom must be removed.
If in doubt, seek help.
The float is likely to be held by a hinge close to the inlet valve. Where possible, turn the housing upside down before removing the hinge pin to gain access to the inlet valve. Otherwise, ensure that the needle, which will fall out as the float is removed, is not lost.
If you cannot remove the body of the inlet valve, try to clear the valve by blowing through it from the float chamber towards the inlet pipe.

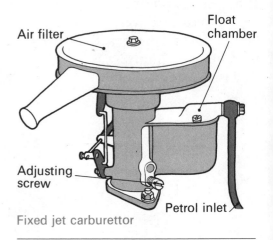

Fixed jet carburettor

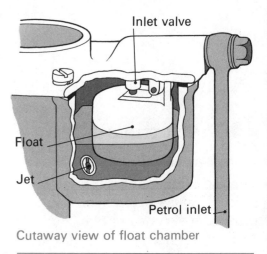

Cutaway view of float chamber

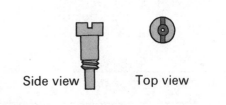

Side view   Top view

Carburettor jet

HOW TO AVOID TROUBLE

Most fuel faults can be prevented by frequent inspection and maintenance. Pipe unions should be tight and all filters clean.

The petrol level in the tank should never be allowed to get too low, for this will draw up sediment. Sometimes, the inside of the petrol tank deteriorates. Suspect this when the filters quickly become blocked with dirt. Have the tank steam-cleaned, or replace it.

The main jet

It is rare for a main jet to become blocked, or even partly blocked, unless water and dirt from the fuel tank build up in the float chamber. And that is likely to happen only after running out of petrol.

A blockage in the jet can often be cleared without dismantling the carburettor, provided that the engine will run.

Remove the air filter.

Start the engine.

Hold the throttle linkage with one hand so that the engine runs at about half maximum rpm.

Place the other hand flat over the carburettor inlet from which the air filter was removed.

Suction, which may clear the jet, will be felt on the hand and the engine will falter.

Before the engine can stop, take the hand away quickly but hold the throttle linkage in the same position until the engine picks up.

If the engine stops, there is a slight risk of a flash-back from the carburettor.

Restart the engine by the procedure followed to start a 'flooded' engine (p. 16).

Replace the air filter.

If the engine is not running and cannot be started, call the AA or a garage.

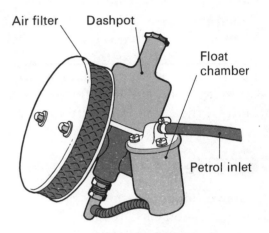

Variable jet carburettor

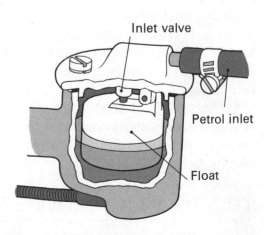

Cutaway view of float chamber

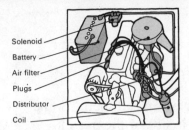

Solenoid
Battery
Air filter
Plugs
Distributor
Coil

Engine will not start

When an engine fails to start after a few attempts, do not continuously operate the starter as this will quickly run the battery flat. Switch off the ignition and look for the fault. If the engine was running normally when it was last used, the failure will probably be caused by a simple fault such as damp ignition leads, failure of the choke to operate, or excessive spark plug gaps.

Effects of the weather

Damp or foggy weather

Dampness on certain parts of the ignition system can cause electric current to leak away, and the plugs will fail to spark. The simplest cure is to spray the whole system – plugs, plug leads, coil and distributor top – with a damp-repellent aerosol. Another way is to go over the system with a dry cloth. Remove the plug caps one at a time to dry them or to spray the inside. Replace each one before removing another.

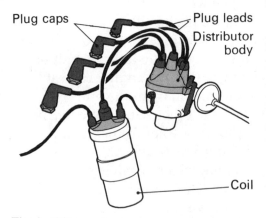

Plug caps · Plug leads · Distributor body · Coil

The ignition system

Flooding

Abortive attempts to start up may result in flooding: spark-plugs and inside the combustion chamber become damp with petrol and with condensation.
To clear this, push in the choke, hold the accelerator pedal right down on the floor (do not pump it) and try again.

Release the pedal and pull out the choke as soon as the engine starts.

Petrol

Check that there is petrol in the tank. Do not rely on the gauge. Remove the petrol filler cap, rock the car, and listen for a 'sloshing' sound in the tank.

TRY TO START THE ENGINE

If it still fails, carry out the following tests . . .

② Check the battery

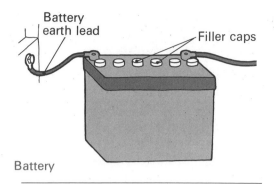

Battery earth lead — Filler caps

Switch on the ignition. If the red warning light fails to come on, there is no power supply, meaning either that the battery is flat or the connections are faulty.

Battery

Check the connections. Take off both battery leads (thick wires) even if they appear tight. They are fitted with a screw or held by a nut and bolt.

Clean the battery terminals and leads with a file or emery cloth. Replace connections. Coat terminals with Vaseline as soon as convenient.

Post-type terminal

Check that the earth lead (often a braided cable) is securely attached to the body or chassis. If in doubt, remove the cable, scrape both surfaces clean, then refit.

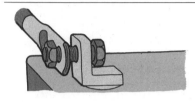

Bolt-type terminal

TRY TO START THE ENGINE

If the ignition light still fails, the battery is flat and will need recharging. Call the AA or a garage. If the light comes on, but the engine will not start

③ Check the starter motor

When the starter is operated the starter motor may do one of four things:

It may turn the engine at normal speed, but not start it
This means the fault is elsewhere in the ignition or petrol systems. Carry out the tests starting on pp. 6 or 10.

It may turn the engine very slowly
This means the battery is low and needs recharging. The engine, however, can be started by pushing the car or giving it a 'boost start' (see p. 18).

PUSH START

Ask for help to push the car. Depress the clutch pedal, engage second gear and switch on the ignition. When the car is rolling. well, sharply release the clutch pedal. As the engine fires depress the clutch quickly, disengage gear and press the accelerator.

BOOST START

This means connecting your battery to that of another car with thick booster cables. Do not use thin wires: they are certain to overheat.

Start the engine of the other car. No matter how the batteries are earthed, connect the two negative terminals with the black lead of the booster cables and the two positive terminals with the red. Turn on the ignition and start the engine. Remove the cables when your car has started.

On a car with an alternator, do not disconnect the battery while the engine is running.

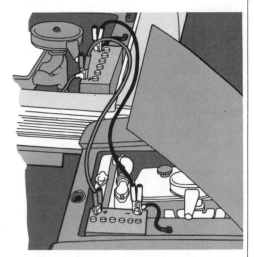

Booster cables connecting two batteries. It is important to connect the negative (−) terminals with one cable, and the positive (+) with the other cable.

The starter motor may whirr but not start the engine

This means that the starter motor and the engine are not engaging, because part of the starter motor is jammed. This can often be freed by a sharp tap on the squared end of the starter motor. If this does not work, push-start the car or call the AA or a garage.

The starter motor may make a single 'clunk' sound

This is usually an indication of a jammed starter. Select top gear, release the handbrake, and rock the car backwards and forwards. If this is unsuccessful or difficult, free the starter by turning the squared end of the starter motor armature clockwise with a spanner.

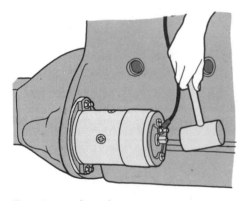

Tapping to free the starter motor

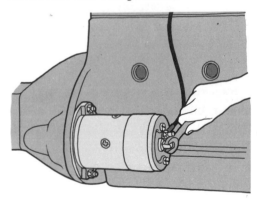

Turning to free the starter motor

TRY TO START THE ENGINE

If it starts and the gears engage, but the car will not move, there is a major fault. Call the AA or a garage.

If the engine still does not start, carry out the following tests . . .

4 Check sparking at the plugs

Testing for the presence of a spark at the plug is simple and can be done without removing the plug; but the spark may be too weak to cross the plug gap if the gap between the electrodes is greater than is recommended. This could prevent starting, especially if the car has stood for a few hours in extremely cold weather.

Testing for sparking

Take off one of the plug caps and clean it thoroughly.
Insert a roll of tinfoil (cigarette foil) into the connector so that it projects beyond the cap.
Hold the connector so that the end of the tinfoil is about $\frac{1}{8}$ in. away from a good earth (any clean metal part of the car except the rocker box cover and carburettor).
Switch on and turn the engine.
Turn the engine by operating the starter – or get someone to operate it for you. Look for a spark between the tinfoil and the earth.

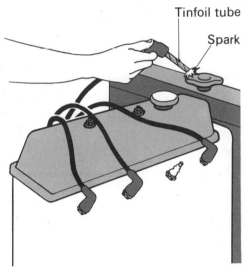
Testing for a spark with tinfoil

If there is a spark

The fault may be excessive spark-plug gaps, or in the fuel supply. Test the fuel supply as detailed on pp. 10–15.

If there is no spark

The fault will be in the ignition system, between the battery and the plugs. Carry out the tests described on pp. 6–9.

Adjusting the gap

Unscrew each plug, making sure that the plug spanner does not tilt and damage the ceramic insulation. Check that each plug is dry.
Adjust the plug gap by gently tapping in the electrode joined to the metal body of the plug.
If there is any doubt about the correct width of the gap, adjust it temporarily to the thickness of a plastic credit card. Correct this to its recommended width as soon as possible.

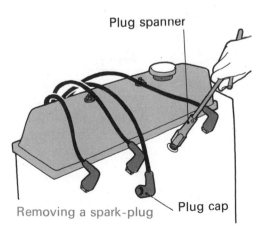
Removing a spark-plug

Avoid connecting leads to the wrong plugs by replacing each plug and its lead before starting on another.

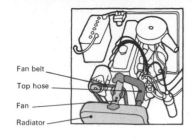

Fan belt
Top hose
Fan
Radiator

The engine overheats

There is no substitute for anti-freeze to protect the cooling system during the winter months.

If you see steam rising from the bonnet, get a higher reading on the temperature gauge, or the warning light comes on, pull off the road as soon as possible and stop.

The engine is overheating because water has been lost through a leak or because water is unable to circulate through the system.

Overheating from a sudden loss of water, such as from a burst bottom hose, may be only briefly indicated on the temperature gauge. The gauge may even continue to give a normal reading, and sometimes a lower one, in such an instance.

If the heater is switched to hot and starts to blow cold, or the engine suddenly loses performance and runs irregularly, suspect a complete loss of water, which can only lead to overheating.

❶ Look for leaks in the cooling system

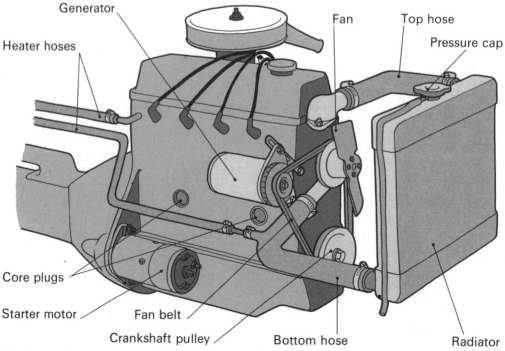

Generator

Fan

Top hose

Heater hoses

Pressure cap

Core plugs

Starter motor

Fan belt

Crankshaft pulley

Bottom hose

Radiator

Typical cooling system

Once the car is off the road, switch off the ignition and open the bonnet.

Do not remove the radiator cap yet. Look for steam or water coming from the top or bottom hose, the radiator, the thin hoses that carry the coolant to and from the heater, the joints at the water pump and cylinder head, the expansion tank and pipe (where fitted).

A less likely cause is a lost or seeping core plug.

② Check the water level in the radiator

Do not try to take off the radiator pressure cap until the engine has cooled a little. Scalding water or steam may spurt out.
Cover the cap with a thick cloth, turn your face away and, with the flat of the hand, turn the radiator cap about an eighth of a turn.
Wait until any hissing of escaping steam has stopped, then turn the cap further and remove it.
Always top up after a water loss, but never add cold water to a hot engine: it will result in rapid cooling and may damage the engine.
Wait at least half an hour for the engine to cool, with the bonnet up and the radiator cap off.
Switch the heater on to the hot position, start the engine and maintain a fast tickover.
Feel both the heater hoses. When they are hot, the heater will be full of water.
Top up again as necessary to bring the water up to the correct level, which is 1 in. below the top of the radiator.
If the car has a sealed system (with separate header tank), remove the header tank cap and top up as described for radiator.
Once you have topped up, look again for leaks.

When there is a leak . . .

Leaking radiator This is difficult to repair, but if it is a slow leak the car can be driven home. If the leak is serious, call the AA or a garage.

Leaking hoses If water is oozing from the connections, check the clips and tighten as necessary.
If the end of the hose has split, see if there is sufficient length of hose for it to be reconnected if the damaged part is cut off.
In an emergency, a split or holed hose can be bound with plastic insulating tape, or a bandage, to get you to a garage. Drive with the radiator cap loose, check the water level and top up at least every 5 miles, and restrict your speed to 40 mph.

Leaking from the engine There are several places where water can leak from the engine, but often the leak will be a slow one which has gradually emptied the system.

Top up the radiator then look round the engine. If water gushes out, do not move the car. Call the AA or a garage.
If the water does not gush out, drive to the nearest garage.

If there is no leak . . .
Carry out the following tests . . .

③ Check the fan belt

The fan belt is at the front or side of the engine between the engine and the radiator. It usually connects three pulleys, so that when the engine is running it drives the water pump and fan (to cool the engine) and the generator (to provide electricity). The first sign of fan-belt failure is usually that the ignition warning light comes on. Failure of the fan belt can be for two reasons: it may have broken (which means it will have fallen off) or it may be slipping.

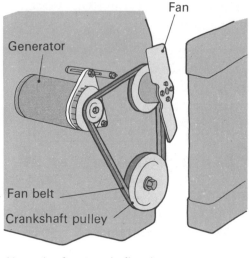

How the fan belt is fitted

If the fan belt is broken

Fit a new belt. On no account start the car before this is done.

FITTING A NEW FAN BELT
Slacken the three bolts holding the generator. Push the generator close to the engine. Remove the existing belt, easing it off the generator pulley first.

Loop the new belt over the fan and on to the water-pump pulley, then over the crankshaft pulley. To guide it on to the generator pulley, turn the fan by hand.

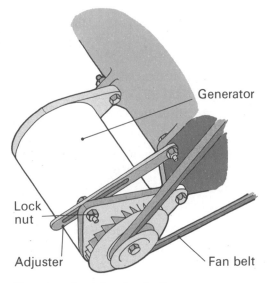

How to adjust the fan belt

Adjust the tension of the belt. To do this, look for the longest length of belt between two of the pulleys. Take hold of the middle of the belt between finger and thumb. Push the belt in and out between the two pulleys. The total in-and-out movement should be $\frac{1}{2}$–$\frac{3}{4}$ in. Adjust by moving the generator away from the engine.

Tighten the generator bolts while holding the generator. A new belt may stretch, and so begin to slip, during the first 100 miles – so check the tension again later.

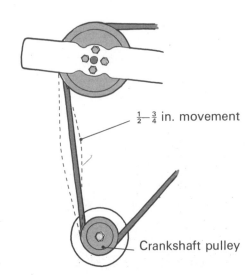

Fan-belt tension

If the fan belt is slipping

The belt may be split or stretched, or the pulleys greasy or oily. Test the tension of the belt (as described on the opposite page). If it is too tight or slack, adjust.

If the belt is still slack when the generator has been pushed to its limit, the belt must be replaced.

If the belt tension is correct but the belt slips at high engine speeds look carefully for a split. If there is one, replace the belt (see opposite page).

If there is no split. Check for oil on the fan belt. An oily belt must be replaced.

START THE ENGINE

If the ignition warning light goes out the belt is working correctly. Start driving the car. If it is still overheating the fault may be in the water pump or the thermostat. Call the AA or a garage.

If the light stays on, or the ammeter shows a continuous discharge or the battery condition indicator gives a low reading, there is probably a failure in the charging system.

Charging failure

Test the operation of the charging system by observing the brilliance of the headlights when the engine is accelerated from tickover. If the light from the headlamps gets brighter, the charging system is working. If it does not, and the fan belt is found to be in good condition, the system needs the attention of a competent electrician.

Getting home It may be possible to continue driving if the battery is fully charged.
A daylight journey should not exceed five hours. A night journey can be continued for one hour with the headlights in use, provided that no other electrical equipment, such as the heater fan, is used. Do not stop the engine unless there is no alternative.

Slipping clutch

Clutch slip occurs when the engine is not coupled firmly to the gearbox. When the accelerator is operated to increase the engine rpm, there is no comparative increase in the road speed. This results from excessive wear of the soft lining material on the clutch plate or contamination of that material by oil.

Getting home If the clutch is adjustable, the method of adjustment will usually be found in the car handbook. If it is not adjustable, it is important that slipping should be minimised.
Use as high a gear as possible, do not exceed 40 mph in top gear, and accelerate as slowly as you can without sudden changes of speed.

23

Rough or noisy running— is it safe to go on?

Unusual noises, loss of power and rough or hesitant running are all signs of potential danger. The following checks give a rough guide as to whether it is safe to drive on.

If in doubt, do not drive the car. Call the AA or a garage. To make the checks, pull the car off the road, take it out of gear and switch off the engine.

1 Noises—a nuisance or a serious fault?

Any unusual noise from a car, particularly one that starts suddenly, should be investigated immediately, as it could indicate a serious fault.

Stop the car, but before calling the AA or a garage, check whether the noise is something simple which does not affect the safe running of the car.

Open the bonnet and look for loose components or fittings, such as the air filter, battery, bonnet stay, fan belt or fan.

Check that the bonnet is properly closed. If the catch is loose or faulty the bonnet will vibrate.

Check that there is nothing rolling about in the boot, particularly if the noise occurs when cornering.

Noises which may mean something is seriously wrong

The car should not be driven under any circumstances when the fault is serious. This is indicated by one of the following sounds:

Heavy knocking from the engine when the car is accelerated. This could be a worn big-end bearing.

Heavy rumbling from the engine when the engine is put under strain – such as being driven up a hill in too high a gear. This could be caused by worn main bearings.

Squeal or judder when the brakes are applied. This may simply mean the linings or pads are dirty, but

it could also be caused by worn linings, or distorted brake drums or discs. These noises could indicate faults leading to serious damage or to brake failure.

Clanking when rolling slowly forward. This could be caused by a worn or loose propeller shaft or rear axle.

Rattles or rhythmic thuds from one wheel. This could be due to loose wheel nuts. Remove hub cover to check. Tighten the nuts with wheel brace if necessary. Make sure the nuts are on the right way – with the bevelled end towards the wheel.

Other noises which could mean a serious fault . . .

In these cases the car can probably be driven slowly to the nearest garage, but if the noise gets worse stop and call the AA or a garage.

Grinding noise when the clutch pedal is depressed. This could be due to worn parts in the clutch.

Rattle from the engine when the car corners – low oil level or loose component. If the oil level needs topping up, the oil indicator light should have flickered on when the noise was heard. If the oil level is correct, look for a loose component.

Whirring noise which stops when clutch pedal is depressed. This is probably due to a worn clutch release bearing. Drive slowly to a garage.

Rattling or clanking from the front of the engine. This is probably due to a worn timing chain or worn water pump.

Rattling or slapping sound when starting from cold. This means the oil pump is slow in circulating oil, or the pistons are slapping in the bores.

Noises which mean you can probably drive on safely . . .

Rattles from windows, doors, the boot or bodywork generally.

Light tappings from the engine on tickover – probably loose tappets (see p. 35).

Spluttering from the exhaust pipe or silencer.

Chuffing or hissing sounds when the engine is revved – probably

due to a leak in the exhaust system or an air leak from the inlet manifold (see p. 34).

Screeching from the engine near the radiator. This could be the fan belt slipping (carry out checks listed on p. 22) or a worn water pump bearing. Drive slowly to a garage, keeping an eye on the engine temperature.

2 Lack of power or rough running

A sudden loss of power or rough running is usually caused by a simple fault, which can often be put right at the roadside.
Whatever the cause it will be safe to drive on slowly to the nearest garage *unless* the engine is overheating (see p. 20) or *unless* there is a petrol leak (see p. 10) or *unless* there is a lack of oil pressure.
Before driving on look for an obvious fault:
A plug lead or battery connection may have worked loose.
Look for a petrol leak (see p. 10).
If there is one, call the AA.

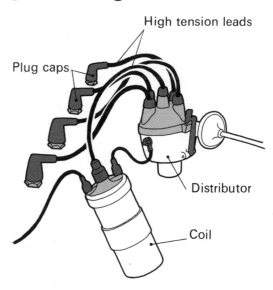

High tension leads

Plug caps

Distributor

Coil

Diagram of the ignition system

Lighting failures

If any of the lights fail, get the car off the road as soon as possible. It is both illegal and dangerous to drive without lights. A failure in the lighting can be due to one of several faults: a blown fuse or bulb (easy to replace), a frayed or loose wire (not so easy to find), a broken switch or bad earth (difficult to detect). The number of lights that fail help to indicate the fault. If more than one fails see p. 27, otherwise . . .

① Tracing the fault if one light fails

The failure of one light can arise from a blown bulb, corrosion of terminal connectors, or a bad earth.

Side-light If a side-light fails and you cannot park without lights, drive to the nearest garage using dipped headlights.

Rear lights The failure of any rear light could lead to a rear collision, especially on a motorway. Fit a new bulb at the first opportunity. It is a good plan to check these lights before starting any stage of a journey in darkness.

Inspect the bulb . . .
The condition of the bulb will usually indicate the fault.

Glass is blackened or milky
If the glass is blackened, it has become coated with metal from the filament. If it is milky, air has got in through a crack. In either case, fit a new bulb.

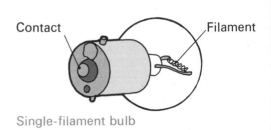
Single-filament bulb

Glass is clear Inspect the filament. If it is broken, fit a new bulb. In case of doubt, test the bulb (see opposite page).

Corrosion If a bulb is corroded and difficult to release from its holder, always clean the holder before fitting a new bulb.

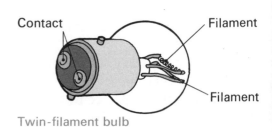
Twin-filament bulb

If it is not obvious that the bulb has blown, the bulb can be tested with a piece of wire. (See diagram.)

If the bulb lights, the contacts on the bulb or bulb-holder were corroded or dirty. Clean the contacts by scraping them.
If the light still does not work, there is probably a wiring fault.

If a headlight fails Check whether it is a sealed-beam unit or is fitted with a bulb.
A scaled-beam unit will have to be replaced with a complete new unit, and the beam setting must be checked by a garage.

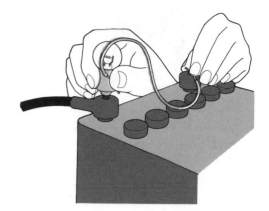

How to test a bulb. Connect one end of a piece of wire to the side of the bulb and the other end to a battery terminal. Place the base of the bulb on the other terminal.

A faulty bulb is easily replaced on most cars.

② If more than one light fails

This could be a blown fuse causing one circuit (such as both headlights) to fail. Most modern cars have a fusebox with a fuse for each circuit, but some cars have fuses built into the wiring that can be difficult to find.
If the car has a fusebox (the car handbook will show where it is) look for a blown fuse. If the replacement fuse blows when the light is again switched on, there is a short circuit in the system and AA or garage help is necessary.

Some cars have bullet connectors on each side of the engine compartment and in the boot. Check that none has worked loose.

If you cannot find the fault
Park the car well off the road or under a street light and facing the same direction as passing traffic. Call the AA or a garage.

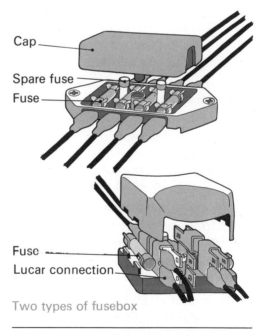

Cap

Spare fuse

Fuse

Fuse

Lucar connection

Two types of fusebox

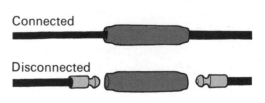

Connected

Disconnected

Bullet connection

Remember, it is illegal to drive without the proper lights and there are places where it is illegal to park without lights.

Spotting trouble by the instruments

The lights and dials on an instrument panel can give a warning that something is wrong – in time for the motorist to take action before the fault gets worse, making it necessary to carry out a costly repair. Instruments with calibrated dials give more information than warning lights.

However, if a warning light comes on when driving, stop and investigate the cause.

Ignition warning light

This lights up as soon as the ignition is switched on, showing that the battery is supplying current. The light should go out as soon as the engine speed reaches a fast idle – showing that the generator is working and supplying current to the battery and the electrical system.

Danger sign When the light stays on above fast idling speed.

Action Check that the fan belt is not broken or slipping. (See check list on p. 23.) The fan belt drives the generator (to supply current) and the water pump and fan (to cool the engine) – see Fitting a new fan belt, p. 22.

Ammeter

This does the same job as the ignition warning light, but gives much more information.

Immediately the ignition is switched on, the ammeter needle should point towards negative (–) indicating that there is a slight discharge of electricity. When the engine is running above tickover the needle should point to positive (+), indicating that the battery is being charged. After prolonged use of the starter and other electrical equipment, the ammeter will show a 20–30 amp. charge for a few seconds, but the reading should quickly settle down to 1–2 amps. A higher reading can be expected if the battery is in a low state.

Danger signs Continuous discharge, a high charge or a flickering needle.

Action With a continuous discharge, check the fan belt. If it is slipping it will not be turning the generator under load (see p. 23). A continuous high charge may indicate a generator control box fault, which will need attention by a competent electrician. A flickering needle means that there is a fault in the system or a loose connection. Switch on each circuit in turn (with the engine not running) – lights, horn, indicators and so on. The ammeter may show, by a high discharge or a zero reading, which system is faulty.

Battery-condition indicator

This instrument is gradually replacing the ammeter. Instead of showing the flow of electricity into or out of the battery, it indicates the voltage state of the electrical system. With the engine running above idling speed, the dial, which is marked in volts from 11 to 15, shows the charge voltage. This should be 13–15 volts if the battery is in good condition. When the engine is not running, with the ignition switched on the indicator shows the terminal voltage of the battery, which should be 12–13 volts.

Danger signs Readings below 12 volts off charge (when the engine is not running) and above 15 volts on charge (after more than 10 minutes running).
Action An off-charge reading below $11\frac{1}{2}$ volts indicates a discharged battery. Check that there is no loose or dirty connection and that the battery is topped up. If these checks reveal no fault, the battery may need replacing.
A charging reading above 15 volts may indicate a generator control fault, which will need expert attention.

Oil-pressure warning light

This light should come on when the ignition is switched on and go out when the engine is running. It should stay out until the engine stops. If it fails to light up, check the bulb and the connector on the pressure switch.

Danger signs The light comes on during normal driving or flashes when cornering or braking.
Action Check the oil level with the dipstick. Top up with oil if necessary. If the level is correct expert help will be needed.

Oil-pressure gauge

This shows the pressure of the oil in the engine in pounds per square inch. On starting the engine, the gauge should show an immediate rise to normal operating pressure (see the car handbook). When a hot engine is ticking over, it is not abnormal for the oil pressure to be lower than when the engine is cold.

Danger signs When the needle shows an abnormal reading – it drops gradually, fluctuates or stays high.
Action Most of these signs show a fault which requires garage attention, but check the oil level. If the level is correct, drive slowly to a garage. If the pressure drops to zero, call the AA or a garage

Water-temperature gauge

This shows the temperature of the water in the cooling system – usually at the hottest part of the engine. The correct operating temperature varies from car to car, but as a general guide it should be around 90°C (194°F). Some cars have a simpler gauge marked C (cold), N (normal) and H (hot). The engine is overheating when the needle enters the red zone.

Danger signs Engine temperature rises several degrees and stays there; or the engine temperature rises and then drops to cold.
Action If there is any serious fluctuation in the temperature, stop immediately. If the needle is above boiling point, or if the gauge registers zero, all the water has leaked or boiled away. Carry out the checks listed on p. 20.

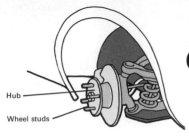

Hub

Wheel studs

Changing a wheel

WARNING: As soon as a tyre deflates, change the wheel. Do not wait until the tyre is completely flat – driving on a soft tyre can affect steering, causing the car to slew off the road or into other traffic.

Get the car into a safe place – well on to the hard shoulder on a motorway or out of the traffic on any other road. Put down a warning triangle at least 50 yds behind the car – 150 yds on a motorway. Walk along the grass verge of a motorway, not the hard shoulder.

Make sure the handbrake is on and chock the wheel opposite the one to be changed with a lump of wood.

Prise off the hub cover with the chamfered end of the wheel brace or with a screwdriver.
Slacken the wheel nuts about one turn with the wheel brace before jacking up the car.

Fit the jack into the place provided, which varies slightly according to the model of car. A side-lift jack will fit into a hole (sometimes covered with a plug to keep out dirt) under the side of the car. The fitting for a scissor jack varies. (The car handbook will show

where and how to fit the jack.) On soft ground put something solid under the jack, such as a piece of wood or a brick.

Jack up the car until the wheel is well clear of the ground. Remove the wheel nuts.
Put on the spare wheel and replace each wheel nut, making sure that the bevelled side faces inward. Tighten the nuts until finger tight, starting at the top and working diagonally (so that the wheel is not pulled to one side).

Lower the car until the weight is on the wheel, then finish tightening with the wheel brace.

Remove the jack. Replace the hub cover by slotting it on at the bottom first, then giving the top of the cover a sharp thump with the heel of the hand to click it into place.

As soon as possible, check that the pressure of the spare tyre is correct. A wrongly inflated tyre can affect braking and steering.

Side jack located under the car

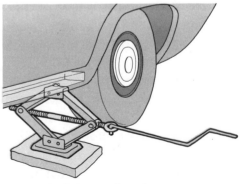

Scissor jack located under car

Towing

DANGERS IN TOWING. A motorist should consider all the hazards before offering or accepting a tow. Many modern cars have no safe place to attach the tow rope, and considerable damage can be caused by fixing a rope wrongly. The only safe way is to get a tow from the AA or a garage breakdown service. A wrongly fitted tow rope can rip off the number plate, affect the steering or damage the suspension.

NEVER attach it to the steering linkage; this can affect the steering.

NEVER attach it to an exposed drive shaft (some drive shafts do not run inside a fixed casing) as the rope may wind on to the shaft or slip along it and cause damage.

NEVER tow a car with automatic transmission before checking in the car handbook that it is possible to do so without causing damage.

If you decide to tow . . .

If possible, use a tow rope of nylon or of plastic material with an elastic quality.

If in doubt about where to attach a tow rope, fasten it to a bumper. It is better to risk damaging a bumper and bodywork than the steering or suspension, where any damage is likely to be unnoticed with possible serious consequences. The distance between cars when one is towed is limited by law to 15 ft. Too short a rope makes it more difficult for the driver of the towed car.

The rope must be clearly visible to other drivers and to people who might walk between the cars. Tie pieces of coloured material along the tow rope.

The law does not now require the towed vehicle to carry a notice 'On tow', but it is still advisable. This will indicate to drivers behind that they cannot overtake and squeeze in between the two cars.

If you are towing a car . . .

On starting, take up the slack gently to prevent breaking the rope or damaging the cars.

Keep the rope taut. If it is allowed to sag, the towed car may run over it and wrap it round a wheel. Warn approaching traffic by keeping your headlights on.

If you are being towed . . .

Keep the rope taut, even if it means touching the brakes lightly.

Be ready for the car towing you to change gear – it will momentarily lose speed and the rope will sag. Going downhill, keep the rope taut by applying the brakes. On a straight road move nearer the centre of the road than the car towing you, to give yourself an un-obstructed view.

Car terms and their meaning

This list defines the technical terms used in the preceding pages on breakdown repairs—and identifies some of the items listed on a garage bill.

A

Accelerator pump Mechanism in some types of carburettor which injects extra petrol into the engine for rapid acceleration, when the accelerator is suddenly depressed.

Air cleaner Filter which removes dirt from the air before it is drawn into the carburettor. The filtering agent may be oil, oil-soaked metal gauze, felt or paper.

Alternator An engine-driven generator which produces alternating current. It has a higher output than a dynamo at low engine speeds, and unlike a dynamo will charge the battery when the engine is idling.

Anti-freeze Chemical mixture, usually an ethylene glycol compound, added to the water in the cooling system to lower the freezing point of the coolant. A 25 per cent content of anti-freeze in the water gives usually enough protection in Britain.

Anti-roll bar A metal rod attached to the suspension across the car to resist a car's tendency to roll on corners.

Automatic choke A device in the carburettor which gives a richer mixture when the engine is cold and gradually weakens it as the engine warms.

Automatic cut-out See Control unit

Automatic transmission Gearbox in a 'two-pedal car' (one without a clutch pedal) which automatically changes gear to suit the car's speed and the gradient of the road. For instance, it will select a low gear when the car climbs a hill.

B

Ball joint Coupling of two components, end to end, so that either can pivot in any direction relative to the other.

Bendix pinion Gearwheel which moves along a spirally grooved shaft when the shaft turns. On the starter motor, the Bendix pinion engages with a toothed ring on the flywheel. Once the engine starts, the pinion 'jumps' back so that the starter motor disengages.

Big end The part of the connecting rod in the engine which is attached to the crankshaft. The small end is attached to the piston. See *Piston illustration, p. 34.*

Big-end bearing The shell bearing which encircles the crank pin, held in place by a cap bolted to the bottom of the connecting rod. See *Piston illustration, p. 34.*

Box spanner Tubular spanner. One or both ends fit over a bolt head or nut. A tommy bar fits into holes in the spanner to turn it.

Box spanner

Brake fluid Synthetic fluid used in a hydraulic braking system. The fluid is harmless to the system's rubber seals and is not affected by high temperatures.

Brake lining A layer of hard friction material, bonded or riveted to a brake shoe. See Drum brake.

Brake pad Hard friction material bonded on to metal plates which are pressed on to the brake discs. See Disc brake.

Brush Small piece of carbon or other material used to make electrical contact between a stationary component and a moving one.

C

Caliper Component of disc brake assembly which holds the pads against the disc. See Disc brake.

Cam A projection on a shaft. As the shaft turns, the cam pushes away another component which touches it, so converting the shaft's rotary action into up-and-down or side-to-side motion.

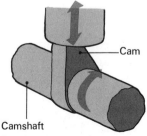

Camshaft
Section of camshaft

Camber angle Angle at which wheels are tilted from the vertical. With positive camber the wheels are further apart at the top, and with negative camber they are closer together at the top. A wheel with negative camber gives more stable cornering at speed.

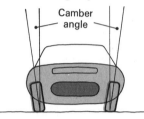

Car with positive camber

Cam follower Component that bears directly on to a cam operating a valve or push rod. Otherwise called a tappet.

Camshaft A revolving shaft operating the valves through a series of cams. Sometimes it also operates the distributor through skew gears, and mechanical fuel pump.

Carburettor A component in the fuel system which mixes petrol and air in the correct proportions for combustion.

Castor angle Angle by which the steering pivots of the front wheels lean back from the vertical so that the wheel has a self-centring effect causing it to return to the straight-ahead position after cornering.

Chassis Steel frame to which the engine and body are attached. Most modern cars have no chassis.

Choke Butterfly valve which restricts the intake of air into the carburettor, so enriching the mixture for cold starting.

Clutch Mechanical means of disconnecting the engine from the gearbox when a car is changing gear or starting from rest.

Coil Electrical unit for converting the low voltage of the battery (6 or 12 volts) into the high voltage – as much as 30,000 volts – necessary to produce a spark at the plugs.

Combustion Burning of the petrol/air mixture in the combustion chambers producing expanding gases which drive the piston on the power stroke.

Compression Increasing the pressure of a gas by reducing its volume, as during the compression stroke – the second stroke in the four-stroke cycle – in an engine.

Compression ratio The ratio between the volume of gas in the cylinder before and after compression. If the mixture is compressed to one-ninth of its original volume, the compression ratio is 9:1.

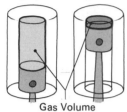

Gas Volume

Compression ratio

Condenser An electrical component for storing electricity. Used in the distributor to stop arcing (electricity jumping a gap) at the points when they open.

Connecting rod A forged steel or alloy rod which is attached by its small end to the piston and by its big end to the crankshaft. See *Piston illustration, p. 34.*

Constant velocity joint A type of universal joint fitted mainly on the drive shafts of front-wheel-drive cars, to allow judder-free drive to the wheels when steering.

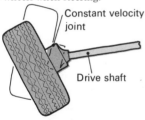

Constant velocity joint

Drive shaft

Position of constant velocity joint

Contact breaker Mechanically operated switch in the distributor which interrupts the low-tension current to the coil. This action induces the high-tension current in the coil – as much as 30,000 volts – needed for the spark-plugs.

Contact breaker gap The distance between the points in the distributor when they are fully open.

Control unit A sealed unit in the electrical system containing an automatic cut-out (to stop the battery discharging itself back through the dynamo), a voltage regulator and current control.

Core plug Round plug, shaped like a small tin lid. Used to seal off the casting holes in the block.

Crankshaft A strong, heavy metal shaft with a crank for each cylinder. It converts, through the connecting rods, the up-and-down movement of the pistons into a rotary motion to drive the road wheels.

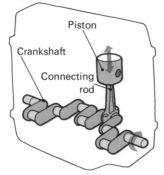

Piston

Crankshaft

Connecting rod

Crankshaft and piston

Crown wheel and pinion Two gears in the final drive unit which transmit the drive from the propeller shaft through a right angle to the road wheels. See *Rear axle illustration, p. 35.*

Cylinder block Casting of iron or aluminium alloy containing the cylinders. The space between the cylinders and the outside walls of the block of a water-cooled engine contains the water jacket through which water circulates to cool the engine. The block of an air-cooled engine has fins for cooling.

Cylinder head Casting of iron or aluminium alloy bolted on to the cylinder block and usually containing the combustion chambers, water jacket, spark-plugs, valves and valve gear.

Cylinder head gasket A seal between the block and cylinder head to prevent the leakage of gases and water. It is often of asbestos with a thin steel or copper covering.

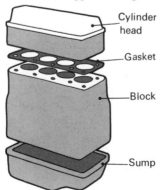

Cylinder head

Gasket

Block

Sump

Main parts of the engine

Cylinders Circular cavities in the cylinder block in which the pistons move up and down and in which combustion takes place.

D

Damper A unit fitted to control the movement between the body of the car and the suspension. Often called a shock absorber.

Differential Arrangement of gears in the final drive which, when a car is turning a corner, allows the inside wheel to travel more slowly than the outside wheel which has to cover a greater distance.

Disc brake Type of brake in which two pads are pressed against a metal disc which is attached to and revolves with a road wheel.

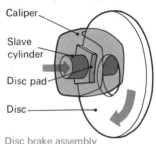

Caliper

Slave cylinder

Disc pad

Disc

Disc brake assembly

Distributor Unit in the ignition system which helps to convert low-tension current into high-tension current. It then distributes the current to each spark-plug in turn through the rotor arm.

Drive shaft Another term for half shaft, usually applied to shafts not enclosed in the axle casing.

Drop arm Part of the steering linkage. See Steering, p. 35.

Drum brake A brake consisting of two curved metal shoes faced with friction material; the shoes are forced outwards on to the inside surface of a drum which is attached to a road wheel.

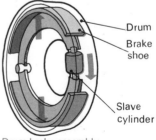

Drum

Brake shoe

Slave cylinder

Drum brake assembly

Dynamo Generator which produces direct current electricity, above idling speed.

E

Earth Connection from electrical equipment to the car body or chassis to complete an electric circuit.

F

Fan Rotating blades which draw air through the radiator. In an air-cooled car it blows air directly on to the engine.

Feeler gauge Strips of flat metal of varying thickness, marked in thousandths of an inch, used for measuring clearances.

Feeler gauge

Final drive Unit in the transmission usually including crown wheel and pinion and differential. See *Rear axle illustration, p. 35.*

Firing order Order in which the spark is produced in the cylinders from front to rear. In a four-cylinder engine the order is usually 1, 3, 4, 2, but sometimes 1, 2, 4, 3.

Float Buoyant component in the carburettor which opens and closes a valve to control the flow of petrol.

Flywheel Heavy disc bolted to the rear end of the crankshaft to smooth out the individual pulses of the pistons. By storing energy in the form of momentum, it maintains a steady rotation of the crankshaft. Around the flywheel is a toothed ring which engages with the starter motor.

Fuel pump Electrical or mechanical device which transfers petrol from the tank to the carburettor.

G

Gasket Layer of metal, fabric, cork, paper, rubber or composition sometimes sandwiched between two metal surfaces, to make a gas-tight or liquid-tight joint.

Gearbox The unit containing sets of gears which convert the high speed of the engine crankshaft into various lower speeds for the drive shaft. For instance, the lower gears allow the wheels to turn slowly while the engine is running fast.

Generator A unit, either a dynamo or alternator, which produces electricity to charge the battery.

Gudgeon pin Steel pin which connects the pistons to the small end

of the connecting rod. See *Piston illustration.*

H

Half shaft Metal shaft connecting the drive from the final drive to one of the road wheels. See *Rear axle illustration, p. 35.*

Hydrolastic A suspension system on a range of British Leyland cars which serves the purpose of both springs and dampers. Fluid in the system works in conjunction with rubber cone springs to provide an interconnection of front and rear suspension units.

I

Ignition system Electrical system which produces the sparks at the plugs to ignite the petrol/air mixture in the cylinders.

Ignition timing The relationship between the contact breaker points opening in the distributor and the compression stroke in the cylinder which ensures that each plug produces a spark at the correct time in the four-stroke cycle. See *Illustration, p. 8.*

J

Jet A component inside a carburettor which ensures the correct flow of fuel. Usually a brass screw with a hole in the middle. See *Illustration, p. 14.*

Jump leads Wires, usually with a crocodile clip at each end, used for finding a fault in an electric circuit, by cutting out a part of it. Similar, but thicker, wires called booster cables are used for starting a car which has a flat battery.

M

Main bearings Bearings which support the crankshaft. They are made in halves of steel lined with alloy, grooved to transfer oil to big-end bearings.

Manifold A branching arrangement of pipes through which air or gases flow. The inlet manifold carries the petrol/air mixture to the cylinders. The exhaust manifold allows exhaust gases to escape into the exhaust pipe.

Exhaust manifold

Master cylinder A unit in the hydraulic systems of either brake or clutch which, when a foot pedal is depressed, forces hydraulic fluid through the system (to apply the brakes or disengage the clutch).

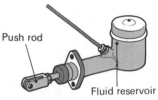
Push rod
Fluid reservoir
Master cylinder

N

Negative earth A system in which the battery's negative terminal (−) is earthed. In some cars the positive terminal (+) is earthed.

O

Overhead camshaft A camshaft mounted over the cylinder head operating the valves directly instead of through a system of push-rods and rockers.

P

Petrol pump See Fuel pump

Piston Component which moves up and down inside a cylinder. It turns the crankshaft through a connecting rod.

Piston rings Thin bands of iron or steel which fit into grooves round the piston. Each ring is sprung so that it presses outwards in the cylinders, making a gas-tight seal.

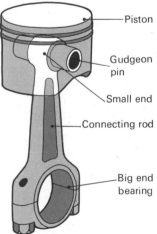
Piston
Gudgeon pin
Small end
Connecting rod
Big end bearing
Piston assembly

Points See Contact breaker

Pressure cap The cap on the radiator which maintains a predetermined pressure in the cooling system, and so raises the boiling point of the water.

Propeller shaft The shaft in front-engine, rear wheel drive cars which transmits the drive from the gearbox to the back axle.

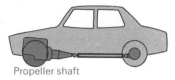
Propeller shaft

Push-rod Metal rod which is part of the valve-operating gear. See *Valve illustration*.

R

Radiator Unit for dissipating heat from water in the cooling system.

Rear axle The two drive shafts to the rear wheels and the casing in which they are contained.

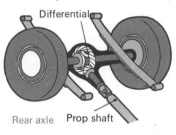
Differential
Rear axle   Prop shaft

Regulator See Control unit

Rockers Pivoted levers moved by the push rods to open and close the engine valves. See *Valve illustration*.

S

Sealed-beam unit Headlamp with reflector, lenses and filament forming one sealed unit. It is more efficient than a headlamp with a removable bulb.

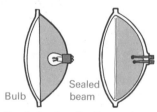
Bulb   Sealed beam

Shock absorber See Damper

Short circuit Electric current taking a 'short cut' to earth instead of flowing through the system, resulting in the failure of an electrical component.

Slave cylinder Small unit at the end of a hydraulic system (brakes or clutch) which converts hydraulic pressure back to mechanical effort.

Solenoid Electro-magnetic device which usually acts as a remote-controlled heavy-duty switch – as for the starter motor.

Spark-plug Device which produces the spark needed to ignite the petrol/air mixture in the cylinder, by making high-tension current jump between two electrodes.

Steering A mechanical system for changing the car's direction of travel by turning the front wheels. All systems have a steering wheel and steering column. The column is connected either to a steering box or to a rack and pinion. Steering-box arrangements have a drop arm which moves track rods connected to the wheels. Rack-and-pinion arrangements are connected to the wheels through ball joints and track rods.

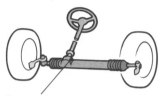
Rack and pinion

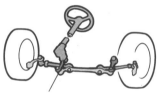
Steering box
Two types of steering assembly

Sump Container bolted to the bottom of the engine to hold the oil which is pumped round the engine to lubricate bearings and moving parts.

Suspension The springs and dampers or hydraulic system which supports the car body and minimises vibrations from the road.

Synchromesh Mechanism which equalises the speed of a gear and the shaft it is on before locking them together. Used in gearboxes to make easy gear changes.

T

Tappet Steel cylinder which is part of an engine's valve-operating mechanism.

Thermostat Automatic temperature regulator which prevents the coolant circulating through the radiator until the engine has reached working temperature.

Throttle Butterfly valve in the carburettor which regulates the amount of petrol/air mixture flowing into the cylinders. It is operated by the accelerator pedal.

Track The distance between a pair of wheels, measured between the centres of the tyre treads where they meet the road. A car's front-wheel track may not be the same as its rear-wheel track.

Track rod See Steering

Transmission General term applied to the clutch, gearbox, propeller shaft, differential and rear axle, through which engine power is transmitted to turn the wheels.

Trickle charger Accessory for recharging a car battery from the electric mains. It converts the mains' alternating current to direct current and lowers the voltage to suit the battery (6 or 12 volt).

U

Universal joint Flexible joint connecting two shafts, but allowing one to pivot in relation to the other.

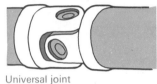
Universal joint

V

Valve Device for controlling the flow of liquids or gases. Several different types are used in a car, but 'the valves' usually refer to those in the cylinder head which control the entry of the mixture and the exit of the exhaust gases.

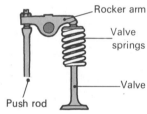
Rocker arm
Valve springs
Valve
Push rod
Valve gear

Valve clearance The free movement between the rocker arm and the valve stem when the valve is fully closed.

Valve springs Coil springs, usually in pairs, one inside the other, for closing the valves.

W

Water pump More correctly, a water impeller, which pushes water round the engine.

Wheel alignment Adjustment of the front wheels to counteract their tendency to run out (splay out). Wrongly aligned wheels cause uneven and rapid tyre wear.

LAW AND THE MOTORIST

What to do after an accident

The first action to take after an accident is to warn other traffic so that more vehicles do not pile into the crash (see p. 4).

Next attend to the injured (see p. 65).

Finally start dealing with the legal and insurance problems. Take names and addresses of other people involved and of witnesses, and note important facts about the accident (see opposite page).

Exchanging names and addresses

If you are involved in an accident that has caused damage or injury to another person or vehicle, to property, or to any animal (horse, cattle, ass, mule, sheep, pig or dog) not being carried in your vehicle, the law requires you to give your name and address, as well as those details of the owner of the vehicle if it is not you, to anyone with reasonable grounds for requiring that information. This usually means anyone else involved in the accident.

In an accident involving personal injury, you must, if required, also produce your certificate of insurance.

Reporting to the police

If, for any reason, you have not given your name and address at the scene of the accident, or if, in the case of personal injury, you have not produced your certificate of insurance, you must report the accident to a police constable or at a police station. This must be done as soon as is reasonably practicable, in any case within 24 hours of the accident (this does not mean automatic entitlement to 24 hours). Failure to do so is an offence for which there can be a fine of up to £100 as well as disqualification from driving.

If you have not got your driving documents with you when reporting an accident to the police, you will be allowed to produce them at a police station of your choice within five days. Failure to do so is also an offence that can lead to a fine of up to £100.

You may wish to call the police for an independent record of the circumstances, but they are under no obligation to attend the scene of every accident. Even if they respond to such a call, you have no power to detain another driver until the police are on the spot.

Avoid getting involved in discussions about the cause of the accident.

A safe general rule is: say as little as possible either to the other driver or to the police. In particular, never admit blame – it could provide prosecution evidence, and if you are in an agitated frame of mind, you may be admitting more than the facts warrant. You do not have to make a statement – written or verbal – to the police, either at the scene or at a police station. If you do wish to make a written statement, perhaps blaming the other driver, write it yourself if you feel confident enough to do so – or make sure that a policeman writes the statement in your words rather than his own. Read it carefully before signing it. Initial all additions or corrections that you make.

In a case of any seriousness it is better just to give your name and address and insurance particulars and state that you do not wish to say anything more and you will be getting in touch with your solicitor as soon as possible. Then, as soon as you can, make a written account of the incident.

Informing the insurance company

As soon as possible after being involved in an accident (and certainly within a week), notify your insurance company or broker.

Details of what can be claimed are given on the policy. It normally covers the driver against claims made against him. A driver may also be able to claim from his insurance company the cost of repairing any damage to his own car. Give the date, place and time of the accident, the estimated speeds of the vehicles involved, and describe the road conditions and visibility. Include a copy of any sketch map or photo-

graphs, give the names and addresses of any passengers or witnesses, and state whether or not the police were at the scene.

Keep your insurance company informed of any developments arising out of an accident. Immediately send to them, unanswered, any letter, summons or claim against you.

An injured passenger may be able to claim damages against the other driver involved, the driver of the car in which he was travelling, or both. To succeed, he must prove that a driver was negligent or at least partly to blame.

What to carry with you

A prudent motorist accepts that one day he may be involved in an accident. Ideally he should carry in his car (in addition to the first-aid equipment described on p. 71) the following items for recording information:

1 Notebook and pen or pencil.
2 Steel tape measure.
3 Chalk.
4 Flashing torch.
5 A loaded camera.

Recording evidence on the spot

A driver involved in an accident should note the relevant facts in case there is a court action or a claim for compensation at a later date. Record the following information:

1 Names and addresses of other people involved in the accident and of any witnesses. Any other driver involved must give his name and address, but witnesses or passengers are not bound to give this information to anyone but a police officer.

2 Registration numbers of any other vehicles involved.

3 The name and address of the other driver's insurance company, and his insurance certificate number if known.

4 The amount of traffic at the time of the accident.

5 The time of day and weather conditions (and, after dark, positions of street lights).

6 The positions of other vehicles. Make a sketch, or take photographs, if possible. Unless a vehicle is causing a dangerous obstruction, do not move it until the police have taken measurements at the scene. If the vehicle is a danger to other road users its position at the time of the accident should be marked on the road in chalk, and then it should be moved to a safe place near by.

7 Note also such other features as broken glass in the road, skid marks, road signs and obstructions.

Making a plan of an accident

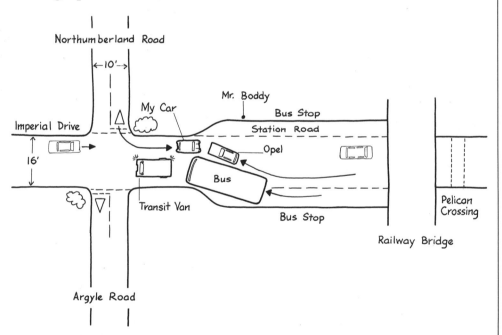

At 1 p.m. on August 13 I drove my Mini – WFC 159K – down Northumberland Road. I stopped at the junction, then turned left into Station Road. I had to keep close to the nearside as there was a Ford Transit waiting to turn right off Station Road into Northumberland Road. As I turned I noticed a 14A bus leaving the bay opposite causing a following motorist (Opel Ascona WAP 952H) to swerve sharply to avoid colliding with the rear of the bus. I braked violently but still could not avoid a collision with the swerving Opel. I incurred damage to my headlights, grille and windscreen, which was shattered. The driver of the Opel was Mr H. Smith of 14 High Street, who is insured with the Acme Insurance Company of Birmingham. His car was severely dented in the front and nearside. Mr Arthur Boddy, of 100 Belgrave Road, witnessed the accident. The weather was sunny and the surface of the road dry.

Repairing your car after an accident

If you are involved in an accident and your insurance policy entitles you to claim for repairs, get a detailed estimate of the probable cost from a garage of your choice and send it to the insurance company.

In most cases, repair work can then begin. In some cases, however, insurance companies require their own engineer to inspect the damage before the garage is authorised to begin work. A telephone call to your insurance company will tell you when the repair work can be put in hand. After the repairs have been done, the policy holder is generally asked to sign a form stating that he is satisfied with the work. Do not sign such a form until you have inspected the work and found it satisfactory.

If it costs more to repair a car than the car is worth on the open market, it is written off by the insurance company. In this case the insurance company is entitled, under a comprehensive policy, to offer a single lump-sum payment instead of paying for repairs. This payment represents the market value of the car at the time of the accident (less any hire-purchase payments still owing), unless it is insured for a smaller amount or there is an 'agreed-value' clause in the policy. If the policy holder agrees to the offer of the insurance company, the company is entitled to take what is left of the vehicle and sell it as scrap.

Private claims

There are three reasons why a motorist may wish to bring a private claim against another driver or his insurance company rather than claim on his own insurance.

1 To preserve his no-claim bonus.

2 To recover any money which he cannot claim from his insurance company because of an 'accidental damages excess' clause in his policy. This means that, usually in return for a reduced premium, a driver has undertaken to pay the first part (say £15 or £25) of any claim for accidental damages to his car, called the excess.

3 Because he has only Third Party insurance, which does not cover him against damage to his own car.

But even if he intends to make a private claim, the driver must still notify his insurance company.

This leaves him free to make a claim on his own insurance later if the circumstances change. Be wary if another driver admits responsibility for causing damage to your car and offers an 'on-the-spot' settlement.

What appears to be only a minor external dent may have caused other damage, so wait until a garage makes a proper estimate of the likely cost of repairs, and then make your damages claim. Do not accept another driver's offer to have your car repaired by his garage and at his expense. You have no control over the quality and time taken for such work.

To make a claim for repairs to your car, first get an estimate of the probable cost. Then write to the other driver or his insurance company, saying you are holding him responsible and enclosing a copy of the estimate and details of any other claim (such as the cost of hiring a car while yours is damaged).

Keep a copy of this and all other correspondence. Do not wait more than a week for a reply to your initial letter, or more than two weeks for a reply to a letter setting out full details of your claim. If there is a delay, send a firm reminder threatening legal action. If you still get no response, consult your insurance company or your solicitor. Often a personal visit to the other driver's insurance company achieves the quickest results.

The company may settle the claim immediately by paying the estimated repair costs. But it may make an offer which you regard as too small.

Or it may offer to consider the claim only after the repairs have been done and a final account drawn up – and then it could refuse to settle. If such difficulties arise, put the matter in the hands of your own insurance company.

What to claim

A motorist who is free from blame in an accident can generally claim the cost of repairs, any towing charge, and fares on public transport or the cost of hiring a vehicle, if this is essential, while his vehicle is being repaired.

Hire charges must not include the cost of petrol used, and the cost of fares on public transport must be reduced by the amount which normally would have been spent on petrol to make those journeys.

When you receive what you regard as a reasonable offer, write accepting it, but make it clear that you are not admitting any liability yourself. Make sure that any agreement to settle without involving insurance companies is made for the full amount and within a specified time.

Claims against you

Before deciding to settle a private claim made against yourself, make sure what is involved. Even quite minor damage to a car's bodywork can be expensive to repair, and a claim for personal injury could ultimately be estimated at thousands of pounds.

But a reasonable and straightforward claim for repairs which is less than your no-claim bonus can be met, although you should still inform your insurance company of your intentions. Get the claimant to supply an estimate, try to settle immediately, and make it clear that the payment is 'final and in full' and is made without admitting any liability. If the claim seems too high and the other driver refuses to reduce it, or to get another estimate, refer the matter to your own insurance company or seek legal advice.

If only a few pounds are in dispute it is probably better to pay up than to lose your no-claim bonus or meet legal costs.

When a driver must stop

A driver must stop if signalled to do so by any of the following:

1 A policeman in uniform.

2 A traffic warden who is controlling moving traffic or pedestrians.

3 A school crossing patrol.

A driver who disobeys such a signal may be fined up to £100.

A workman controlling traffic at roadworks with a Stop–Go sign has no power to stop a motorist except in the control of traffic, and in that instance his instructions must be obeyed.
Having stopped, a motorist must not drive on until signalled to do so.

A driver is also obliged by law to stop in the following circumstances:

At the scene of an accident;

IF any person, outside or inside the car, is injured;

IF any other vehicle is damaged;

IF any roadside property is damaged – for example, a road sign, street lamp or wall of a house.

IF any animal – cattle, dog, goat, horse, ass, mule, pig or sheep – not in his vehicle is injured.

The driver must remain at the scene of an accident long enough to enable particulars to be given to any person who is reasonably entitled to demand them.

If the police have been called to the scene, the driver should wait until they arrive.

Failure to stop after an accident is a serious offence that can incur a fine of up to £100, an endorsement and disqualification.

Powers of a traffic warden

The function of traffic wardens is to assist the police in the regulation and control of traffic and pedestrians. They have the same powers as the police to require alleged offenders to provide their name and address. They cannot, however, ask a driver to produce his driving licence except when employed at a car pound, when refusal would be an offence regardless of the reason for the car's removal.
Traffic wardens can issue fixed-penalty tickets for all parking offences (except those of causing wilful or unnecessary obstruction), for leaving vehicles after dark without lights, and for failure to display a valid excise licence.

Searching a vehicle or driver

The police can stop and search any vehicle if it is suspected that the driver is in possession of stolen goods, a firearm, certain drugs, or game or wild birds that have been obtained unlawfully.

Police powers of arrest

A police officer may arrest on the spot any driver who:

1 Drives, attempts to drive, or is in charge of a motor vehicle while under the influence of drink or drugs.

2 Drives, attempts to drive, or is in charge of a car when his blood-alcohol concentration is above the prescribed limit.

3 Refuses to take a breath test.

4 Has a positive result in a breath test.

5 Is to be charged with reckless or careless driving, if the driver does not supply his name and address or is unable to produce his driving licence.

6 Drives while disqualified.

7 Takes a vehicle without consent of the owner or other lawful authority.

In many cases, a motorist can be arrested even if he is not actually driving. It is enough that he may be about to attempt to drive or that he is in charge of the vehicle.
Where the police believe that a car may have been stolen – perhaps because the driver cannot remember the registration number or cannot prove that it is hired or borrowed – they may ask him to go to the police station. He is not obliged to do so unless he is arrested, but failure to help the police may complicate the situation and antagonise the officers involved. A person who has an innocent explanation is usually best advised to co-operate.

If you are stopped by the police

1 The police are entitled to demand from a driver his name, address and the name and address of the vehicle's owner.

2 The police can also ask for the name and address of the person who was driving the vehicle when it was involved in a previous accident or an alleged traffic offence.

3 A uniformed policeman can also ask for and examine a motorist's driving licence. If a driver is not carrying his licence, he can be instructed to take it to a police station nominated by the driver within five days.

4 A driver must also produce on request his insurance certificate and the annual vehicle (DoT) test certificate, if applicable, or take them to a nominated police station within five days of being asked for them.

Warning of intended prosecution

When a driver is stopped for certain offences, the police must either warn him that the matter will be reported, and be considered with a view to prosecution, or, within 14 days, they must send him or the owner of the vehicle a notice of intended prosecution giving details of the alleged offence.

If the police have not complied with this rule, the driver cannot be convicted. But it is the driver who has to prove that no warning, verbal or written, was given: the warning is deemed to have been given unless the contrary is proved.

No police warning is required where a driver has been involved in an accident.

A warning must be given for:

1 Reckless or careless driving.

2 Speeding.

3 Failure to obey traffic signs or directions, including double white lines.

4 Leaving a vehicle in a dangerous position.

When to get legal advice

As soon as a driver receives warning of intended prosecution, it is in his best interests to get legal advice. A member can apply to the AA for legal advice and representation in court. He should send to the Association's legal department, at the appropriate Regional Headquarters, any summons or notice of intended prosecution (see AA Members' Handbook).

Speeding offences

There are two classes of speeding offence – exceeding the *vehicle's* speed limit and exceeding the limit set for the *road*.

1 Ordinary passenger vehicles (unless adapted to carry more than seven passengers or when towing trailers) are not subject to any 'vehicle' speed limit; nor is there a limit for dual-purpose vehicles – for example, shooting brakes.

Goods vehicles or vehicles drawing trailers are subject to limits according to their size.

2 A limit of 30 mph is imposed in all 'built up' areas, i.e., where street lighting is from lamps not more than 200 yds apart, unless a higher limit or derestriction is indicated.

Derestriction signs do not indicate that there is no speed limit. They impose the national limit of 60 mph on single carriageways and of 70 mph on dual carriageways and motorways.

Police methods

Methods used by police to detect speeding include the use of radar and Vascar. The radar device is set at the roadside to bounce a beam of radio waves off passing vehicles and record their speeds on a meter.

Vascar (Visual Average Speed Computer and Recorder) is a method of remote calculation of a vehicle's speed by a device mounted on a following police car.

A common method still practised is for police to keep an even distance from the speeding vehicle until the speed is established.

Although the law requires evidence of speeding to be corroborated, i.e. supported by other evidence, this does not limit that evidence to be given by two police witnesses. It has been held that the evidence of a police speedometer can provide corroboration of a single police witness. If you are stopped for speeding, always ask the method used and the precise speed alleged. If you dispute it, make sure that a note is taken by the police of your denial and get your speedometer checked as soon as possible.

Penalties

Endorsement of licence is virtually automatic for a speeding offence. Fines for speeding are about £1.50 per mile above the limit – that means, for example, a fine of £30 for driving at 60 mph in a 40 mph limit – and the maximum is £100. An excess of more than 30 mph over the limit may result in a proportionately higher fine as well as greater likelihood of disqualification. Speeds in excess of 80 mph on motorways regularly involve disqualification, even on a first offence. 'Totting up' disqualifications, i.e. where the driver has had two endorsements within the three years preceding the latest offence, are most common for speeding offences.

What to do when stopped for speeding

1 The police do not have to tell the driver his alleged speed, but you should always ask what they think it was. If you dispute the speed, say so at once and see that the police write down your reply.

2 If you intend to plead not guilty to a possible speeding charge, have your speedo-meter tested straight away. Do not wait until the arrival of a summons.

3 Get the tester to provide a written statement which can be submitted as evidence.

4 Because speeding charges are among the most difficult to defend, seek legal advice.

Taking a breath test

It is in your interest to bear these simple points in mind if stopped by the police and asked to take a breath test.

1 Ask the reasons for requiring a breath test.

2 Tell the police when you last had a drink and ask for the test to be delayed if drink was taken within 20 minutes of being stopped – to avoid an excessive reading due to mouth alcohol. (You can be arrested if the reading is above the limit.)

3 Police procedure is to use the filing hole in their box to break off both ends of the breathalyser. The bag is fixed to the green end, the mouthpiece fastened to the white-band end of the tube. The bag should be inflated in 10–20 seconds with one breath (make sure that you wipe your lips to remove any alcohol).

4 Ask to see the tube if the test is positive. If it is difficult to see by street lighting, the police will show it to you by the car's lights or under torchlight.

5 After arrest, the tube will be taken to the police station to be shown to the officer in charge.

Drinking and driving offences

The law says that a uniformed police officer may require any person driving or attempting to drive a motor vehicle on a road or other public place, to provide a specimen of breath there or near by if the officer has reasonable cause to suspect him of

1 Having alcohol in his body, or

2 Having committed a moving traffic offence.

Note that the test will normally be carried out publicly on the spot 'or near by'. If a traffic offence is alleged, the test must be made as soon as is reasonably practicable.

Random tests are not permitted, but a driver may be suspected of having alcohol in his blood after being stopped for any good reason: for example, the policeman may smell alcohol on a driver's breath when he speaks to him. Failure to supply breath or sufficient breath is an offence – unless the driver can prove a reasonable excuse for his refusal or inability. The maximum fine is £50.

The detailed police procedure requires that the arrested driver be first asked for a specimen of blood. If he refuses he must be asked for two specimens of urine to be given within an hour, the first specimen to be discarded. If he fails, or refuses within an hour, he must be asked again to provide a specimen of blood.

A doctor, usually the police surgeon, will be called and will ask the motorist's consent to take a blood specimen – normally from a finger or vein in an arm. The motorist cannot dictate the method, nor can he insist on having his own doctor or his solicitor present.

The police must offer the motorist a part of the specimen he has given. Their part is sent for laboratory analysis, and the result of the analysis is sent to the driver, usually within three weeks. If there was an excess of 80 mg of alcohol in 100 ml of blood – or the equivalent in the urine – the driver will be prosecuted.

At the police station

If the roadside breath test is positive – or it has been refused or failed – the driver is arrested and taken to a police station. He must there be offered the opportunity of a further breath test. (Agreeing at the station to take a test does not, however, excuse an earlier refusal at the roadside.) At least 20 minutes must have elapsed since the roadside test. If the second test proves negative the driver must be released, unless police propose to prefer a charge of being 'unfit' to drive.

A blood or urine test

When a person has given a positive breath specimen at the police station, or has failed to give a breath specimen, he is asked to give a specimen of blood or urine. He must be warned that refusal carries a maximum penalty of £1000 and imprisonment and obligatory disqualification for at least 12 months.

Accidents and breath tests

If an accident occurs because of the presence of a motor vehicle on a road or other public place, a uniformed policeman may require any person who he has reasonable cause to believe was driving or attempting to drive the vehicle at the time of the accident to provide a specimen of breath for a breath test.

Such a breath test may be on the spot or at a police station. If a driver is admitted to hospital, the permission of the patient's doctor must be obtained; and if the breath test is positive, the hospital doctor is asked to allow a blood or urine specimen to be taken by the police doctor.

How much can you drink?

It is better not to drink at all before driving. There is no simple way of knowing how much a person can drink before the amount of alcohol in his blood exceeds the legal maximum of 80 mg per 100 ml of blood. The concentration depends on how much exercise he has had, as well as what he has eaten and drunk and how quickly.

As a general rule, eating before or during drinking slows down the rate at which alcohol is absorbed into the blood. Alcohol usually has more effect on someone of small build and is absorbed into the blood more quickly the quicker it is drunk.

Spirits are absorbed rapidly when taken neat or diluted – and even more quickly when taken with soda water, because aeration keeps the alcohol circulating in the digestive system.

Beer is absorbed slowly. It is a diluted form of alcohol because of its high content of soluble nutrients. Doctors assume that the blood-alcohol level will be only one-third of that when the same amount of alcohol is drunk as spirits.

Wine is absorbed slowly because of its sugar content.

Penalties

For driving or attempting to drive with excess alcohol in the blood, the maximum penalty is a fine of £1000 or imprisonment up to six months, or both. Disqualification for at least 12 months is obligatory and can be increased in proportion to the excess, e.g. 160 mg of alcohol may result in two years' disqualification. For being in charge of a vehicle (as opposed to driving), the maximum fine is £500 and/or three months' imprisonment, and disqualification is at the court's discretion.

The alternative law

Any person who drives or attempts to drive a motor vehicle on a road or other public place when he is 'unfit to drive' through drink or drugs, is guilty of an offence. This means that without any breath test a motorist may be arrested as unfit to drive.

A driver is taken to be 'unfit to drive' if his ability to drive properly is for the time being impaired. He will normally be offered a blood or urine test at the police station, and refusal may be treated as evidence against him. A doctor will be called and may examine him.

The penalty for being unfit is the same as for an excess of alcohol – a fine of up to £1000 and/or up to six months' imprisonment and obligatory minimum of 12 months' disqualification.

Drunk in charge

It is an offence simply to be 'in charge' of a vehicle while 'unfit to drive' or with excess alcohol in the blood.

Normally a person remains in charge of his car unless and until he passes it over to someone else. But the law says that a person shall not be considered to be in charge if he proves that at the time there was no likelihood of his driving as long as he remained unfit, or as long as there was any probability of his having excess alcohol in his blood. The penalty for being 'in charge' (as opposed to driving or attempting to drive) is a fine up to £500 and/or three months' imprisonment with disqualification at the court's discretion.

When police may check your car

Authorised police officers and Department of Transport examiners are empowered to conduct a roadside check on any vehicle for defects. The motorist is entitled to require the police or examiner to produce his authority. An ordinary police warrant card is not enough; the officer should carry a certificate which authorises him to inspect motor vehicles.

A driver is normally entitled to ask for a test check to be deferred for up to 30 days and to choose where it is to be carried out. He must give the police an opportunity to inspect the car within a seven-day period before the end of the 30 days. But if the car has been in an accident or the policeman believes that it is unsafe the police can insist on a check without further delay.

A car on private premises cannot be tested unless the owner of the premises gives his consent, or the car owner has been given at least 48 hours' notice. No notice or consent is required if the police believe that the car has been involved in an accident within the last 48 hours.

Police can apply for a magistrates' warrant if the owner of premises refuses to allow them to check a vehicle.

When the police conduct a check they may examine the general condition of a car as well as the specific points governed by Construction and Use Regulations. These are detailed Government standards laid down for brakes, steering, tyres, suspension, lights, seat belts and the exhaust and silencer system. Both the driver and owner of a vehicle who allows it to be used are responsible if any of these items are defective. The maximum penalty for using a vehicle in a dangerous condition is £100 with endorsement and unlimited disqualification, unless a driver can prove that he was not aware of the vehicle's condition and had no reasonable cause to suspect it. There is a similar penalty for using a vehicle with defective steering, brakes or tyres.

READING ROAD SIGNS

Motorway hazard signs

Motorway signs are kept simple for easy recognition at high speed, and most of them indicate that there is a hazard ahead; for example, an accident, fog or a risk of skidding. These signs consist of flashing lights, numbers and symbols. Some motorways have other special signals – such as on the Severn Bridge, to warn of high winds. Always: STOP at a flashing red light and SLOW DOWN to the advised speed when amber lights are flashing. Slow down even further when you see the danger, and do not resume normal speed until certain all is clear.
If the earlier type of signals (see below) are flashing, keep below 30 mph.

Above the lanes

Advised maximum speed. If flashing amber lights change to flashing red, stop at the sign

Move to lane on left (reversed for move to right)

Leave the motorway at the next exit

Restrictions at an end (also shown beside carriageway)

Beside the carriageway

Earlier-type sign

Signs at entrances advise maximum speed. If flashing amber lights change to flashing red, stop at the signal

Signs on central reservation may show maximum speed or (as here) indicate that a lane is closed ahead

Flashing amber lights indicate that the advised maximum speed is 30 mph and warn of some danger ahead (such as an accident, fog or ice)

Information signs

Signs giving information on motorways and other roads are *always* rectangular, whereas signs giving orders are *mostly* circular.

No through road

Recommended for pedal cycles

Parking place

Meter ZONE

Mon-Fri 8·30 am-6·30 pm
Saturday 8·30 am-1·30 pm

Entrance to controlled parking zone

'Count-down' markers at exit from motorway or primary route (each bar represents 100 yds to the exit)

You have priority over vehicles from opposite direction

Bus lane

Bus lane at junction ahead

Appropriate traffic lanes at junction ahead

Direction signs

Motorways

Turn-off ½ mile ahead for town indicated. The motorway junction number is in the bottom left-hand corner

Primary routes

Turn-offs ahead for towns indicated; width of symbol shows importance of road

Other routes

Places on roads extending from junction ahead

Local routes

Junctions ahead leading to place indicated; width of symbol shows road importance

Warning signs

The symbol inside a red triangle denotes the kind of danger ahead. The only two inverted triangles warn of further signs giving orders.

JUNCTION SIGNS Priority is indicated by thickened line

Distance to
STOP
sign ahead

Distance to
GIVE WAY
sign ahead

Children

Plate used with
sign near
school . . .

Patrol
200 yds

. . . and plate used
near school
crossing

Road narrows on
offside (nearside
if symbol
reversed)

Single file
traffic

Single file in
each direction

Single track
road

Road wide
enough for only
one line of
traffic

 Road narrows
on both sides

 Dual carriageway
ends

Two-way traffic
straight ahead

 Two-way traffic
crosses
one-way road

 Roundabout

 Change to
opposite
carriageway
(may be reversed)

 Right-hand lane
closed (symbols
may be varied)

 Traffic merges
from left

 Traffic joins
from right

 Bend to right
(reversed for left)

 Double bend
(starting left)

 Steep hill

Signs giving orders

Blue discs and red circles give commands. In GIVE WAY and STOP signs the triangles are inverted to emphasise their importance.

Give way to traffic
on major road

All vehicles
prohibited

No entry

Give way to
vehicles from
opposite direction

 Turn left
ahead

 Turn right
ahead

 Turn left

 Turn right

Ahead only

 Mini
roundabout

Stop and
give way

Play Street
8 am to sunset
except for
access

Details of
prohibition

No U turns

No right turn
(no left turn
if reversed)

 Keep left

 Keep right

 Pass either
side

Overtaking
prohibited

Goods vehicles over
unladen weight
shown prohibited

Vehicles with
more than 12
seats prohibited

No cycling

 Minimum speed

 End of minimum
speed

 Pedal cycles
only

All motor
vehicles
prohibited

Total weight
limit

National speed
limit applies

Maximum speed

 School crossing
patrol. Vehicles
must stop

 Hand-operated
roadworks sign

 No stopping
(clearway)

Pelican crossings

At these crossings the pedestrian controls the lights with a push button. The difference compared with normal traffic lights, is that the motorist sees a flashing amber light before the green instead of a red-with-amber. This means he can proceed, but must give priority to pedestrians.

 Green means that drivers have priority to cross

 Amber means stop, unless it is unsafe to do so

 Red means stop pedestrians have priority

 Flashing amber means drivers can proceed only if crossing is clear

Pedestrian crossing ahead

Road works

Slippery road

Uneven road

Falling or fallen rocks

Cattle

Wild horses or ponies

Wild animals

Opening or swing bridge

Quayside or river bank

Low-flying aircraft or sudden aircraft noise

Height limit (e.g. low bridge)

Overhead electric cables

Other danger

Worded warning sign

Available width of headroom indicated

Plate indicating maximum safe height for vehicles

Safe height 16'-6"

Plate indicating nature of danger

Surveying

1 mile
Distance to hazard

For 2 miles
Extent of the hazard

Railway crossings

Flashing red signal means STOP

'Count down' markers approaching concealed level crossing

Level crossing with gate or barrier ahead

Location of level crossing without gate or barrier

Level crossing without gate or barrier ahead

Road markings

WHITE LINES Do not cross solid white line. If line is broken (right) on your side of road, cross line only if safe to do so

Do not enter marked area unless safe

Lane line

Centre line

Warning line

Along the carriageway edge

1. Junctions with Give Way lines. 2. Other junctions and lay-bys.
3. Bends and other hazards. 4. Elsewhere.

NO WAITING (except for loading and unloading) at times shown on nearby plates or entry signs to parking zones

1. During every working day. 2. During every working day and additional times. 3. During any other periods.

Across a carriageway

Advance warning of GIVE WAY just ahead

Box junction. Do not enter if exit is blocked

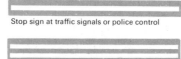
Stop sign at traffic signals or police control

Stop line at STOP sign

Give way lines (single at roundabouts)

On the kerb or edge of the carriageway

NO LOADING
1. During every working day.
2. During every working day and additional times.
3. During any other periods.

ZIGZAG CROSSING
Stop at the broken line before the zebra markings if pedestrians are crossing. Do not overtake, wait or park within the zigzag markings.

WEATHER HAZARDS

How to avoid trouble-spots on motorways

A motorist planning a long motorway journey might avoid hazards and delays caused by bad weather if he studies the maps on these and the following pages before setting out.

Bad weather probably blankets a large area—but, whatever might be the general situation, certain stretches of a motorway are more liable than others to crosswinds, fog or snow. This map is designed to pinpoint such trouble-spots with the help of radio weather forecasts or area forecasts obtained by dialling the appropriate number given below or on p. 48.

Police signs indicate alternative routes when sections of motorway are closed. But by then the motorist is caught up in the congestion and it is too late for him to choose another road.

The suggested alternative routes given on these maps are for drivers who are *planning ahead* to avoid possible bad-weather stretches of motorway.

The effectiveness of these alternatives might depend on traffic conditions at a particular time of day or road works, so a cross-reference to the appropriate road map is given for the motorist to choose his alternative route.

Motorway strip maps—see pp. 117–26.
Road conditions—telephone numbers for certain areas are given on the map flaps on pp. 139–263.

Forecasts by telephone

A motorist can get weather forecasts for the various stages of his route by telephoning the following numbers before setting out or en route:

Glasgow	041 246 8091
Edinburgh	031 246 8091

Tyne-Tees
   Newcastle upon Tyne 8091

Continued on p. 48.

M 8

JUNCTIONS 2–3
Fog

JUNCTIONS 3–5
Cross-winds on exposed parts

JUNCTIONS 4–5
Snow and ice

Alternative routes A89, B7066

See map 232

M 8

JUNCTION 5, west for $1\frac{1}{2}$ mls. Fog, snow and ice

JUNCTION 5, east for 2 mls. Fog, snow and ice, cross-winds

Alternative route B7066

See map 232

M 8

JUNCTIONS 8–9
High winds and ice on viaduct

JUNCTIONS 10–11
Strong cross-winds, ice and fog

See map 232

M 74

JUNCTIONS 2–3
Snow and ice

JUNCTIONS 4–5
Fog

JUNCTIONS 1–2, 4–5
Cross-winds
Alternative route B7078 A72 B7071
See maps 226, 232

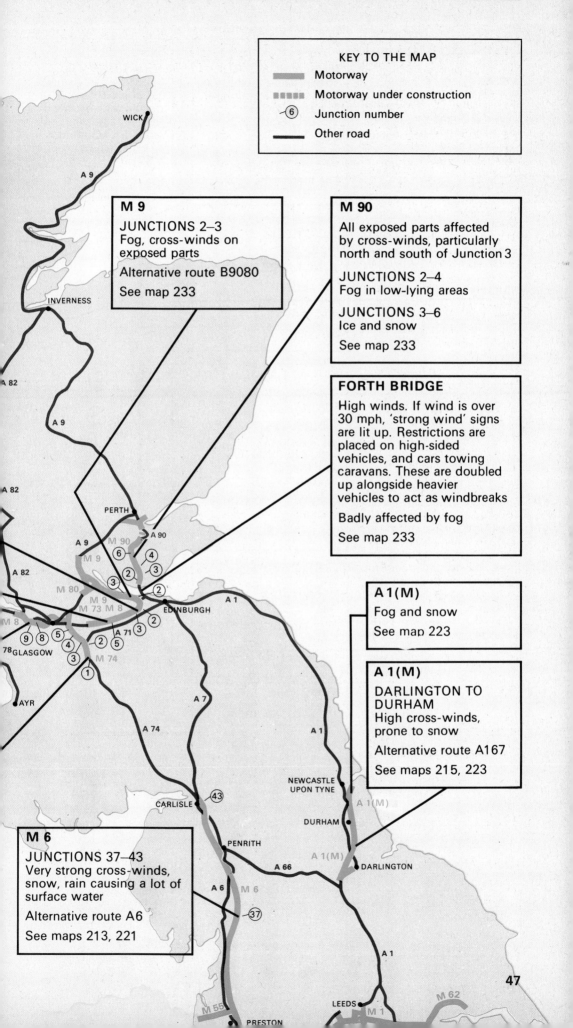

KEY TO THE MAP

Motorway

Motorway under construction

⑥ Junction number

Other road

WICK

A 9

M 9

JUNCTIONS 2–3
Fog, cross-winds on exposed parts

Alternative route B9080

See map 233

M 90

All exposed parts affected by cross-winds, particularly north and south of Junction 3

JUNCTIONS 2–4
Fog in low-lying areas

JUNCTIONS 3–6
Ice and snow

See map 233

INVERNESS

A 82

A 9

A 82

FORTH BRIDGE

High winds. If wind is over 30 mph, 'strong wind' signs are lit up. Restrictions are placed on high-sided vehicles, and cars towing caravans. These are doubled up alongside heavier vehicles to act as windbreaks

Badly affected by fog

See map 233

PERTH

A 9   M 90   A 90

M 9

A 82   ⑥   ④

M 80   ③   ③

②

M 9   ③   ②

M 73 M 8

M 8   EDINBURGH   A 1

⑨ ⑧ ⑤   A 71   ③   ②

78 GLASGOW   ④   ②   ⑤

③

A 1(M)

Fog and snow

See map 223

A 1(M)

DARLINGTON TO DURHAM
High cross-winds, prone to snow

Alternative route A167

See maps 215, 223

M 74

AYR

A 7

A 74

A 1

NEWCASTLE UPON TYNE

CARLISLE   ㊸

DURHAM

A 1(M)

PENRITH

A 1(M)   DARLINGTON

A 66

M 6

JUNCTIONS 37–43
Very strong cross-winds, snow, rain causing a lot of surface water

Alternative route A6

See maps 213, 221

A 6   M 6

㊲

A 1

47

M 55

LEEDS   M 62

PRESTON   M 1

Forecasts by telephone

A motorist can get weather forecasts for the various stages of his route by telephoning the following numbers before setting out or en route:

Lancashire (coast)
061 246 8092
Lancashire (central)
Blackburn 8091

South Lancashire
051 246 8091

Leeds   Leeds 8091

Sheffield   Sheffield 8091

North Lincolnshire
Lincoln 8091

Notts & Derby
Nottingham 8091

Norfolk & Suffolk
Ipswich 8091

Bedford   01 246 8099

Birmingham   021 246 8091

South-west Midlands
Gloucester 8091

Cardiff   Cardiff 8091

Thames Valley   01 246 8090

Bristol   Bristol 8091

London   01 246 8091

Kent coast   01 246 8098

South Devon   0392 8091
                 0803 8091

Isle of Wight & S Hants
Southampton 8091

Sussex coast   01 246 8097

M 6
North of JUNCTION 15 Thick fog mixed with smoke from diesel lorries on incline
JUNCTIONS 14–15 Fog
Alternative route A34
See maps 190, 202

M 6
JUNCTIONS 12–13 High winds
JUNCTIONS 10–11 Mist, fog
Alternative routes A34, A449
See map 190

M 6–M 1 Midland link
JUNCTIONS 1–4 Fog
JUNCTIONS 2–4 High winds (particularly Longford viaduct at Junction 3)
Subject to surface water
High winds on elevated sections
See maps 180, 191, 192

M 5/50
JUNCTION 8 Fog
Alternative routes A38, A449
See map 178

M 5
JUNCTIONS 14–15 High winds
Alternative route A38
See maps 166, 167

M 62
JUNCTIONS 21–22 Strong winds, heavy fog, thick snow (mainly around Windy Hill and across Moss Moor but sometimes on other stretches of M62)
See map 208

M 5
JUNCTIONS 3–4 Fog
Alternative routes B4551, A38
See maps 179, 191

SEVERN BRIDGE
High winds
See map 166

M 5
4 miles north of JUNCTION 22 Fog
See maps 153, 166

KEY TO THE MAP
Motorway
Motorway under construction
(5) Junction number
Other road

A 5
CARMARTHEN
SWANSEA
CARDIF
M 4
M 5   A 3
EXETER
A 30
PLYMOUTH
A 379
PENZANCE

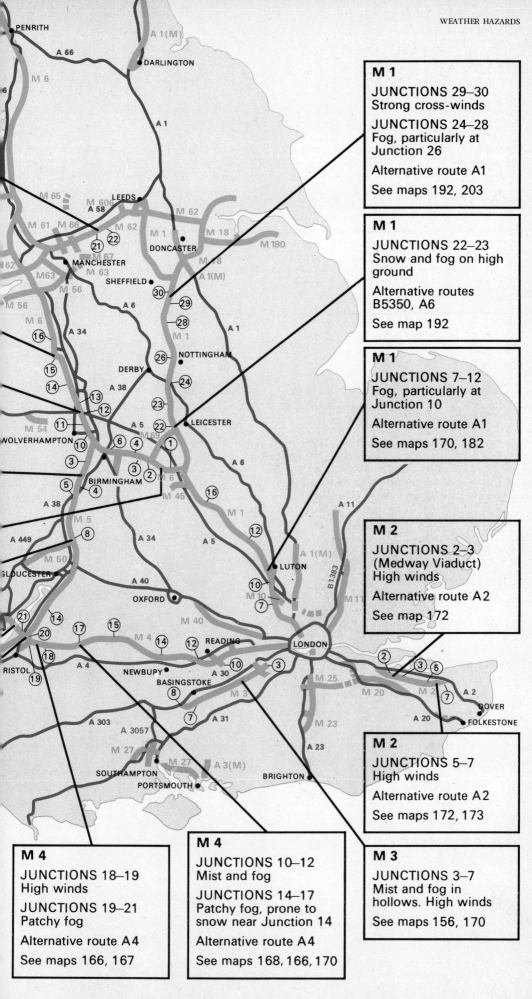

M 1

JUNCTIONS 29–30
Strong cross-winds

JUNCTIONS 24–28
Fog, particularly at
Junction 26

Alternative route A1

See maps 192, 203

M 1

JUNCTIONS 22–23
Snow and fog on high
ground

Alternative routes
B5350, A6

See map 192

M 1

JUNCTIONS 7–12
Fog, particularly at
Junction 10

Alternative route A1

See maps 170, 182

M 2

JUNCTIONS 2–3
(Medway Viaduct)
High winds

Alternative route A2

See map 172

M 2

JUNCTIONS 5–7
High winds

Alternative route A2

See maps 172, 173

M 4

JUNCTIONS 18–19
High winds

JUNCTIONS 19–21
Patchy fog

Alternative route A4

See maps 166, 167

M 4

JUNCTIONS 10–12
Mist and fog

JUNCTIONS 14–17
Patchy fog, prone to
snow near Junction 14

Alternative route A4

See maps 168, 166, 170

M 3

JUNCTIONS 3–7
Mist and fog in
hollows. High winds

See maps 156, 170

DRIVING IN ALL WEATHERS

How to prepare for safer journeys

A few minutes' study of the lines and symbols on a weather map may help a motorist to time a long journey so as to avoid the worst of the weather on different parts of his route. Weather maps show the present weather and indicate how it is moving and developing. The lines, called isobars, show variations in pressure in the same way as contours on a map show variations in height. Areas of high pressure are often associated with fine weather (although in winter they can be associated with fog) and low pressure with bad weather.

The weather reports show in which direction these pressure systems are travelling and at what speed. The closer the isobar lines are together the higher will be the winds round the centres of pressure.

The high-pressure areas are known as anti-cyclones and the low-pressure areas as depressions. A depression may, for example, lie with its centre over the Irish Sea with belts of rain moving from west to east across England. These belts are associated with fronts which pass quickly over the country with light rain setting in ahead of the warm front, followed after a few hours by heavier rain at the cold front and then clearing skies. A front, which is the boundary between two different air masses, is shown on the weather map by a thick black line; a warm front has small rounded black blobs on one side of the line and a cold front has small black triangles. A warm front gives a period of fairly steady rain and a cold front usually brings sharp showers with sunny intervals. Occasionally, a front will be marked on the weather map with blobs on one side of the black line and triangles on the other. This means the front has become stationary.

There is a fourth type of front known as an occluded front, or an occlusion, formed when the cold front has started to overtake the warm front, which usually brings rain. Other map symbols show cloud density and wind speeds.

Blue sky ⭕ Cloudy sky ◑ Rain ⬤ Snow ✳

Fog ☰ Thunderstorm ↯ Temperature 9° (48°)

Wind

The number of feathers on each arrow show wind strength — light air if one short feather, slight breeze if full-length feather, then each additional feather indicates wind force up to Force 10 (whole gale). A dead calm is shown by another circle round the present weather circle.

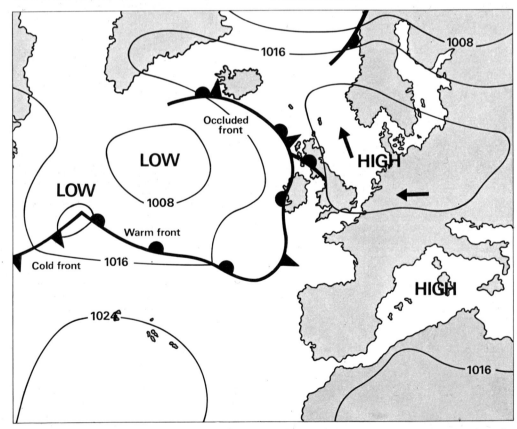

Three types of 'front' – the occluded front is moving into Scotland, bringing rain patches while the warm front is moving north and the cold front south-east. Figures show barometric pressure in millibars.

Clear signs in the sunset

The colours of a sunset are a fairly reliable guide to the following day's weather. There is much scientific truth behind old folklore rhymes such as 'Red sky at night, Shepherds' delight'. The reason is that rays of sunlight passing through the atmosphere are similar to light passing through a prism. The main sky colours depend on the scattering and reflecting of the rays and the number and size of particles of moisture in the atmosphere.

If the atmosphere grows moister, the particles increase in size and number, scattering the blue rays, so that somebody on the ground sees reds and yellows instead.

The reverse occurs on a fine day when these particles are few and small, giving a blue sky.

RED If the red sunset glow is evenly diffused over a clear western sky, the next day should be sunny (frosty in winter). Red-tinged clouds could mean a storm.

YELLOW This is one of the worst colour signs. Such a sunset is a forerunner of gales and heavy rain – although this bad weather may not arrive for 36 hours.

GREEN When this is intermingled with a blue sky, showery weather is probable. The green colour means that the upper atmosphere is very moist.

COPPER This colour is associated with thundery conditions. A coppery colour to the clouds at sunset is a sign that thunder clouds are forming.

GREY A grey, colourless sunset usually means that rain is on the way, particularly when a blue sky during the day changes to a consistent ashy grey before dusk.

DARK BLUE A hard blue, against which clouds are sharply outlined, indicates unsettled weather. A light blue sky merging into a red glow means fair weather.

How to read a barometer

A barometer can be misleading if you look to see only if it is high or low. Sometimes the barometric pressure will be high and the needle will point to 'fair weather' on a rainy day. At other times the needle will point to 'rain' in fine weather. The important thing to note is whether the barometer is rising or falling. Tap the glass and note whether the needle rises, falls or remains steady. Also, note any changes in the wind.

If the barometer is fairly high, but showing a decided fall when tapped, unsettled weather is approaching, especially if the wind is backing (anti-clockwise) to south or south-east. If the barometer is low, but the needle jumps up when you tap the instrument, and the wind has veered (clockwise) from south-west to north-west, expect clearing skies and sunshine. A rapid rise means the weather improvement will only be temporary.

Sometimes the barometer will fall slightly without any rain coming. This usually denotes freshening winds, and any improvement will not last long.

Danger of cross-winds

High cross-winds are particularly dangerous on exposed stretches of motorway and high bridges, such as the Forth and the Severn. The main danger is that a driver who is steering into the wind, particularly when the gusts are strong, may veer sideways in a sudden lull.

Before making a long journey, study the evening weather forecast on television and note the estimated progress of the centre of an approaching depression.

Its speed and direction will give an indication of how long it will take to cross the country and so bring calmer weather behind it.

When driving near the coast watch for gale warnings, which are run up flagstaffs at coastguard stations, pier heads and yacht clubs. Storms are denoted by small black cones:

▲ NORTH CONE, always pointing upwards, means that a gale is about to set in from a northerly direction. This cone is also shown when a gale is starting from east or west, if it is expected to change to the north.

▼ SOUTH CONE, always pointing downwards, denotes a gale starting from or changing to a southerly direction.

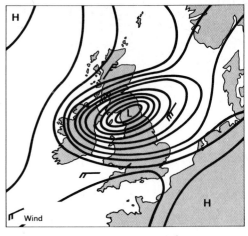

Isobars are close, indicating strong winds.

If a full gale is forecast, it is safer to keep off a motorway, or at least to keep the car's speed below 50 mph. Keep down to 40 mph on any exposed stretches.

In very strong winds keep well clear of high vans which can be blown over. It can also be extremely hazardous towing a caravan in strong winds. Wait until the wind dies down.

Winds on the motorway

As a car draws alongside a high-sided van, turbulent air around the van tends to draw the two vehicles together, and the driver compensates by steering slightly away from the van. The 'attraction' is lessened if there is a clear lane between the vehicles. After passing, the driver must be prepared to compensate for any cross-wind.

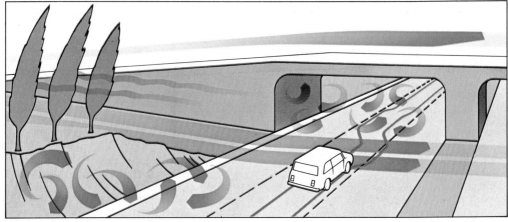

Avoid making a third lane of traffic in strong wind when going into a motorway cutting or under a bridge. The cars in the other lanes are liable to swing sharply off course as they are momentarily blanketed from the wind. This is because the drivers have been compensating their steering to counteract the side pressure of the wind.

Signs of fog ahead

Fog often forms when a layer of warm air rests above a layer of cold air, and forms a kind of ceiling, so keeping moisture-laden cool air close to the ground. When the wind drops to a calm and the temperature falls rapidly after dusk, fog will often form and become dense by morning. In some areas it may persist all day. The most common areas of fog are in valley bottoms and near rivers and lakes and industrial areas which are not within a smokeless zone.

In winter, when an anticyclone, with its light winds, covers the British Isles, fog will probably be widespread. The only places where winter fog is rare are on the south coasts of Devon and Cornwall. However, sea fog occurs in the West Country, particularly in early summer.

This fog rolls inland, but usually clears as it crosses warm ground. Early morning summer fog, which usually forms in valleys near rivers and streams, does not extend very high – unlike winter fog – and from high ground church spires can often be seen thrusting above it.

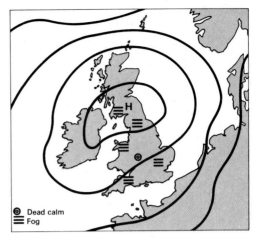

⊚ Dead calm
≡ Fog

A typical autumn map forecasting fog.

How to drive safely in fog

Fog produces one of the most dangerous driving conditions, as an accident can quickly involve several other cars. Immediately you find yourself approaching fog, switch on your side-lights as well as dipped headlights or fog lights. Switch on the windscreen wipers and wash the screen; wipe the inside of the screen as well. Open the driver's window so that you can hear what is going on around you; often you will hear another car before you see it.

Keep the heater going to avoid misting of windows. The build-up of hot air will prevent cold air coming in.

If you catch up with another car do not be tempted to overtake or get nearer. Keep far enough behind so that if the car ahead hits something or stops suddenly you have enough room to pull up safely.

The slightest film of dirt on any headlamp reduces its efficiency, so clean the headlamps often. If your fog lamps are fitted with covers, remove them as soon as fog is forecast.

With normal rear lights

At 30 ft distance   *At 20 ft distance*   *At 10 ft distance*

With a rearguard fog light

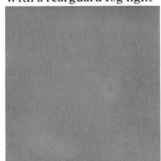

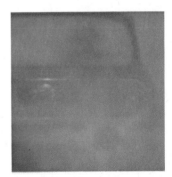

At 30 ft distance   *At 20 ft distance*   *At 10 ft distance*

Even with the best rear fog light available you must drive slowly. The car 30 ft ahead is just visible, but at 30 mph your stopping distance is 75 ft, which makes a collision inevitable if the car ahead stops suddenly.

Hidden danger of black ice

Black ice is particularly dangerous because it usually catches a motorist unawares. He may have driven along miles of wet roads then suddenly reach a stretch where the temperature of the ground is below freezing.

There seems to be no apparent change in the surface, but the road has frozen over and is covered with a sheet of ice, which is not visible because there is no white hoar frost. Black ice is sometimes caused by rain freezing as it hits the ground.

When driving, if the temperature is about freezing point, keep your speed down in case patches of ice have formed. The first indication of black ice may be that the steering suddenly feels light.

Hoar frost is usually associated with clear skies in winter. The hardest frosts may be expected on calm, cloudless nights when the wind direction on the weather map is from the east or south-east, bringing wintry conditions from the Continent. A thaw during the day can be followed by freezing again at night, making the roads slippery and dangerous.

When snow makes driving treacherous

In winter, snow may be expected if the weather map shows an area of high pressure across the north of Europe, and low pressure over the Bay of Biscay and the Mediterranean. This brings a flow of polar air sweeping across the British Isles. The south of England then gets the brunt of the continental wintry conditions. In the early stages of a snowfall, before the snow has been pressed hard on to the road surface by the traffic, driving is not too difficult, although visibility might be affected. But if the snow freezes hard, roads become very treacherous.

When falling snow, fog or heavy rain causes bad visibility during daylight hours, it is compulsory for drivers to switch on side-lights as well as either dipped headlights, a pair of fog lights or a matched fog light and spot light.

How to control a skid

A car will skid when the force acting on it, either from the side or in a straight line, is greater than the grip of the tyres on the road – which simply means you are going too fast with too little space and too little time to do as you wish. Consequently, the sudden and violent use of the brakes, steering and accelerator will make a skid worse. Try to relax; a tense driver will grip the wheel too tightly and lose his 'feel' of the road. Check that you are not driving too fast or too close to the vehicle ahead. Never allow speed to be dictated by an impatient driver behind.

Cars driven through the rear wheels will skid rear first, while front-wheel-drive cars skid front first. The correction technique is completely different.

A. The start of a skid . . . the back wheels slide to the nearside.

B. The driver fails to steer into the skid, and is probably accelerating.

C. The car is now broadside on, and still skidding.

D. The driver has lost control and the car has spun right round.

Rear-wheel skid

The feeling is that the car is trying to spin, and if you do nothing to prevent it, that is what it will do. In a left-hand bend the rear of the car will break away to the right; in a right-hand bend, to the left. The simplest method of correction is to lift the foot from the accelerator and at the same time steer in the direction the rear of the car is moving.

Do not touch the brake or clutch pedals or you will lose all directional control of the car. Wait until the skid is held and then straighten the steering wheel. Do not re-apply the accelerator until all four wheels are again in line.

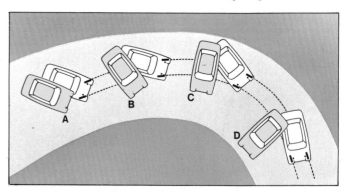

The white car has successfully recovered from the skid and safely negotiated the bend . . . while the orange car, shown in relation to the orange car in the four pictures above, has run off the road.

Controlling a car in heavy rain

At 60 mph on a wet road, the tread pattern of an average-sized tyre needs to move more than 1 gallon of water out of the way every second – 2 gallons a second in heavy rain. A worn tyre cannot channel away the water and a situation called aquaplaning can develop. Water builds up in front of the tyre causing it to lift and slide on the surface of the water. Even with a moderate amount of tread, a tyre's grip on a wet road decreases appreciably as the speed increases, and it may still aquaplane.

Aquaplaning becomes evident when the wheels do not respond to steering movements. The cure is to decelerate until the tyres drop back on to the road. DO NOT BRAKE SHARPLY.

Thunderstorms

Thunderstorms over the British Isles can occur at any time of the year, although they are more common in summer than in winter. Summer thunderstorms develop within a warm, moist air mass, which is heated, perhaps locally, by an even warmer earth. In winter, storms generally form ahead of a strong cold front but they are short-lived. The closeness of a storm can be judged by the time lag between a flash of lightning and a thunderclap. The sound of thunder travels at only 12 miles a minute – or 1 mile in 5 seconds. The greatest distance at which thunder can be heard is about 10 miles.

It is usually safer to carry on driving than to get out of the car to seek shelter, as the car's tyres act as insulators.

Floods

After heavy rain it is possible to get caught on a flooded stretch of road.

Slow down, change into a lower gear and keep the engine revolutions high, slipping the clutch if necessary to keep the car moving slowly. If you drive fast through a deep puddle the bow wave will cause a surge of water into the engine compartment which, if it reaches the fan, will be flung over the engine probably causing it to stall in the middle of the flood.

After driving through a flood, drive for a few seconds with your foot on the footbrake to dry out the brakes.

Four-wheel skid

This can happen to front-wheel or rear-wheel-drive cars, and is caused by sudden hard braking, giving the feeling you are going faster than before you braked. Correct by releasing the brake to allow the wheels to roll and then re-apply the brakes with a smooth dabbing action sufficient to bring the wheels almost to the point of locking, and then release them momentarily. Remember that while all four wheels are locked you have no control of the steering.

The brakes of most cars are powerful enough to lock all four wheels, even on a dry road; but usually the rear wheels lock first and the car skids before the driver has applied enough brake pressure to lock the front wheels as well.

Front-wheel skid (with a front-wheel-drive car)

Here, the feeling is, that the car is going straight on with a complete loss of steering control.

The method of correction (with a front-wheel-drive car) is to keep the front wheels pointing in the direction you wish to go. Remove the foot from the accelerator immediately. As the car loses speed, due to the scrubbing effect of the front wheels on the road, steering control will be regained. Braking will only heighten the effect and reduce control even further.

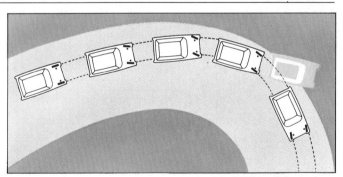

The driver of the orange car has lost control and is skidding off the road. In contrast, the driver of the white car shows how, by decelerating, not braking, and by steering into the corner, the skid is controlled.

Skid pans where motorists can practise in safety

Greater Manchester Transport Centre, Hyde Road.
Greater Manchester Council, Area 5, Grove House, Skerton Road, Old Trafford.
Tel. 061 872 8328

Thruxton Skid Pan, near Andover, Hants.
Mike Reed, Audubon, Bradcuts Lane, Cookham Dean, Berks. SL6 9AA.
Tel. Bourne End 27387

Lightwood Traffic Training Centre, Sheffield.
S. Yorkshire County Council, Norton Avenue, Sheffield S8 8BB.
Tel. Sheffield 396715

Goodwood Circuit, near Chichester, W. Sussex.
Image Race Cars, Super Shell Building, Goodwood Motor Circuit, Chichester PO18 0PH.
Tel. Chichester 527011

Marston Moor Autodrome, North Yorkshire.
SOS Driver Training Centre Ltd, Control Tower Offices, Marston Moor Autodrome, Tockwith YO5 8QF.
Tel. Tockwith 346

CALENDAR OF EVENTS
What's going on from month to month

This calendar lists major festivals and ceremonial, cultural and sporting events in Britain. The demand for tickets for some events is so great that bookings must be made months in advance. For the events listed below, book in the month indicated by *italic* type:

January: The Derby (June); Wimbledon Tennis (June/July); National Brass Band Festival (October).
February: International Musical Eisteddfod (July); Stratford-upon-Avon Shakespeare Season (April).
March: Cheltenham Festival (July); Royal Ascot (June).
April: Braemar Gathering (September); Glyndebourne Festival (May); Bath Festival (May); Aldeburgh Festival (June); Chichester Festival (May); Edinburgh International Festival (August).
June: Horse of the Year Show (October); The Proms (July); Three Choirs Festival (August).

The British Tourist Authority, 64 St James's Street, London SW1A 1NF (01 629 9191) gives information on all coming events.
The English Tourist Board, 4 Grosvenor Gardens, London SW1W 0DU (01 730 3400) has set up eleven regional boards to provide information about their respective areas. The addresses and telephone numbers of these boards, and of the information offices in most big towns, can be obtained from the British Tourist Authority at the above address.
Addresses of other national boards are:
Scottish Tourist Board, 23 Ravelstone Terrace, Edinburgh EH4 3EU (031 332 2433);
Wales Tourist Board, Welcome House, Llandaff, Cardiff CF5 2YZ (Cardiff 567701);
Northern Ireland Tourist Board, River House, 48 High Street, Belfast BT1 2DS (0232 31221);
Republic of Ireland, Bord Failte Eireann, Baggot Street Bridge, Dublin (0001 65871).

January

New Year customs

FIRST-FOOTING, Scotland This is a custom in Scotland and the north of England of visiting friends after midnight has struck on New Year's Eve. For good luck, the first person to cross the threshold of a house in the New Year should be a dark man; the belief that a fair man brings ill-luck is perhaps a relic of ancient Norse invasions. A first-footer should bring a 'handsel', a gift of a piece of coal, some money – or a bottle of whisky.

AULD LANG SYNE, London The old year is seen out in Trafalgar Square, when crowds sing 'Auld Lang Syne' and dance around, and sometimes in, the fountains.

TAR BARREL BURNING, Northumberland Men in fancy dress parade through the streets at Allendale Town carrying tubs of burning tar on their heads in a ceremony dating back to pagan times which signals the end of the old year, and ensures the return of the sun the following spring. A bonfire in the market-place is lit by the burning barrels at midnight.

First week

HAXEY HOOD GAME, Lincolnshire A violent form of Rugby football is played at Haxey on January 6, with rolled-up pieces of canvas and leather called 'hoods'. Players are called 'boggans' – men from the fenland bogs. The game recalls a 13th-century lady's loss of her hood while riding near Haxey church, and its recovery by 13 labourers.

GLASTONBURY THORN, Somerset January 6 (old Christmas Day) brings visitors to Glastonbury to see the holy thorn. This is a cutting of a tree said to have been planted by Joseph of Arimathea in 663. It is reputed to flower on the old Christmas Day, but it may flower earlier.

BOAT SHOW, London The ten-day International Boat Show at Earl's Court features boats and equipment exhibited by more than 400 British and foreign firms. Displays ranging from do-it-yourself canoes to luxury ocean-going craft, anglers' equipment and sailing fashions are usually centred around a large indoor pool.

Second week

BURNING THE CLAVIE, Grampian On the night of Auld Hogmanay (January 11), inhabitants of Burghead carry a burning 'clavie' round the town. The clavie is made from a tar barrel sawn in half which is fixed to a 6 ft stave with a nail driven in with a stone – legend has it that bad luck will follow if the nail is touched by iron. The clavie is filled with tar and pieces of wood, then lit by a piece of peat from a household fire and carried to the top of a local hill where it is allowed to burn out. Pieces of the clavie and embers are scrambled for, as each piece is said to bring good luck to its owner for the rest of the year.

Third week

BLESSING THE PLOUGH On Plough Sunday, the beginning of the ploughing season is marked with services at Chichester Cathedral and a number of churches throughout Britain. A plough is dragged to the steps of the chancel and blessed, and prayers are offered for all who work on the land.

Fourth week

BURNS NIGHT January 25, the birthday of Scottish poet Robert Burns, is celebrated by about 700 Burns Clubs in all parts of the world. The highlights of a traditional Burns Night supper are the toast to the 'Immortal Memory' of the poet and the piping in of the haggis, when a piper precedes the steaming dish to the table.

UP-HELLY-AA, Shetland On the last Tuesday of the month several hundred men dressed as Vikings accompany a 30 ft model of a Viking galley in a torchlight procession through the streets of Lerwick. When the procession ends the torches are hurled into the galley to make a bonfire, and revels follow. It is called Up-Helly-Aa, and is claimed to be a Viking fire festival, although it originated in the last century.

CHARLES THE MARTYR, London Wreaths are laid at the foot of the statue of Charles I at Charing Cross on January 30, to mark the anniversary of his execution in Whitehall in 1649.

February

First week

HURLING THE SILVER BALL, Cornwall The mayor throws a wooden ball covered with silver leaf from the wall of the parish church at St Ives at 10.30 a.m. on Feast Monday in the week of Candlemas (February 2). The ball is thrown from person to person as the game proceeds and whoever holds it at noon receives a prize from the mayor. The game is thought to be a relic of pagan sun worship.

Second week

CRUFT'S DOG SHOW, London Seven thousand dogs of about 120 breeds, from Afghan hounds to Yorkshire terriers, are entered for Cruft's Dog Show, held over two days at Earl's Court. Probably the world's best-known dog show, it is organised by the Kennel Club and entrants must be prize winners at shows held in the previous year under Kennel Club rules. The supreme champion can be of any breed. Details from: Cruft's Dog Show Society, 1 Clarges Street, London W1.

Shrovetide customs

Shrove Tuesday was originally the day when people went to confession to be shriven or shroven – that is, gain absolution – before Ash Wednesday, the first day of Lent. It has been associated with pancakes since pre-Reformation times, when it was the day on which fats and eggs, foods forbidden during Lent, were commonly used up in making pancakes.

PANCAKE DAY RACES, Buckinghamshire A pancake race for women at Olney has taken place for 500 years over a 415 yd course from the market square to the church door. The pancake is tossed three times and the winner is rewarded by a kiss from the church bellringer. Other pancake races take place at Bodiam, East Sussex, and North Somercotes, Lincolnshire.

SHROVETIDE FOOTBALL Shrovetide football, a game with few but greatly varying rules, has been played in England since medieval times, and perhaps much earlier. Matches are held at Ashbourne, Derbyshire; Alnwick, Northumberland; Sedgefield, County Durham; Atherstone, Warwickshire; and Corfe Castle, Dorset.

...AND SKIPPING At Scarborough, North Yorkshire, long skipping ropes are set up on the foreshore in the early afternoon and all who wish can skip until dusk.

HURLING THE SILVER BALL, Cornwall Hurling the Silver Ball at St Columb Major and Minor is quite different from the similarly named game at St Ives. Two teams of up to 1000 players each join in a wild form of Rugby where the goals are a mile apart. The game usually ends without a score.

March

First week

WHUPPITY SCOORIE, Strathclyde An oddly named Whuppity Scoorie ceremony at Lanark on March 1 seems to be a relic of a pagan ritual to chase away winter spirits. Children armed with paper balls tied on strings circle three times around the church as the church bell tolls and then engage in mock battle, which ends in a scramble for coins thrown by town officials.

ST DAVID'S DAY, Wales Every member of a Welsh regiment is ceremoniously presented with a leek, the national emblem of Wales, on St David's Day (March 1). Legend says that Welshmen wore leeks in their caps on the advice of St David to distinguish their comrades from the enemy, bringing them success in battle against the Saxons. The patron saint of Wales is also commemorated by a special service at the diminutive cathedral bearing his name at St David's, Pembrokeshire, where he is said to have settled in the 6th century and made it the principal seat of Christianity in the West. The cathedral was built in the 12th century.

IDEAL HOMES EXHIBITION, London Furnished houses in land-scaped gardens, displays of furniture, home improvements and domestic equipment are featured at the three-week exhibition at Olympia or Earl's Court.

Third week

KIPLING COTES DERBY, Humberside The Kipling Cotes Derby, reputed to be the oldest flat race in Britain, has been run on the third Thursday in the month since 1519. The race starts at noon over a 4 mile course, from South Dalton to Kipling Cotes Farm, between Market Weighton and Middleton. Paradoxically the prize for second place is greater than for the winner because the second rider collects all the entrance money.

ST PATRICK'S DAY, Ireland Irishmen everywhere celebrate St Patrick's Day (March 17). Pilgrimages are also made to the traditional burial place of Ireland's patron saint at Downpatrick, County Down, and to nearby Saul, where he founded the first church in Ireland.

CAMDEN FESTIVAL, London Rare works of music and opera are performed during the two-week Camden Festival in North London; there are also choral and symphony concerts, art exhibitions, poetry and drama.

Fourth week

TICHBORNE DOLE, Hampshire Villagers at Tichborne and near-by Cheriton receive flour on Lady Day (March 25) under a 12th-century bequest of Lady Mabella Tichborne. On her death-bed she asked her husband to give sufficient land to provide an annual gift of bread to the poor. He agreed to grant as much land as she could encircle while carrying a burning faggot before the flame died. Too weak to walk, she crawled around 23 acres and the land, known since as The Crawls, was set aside for charity.

Last week

ORANGES AND LEMONS DISTRIBUTION, London. Local children receive gifts of fruit at a special service on the Thursday nearest to March 31 at St Clement Danes, the church of 'Oranges and Lemons' nursery-rhyme fame.

GRAND NATIONAL, Merseyside Probably the world's best-known steeplechase, the Grand National, is run in late March or early April over a course of approximately 4½ miles, that is twice round the circuit at Aintree, near Liverpool. The horses have to tackle a total of 30 fences, most of which are particularly difficult because the ground drops down steeply after the horses have cleared them.

BOAT RACE, London The famous annual contest between rowing eights from the universities of Oxford and Cambridge is held in late March or early April over a 4¼ mile stretch of the River Thames, upstream from Putney Bridge to Mortlake. The race was first rowed at Henley in 1829, and transferred to the present course in 1845. The Boat Race can be watched from many points along the river bank or from launches that leave from Westminster Pier and follow the crews.

HEAVY HORSE SHOW, Cambridgeshire About 150 working draught horses from farms, breweries and other places, in teams of two, four, six and eight horses, are on display at the one-day National Shire Show held in late March or early April at the East of England Showground, at Alwalton, near Peterborough.

Easter customs

MAUNDY THURSDAY The Queen distributes the Royal Maundy Money, specially minted for the occasion, on the Thursday before Good Friday. This royal charity dates back to the time of Edward III when the monarch washed the feet of the poor and gave them clothes and food. Since the 18th century money has been substituted for the gift and the washing ceremony has been dropped. The distribution takes place in a different church each year.

HOCKTIDE FESTIVAL, Hungerford, Berkshire On the second Tuesday after Easter, Hungerford's special fishing and grazing rights are commemorated by the meeting of the Hocktide Court. Two Tuttimen and an Orange Scrambler are elected and later the Tuttimen are given tall staves, called Tutti Poles, festooned with ribbons.

BACUP NUTTERS DANCE, Lancashire A team of Garland and Coconut Dancers, or 'Nutters', dance in the streets of Bacup on Easter Saturday. The origins of both dances are obscure. The Garland Dance, involving a garland of paper flowers, is believed to be connected with the rebirth of spring. For the Coconut Dance, the black-faced performers have small wooden discs (the coconuts) attached to the hands, waists and knees and these are clapped in rhythm as they dance. One performer, called the 'Whiffler', stays in front of the others to drive away evil spirits.

EASTER PARADE, London Bands and decorated floats take part in a spectacular parade in Battersea Park at 3 p.m. on Easter Sunday. The theme of the parade usually relates to the history and attractions of London.

HICKSTEAD EASTER MEETING, West Sussex Riders and horses from Britain and Europe compete during five days in Easter week at the International Show-Jumping Meeting held at the All-England Jumping Course at Hickstead, near Bolney.

BIDDENDEN DOLE, Kent The distribution of the Biddenden Dole on Easter Monday at Biddenden commemorates the Siamese twins Eliza and Mary Chulkhurst who were born in the village c. 1100 and lived joined together at the hips and shoulders for 34 years. On their death they left a bequest of 20 acres of land, the income from which was to provide bread, cheese and a small sum of money for the needy. Biddenden Cakes, biscuits fashioned to resemble the twins, are distributed to people attending the ceremony.

PACE-EGGING, Lancashire Egg-rolling or Pace-Egging takes place on Easter Monday afternoon at Preston, when children roll hard-boiled brightly coloured eggs down a slope in Avening Park. This is a religious custom said to commemorate the stone being rolled away from Christ's tomb.

WORLD COAL-CARRYING CHAMPIONSHIP, West Yorkshire Competitors carrying 1 cwt bags of coal race over an uphill course at Gawthorpe, near Dewsbury, on Easter Monday for the World Coal-carrying Championship. The course distance is slightly under 1 mile and the race has been won in times of little more than $4\frac{1}{2}$ minutes. The winner receives a silver cup which is held for a year and a medal which is kept.

HARNESS HORSE PARADE, London A wide variety of horses, ponies and vehicles can be seen at the London Harness Horse Parade held on Easter Monday in the Inner Circle, Regent's Park. Judging takes place from about 10 a.m.

TUPENNY STARVERS, Avon Huge buns known as Tupenny Starvers are distributed to the choirboys of St Michael's Church, Bristol, during the morning of Tuesday in Easter week. The custom dates back to at least 1750, and it is thought that the buns were intended as a treat for choirboys in the days when black bread was a staple food.

BOTTLE-KICKING, Leicestershire A hare pie is cut up by the rector of Hallaton on Easter Monday, and some portions are distributed among the villagers. The remaining portions are scattered over the ground on Hare-Pie Hill and scrambled for. Then three 'bottles' – wooden casks, two full of beer, the other empty – are fought for by the youths from Hallaton and Medbourne who attempt to carry the bottles over a stream and into their own parish. Afterwards, the opposing factions join forces to enjoy the contents of the bottles. These ceremonies appear to have their origins in a fertility rite.

April

First week

SHAKESPEARE SEASON, Warwickshire The annual Shakespeare season at the Royal Shakespeare Theatre, Stratford-upon-Avon, opens near the beginning of the month and continues until December. Five or more productions of Shakespeare's plays are presented. Booking opens in early February at the Box Office, Royal Shakespeare Theatre. Early application is advisable.

Third week

BACH FESTIVAL, Oxford and London Not only Bach, but Handel, Beethoven, Stravinsky and other composers are featured in the English Bach Festival which takes place in various historic buildings in Oxford and London from mid-April to mid-May. Details from: English Bach Festival, Dept. BT, 15 South Eaton Place, London SW1.

Fourth week

ST GEORGE'S COURT, Lichfield, Staffordshire At noon on St George's Day (April 23) the Court of Review of Frank Pledge and the Court Baron of the Burgesses are held in the Guildhall at Lichfield. A jury is present to hear complaints and to appoint two High Constables, a Bailiff and other officers. The courts date from about 400 years ago, when Edward VI transferred the manorial right of the city from the Bishops to the Mayor, Sheriff and Aldermen.

May

May Day festivals

PADSTOW 'OBBY 'OSS, Cornwall The 'Obby 'Oss, or hobby horse, in a black costume and grotesque mask, is carried through the streets in a dancing procession at Padstow. Sometimes it snatches at women – a sign of good luck. The celebrations begin with a traditional song welcoming summer. Later there is maypole dancing. At the end of the day the 'Oss is ceremonially killed.

MAY MORNING CEREMONY, Oxford Choristers at Magdalen College greet the May Day sunrise with a 17th-century hymn in Latin sung from the college tower. Later there is Morris dancing in The High.

MINEHEAD CELEBRATIONS, Somerset Three days of entertainments and festivities begin at Minehead on May Day, when a bearded hobby horse is led through the streets by dancers and musicians.

MAY FAIRS Fairs are held on different dates in May at: Great Torrington, North Devon; Knutsford, Cheshire; Ickwell, Bedfordshire; Boston, Lincolnshire; Rhyl, Clwyd; Berwick-upon-Tweed, Northumberland.

First week

BRIGHTON ARTS FESTIVAL, East Sussex A two-week festival of music, theatre and visual arts at Brighton is held in the Royal Pavilion and various halls.

CHICHESTER FESTIVAL, West Sussex One of Britain's most successful drama festivals, the Festival Theatre season at Chichester, lasts from May to September. Postal bookings, direct from the Festival Theatre, Chichester, W. Sussex.

FLORA DAY, Cornwall The Furry, or Flora, Dance, said to have originated in a Celtic ceremony welcoming the growing season, takes place at Helston on May 8 or, if that falls on Sunday or Monday, the preceding Saturday. Dancing through the streets and gardens starts early in the morning.

OPEN-AIR EXHIBITION, London Artists show their work at Victoria Embankment Gardens for two weeks.

Second week

PLANTING THE PENNY HEDGE, North Yorkshire The Penny Hedge, a fence strong enough to withstand three tides, is built on the shore at Whitby on Ascension Eve. This custom continues a 12th-century penance imposed by the Abbot of Whitby after local huntsmen killed a priest who tried to protect a wild boar. The name of the ceremony is a corruption of the original 'Penance Hedge'.

WELL-DRESSING, Derbyshire A thanksgiving for water is still observed in the custom of decorating Derbyshire wells with floral religious pictures. One of the best-known ceremonies is at Tissington, on Ascension Day.

SPALDING TULIP PARADE, Lincolnshire Spalding Tulip Parade is held on about May 7, according to the weather and condition of the blooms. About 7 million tulip heads are used to decorate the floats. A one-way route round the tulip fields is signposted by the AA.

ROYAL WINDSOR HORSE SHOW A four-day horse show is held in the Home Park, below Windsor Castle, Berkshire.

GARLAND DAY, Dorset Garlands of flowers are carried through the streets at Abbotsbury on May 13 (if a Sunday, May 12) in a custom originating from the blessing of fishing boats. The garlands were once cast into the sea in the hope of ensuring a good fishing season, but they are now placed on the war memorial.

Third week

GLYNDEBOURNE FESTIVAL, East Sussex The Glyndebourne Festival of opera is held 2 miles from Glynde village, near Lewes, and lasts until mid-August. Operas are sung in the original language by international casts. Long intervals give time for dinner or a stroll in the grounds. Postal bookings from Glyndebourne Festival Opera, Glyndebourne, E. Sussex, open early in April.

BIGGIN HILL AIR FAIR, Kent The two-day International Air Fair is held at Biggin Hill. The race is a handicap event for light aircraft, ranging from two-seater to executive-class aircraft, over a 300–400 mile course finishing at Biggin Hill. The event is part rally, part race, and is mainly a test of navigating skill.

ROYAL ACADEMY SUMMER EXHIBITION, London Almost 2000 selected new paintings and other works of art submitted to the Royal Academy are on display at Burlington House until mid-August.

SHROPSHIRE AND WEST MIDLAND SHOW A two-day agricultural show is held at Shrewsbury.

MAYORING DAY, East Sussex At noon on Mayoring Day, the new Mayor and other council officials of Rye throw hot pennies from the town hall windows to children below. The custom dates from when the town minted its own coins.

SURFING CHAMPIONSHIPS, Cornwall The National Surfing Championships are held on Cornwall's Atlantic Coast.

Fourth week

MAY EIGHTS WEEK, Oxford The University rowing races, known as the Eights, take place on the Isis, a local stretch of the Thames.

CHELSEA FLOWER SHOW, London Exhibits from all over the country, and covering all aspects of gardening, are shown at the Chelsea Flower Show, Britain's most important horticultural show. It is open to the public for three days in the grounds of the Royal Hospital, the home of the Chelsea Pensioners. Centrepiece of the show, organised by the Royal Horticultural Society, is a spectacular exhibition of flowers, shrubs, fruit and vegetables in a $3\frac{1}{2}$ acre marquee.

GARLAND FESTIVAL, Derbyshire A procession at Castleton on Oak Apple Day (May 29) is believed to commemorate the escape of Charles II from the Roundheads in 1651. The Garland King wears a huge cloak of flowers and foliage.

GROVELY FOREST RIGHTS, Wiltshire On May 29 the villagers of Wishford Magna celebrate a right, granted in the 17th century, to gather wood in Grovely Forest by carrying branches and twigs in a procession through the village. General festivities follow.

BEATING RETREAT, London The massed bands of the Household Division march and counter-march on Horse Guards Parade on three evenings in late May/early June.

MILK RACE TOUR OF BRITAIN The starting point varies for a two-week cycling event in daily stages covering 1100 miles of England and Wales, sponsored by the Milk Marketing Board.

ROYAL ULSTER SHOW The Royal Ulster Agricultural Society Show and Industrial Exhibition is held at Balmoral, Belfast.

BATH FESTIVAL, Avon A two-week festival of music in the 18th-century buildings of Bath, together with a variety of other activities. Postal bookings are available from the Bath Festival Office, Linley House, 1 Pierrepont Place, Bath, Avon, from early April.

What's on at Whitsun

CHAMPIONSHIP CAR RACES, Northamptonshire International motor racing is included in the seven meetings held each year on the 3 mile circuit at Silverstone, near Towcester. More than 20 other meetings are held on the shorter Club Track.

COURT OF ARRAYE, Staffordshire Youths in ancient coats of mail parade for inspection by town officials at Lichfield, Staffordshire, recalling the medieval military Court of Arraye's annual inspection of the town's preparations for national defence.

RAM ROASTING, Devon The Ram Roasting Fair at Kingsteignton is said to originate from a drought in pagan times, when water was found after the sacrifice of a ram.

FOLK EVENTS Morris dancing can be seen in London at St Paul's and Hampstead, and at fairs and festivals in the Thames Valley, Oxfordshire, and east Kent. Traditional fairs and carnivals are held at Morecambe, Lancashire; Faversham, Kent; Southwold, Suffolk; Lowestoft, Suffolk; Littlehampton, West Sussex; Pwllheli, Gwynedd.

RUSH SUNDAY SERVICE, Avon The Lord Mayor of Bristol goes in procession to a Rush-service at St Mary Redcliffe Church, Bristol, on Whit Sunday. The service continues a 15th-century mayor's bequest for the church to be strewn with rushes to lessen the cold.

BREAD AND CHEESE THROWING, Gloucestershire At St Briavels, in the Forest of Dean, a forester standing on a wall scatters bread and cheese among the congregation leaving church on Whit Sunday. The custom is said to commemorate rights of land tenure which King John granted the villagers in 1206.

JOUSTING, Hertfordshire A medieval jousting tournament is held over two days at Knebworth House, Knebworth.

59

June

Summer fairs and festivals

ALDEBURGH FESTIVAL, Suffolk A three-week annual festival of music and the arts begins at Aldeburgh early in June. The festival was founded by the composer Benjamin Britten in 1948, and concerts and operas are given in the Maltings, at Snape, 4 miles inland from Aldeburgh, at various local churches and Aldeburgh Jubilee Hall. Bookings start in late April from: Festival Office, Aldeburgh.

COVENTRY CARNIVAL, Warwickshire A carnival is held in Coventry on or near June 12. Lady Godiva is occasionally featured on a float to commemorate the bargain said to have been made in the 11th century that she would ride naked through the streets if her husband, the Earl of Mercia, would reduce oppressive taxes on the town.

CARNIVAL TIME Carnivals are also held during the month at Lytham St Annes, Lancashire; Wallingford, Oxfordshire; Nuneaton, Warwickshire; Bury, G. Manchester; Babba-combe, Devon; Biggleswade, Bedfordshire. A 17th-century Fair is held at Basildon, Essex, a five-day Continental Festival at Scarborough, North Yorkshire, and Fair Week at Alnwick, Northumberland. Details from the Council Clerk in each district.

AGRICULTURAL SHOWS Royal Bath and West, Shepton Mallet, Somerset (four days, May to early June); South of England, Ardingly, West Sussex (three days, second week); Three Counties, Malvern, Hereford and Worcester (three days, second week); Royal Highland, Ingliston, near Edinburgh (six days, third week); Royal Norfolk, New Costessey, Norwich, Norfolk (two days, last week).

First week

TROOPING THE COLOUR, London The colour of one of the five regiments of Foot Guards is trooped on Horse Guards Parade on the Queen's official birthday, usually the second Saturday in June. The Queen rides side-saddle for a 20-minute inspection of the Household Division, who then march and counter-march to the music of massed bands. The ceremony is a personal salute to the sovereign and dates from the 17th century when it was the practice to carry the regimental colours through the lines at nightfall to ensure that the men would know which colour to rally round in the next day's fighting.

ROYAL SALUTES, London The Queen's official birthday is marked by Royal Salutes from the Tower of London (62 guns fired by the Hon. Artillery Company) and Hyde Park (41 guns fired by the Royal Horse Artillery). The extra 21 guns fired from the Tower are on behalf of the City of London.

THE DERBY, Surrey The Derby, Britain's richest 'classic' race for three-year-old colts and fillies, is run over 1½ miles on Epsom Downs. The race, named after the 12th Earl of Derby, began in 1780, a year after the Oaks, a race for fillies, run over the same distance at the same meeting. The race can be watched from the Hill, while standing near gipsy caravans and merry-go-rounds, or from the stands. Application for admission to the stands and enclosures should be made from January 1 to: Epsom Grandstand Association, Racecourse Paddock, Epsom. Morning dress is compulsory in the Club Enclosure on Derby Day only.

TT RACES, Isle of Man International Tourist Trophy motor-cycle races are held over four days.

LLANDAFF FESTIVAL, South Glamorgan A ten-day festival of choral, chamber and orchestral music at Llandaff. Details can be obtained from the Secretary, Llandaff Festival, Well House, Penylan Newton, Cowbridge, S. Glamorgan.

MINACK THEATRE, Cornwall An open-air theatre built in Classical Greek style on a cliff near Porthcurno is the setting for a season of Greek, Shakespearean and modern drama, lasting until early September.

DUBLIN FESTIVAL A festival of Abbey Theatre and international plays. It generally lasts until October.

Third week

COMMON RIDINGS Common Ridings or Ridings of the Marches by a procession of horsemen are the Scottish equivalent of the English custom of 'Beating the Bounds' to check local boundaries. This medieval custom is a popular attraction in many Border towns, including Hawick and Selkirk.

DICKENS FESTIVAL, Kent People at Broadstairs walk through the streets in Victorian dress, during a one-week Dickens Festival, founded in 1937.

GARTER CEREMONY, Windsor A service for the Order of the Garter, the highest order of chivalry, is attended by the Queen at St George's Chapel, Windsor Castle. There is a procession of the Knights of the Order, the Household Cavalry and Yeomen of the Guard. The ceremony dates from the 14th century.

ELECTION OF THE MAYOR OF OCK STREET, Oxfordshire Morris dancers of Abingdon dance along Ock Street on the Saturday nearest June 20, halting for a drink at each inn. There is also a traditional ceremony in which residents of Ock Street elect an honorary mayor, who holds office for only one day.

Fourth week

WIMBLEDON TENNIS, London The All-England Lawn Tennis Championships at Wimbledon, from late June to early July, attract the world's leading tennis players. Demand for the Centre Court enclosure and 8700 Centre Court tickets is so great that a ballot is held. For a ballot form apply before February to: All England Lawn Tennis Club, Church Road, Wimbledon, London SW19 5AE.

LUDLOW SUMMER FESTIVAL, Shropshire A festival of drama, music and art at Ludlow lasts until mid-July. Shakespearean plays are performed in the massive Norman castle and concerts are given in the cathedral-like Church of St Lawrence. Details can be obtained from the Secretary, Ludlow Festival Society, Castle House, Ludlow.

HENLEY ROYAL REGATTA, Oxfordshire The Henley Royal Regatta, founded in 1839, is held on a straight 1½ mile stretch of the Thames at Henley-on-Thames over four days in late June/early July. About 1000 oarsmen compete in the heats and finals of a dozen events. Tickets from: Henley Royal Regatta, Henley-on-Thames. Booking opens in May.

ROYAL ASCOT, Berkshire Fashion attracts as much attention as the horses at the four-day race meeting at Ascot. Royal Ascot was inaugurated by Queen Anne in 1711 and since then has always been attended by the sovereign and members of the royal family who drive from Windsor each day in open carriages. Applications for admission to the Royal Enclosure should be made before the end of April to Her Majesty's Representative, Ascot Office, St James's Palace, London SW1; first requests must be signed by a sponsor, who has already been accepted in the enclosure.

MIDSUMMER BONFIRES, Cornwall A chain of fires is lit on St John's Eve, June 23, along the hills of Cornwall, the first one at Carn Brea, near Redruth. Blessings are spoken in Cornish and flowers thrown on the fire. The ceremony is believed to originate from a pagan custom.

WORLD CABER-TOSSING CHAMPIONSHIP, Aberdeen The Highland Games at Hazlehead Park include the World Caber-Tossing Championship. Tossing the caber, or 'tossing the bar', is thought to originate from the technique used by woodsmen to hurl a tree trunk across a stream. They tried to make the trunk land on the other bank, then fall forwards and not backwards into the water.

CHESTER FESTIVAL, Cheshire The two-week festival is opened with a procession of floats through the town.

THE HOPPINGS, Newcastle upon Tyne A fair is held for a week on a common just north of the city centre.

DRUIDS' CEREMONY, Wiltshire At Stonehenge, Companions of the Most Ancient Order of Druids keep a midnight vigil on Midsummer's Eve and honour midsummer day with a service when the sun, seen from the Altar Stone, rises over the Heelstone. In the centre of Stonehenge are two rings of sarsen stones which came from Marlborough Downs. The fallen Altar Stone in the centre is one of 80 bluestones which are believed to have been brought from the Prescelly Hills in Dyfed. The arrangement of the stones was changed

between 1800 and 1500 BC. Sun-worshipping ceremonies are believed to have been held here nearly 4000 years ago.

WALL PULPIT SERMON, Oxford On the Sunday nearest St John the Baptist day, a sermon is delivered from a pulpit set in the wall of the first quadrangle of Magdalen College. The ceremony goes back about 500 years to commemorate that a Hospital of St John the Baptist stood on the site.

July

First week

TYNWALD CEREMONY, Isle of Man An open-air parliament founded by the Vikings in the 10th century is held on Tynwald Hill, St John's. A sword-bearer, carrying the Manx sword of state, leads a procession to the hill, where laws passed during the year by the House of Keys, the island's parliament, are read in Manx and English. The House is claimed to be the world's oldest parliamentary assembly.

WIMBLEDON TENNIS The Wimbledon lawn tennis championships continue (see *June Calendar*) with finals on the Centre Court on Friday and Saturday.

BRAW LADS GATHERING, Borders A colourful two-day Border festival, the Braw, or brave, Lads Gathering at Galashiels, recalls the town's history in a pageant on horseback. A highlight is the enactment of an incident during Border troubles in 1337 when the townsmen routed a company of marauding Englishmen.

INTERNATIONAL MUSICAL EISTEDDFOD, Clwyd About 200,000 people attend the six-day International Musical Eisteddfod at Llangollen. More than 200 choirs, groups of folk dancers and 500 soloists, from about 30 countries, take part in the various competitions. Booking opens February 1 from the International Musical Eisteddfod Office, Llangollen.

NATIONAL ROSE SHOW, Hertfordshire Royal National Rose Society's two-day Summer Show at Chiswell Green, St Albans.

ROYAL SHOW, Warwickshire The Royal Show, a five-day agricultural show, is held at the National Agricultural Centre, Stoneleigh, near Kenilworth.

RUSHBEARING, Ambleside, Cumbria On the Saturday nearest to July 2, children parade through the town carrying flowers and woven rushes. After a church service they are given gingerbread. The custom of rushbearing takes place in a number of churches throughout Britain and dates to the time when church floors were strewn with new rushes each year.

THE WHALTON BALE, Whalton, Northumbria On old Midsummer's Eve (July 4), a great bonfire is lit on the village green and there is Morris and sword dancing to the music of fiddlers and pipers. 'Bale' comes from the Anglo-Saxon *bael*, meaning a great fire.

Second week

CHELTENHAM FESTIVAL, Gloucestershire Contemporary British works are featured at a ten-day festival of symphony concerts, chamber music and recitals at Cheltenham. Bookings from late March to Festival Office, Town Hall, Cheltenham.

ROYAL TOURNAMENT, London Spectacular marching, massed bands and demonstrations of military skills are included in the Royal Tournament, a two-week show by the armed forces at Earl's Court, London. Bookings all year round from the Royal Tournament, Horseguards Building, Whitehall, London SW1.

GREAT YORKSHIRE SHOW The Great Yorkshire Agricultural Show at Harrogate lasts three days.

THE QUEEN'S PRIZE, Bisley, Surrey The Queen's Prize is the most important event of the National Rifle Association's two-week meeting at Bisley, near Woking. About 1200 marksmen in the first stage are reduced to 100 for the final,

when each takes 15 shots at 900 yds and 1000 yds. The meeting covers about 200 events for all weapons ranging from pistols to match rifles, including machine-guns.

VINTNERS PROCESSION, London After the installation of the new master at Vintners Hall, the court and company officials go in procession to the Church of St James, Garlick Hill.

ST MARGARET'S FAIR, Tenby, Dyfed The four-day fair is opened by the mayor and council walking round the town walls.

Third week

BRITISH GRAND PRIX The world motor-racing championship is decided each year by the total points won by a driver in ten Grand Prix races. One of these, the British Grand Prix, is held at Silverstone (see *May Calendar*) in odd years and at Brands Hatch, Kent, in even years.

SWAN UPPING A census of the swans on the River Thames between London Bridge and Henley is held for about a week every year. Ownership of the swans is shared by the Queen and two City of London companies, the Dyers and Vintners – a right going back to the reign of Elizabeth I, when swans were a table delicacy. Swan-masters of the Queen and companies record ownership of the swans from skiffs while the crews round them up. Cygnets belonging to the companies are nicked on their bills while those of the Queen are unmarked.

DURHAM MINERS' GALA Thousands of miners from County Durham gather on the racecourse in Durham city for the annual one-day Miners' Gala, which includes brass bands, speeches and a fair.

EAST OF ENGLAND SHOW, Cambridgeshire The East of England Show, a three-day agricultural show, is held at Alwalton, near Peterborough.

Fourth week

DOGGETT'S COAT AND BADGE, London Doggett's Coat and Badge Race, a race for Thames watermen, is rowed over a 4½ mile course from London Bridge to Cadogan Pier, Chelsea. Thomas Doggett was an Irish comedian who, in 1716, left a legacy to provide a cash prize and a scarlet coat with a large silver badge on one sleeve for the champion oarsman. The badge is embossed with the white horse of Hanover because Doggett instituted the race to mark the anniversary of George I's accession to the throne.

ROYAL WELSH SHOW, Powys This three-day agricultural show is held at Llanelwedd, Builth Wells.

ROYAL INTERNATIONAL HORSE SHOW, London Leading show jumpers compete before royalty at the Royal International Horse Show, at the Empire Pool, Wembley.

SON ET LUMIERE, York Minster The history of the 700-year-old cathedral is told in a play using only light and sound.

THE PROMS, London Sir Henry Wood Promenade Concerts at the Royal Albert Hall are given from late July until September. Booking opens in mid-June. Ballots are held for tickets for first and last nights. For a ballot form apply before May 31 to the Box Office, Royal Albert Hall, Kensington Gore, London SW7.

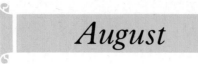

August

First week

COWES WEEK, Isle of Wight Racing yachts of all classes compete on the Solent during Cowes Week which, in fact, lasts nine days. Cowes is the centre for eight regattas held by various clubs. The most important regatta is organised by the Royal Yacht Squadron. Details from Cowes Combined. Clubs, 128 High Street, Cowes.

DUBLIN HORSE SHOW The Horse Show is the outstanding social event in Ireland and attracts thousands of overseas visitors. International jumping competitions and bloodstock sales are held at the Royal Dublin Society's grounds, Ballsbridge. Details from Royal Dublin Society, Ballsbridge, Dublin 4.

THE GREAT GOOSEBERRY CONTEST, North Yorkshire The biggest gooseberry is selected at a Gooseberry Show at Egton Bridge on the first Tuesday in August. The winning gooseberry is often almost as big as a hen's egg and weighs nearly 2 oz.

ROYAL NATIONAL EISTEDDFOD, Wales The foremost Welsh cultural festival, the Royal National Eisteddfod, includes competitions in music, drama, literature, arts and crafts, and a Gorsedd Ceremony which reaches its climax with the chairing and crowning of two Bards. The eight-day festival, held alternately in North and South Wales, is conducted entirely in Welsh. Details from Wales Tourist Board, Llandaff, Cardiff CF5 2YZ.

FESTIVAL OF ST WILFRID, North Yorkshire The return from exile of Bishop (later Saint) Wilfrid of York in the 7th century is commemorated at Ripon. 'St Wilfrid', on a white horse led by a monk, parades through the streets.

HIGHLAND GAMES AND GATHERINGS Highland Games take place at Fort William, Highland; Portree, Isle of Skye; Ballater and Strathdon (the Lonach Gathering), Grampian; Crieff, Tayside; Dunoon (Cowal Gathering) and Oban (Argyll Gathering), Strathclyde.

FOLK FESTIVALS Held at Sidmouth, Devonshire; Broadstairs, Kent; Whitby, North Yorkshire.

NATIONAL TOWN CRIERS' CHAMPIONSHIP, East Sussex Official town criers, some holding offices dating from medieval times, compete at St Leonards for the title of National Champion Town Crier. The winner is chosen on the strength and audibility of voice, and the test piece begins: 'Oyez, Oyez, Oyez. Good people assembled this day . . .'

Second week

BATTLE OF FLOWERS, Jersey Flower-decorated floats parade along the seafront at St Helier on the second Thursday in August. At one time the carnival, first held in 1902 to celebrate the coronation of Edward VII, ended with a battle of flowers torn from the floats. Spectators are now forbidden to touch the floats, which go on public display after the carnival.

SHEEPDOG TRIALS National sheepdog trials are held in England, Scotland and Wales in mid-August. Details from the Press Office, International Sheepdog Society, 64 St Loyes Street, Bedford NK40 1EZ.

CHESS CHAMPIONSHIPS The annual British Championships Chess Congress is held at different venues. Details of the next Congress can be obtained from: British Chess Federation, 4 The Close, Norwich.

NATIONAL ARCHERY CHAMPIONSHIPS, Warwickshire Archers meet for the British Target Championship meeting of the Grand National Archery Society, a two-day event held at Stoneleigh. In a York Round archers shoot 72 arrows from 100 yds, 48 from 80 yds and 24 from 60 yds; in a Hereford Round women shoot 72 arrows from 80 yds, 48 from 60 yds and 24 from 50 yds. Details of meetings can be obtained from the Secretary, Grand National Archery Society, National Agricultural Centre, Stoneleigh, Kenilworth.

Third week

EDINBURGH INTERNATIONAL FESTIVAL A three-week festival of music, opera, drama and cinema is held annually at Edinburgh. Other attractions are the Military Tattoo, on the Castle esplanade, and the Fringe – about 50 groups of young dramatists and actors performing plays, reviews and recitals. Booking opens in mid-April from: Edinburgh Festival Office, 21 Market Street, Edinburgh.

TALL SHIPS RACE The Tall Ships Race, a bi-annual event (in even years) over different routes, was launched with the Torbay to Lisbon race in 1956. Starting dates vary. Details from: Race Director, The Sail Training Association, 5 Mumby Road, Gosport.

MARHAMCHURCH REVEL, Cornwall The Marhamchurch Revel on the Monday after August 12 (the Feast of St Marwenne) commemorates the 6th-century Celtic saint who brought Christianity to this Cornish village. A Queen of the Revel is crowned by Father Time; afterwards there is a procession.

CORACLE RACES, Dyfed Coracle races are held annually on the River Teifi at Cilgerran. Similar small oval boats, consisting of a covered framework made of intertwined strips of wood, were used in pre-Roman Britain.

THREE CHOIRS FESTIVAL Concerts of church choral music and orchestral music are held in annual rotation in the neighbouring cities of Gloucester, Worcester and Hereford. Most of the recitals in the six-day festival, which was founded in the 18th century, are held in the cathedral of the host city, and the choristers at all three cathedrals take part. Booking opens mid-June.

Fourth week

BATTLE OF FLOWERS, Guernsey An annual floral pageant is staged at Saumerez Park in the heart of the island.

OLD-TIME DANCE FESTIVAL, Isle of Man A three-day festival of old-time dancing is held at Douglas.

OFFSHORE POWERBOAT RACE, Isle of Wight The Offshore Powerboat Race from Cowes, Isle of Wight, to Torquay, Devon and back, covers more than 200 miles. The race is on a Saturday between late August and early September; on the Sunday there is a powerboat race round the Isle of Wight.

September

First week

FARNBOROUGH AIR SHOW, Hampshire This week-long trade exhibition of the British aerospace industry is held in even years at Farnborough. There are three open days when visitors see flying displays, sky-diving and exhibitions. Details from: The Society of British Aerospace Companies, 29 King Street, St James's, London SW1.

BRAEMAR GATHERING, Grampian The most famous of the Highland Games, the Royal Highland Gathering at Braemar takes place 8 miles from Balmoral Castle, the Queen's Grampian home. There are competitions in piping, dancing and athletics. Booking opens April 1 from: Braemar Royal Highland Society, Braemar. Other Highland Games in early September are held at Aboyne, Grampian, and at Pitlochry, Tayside.

ST GILES' FAIR, Oxford Busy St Giles Street in Oxford, Oxfordshire, is closed to traffic and becomes a fairground for two days following the Sunday after St Giles' Day, September 1.

Second week

HORN DANCE, Staffordshire Dancers and musicians in Tudor costume perform a dance symbolic of an ancient deer hunt at Abbots Bromley on the Monday following the first Sunday after September 4. The dance is thought to have originated in Norman times in the granting of hunting rights to the villagers, and the dancers carry reindeer antlers on wooden poles. They dance throughout the day accompanied by traditional figures such as Robin Hood and Maid Marion.

BLACKPOOL ILLUMINATIONS, Lancashire Coloured lights are switched on along 6 miles of promenades at Blackpool. The display continues every night until late October.

WIDECOMBE FAIR, Devon, world-famous through the song that recounts the adventures of Uncle Tom Cobleigh and Tom Pearse's unfortunate grey mare, is held on the second Tuesday in September.

BURGHLEY HORSE TRIALS, Lincolnshire The Burghley Horse Trials at Burghley Park, near Stamford, is a three-day test of horses and riders. There are three tests: dressage, speed and endurance, and jumping. Details from Burghley Horse Trials Office, Stamford PE9 2LH.

Third week

BATTLE OF BRITAIN WEEK The defeat of the German Luftwaffe by the RAF in 1940 is celebrated throughout the week starting with September 15 (Battle of Britain Day). On the following Saturday a number of RAF stations stage public ground and air displays, and on the Sunday there are Thanksgiving Services at Westminster Abbey and churches throughout the country.

INTERNATIONAL BOAT SHOW, Southampton Every type and size of boat and piece of equipment is on show for six days at Mayflower Park, near the Isle of Wight ferry landing stage.

CRAB FAIR, Cumbria Apples are distributed in the streets at the Egremont Crab Fair on the Saturday nearest to September 18. Originally the distribution was of crab apples which, because of the distorted facial expressions they produced, gave rise to the World Gurning (face-pulling) Championships that are now held during the Crab Fair.

PIG-FACE DAY, Gloucestershire A feast of wild boar given at Avening by Queen Matilda in 1080 when Avening Church was consecrated is recalled every third year on the Sunday after September 14. After evensong in the church, the feast is re-enacted in the village hall and ham is served.

AUTUMN ANTIQUES FAIRS Antiques fairs are held throughout the country, notably at Chelsea Town Hall, London, at Cheltenham, Gloucestershire, and Harrogate, N. Yorkshire.

DR JOHNSON CELEBRATIONS, Staffordshire The Mayor and Sheriff go in procession to lay a wreath on Dr Johnson's statue in the market-place at Lichfield on the Saturday nearest September 18, the anniversary of his birth there in 1709. In the evening, Dr Johnson's favourite meal, steak and kidney pudding with mushrooms, and apple tart and cream, is served to local dignitaries at a commemoration supper.

CLIPPING THE CHURCH, Gloucestershire Children at Painswick 'clip' or embrace the church by holding hands and dancing round it while singing the Clipping Hymn, on the Sunday nearest to September 19. Villagers afterwards eat Puppy-Dog Pies, named, it is said, after pies once made by a local innkeeper. They are now cakes with china dogs inside. A similar ceremony is held at Wirksworth, Derbyshire, on the Sunday after September 8.

Fourth week

AUTUMN FLOWER SHOW, London The Royal Horticultural Society's three-day Great Autumn Show is held at the Royal Horticultural Society Hall, Vincent Square, Westminster. Details from: Royal Horticultural Society, Vincent Square, London SW1.

CHAMBER MUSIC FESTIVAL, Suffolk The festival at the Maltings, near Snape, is held for one week in September/October.

October

First week

BRITISH SAND YACHT CHAMPIONSHIPS, Lancashire The British Sand (or Land) Yacht championships are staged at Lytham St Annes on the first or second weekend of the month, depending on low tides. Race distances vary, but up to 12 miles may be covered and speeds in excess of 60 mph are far from uncommon.

COSTERMONGERS' HARVEST FESTIVAL, London On the first Sunday in the month, Pearly Kings and Queens in colourful regalia, sewn with hundreds of pearl buttons, assemble for the Costermongers' Harvest Festival Service at St Martin-in-the-Fields. Each 'monarch' takes offerings of fruit, flowers and vegetables to the festival.

HORSE OF THE YEAR SHOW, London British and foreign showjumpers compete in the Horse of the Year Show at the Empire Pool, Wembley. The six-day show includes contests for hunters, hacks and ponies. A ballot is held for the 8000 seats on the final night. For a ballot form apply before June 19 to the Box Office, Empire Pool, Wembley.

Second week

ROUND-UP OF PONIES, Hampshire Foals are rounded-up in Hampshire's New Forest for auction at four sales held during late summer and autumn at Beaulieu Road Station, between Lyndhurst and Beaulieu. About 15,000 ponies, many bred by commoners under ancient laws, are allowed to run wild in the New Forest, and an average of 500 foals are auctioned at each sale. The ponies are broken for hunting, polo and show-jumping.

MOP FAIRS Mop Fairs, though they are now solely pleasure fairs, were once held throughout the country for hiring farmhands and servants. At Stratford-upon-Avon, Warwickshire, one such fair is followed a fortnight later by a Runaway Fair, where servants unhappy with their new masters used to seek jobs again. Other October Mop and Runaway fairs are at Cirencester and Tewkesbury, Gloucestershire; Warwick, Warwickshire; Abingdon, Oxfordshire.

NATIONAL BRASS BAND FESTIVAL, London More than 100 of Britain's best brass bands compete in the National Brass Band Festival, but this number is reduced to about 20 for the championship finals at the Royal Albert Hall. Limited booking opens in January from the National Brass Band Championship, PO Box 58, West Wickham, Kent.

Third week

INTERNATIONAL MOTOR SHOW Latest car models from a dozen countries can be seen on alternate years (1980 at Birmingham) at the International Motor Show. Details from the Society of Motor Manufacturers and Traders, Forbes House, Halkin Street, London SW1.

Fourth week

OYSTER FESTIVAL, Essex To celebrate the opening of the oyster season the mayor and town dignitaries of Colchester set off on the last Friday in October in a fishing vessel to make the first dredge of the season. Afterwards a loyal toast to the Queen is drunk in gin, and gingerbread is served to the officials and guests.

WEXFORD FESTIVAL OPERA, Ireland High musical standards and international artists combine for a festival of opera, including little-known works, at Wexford. Details from Opera Festival Office, Wexford, County Wexford.

November

First week

GUY FAWKES NIGHT November 5, the anniversary of the Gunpowder Plot to blow up Parliament in 1605, is celebrated with numerous fireworks displays. Two of the most spectacular displays are in East Sussex, at Rye and Lewes.

STATE OPENING OF PARLIAMENT, London The Queen is driven from Buckingham Palace along the Mall and Whitehall to the House of Lords in the 120-year-old Irish State Coach for the State Opening of Parliament. A Royal salute is fired in St James's Park during the drive. At Westminster the vaults of the House of Lords, the site of the Gunpowder Plot of 1605, are searched by the Yeoman of the Guard, but this traditional ceremony is not open to the public.

TURNING THE DEVIL'S BOULDER, Devon Villagers of Shebbear go in procession with crowbars and torches on the evening of November 5 to turn over a great stone in the village square. Legend says the stone was quarried for a church 1½ miles away, but it was spirited off to Shebbear by the Devil. Ill-luck is reputed to follow if the stone is not turned.

LONDON TO BRIGHTON VETERAN CAR RUN The Veteran Car Run from London to Brighton, on the first Sunday in November, commemorates the abolition in 1896 of a law requiring a man with a red flag to walk in front of a motor car. The cars depart from Hyde Park at 08.00 and have until 16.00 to arrive at Brighton. Only cars built before 1904 are eligible for the 53 mile run, and there are about 250 entries from more than a dozen countries.

Second week

FIRING THE POPPERS, Buckinghamshire The firing of the Fenny Poppers on November 11 at Fenny Stratford marks the feast day of St Martin, the patron saint of Fenny Stratford church. The poppers, 20 lb. pots made of gun-metal, are charged with gunpowder and fired by applying a red-hot rod at 12, 2 and 4 o'clock. The custom has been observed since the church was built in 1730.

CARAVAN AND CAMPING SHOW, London The International Caravan and Camping Show at Earl's Court lasts ten days (Sundays excluded).

LORD MAYOR'S SHOW, London A 600-year-old London pageant, the Lord Mayor's Show is held on the second Saturday in November. The Lord Mayor, in a 200-year-old gilded coach, is driven in procession from Guildhall to the Law Courts to take the oath of office before the Lord Chief Justice and then returns, by a roundabout route, to the Mansion House. The following Monday evening, the Lord Mayor gives a banquet at the Guildhall at which the principal speaker is normally the Prime Minister.

Fourth week

COURTS LEET AND BARON The Courts Leet and Baron, a survival of the old district courts now replaced by law courts, still ensure than ancient laws are not broken. At Ashburton, Devon, the local Court Leet meets to appoint Ale Tasters to check the quality of ale in the town's inns, Bread Weighers, Pig Drivers and other officials.

ETON WALL GAME, Berkshire A variety of football that is different from any other is played on the Saturday nearest St Andrew's Day (November 30) at Eton College. The 11-a-side game is between the Collegers, the scholarship boys who live in the college, and Oppidans, who live in the town. It is played on a narrow field, and the goals are a gate and a tree. But play mainly consists of scrimmages against a high wall alongside the field, and a goal is rarely scored.

NEWMARKET BLOODSTOCK SALES, Suffolk The public is admitted to the six annual bloodstock sales during autumn and winter at Park Paddocks, Newmarket, the home of the National Stud. About 1500 horses are sold at the biggest sale, a six-day event in late November or early December. Details from: Tattersalls, Knightsbridge Green, Knightsbridge, London SW1.

December

First week

CAGE BIRD SHOW, London There are about 6000 entries from Britain and abroad for the three-day National Exhibition of Cage and Aviary Birds at Alexandra Palace.

SMITHFIELD SHOW, London The Royal Smithfield Show, a five-day agricultural show with the emphasis on beef cattle, is held at Earl's Court.

NATIONAL CAT CLUB SHOW, London About 2000 cats and kittens of 50 or more varieties are on show at Olympia.

Second week

BOSTON BEAST MART, Lincolnshire A proclamation opening the Beast Mart at Boston, under a charter granted in 1573 by Elizabeth I, is read at noon by the Town Clerk. Although sheep are still sold the mart is now mainly a pleasure fair.

VARSITY MATCH, Twickenham, London The annual Oxford v. Cambridge rugby match is played at Twickenham, usually on the second Tuesday of the month. The match is a popular social occasion for lunch parties at the ground before play starts.

CANDLE AUCTION, Berkshire At Aldermaston every third December (1980, 1983, etc.), a candle auction takes place for renting a piece of land known as Church Acre. The vicar usually starts the auction by sticking a pin or nail into a candle, about 1 in. from the top. The candle is then lit, and the successful bid is the last before the pin drops. The

winning bid is the rent payable for Church Acre. Another candle auction is held at Old Bolingbroke, Lincolnshire, on Lady Day (March 25).

Christmas customs

MORRIS DANCING, Surrey The East Surrey Morris Dancers perform at Godstone, Tilburstow Hill and Caterham on Boxing Day.

MUMMERS' PLAY, Avon A troupe of mummers enact an 800-year-old mumming play in the street at Marshfield on Boxing Day. The players disguise themselves in a practice based on an ancient belief that recognition would break the magical power of their dance.

BURNING THE ASHEN FAGGOT, Somerset An ashen faggot, a small bunch of ash twigs bound with green ash bands, is burnt at the Luttrell Arms Hotel, Dunster, on Christmas Eve. As each band burns through and bursts it is the signal for another round of cider. The custom is based on an old belief that ash wood gave protection against witches.

THE DEVIL'S KNELL, West Yorkshire On Christmas Eve the bell at Dewsbury Parish Church is tolled one stroke for every year since the birth of Christ – the holy birth heralding the Devil's death.

CHRISTMAS CAROLS Carol services are held throughout the country at Christmas. One of the best known services is the Festival of Nine Lessons and Carols sung on Christmas Eve at King's College Chapel, Cambridge.

FIRST AID

What to do at an accident

Follow this step-by-step guide **IN THIS ORDER**:

1. Stop other traffic from piling into the crash.

2. Call, or send somebody, for an ambulance.

3. Make a crashed car safe from fire (see p. 66).

4a. Treat a casualty who is not breathing (see p. 67).

4b. Treat an unconscious casualty (see p. 68).

5. Treat casualties who are bleeding (see p. 68).

6. Attend to other injured but **DO NOT MOVE THEM** until an ambulance arrives unless there is a risk of fire.

1. Warn other traffic

- Park your own car safely.
- Switch on four-way flashing indicators or headlights.
- Run back down the side of the road that is blocked to wave traffic down.
- Stop traffic in both directions if casualties are lying in the road.
- Place a warning triangle in the road at least 50 yds behind the accident (150 yds on a motorway).
- At night wear light clothing, wave a torch and shine your headlights on the crashed cars.

DO NOT stand with your back to oncoming traffic.

DO NOT walk across the lanes of a motorway.

On a motorway

On a motorway, park your car on the hard shoulder – but not by the crashed cars as this will reduce the road width – and switch on four-way flashing indicators or get a passenger to press rhythmically on the brake pedal to flash the stop lights.

If you have to stop behind the accident at night or in fog, direct your headlights on to the crash. Get out quickly and carefully in case other traffic is streaming by.

Place a warning triangle 150 yds back from the accident and if you have a torch try to wave down traffic.

Keep to the inner edge of the hard shoulder when running back to place the triangle. At night hold the triangle in front of you so that the lights of oncoming traffic pick up its reflectors.

Send somebody to telephone for help. If you are alone, hurry to the emergency phone. Marker posts indicate the nearest telephone. Drive to the phone if it is possible to get past the crash. The police will answer. Motorways are constantly patrolled by the police, who will arrive quickly and stop other traffic from piling into the crashed cars. The first priority always at a motorway accident is to CALL THE POLICE.

2. How to call for help

- Call, or get somebody to call, an ambulance by dialling 999.
- Give the ambulance service an accurate location of the accident.
- Give details of the crash: how many are hurt, how many are trapped and if petrol is leaking.

DO NOT assume that somebody else has called an ambulance.

What to remember when telephoning

In a town, look for a telephone in the nearest house, shop or public house if you cannot find a call box quickly. In the country follow telephone wires to the nearest house or inn. Give the ambulance details about the type of crash and the number of injured so the operator can decide whether to send more than one ambulance. The operator will alert the police and also the fire brigade if anybody is trapped or there is a risk of fire.

On the motorway

On a motorway, marker posts indicate the direction of the nearest emergency telephone which is answered by the police. Give details and THE LETTER AND NUMBER on the side of the telephone box, as this is how the location of a motorway crash is pin-pointed.

3. Make a crashed car safe

- Turn off the ignition.
- Disconnect the battery if there is any electrical smouldering.
- Apply the handbrake firmly.
- Stop everyone from smoking in case of petrol leaks.
- If you see flames or smoke, get the occupants out as quickly and carefully as possible.

DO NOT move casualties before expert help arrives unless there is real danger, such as fire.

DO NOT allow anyone to run about if his clothing is on fire. Lay him down and smother the flames, or roll him over quickly to prevent flames reaching his face.

DO NOT allow any casualty to keep on petrol-soaked clothing. It might ignite later. Remove it or cut it off and cover the casualty with a coat or blanket.

How to lift a casualty from a blazing car

Fire at accidents is not common, but is a definite risk. Petrol running along the gutter can be ignited by a spark or cigarette from a distance. If you are alone and cannot get any help when fire really threatens lift a casualty out from behind by putting your arms under his armpits, and take his weight on one of your legs. Attack a fire by aiming an extinguisher at the base of the flames. If the fire is in the engine, lift the bonnet an inch, aim a liquid extinguisher through the gap and then close it again. With a dry powder extinguisher the bonnet may be opened further and the powder sprayed all over the affected area. Take great care in using extinguishers near people in an enclosed area.
Use dry sand, soil or a heavy blanket to smother flames if an extinguisher is not available. Take care in approaching a lorry with a leaking load. Corrosive and poisonous substances and fumes can cause serious injury.

4. Attend quiet casualties first

a. When breathing stops

- Look at the quiet casualties first.
- Listen for breathing by putting your ear right against a casualty's mouth.
- If the casualty is blue in the face or is not breathing, lift the chin and tilt the head back.
- If breathing does not then start immediately, clear any obstruction from the mouth, such as dentures, and start mouth-to-mouth artificial respiration – the kiss of life.

Giving the kiss of life

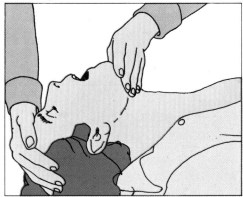

Put the casualty's head at an angle by pressing the forehead down and lifting the chin. Pinch the nostrils closed (except in the case of a small child). Take a deep breath.

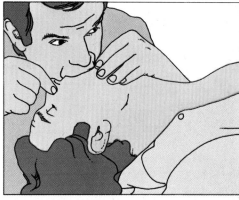

Cover the victim's mouth with yours (for a child, cover the nose also with your mouth). Blow gently. Look for rising of the chest. Remove your mouth.

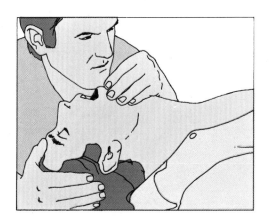

Take a deep breath while his chest deflates.
Repeat blowing procedure six times quickly, then ten times a minute (for a child, 20 shallow breaths a minute).

Once started, keep going until help arrives or the patient starts to recover. When recovery starts, turn the patient on to his side in case he is sick. Breathing may stop after suffocation, drowning, electrocution, inhaling exhaust fumes or even after a heart attack.

Delay is fatal – four minutes without breathing means death.

If after an injury a casualty is not breathing, has no pulse and has wide unmoving pupils he may be dead. If there is no response to artificial respiration within a few minutes you *may* be able to do more good by caring for other casualties, although it is not an easy decision to make. If at all possible, artificial respiration should be continued until a doctor decides otherwise.

When a casualty is unconscious – see next page

Attend quiet casualties first (continued).

b. When a casualty is unconscious

- Turn an unconscious person on to his side carefully. This is called the recovery position.
- Remove any dentures.
- Lift the chin to tilt the head back.
- Keep the mouth clear.

DO NOT leave an unconscious patient lying on his back.

DO NOT leave an unconscious patient alone.

How to place an unconscious person in the recovery position

An unconscious person lying on his back with a coat behind his head as a pillow may choke and die as his tongue falls back. Since an unconscious person *may* have an injured spine turn him carefully with help so that the hips, shoulder and head turn together. Further damage to the spine will then be avoided and the patient will not choke to death.

The casualty does not have to be moved far to do this – just rolled over gently. It can be done in the road or in a vehicle with the patient lying across the seats.

Never leave an unconscious person alone because he may suddenly stop breathing, or roll over on to his back again.

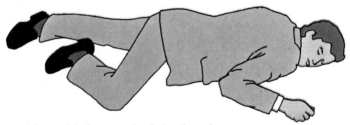

The recovery position, with the casualty lying face down

---

5. Treat casualties who are bleeding

- Cover the wound with a dressing or a CLEAN handkerchief.
- Press firmly and evenly over the dressing to control bleeding.
- Maintain the pressure with a bandage or ask the casualty to press on it with his hand.
- If possible, raise a bleeding arm or leg.
- If blood soaks through the first dressing, put another one on top.
- If there is glass in the wound press around the wound edge, not over it.

DO NOT tie a tourniquet around a limb.

DO NOT disturb a dressing.

DO NOT put cotton wool or lotion on to a wound.

Keep a firm, even pressure on the wound

Most bleeding can be controlled by covering the wound and applying a firm, even pressure and maintaining it.
Moving a dressing disturbs the clot that is forming to seal the damaged blood vessels. If blood soaks through keep the dressing in place and put another dressing on top and resume the firm, even pressure.
A tourniquet seldom controls bleeding properly in unpractised hands. It can damage vital structures and should not be used. Cotton wool is easy to apply but difficult to remove.

6. Attend conscious casualties

- Ask the casualty where he feels pain.
- Feel gently for painful areas.
- Apply a bandage or sling if necessary.
- Reassure the casualty that help is coming.

DO NOT move an injured person.

DO NOT allow anyone to bundle a casualty into his car and drive off to hospital. It is always better to wait for an ambulance. The casualty can then be placed on a stretcher and treated on the way to hospital.

DO NOT give tea, brandy or other drinks to casualties. If you do, it would mean a delay of up to four hours at hospital before an anaesthetic can be given.

DO NOT lift a car if anyone is trapped under it. Lifting may cause another part of the car to press on a casualty, or the car may slip over and cause more injury. Treat him where he is until expert help arrives.

Many injuries may be made worse by dragging a casualty out of the wreckage. All injuries, especially those of the spine, chest, pelvis and legs, need skilful handling to avoid causing further pain or damage. There is no point in taking a person out of one car to sit him in another or to lay him on a cold and draughty bank. In cold, wet or windy weather, cover the patient with a coat or blanket to prevent chilling. But do not attempt to warm a shocked, shivering patient with hot water bottles or by giving him hot drinks or alcohol. This could reverse the body's protective mechanism that is compensating for severe bleeding.

a. Dealing with injured limbs

- Put an injured arm into a sling or ask the patient to cradle one arm with the other – but only if the elbow is already bent.
- Bandage an injured leg against the good one. (See below)

DO NOT encourage a casualty to bend his elbow if it is painful.

DO NOT attempt to straighten a broken limb.

DO NOT tie bandages and slings too tightly.

Supporting a broken limb

A bone may be fractured if the area is swollen, painful, deformed or will not move normally. If in doubt as to what to do, help the patient to support the injured limb and wait for aid to arrive.

If a broken elbow is bent the circulation may be cut off and careless handling of a broken lower leg may cause the bone to come through the skin.

When putting a splint on a leg, always move the good leg to lie alongside the injured one and put padding between the knees and ankles to prevent chaffing. Tie the bandage round the foot and ankle first. Moving a person with fractured bones adds to his pain and shock so keep movement to a minimum.

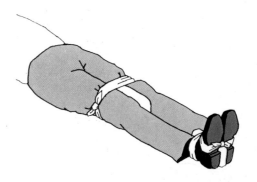

The correct method for strapping the legs

b. How to deal with fire burns

- Cool the burn with clean, running water if possible.
- Cover with a sterile or clean dressing.

DO NOT put cotton wool or a lotion on to a burn.

DO NOT attempt to pull off anything that is sticking to the skin.

c. How to deal with chemical burns

- Wash the burns with running water if possible.
- If an eye is affected, wash it immediately and thoroughly until all traces of the chemical have been removed. Turn the head so that the water does not pass from the affected eye into the other.
- Remove contaminated clothing. Cut or tear it off if necessary. Petrol-soaked clothing can still catch fire a long time after the accident.
- Skilled assistance is essential. So make sure that whoever calls the ambulance reports that a casualty has chemical burns.

Drowning – what to do

- Treat the casualty as for WHEN BREATHING STOPS (see p. 67).
- Feel the pulse in the neck or wrist.
- If stopped apply external heart massage as well.

DO NOT waste time tipping the patient upside-down to drain water out. If there is no pulse apply external heart massage as well as giving the kiss of life.

Giving heart massage

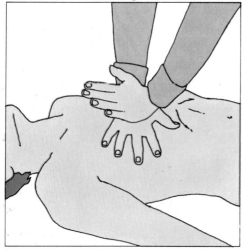

The position of the hands in heart massage.

1. Press with the hands over the lower half of the breastbone avoiding the lower end.

2. Press down firmly expecting about 1–2 in. of movement.

3. Relax pressure fully between each compression.

4. Repeat at about 60 times a minute.

5. Give two mouth-to-mouth inflations then 15 compressions alternately.

6. Use less pressure and press more rapidly for a child.

Heart massage is best left to a person with some knowledge of first aid, since it is advisable to have practised on a dummy. This can be done as part of a short first aid course given by the Red Cross and the St John Ambulance or St Andrew Ambulance Service.

The equipment you need

1. A torch.
2. A warning triangle suitable for day or night use. (BS AU: 47)
3. A fire extinguisher which contains a minimum of 2 lb. of dry powder or 24 oz. (680 cc.) of liquid suitable for petrol and electric fires.
4. A first aid set which can be packed in a plastic sandwich box.

It should contain:
6 No. 15 large pad and bandages;
6 No. 14 medium pad and bandages;
2 crepe bandages (7·5 cm.);
6 triangular bandages;
2 conforming bandages (10 cm.);
2 packets of 10 cm. × 10 cm. sterile gauze;
1 pair of scissors;

1 pair of forceps;
1 packet of assorted safety pins;
1 roll of 2·5 cm. adhesive plaster;
1 packet of assorted plasters;
1 plastic bottle of distilled water for washing out eyes;
antihistamine cream for stings, calamine lotion for sunburn and antiseptic cream for grazes.

TO BE SEEN AT NIGHT make a safety jacket from a pillow case. Cut along each side and cut a hole for the head at the closed end. Attach a tying string to each bottom corner. Keep the jacket and two children's reflective fluorescent arm bands in a handy place in the car so that they can be slipped on quickly.

How to deal with bites and stings

● If the victim of a bite or sting shows signs of acute distress, such as face-swelling, shortness of breath or extreme pain, call a doctor and ambulance immediately.
● Keep the victim as still and quiet as possible until he can receive medical attention. If possible put ice or a cloth soaked in cold water on the wound.

Bee, wasp and hornet stings

Take out a bee sting by stroking it with the side of a needle or pin. Apply antihistamine cream to any sting to relieve the pain. With these stings venom injected into the skin causes inflammation and local pain. In rare cases the venom can spread through the body, causing extreme pain and shortness of breath. The victim should have immediate medical treatment.

Snake bites

The adder or viper (see p. 399 for identification), is the only poisonous snake native to Britain.
Wash the wound with soap and water and apply a dry dressing. Assure the victim that there is no need to worry – many people show signs of panic after being bitten. Arrange for him to be taken to hospital on a stretcher.

DO NOT allow him to move the bitten part.
DO NOT give him anything to eat or drink.

Jellyfish stings

Treat simple stings with antihistamine cream or with calamine lotion. If the victim suffers shortness of breath, or faints, get him to hospital as quickly as possible.
The common jellyfish found in the sea around Britain inflicts a sting that causes a burning sensation and swelling. Only in a few sensitive people do the stings cause fainting and shortness of breath.
Anybody stung by the dangerous Portuguese man-o'-war, a large, purple-red jellyfish that occasionally reaches the south-west of England, should receive immediate medical attention.

Animal bites

Bites from a dog or any other animal are painful, as the skin is crushed and punctured. Animals' teeth are dirty and so wounds often get infected. Rest the injured part and apply a dressing. Seek medical treatment within six hours for an anti-tetanus injection.

TOWN PLANS

Roads and amenities for 109 major towns

The following list of 109 major towns and cities in the British Isles is an index to the town plans in this section and also to those plans which appear alongside the relative maps on pp. 138–264.

The plans on pp. 74–115, which are based on up-to-date information supplied by the Automobile Association, are divided into two categories. The main conurbations are dealt with initially and are covered by a large-scale plan of each central area showing amenities and one-way streets. Each of these plans is accompanied by a smaller-scale plan of the suburbs to give an accurate picture of through-routes into and around the city. In the second category are detailed large-scale plans of the central areas of the remaining major towns throughout England, Wales, Scotland and Ireland.

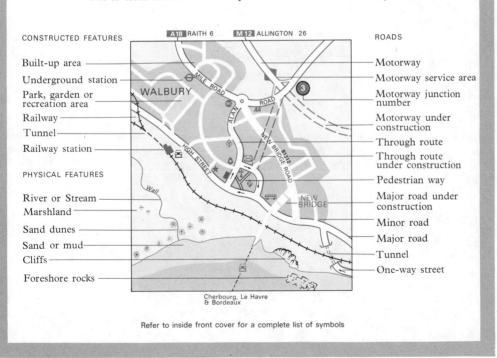

SYMBOLS USED ON THE TOWN PLANS

⊠ Post Office   ★ Theatre   ⚕ Police Station

✝ Church   ⊚ Public convenience   ▬ Public building

⊕ Tourist Information   AA **AA service centre**   🚗 Motorail terminal

🚌 Bus or coach station   ⊕ Car park   🚢 Car ferry route

CONSTRUCTED FEATURES

Built-up area

Underground station

Park, garden or recreation area

Railway

Tunnel

Railway station

PHYSICAL FEATURES

River or Stream

Marshland

Sand dunes

Sand or mud

Cliffs

Foreshore rocks

ROADS

Motorway

Motorway service area

Motorway junction number

Motorway under construction

Through route

Through route under construction

Pedestrian way

Major road under construction

Minor road

Major road

Tunnel

One-way street

Refer to inside front cover for a complete list of symbols

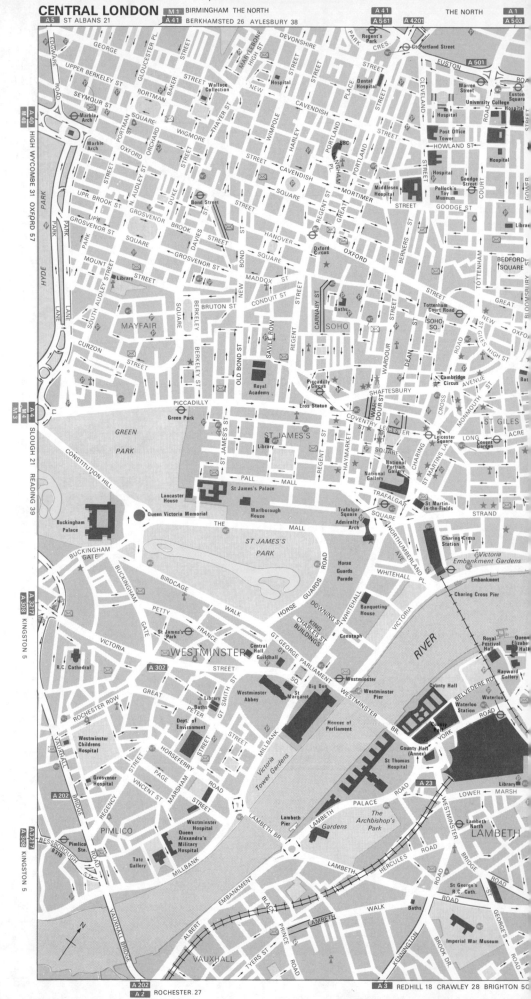

CENTRAL LONDON

A 5 ST ALBANS 21

M 1 BIRMINGHAM THE NORTH
A 41 BERKHAMSTED 26 AYLESBURY 38

A 41 THE NORTH

A 1

A 561 A 4201 A 503

A 202 ROCHESTER 27
A 2

A 3 REDHILL 18 CRAWLEY 28 BRIGHTON 50

A 40 M 40 HIGH WYCOMBE 31 OXFORD 57

A 4 M 4 M 3 SLOUGH 21 READING 39

A 3217 A 308 KINGSTON 5

A 3217 A 308 KINGSTON 5

B513

0 ¼ ½
MILE

EVERSHOLT ST
Euston Station
EUSTON
SOMERS TOWN
St Pancras Station
MIDLAND RD
YORK WAY
Kings Cross Station
CALEDONIAN ROAD
WYNFORD RD

University College
Town Hall
Kings Cross & St Pancras
ROAD

TAVISTOCK
WOBURN PL
ST PANCRAS
BARNSBURY ROAD

A501 PENTONVILLE ROAD
HIGH ST
Angel

BLOOMSBURY
Coram's Fields
KINGS CROSS ROAD
PENTONVILLE
SWINTON ST
UPPER ST

University of London
Russell Square
RUSSELL SQUARE
GUILDFORD STREET
Royal Free Hospital
Eastman Dental Hospital
AMWELL STREET
FINSBURY

British Museum
MONTAGUE ST
SOUTHAMPTON ROW
Great Ormond Street Hospital
Dickens's House
Mount Pleasant (Postal sorting office)
A401
Town Hall
ST JOHN
CITY ROAD

RUSSELL STREET
BLOOMSBURY WAY
THEOBALD ROAD
Library
Conway Hall
Gardens
ROSEBERY
CLERKENWELL
CLERKENWELL ROAD
GOSWELL
A1

HIGH
HOLBORN
HOLBORN
Gray's Inn
GRAY'S INN ROAD
HATTON GARDENS
FARRINGDON
St John's Gate
Farringdon
OLD STREET

GT QUEEN ST
KINGSWAY
A40
Sir John Soane's Museum
Staple Inn
Chancery Lane
ST JOHN ST
Charterhouse
BEECH

LANE
Lincoln's Inn Fields
Lincoln's Inn
CHANCERY LANE
Holborn Circus
FETTER LANE
CHARTERHOUSE STREET
Smithfield Market
Barbican
BARBICAN
ALDERSGATE

ALDWYCH
Royal Courts of Justice
STRAND
Aldwych
St Clement Danes
FLEET STREET
Prince Henry's Room
Dr. Johnson's House
A4
Holborn Viaduct
Holborn Viaduct Station
OLD BAILEY
St Bartholomew's Hospital
LONDON
Museum of London
Moorgate

SURREY ST
Temple
Inner Temple Church
St Bride
NEW BRIDGE ST
FARRINGDON ST
NEWGATE ST
Central Criminal Court
ST MARTINS LE GRAND
Guildhall

EMBANKMENT
M S Discovery
Inner Temple Gardens
LUDGATE HILL
ST PAUL'S CHURCH YARD
St Paul's Cathedral
St Paul's
CHEAPSIDE
MOORGATE
WALL

THAMES
Blackfriars
Blackfriars Station
QUEEN
VICTORIA
UPPER THAMES
CANNON
Mansion House
POULTRY
CITY
PRINCES ST
Bank of England
Stock Exchange

UPPER GROUND
Waterloo Hospital
STAMFORD STREET
BLACKFRIARS BR
A3200
Mansion House
Bank
THREADNEEDLE ST
Royal Exchange
CORNHILL
LEADENHALL

THE CUT
Waterloo Sta (Eastern)
SOUTHWARK
ROAD
Cannon Street
Cannon Street Station
KING WILLIAM ST
GRACECHURCH ST
Monument
FENCHURCH STREET
Leadenhall Market

St Georges Circus
UNION STREET
SOUTHWARK BR
The Monument
LONDON BRIDGE
LOWER THAMES STREET
EASTCHEAP

BLACKFRIARS ROAD
Library
Southwark Cathedral
DUKE HILL
A3
Billingsgate Market

Royal Eye Hospital
Hospital
UNION STREET
HIGH STREET
London Bridge
London Bridge Station
TOOLEY ST
The Tower
London Bridge

BOROUGH
SOUTHWARK
BRIDGE
Borough
BOROUGH
Guy's Hospital

75

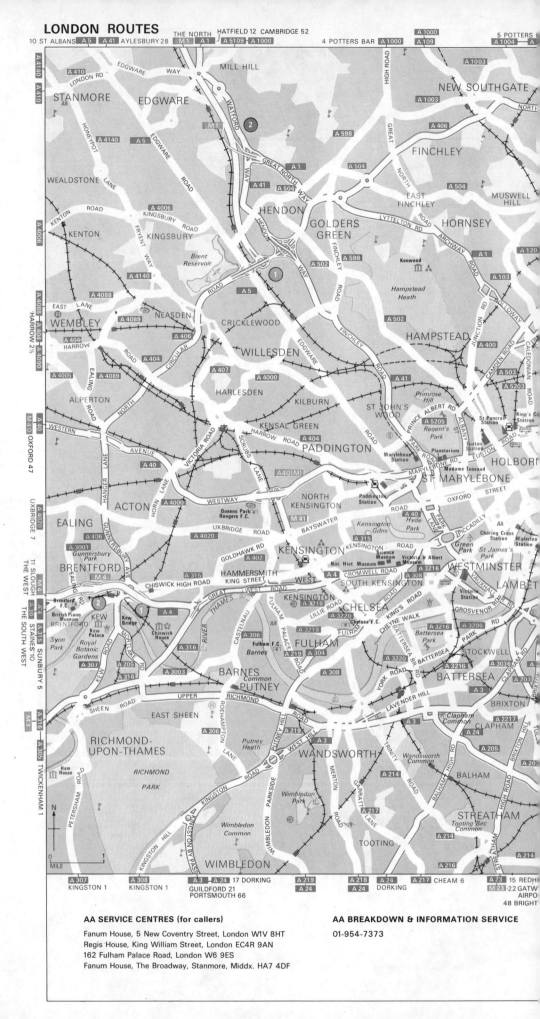

LONDON ROUTES

AA SERVICE CENTRES (for callers)

Fanum House, 5 New Coventry Street, London W1V 8HT
Regis House, King William Street, London EC4R 9AN
162 Fulham Palace Road, London W6 9ES
Fanum House, The Broadway, Stanmore, Middx. HA7 4DF

AA BREAKDOWN & INFORMATION SERVICE

01-954-7373

76

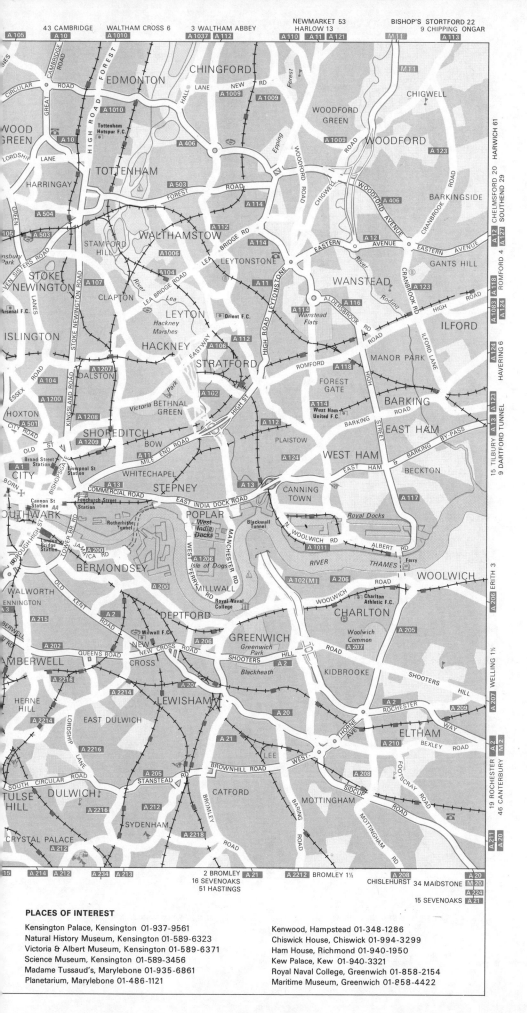

43 CAMBRIDGE WALTHAM CROSS 6 3 WALTHAM ABBEY
A 105 A 10 A 1010 A 1037 A 112

NEWMARKET 53
HARLOW 13
A 110 A 11 A 121

BISHOP'S STORTFORD 22
9 CHIPPING ONGAR
M 11 A 113

PLACES OF INTEREST

Kensington Palace, Kensington 01-937-9561
Natural History Museum, Kensington 01-589-6323
Victoria & Albert Museum, Kensington 01-589-6371
Science Museum, Kensington 01-589-3456
Madame Tussaud's, Marylebone 01-935-6861
Planetarium, Marylebone 01-486-1121

Kenwood, Hampstead 01-348-1286
Chiswick House, Chiswick 01-994-3299
Ham House, Richmond 01-940-1950
Kew Palace, Kew 01-940-3321
Royal Naval College, Greenwich 01-858-2154
Maritime Museum, Greenwich 01-858-4422

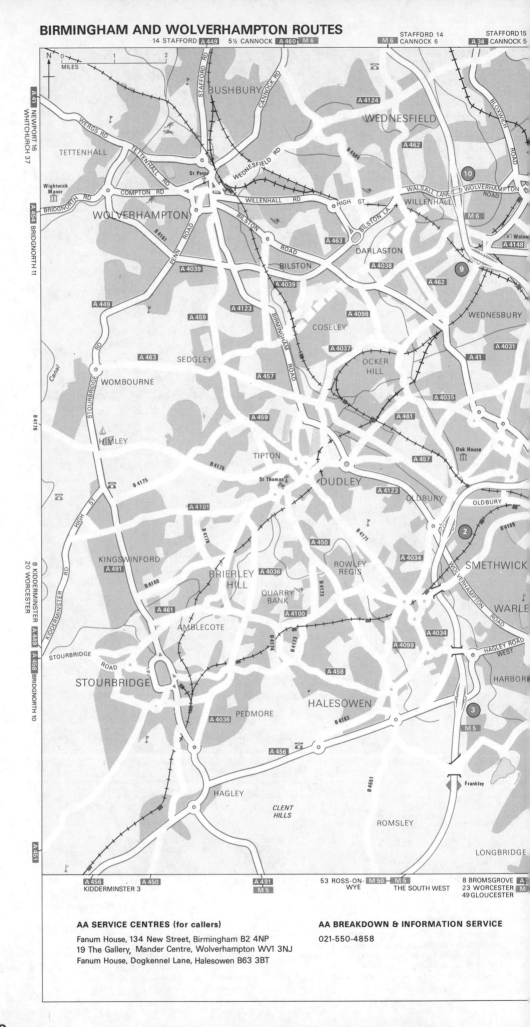

BIRMINGHAM AND WOLVERHAMPTON ROUTES

14 STAFFORD A449   5½ CANNOCK A460 M6   M6 STAFFORD 14 CANNOCK 6   STAFFORD 15 A34 CANNOCK 5

AA SERVICE CENTRES (for callers)

Fanum House, 134 New Street, Birmingham B2 4NP
19 The Gallery, Mander Centre, Wolverhampton WV1 3NJ
Fanum House, Dogkennel Lane, Halesowen B63 3BT

AA BREAKDOWN & INFORMATION SERVICE

021-550-4858

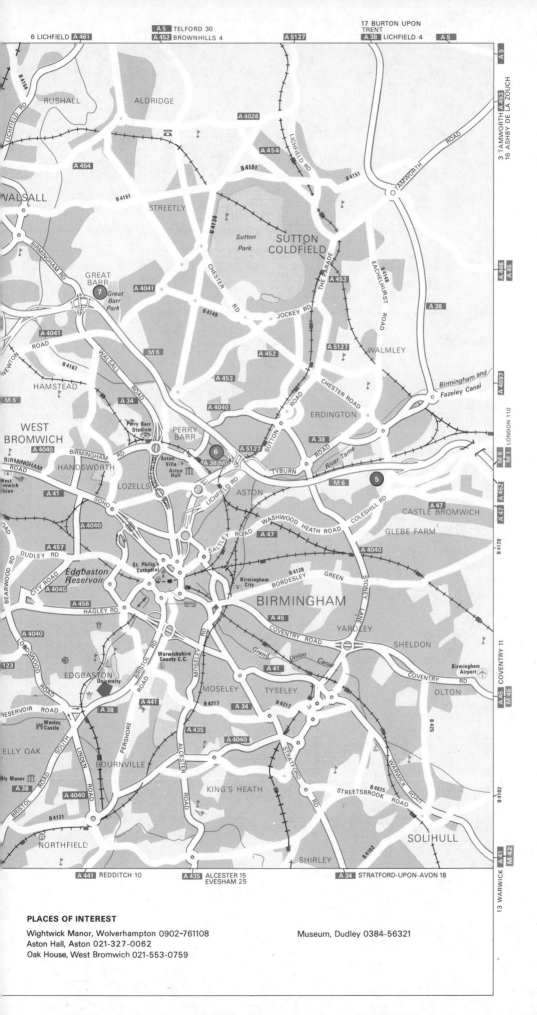

PLACES OF INTEREST

Wightwick Manor, Wolverhampton 0902-761108
Aston Hall, Aston 021-327-0062
Oak House, West Bromwich 021-553-0759

Museum, Dudley 0384-56321

CENTRAL BIRMINGHAM

A 41 WOLVERHAMPTON 13
9 WALSALL A 34
M 6
A 38(M) A 38 LICHFIELD 14 A 4540
A 34

A 457 DUDLEY 8 WOLVERHAMPTON 14
A 456 KIDDERMINSTER 17 M 5

A 4540 LEICESTER 41
18 COVENTRY A 45 COVENTRY 17
21 WARWICK A 41 A 34 STRATFORD UPON AVON 24

CONSTITUTION HILL
HALL ST
SUMMER
LWR LOVEDAY
PRINCIP ST
LANCASTER ST
CORPORATION STREET
ASTON RD
DARTMOUTH MIDDLEWAY
LIVERY
LISTER
WOODCOCK ST
ASTON STREET
PROSPECT ROW
GRAHAM ST
University of Aston
University of Aston
NEWHALL
Canal
St Chad's (R.C.)
St Chad's Circus
Birmingham Canal
NEWHALL HILL ROW
SAND PITS PARADE
Hospital
General Hospital
STEELHOUSE LANE
Law Courts
JAMES WATT QUEENSWAY
JENNENS ROAD
CURZON ST
COLMORE CIRCUS
County Court
MASSHOUSE CIRCUS
Art Gallery & Museum
Council House
St Philip's Cathedral
QUEENSWAY
BULL ST
DALE END
FAZELEY
NEW CANAL STREET
Canal
CAMBRIDGE STREET
Central Lib
Civic Centre
Town Hall
TEMPLE ROW
CORPORATION STREET
HIGH STREET
ALBERT
QUEENSWAY
MERIDEN STREET
FLOODGATE ST
BROAD STREET
NEW STREET
NAVIGATION ST
New Street Station
Moor Street Station
BILL RING
DIGBETH
HIGH STREET
GRANVILLE STREET
HILL STREET
QUEENSWAY
HOLLOWAY CIRCUS
St Martins Circus
St Martin
St Martin's Market
REA STREET
BRADFORD ST
DERITEND
HOLLOWAY HEAD
HORSE FAIR
PERSHORE ST
HURST ST
Ice Rink
Meat Fruit & Vegetable Market
CHEAPSIDE
BATH ROW
BROMSGROVE ST
N

A 38 BROMSGROVE 18 WORCESTER 27

CENTRAL WOLVERHAMPTON

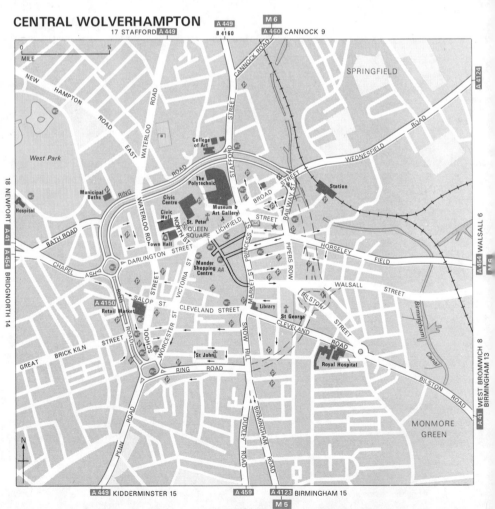

17 STAFFORD A 449
A 449
B 4160
M 6
A 460 CANNOCK 9

18 NEWPORT A 41 A 454 BRIDGNORTH 14

A 4124
A 454 WALSALL 6 M 6
A 41 WEST BROMWICH 8 BIRMINGHAM 13

NEW HAMPTON ROAD
WATERLOO ROAD
CANNOCK ROAD
STAFFORD STREET
SPRINGFIELD
WEST PARK
College of Art
WEDNESFIELD ROAD
RING ROAD
The Polytechnic
Municipal Baths
Station
Hospital
Civic Centre
Civic Hall
Museum & Art Gallery
BROAD STREET
RAILWAY ST
St Peter
QUEEN SQUARE
LICHFIELD
PIPERS ROW
HORSELEY FIELD
BATH ROAD
WATERLOO RD
NORTH STREET
Town Hall
AA
Mander Shopping Centre
MARKET ST
PRINCESS ST
WALSALL STREET
BILSTON
CHAPEL ASH
DARLINGTON STREET
RING ROAD
VICTORIA STREET
MONS HILL
Birmingham Canal
A 4150 Retail Market
SALOP ST
CLEVELAND STREET
Library
St George
CLEVELAND ROAD
BRICK KILN STREET
SCHOOL ST
WORCESTER ST
St John
RING ROAD
DUDLEY ROAD
BIRMINGHAM ROAD
Royal Hospital
BILSTON ROAD
GREAT
PENN ROAD
MONMORE GREEN
N

A 449 KIDDERMINSTER 15
A 459
A 4123 BIRMINGHAM 15
M 5

A 4170 TAMWORTH 20
M 6 A 444 NUNEATON 8
B 4109 BULKINGTON 6
B 4110 A 46 EAST

A 4114
A 45 BIRMINGHAM 18
A 4023 A 45 KNOWLE 11

DRAPER'S FIELD
Naul's Mill Park
Coventry & N.Warwickshire Hospital
HARNALL LANE WEST
STONEY STANTON LANE
SWANSWELL ST
HARNALL LANE EAST
VICTORIA ST
KING WILLIAM
Swanswell Pool
PRIMROSE HILL STREET

Coventry Canal
FOLESHILL ROAD
RADFORD ROAD
BISHOP ST
RINGWAY
WHITE ST
COX ST
Lady Herbert's Gardens
Pool Meadow
FAIRFAX STREET

HOLYHEAD ROAD
BARRAS LANE
DR WELL'S ST
CORPORATION
SMITHFORD WAY
A 4053
HALES ST
TRINITY STREET
BURGES
St Michael's Cathedral
Swimming Baths
Lanchester Polytechnic Lib.

SPON END
WINDSOR ST
RINGWAY
VICTORIA ROAD
St John
★
BROADGATE
MARKET WAY
THE PRECINCT
Library
Council Ho.
St Mary's Hall
Art Gallery & Museum
College of Art

A 46 LEICESTER 24
A 46 M 6 M 1 LONDON 98
A 427 A 428 RUGBY 11

CROFT RD
BUTTS ROAD
Technical College
Ford's Hospital
Ladý Godiva's Statue
HIGH ST
LITTLE PARK ST
EARL ST
JORDAN WELL
Council Offices
GOSFORD
Gulson Road Hospital
GULSON ROAD
Museum

NEW UNION STREET
Grey Friars Green
RINGWAY
LONDON ROAD

HARBOROUGH 28
MARKET
A 45 NORTHAMPTON 31
M 45 M 1 LONDON 94

N
Spencer Park
WARWICK ROAD
STONEY ROAD
QUINTON ROAD
Station

6 KENILWORTH A 444 A 46
27 BANBURY A 423
10 WARWICK A 46

M 62 LEEDS 48
A 576
A 665
A 56 BURY 9
A 664 ROCHDALE 12

N
LOWER BROUGHTON
SUSSEX ST
ST CLOWES ST
SHERBORNE ST
GREAT DUCIE STREET
CHEETHAM HILL ROAD
H.M. Prison
STRANGEWAYS
River Irwell
ST SIMON ST.
A 62 OLDHAM 7

SILK ST
ST SIMON ST
BLACKFRIARS ROAD
GREENGATE
NEW BRIDGE STREET
Victoria Station
MILLER ST
ROCHDALE ROAD
LIVESEY ST

11 BOLTON M 61
A 580 A 6
A 57 M 62

ADELPHI ST
Salford Royal Hospital
Town Hall
Cathedral (R.C.)
CHAPEL ST
Cathedral
CORPORATION ST
WITHY GROVE
SHUDE HILL
ADDINGTON ST
SWAN ST
OLDHAM ROAD
ANCOATS

WARRINGTON 19
LIVERPOOL 33
A 57

IRWELL ST
ORDSALL LANE
EAST
Salford Station
BRIDGE ST
CANNON ST
MARKET
HIGH STREET
CHURCH ST
POLLARD ST
OLD MILL ST
Ancoats Hospital
A 662

Royal Exchange
Law Courts
Library
Stock Exchange
AA
CROSS ST
POLDHAM
NEWTON ST
LEVER ST
DALE ST
STORE ST
ANCOATS STREET
POLLARD ST

River Irwell
NEW QUAY ST
QUAY ST
DEANSGATE
PRINCESS ST
Town Hall
MOSLEY STREET
Art Gallery
LONDON ROAD
Piccadilly Station
A 665

WATER ST
County Court Hospital
Central Lib
PETER ST
PORTLAND ST
Station
FAIRFIELD
A 635 ASHTON-UNDER-LYNE 7

WILBURN ST
City Hall
REGENT RD
LIVERPOOL RD
LWR MOSLEY ST
OXFORD ST
College of Science and Technology
WHITWORTH STREET
MANCUNIAN WAY
Station
A 635

EGERTON ST
CHESTER ROAD
BRIDGEWATER ST
WHITWORTH STREET WEST
Station
CAMBRIDGE ST
MEDLOCK ST
OXFORD ST
BROOK ST
A 57(M)
ARDWICK
SHEFFIELD 38
A 57

8 ALTRINCHAM A 56
HULME
MANCUNIAN WAY
A 57(M)
CAVENDISH ST
UPPER BROOK ST
Town Hall
BRUNSWICK ST
STOCKPORT RD
BRUNSWICK
HIGHER ARDWICK
ARDWICK GREEN SOUTH
HYDE RD
A 6

CHORLTON ROAD
DOWNING ST

MANCHESTER AIRPORT 8 A 5103
M 56 CHESTER 42
M 6 BIRMINGHAM 86
11 WILMSLOW A 34
6 STOCKPORT A 6

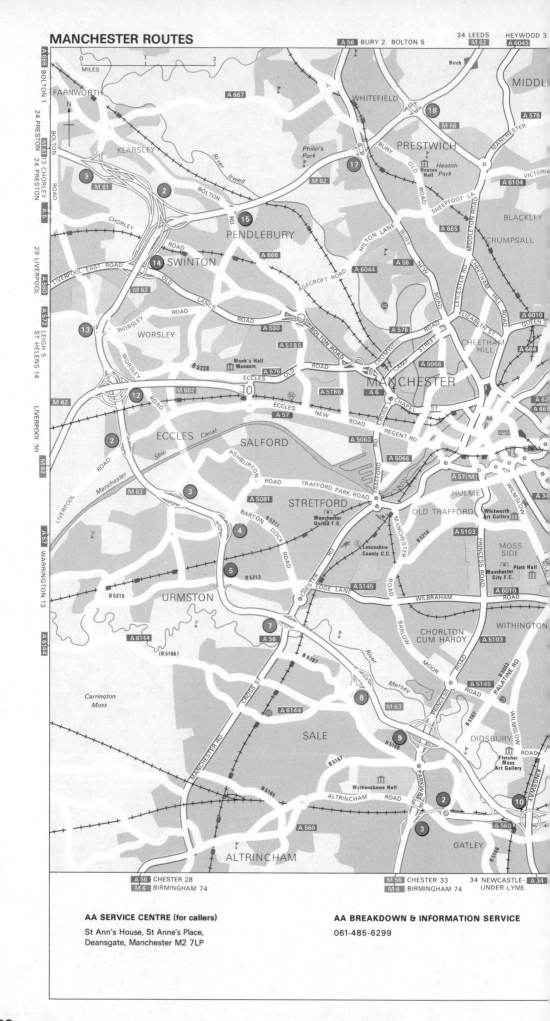

AA SERVICE CENTRE (for callers)

St Ann's House, St Anne's Place,
Deansgate, Manchester M2 7LP

AA BREAKDOWN & INFORMATION SERVICE

061-485-6299

A 669

A 62
16 HUDDERSFIELD
23 LEEDS

CHADDERTON

Oldham Athletic F.C.

A 669

WERNETH

OLDHAM

A 669

A 886

A 670
A 62

B 6189

B 6192

A 6104

A 663

Hollins Road

A 6104

HOLLINWOOD

A 62

MANCHESTER ROAD

BROADWAY

LIGHTBOWNE ROAD

B 6393

AVENUE

A 6104

B 6393

MOSTON

FAILSWORTH

MOSSLEY

B 6194

10 HOLMFRITH A 635

ROAD

ASHTON-UNDER-LYNE

A 627

B 6175

OLDHAM

HULME HALL LANE

A 6010

MILES ATTING

POLLARD ST

DROYLSDEN

A 635

MANCHESTER ROAD

STALYBRIDGE

ASHTON   NEW

A 662

ROAD

A 6018
A 57 SHEFFIELD 29

A 635

OPENSHAW

AUDENSHAW

ASHTON   OLD   ROAD

DUKINFIELD

Newton Hall

HARDWICK

HYDE

GORTON

Gorton Res

Audenshaw Res

A 627

STOCKPORT RD

A 6

DICKENSON RD

MOUNT ROAD

B 5178

A 57

MANCHESTER   ROAD

A 6017

M 57

A 57
SHEFFIELD 29

RUSHOLME

DENTON

BROOM LANE

WELLINGTON ROAD

B 5093

B 5168

LEVENSHULME

River   Tame

HYDE

A 560
25 BARNSLEY
29 SHEFFIELD

KINGSWAY

BURNAGE

A 6017

A 626

MANCHESTER

BREDBURY

B 6104

DIDSBURY

NORTH

RD

ROMILEY

A 626
4 GLOSSOP

Woodbank Park

A 560

STOCKPORT

11

Stockport County F.C.

A 626

MARPLE

CHEADLE

HAZEL GROVE

PLACES OF INTEREST

Wythenshawe Hall, Wythenshawe 061-998-2331   Fletcher Moss, Didsbury 061-445-1109
Heaton Hall, Prestwich 061-773-1231   Newton Hall, Dukinfield 061-308-2721
Platt Hall, Rushholme 061-224-5217

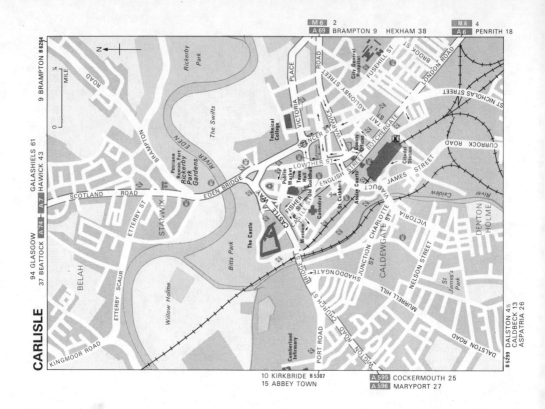

BRAMPTON B 6264

9 BRAMPTON

94 GLASGOW
37 BEATTOCK
GALASHIELS 61
HAWICK 43 A 7
A 74

10 KIRKBRIDE B 5307
15 ABBEY TOWN

A 595 COCKERMOUTH 25
A 596 MARYPORT 27

M 6 2
A 69 BRAMPTON 9   HEXHAM 38

M 6 4
A 6 PENRITH 18

B 5299 DALSTON 4½
CALDBECK 13
ASPATRIA 26

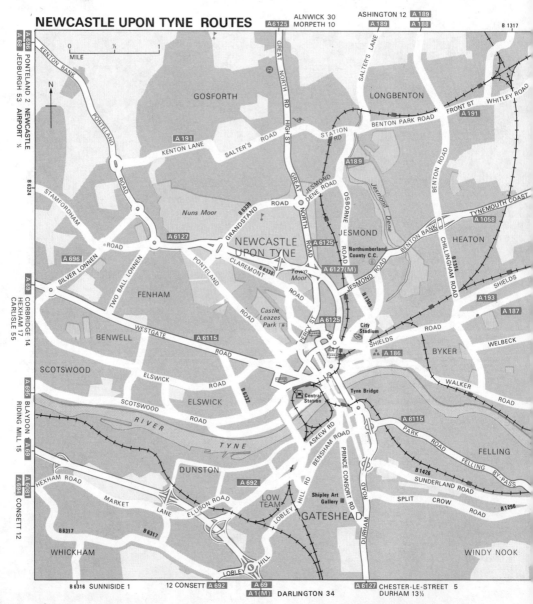

NEWCASTLE UPON TYNE ROUTES

A 6125 ALNWICK 30
MORPETH 10

ASHINGTON 12 A 189
A 189   A 188

B 1317

A 696 PONTELAND 2 NEWCASTLE
A 68 JEDBURGH 53 AIRPORT ½

B 624

A 696

A 69 CORBRIDGE 14
HEXHAM 17
CARLISLE 55

A 695 BLAYDON A 69
RIDING MILL 15

A 6081
A 694 CONSETT 12

B 6316 SUNNISIDE 1   12 CONSETT A 692
A 69
A 1(M) DARLINGTON 34

A 6127 CHESTER-LE-STREET 5
DURHAM 13½

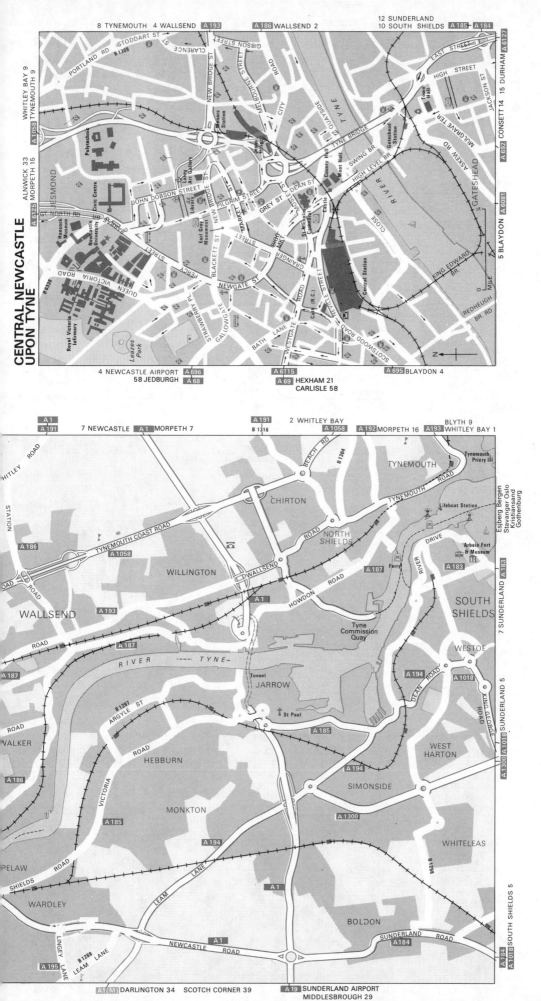

EDINBURGH

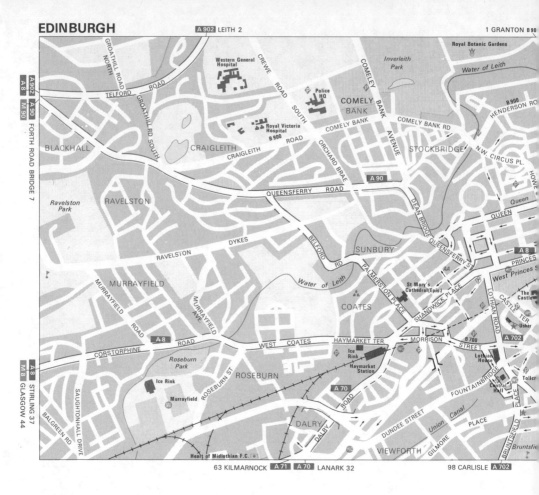

CENTRAL LIVERPOOL

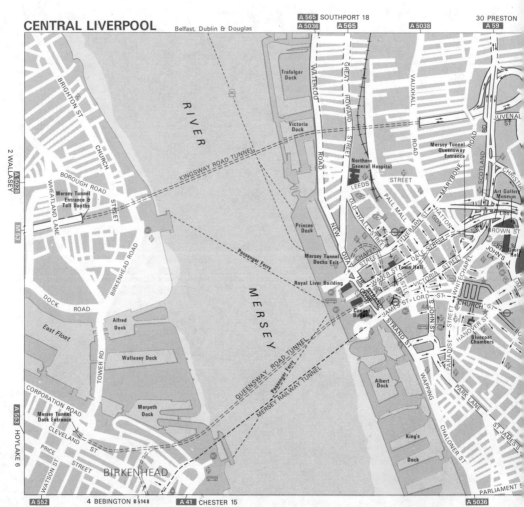

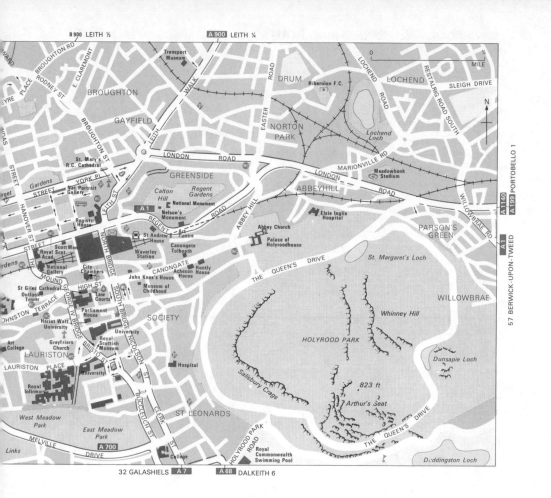

BROUGHTON RD

E CLAREMONT

PLACE RODNEY ST

BROUGHTON

GAYFIELD

Transport Museum

WALK

LEITH

DRUM

Hibernian F.C.

LOCHEND

RESTALRIG ROAD SOUTH

SLEIGH DRIVE

N

LONDON ROAD

NORTON PARK

Lochend Loch

LOCHEND ROAD

St. Mary's R.C. Cathedral

EASTER ROAD

MARIONVILLE RD

Meadowbank Stadium

YORK PL

Nat Portrait Gallery

GREENSIDE

Calton Hill

Regent Gardens

National Monument

ABBEYHILL

LONDON ROAD

WILLOWBRAE RD

A 1

Nelson's Monument

Register House

St Andrew's House

REGENT

ABBEY HILL

Elsie Inglis Hospital

PARSON'S GREEN

A 1   A 199 PORTOBELLO 1   A 1140

57 BERWICK-UPON-TWEED

HANOVER ST

Scott Mon

Royal Scot Acad

Waverley Station

Abbey Church

Palace of Holyroodhouse

St Margaret's Loch

WILLOWBRAE

National Gallery

City Chambers

CANONGATE

John Knox's House

Huntly House

Acheson House

THE QUEEN'S DRIVE

Whinney Hill

St Giles Cathedral

Outlook Tower

HIGH ST

Museum of Childhood

HOLYROOD PARK

Dunsapie Loch

JOHNSTON TERRACE

Law Courts

Parliament House

SOCIETY

SOUTH BRIDGE

NICOLSON ST

Heriot Watt University

Royal Scottish Museum

University

823 ft

Art College

Greyfriars Church

LAURISTON

University

Hospital

Arthur's Seat

Salisbury Crags

LAURISTON PLACE

Royal Infirmary

BRISTO ST

BUCCLEUCH ST

ST LEONARDS

THE QUEEN'S DRIVE

West Meadow Park

East Meadow Park

CLERK ST

HOLYROOD PARK ROAD

Links

MELVILLE DRIVE

A 700

College

Royal Commonwealth Swimming Pool

Duddingston Loch

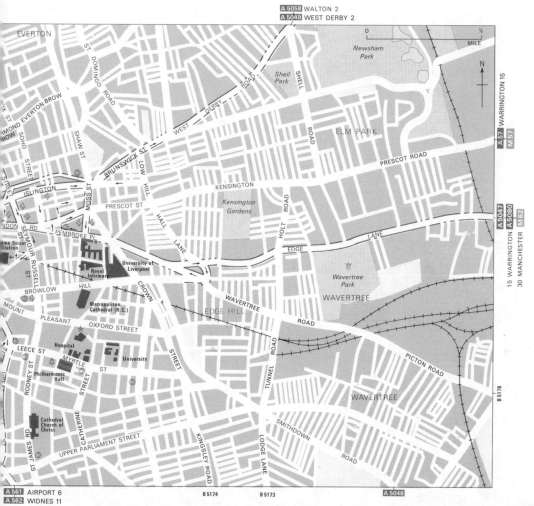

EVERTON

DOMINGO ROAD

Newsham Park

N

EVERTON BROW

SHELL ROAD

Sheil Park

DERBY ROAD

ELM PARK

A 57 WARRINGTON 15   M 57

SHAW ST

BRUNSWICK ST

WEST DERBY ROAD

PRESCOT ROAD

ISLINGTON

MOSS ST

LOW HILL

KENSINGTON

HALL LANE

Kensington Gardens

HOLT ROAD

LANE

A 5047   A 5080   M 62

PRESCOT ST

LONDON RD

SEYMOUR ST

PEMBROKE PL

Royal Infirmary

University of Liverpool

EDGE LANE

15 WARRINGTON   30 MANCHESTER

BROWLOW HILL

CROWN ST

Wavertree Park

WAVERTREE

MOUNT PLEASANT

Metropolitan Cathedral (R.C.)

EDGE HILL

WAVERTREE ROAD

LEECE ST

OXFORD STREET

Hospital

University

STREET

PICTON ROAD

RODNEY ST

MYRTLE ST

Philharmonic Hall

ST

University

KINGSLEY ROAD

TUNNEL ROAD

LODGE LANE

WAVERTREE

ST JAMES RD

Cathedral Church of Christ

ST CATHERINE

UPPER PARLIAMENT STREET

SMITHDOWN ROAD

B 5178

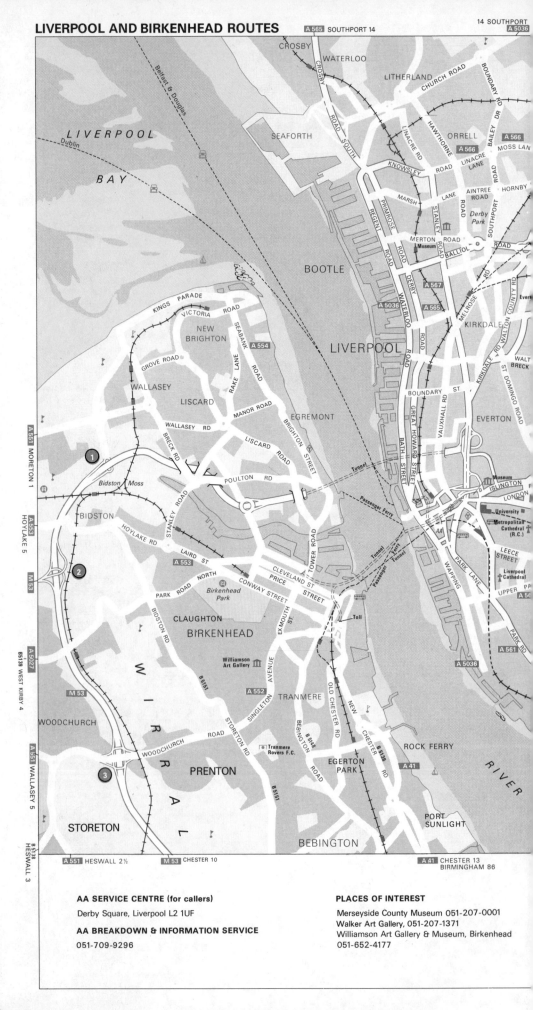

AA SERVICE CENTRE (for callers)
Derby Square, Liverpool L2 1UF

AA BREAKDOWN & INFORMATION SERVICE
051-709-9296

PLACES OF INTEREST
Merseyside County Museum 051-207-0001
Walker Art Gallery, 051-207-1371
Williamson Art Gallery & Museum, Birkenhead
051-652-4177

THE BRITISH ISLES BY ROAD

*The Ordnance Survey is the basis for the maps
of England, Scotland, Wales, Ireland
and the Channel Islands*

SYMBOLS USED ON MAPS

ROADS

Motorway	access / service area / limited access
	See motorway strip plans (pp. 116-126) for details of limited access points
Primary or A road: carriageway single	
dual	
B road	
Other tarred	
Other minor	
Motorway number	M6
A road number	A76
N road number (Republic of Ireland)	N7
B road number	B 1201
Reclassification: old numbers	(A51) (B4044)
Narrow A road with passing places (Scotland only)	
Under construction Motorway	
Other road	
Projected Motorway	
Gradient, 1 in 5 to 1 in 7, steeper than 1 in 5, toll	Toll
Distance in miles	
Roundabout/Interchange	

RAILWAYS

Normal gauge	
Normal gauge (disused)	
Narrow gauge	
Road crossing under, over	
Level crossing, tunnel	
Station, motorail terminal	

BOUNDARIES

National	
County	

SETTLEMENTS

Town with built-up area	
Village or hamlet	

CONSTRUCTED FEATURES

Civil airport (with scheduled services)	
Military airfield (6,000 ft runway or longer)	
Windmill	
Radio or TV mast	
Frontier post (Ireland)	
Lighthouse	
Lightship	
AA or RAC telephone box	
P.O. telephone box in rural area	
Youth hostel	
Observatory	

PHYSICAL FEATURES

Height in feet above mean sea level	Ryder's Hill · 1690
Woodland or forest	
River and lake	canal
Marsh or bog	
Coastal	earth slopes / cliffs / dunes / rock / foreshore / ferry

ANTIQUITIES

Site of Roman antiquities	CANOVIVM
Site of other antiquities	Castle
Ancient fortress	
Site of battle (date)	1066
Roman road (course)	ROMAN ROAD

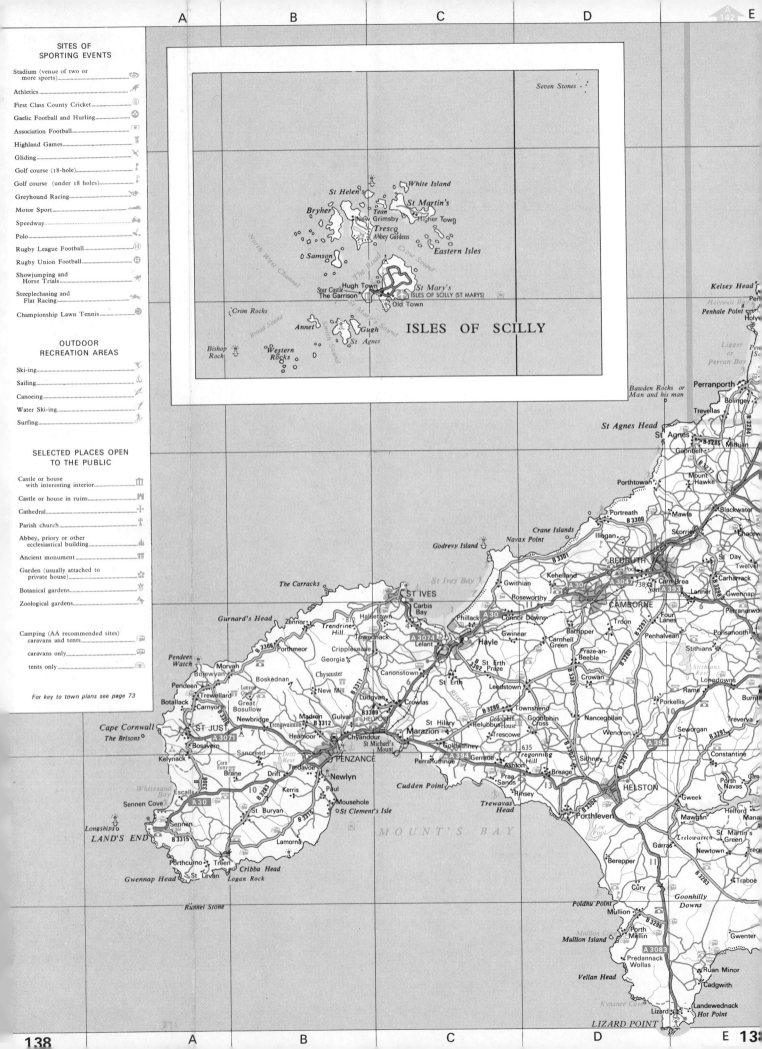

SITES OF SPORTING EVENTS

Stadium (venue of two or more sports)
Athletics
First Class County Cricket
Gaelic Football and Hurling
Association Football
Highland Games
Gliding
Golf course (18-hole)
Golf course (under 18 holes)
Greyhound Racing
Motor Sport
Speedway
Polo
Rugby League Football
Rugby Union Football
Showjumping and Horse Trials
Steeplechasing and Flat Racing
Championship Lawn Tennis

OUTDOOR RECREATION AREAS

Ski-ing
Sailing
Canoeing
Water Ski-ing
Surfing

SELECTED PLACES OPEN TO THE PUBLIC

Castle or house with interesting interior
Castle or house in ruins
Cathedral
Parish church
Abbey, priory or other ecclesiastical building
Ancient monument
Garden (usually attached to private house)
Botanical gardens
Zoological gardens

Camping (AA recommended sites) caravans and tents
caravans only
tents only

For key to town plans see page 73

ISLES OF SCILLY

LAND'S END

LIZARD POINT

FOWEY TO TORBAY

Opening times may vary and should be confirmed by telephone from the number in brackets Map references are shown after each place name

Ashburton see p. 145

Berry Pomeroy see p. 145

Bodmin see p. 143

Brixham see p. 145

Buckfast (Hf) *Abbey* (Buckfastleigh 3301), Norman style, completed by monks in 1938 on the site of a ruined 10th-century abbey

Calstock (Ef) *Cotehele House* (St Dominick 50434), 15th century

Cockington see p. 145

Dartmeet (Gg) Beauty spot where East and West Dart rivers meet

Dartmouth (Je) *Castle*, 15th-century coastal fort, contains a museum

Paignton see p. 145

Plymouth (Ee) *Cathedral*, mid-19th-century Gothic style. *City Museum and Art Gallery* (68000). The 17th-century *Citadel* on the Hoe may be visited by applying to the guide. *Naval dockyards* (553740)

Poundstock see p. 143

Restormel (Bf) *Castle*, 12th-century remains

Saltash (Ee) *Royal Albert Bridge*, designed by Isambard Kingdom Brunel, single railway track over the River Tamar opened in 1859

Stoke Gabriel (Je) *Church of SS Mary and Gabriel*, 15th century with 13th-century tower. The churchyard contains a yew tree said to be more than 1000 years old

Torpoint (Ee) *Antony House* (Plymouth 812191), Queen Anne building, has portraits by Sir Joshua Reynolds

Torquay see p. 145

Totnes (Jf) *Church of St Mary*, 15th century. *Guildhall* (Torquay 862147), part-16th century, museum includes a prison cell, man-traps and stocks. *Castle*, 11th-century ruins

AA SERVICE CENTRE: 10 Old Town Street Plymouth (Plymouth 28004). Breakdown service, Plymouth 69989, 24 hours

A town plan of PLYMOUTH is on p. 140; of TOTNES on p. 145

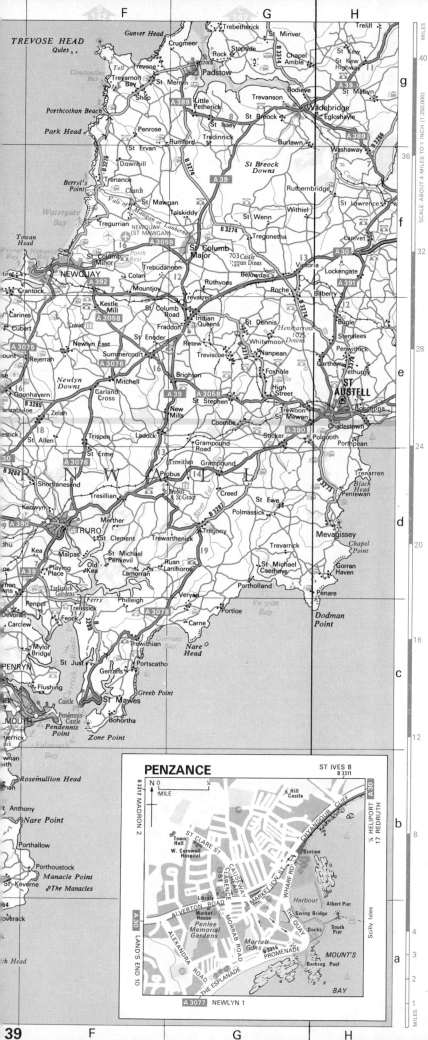

WESTERN CORNWALL

Opening times should be confirmed by telephone from the number in brackets. The exchange is given only if it differs from the place name at the beginning of the entry
Map references are shown after each place name

Camborne (Dc) *Camborne School of Mines* (714866), geological museum with extensive collection of specimens.

Castle an Dinas (Gf) Iron Age fort

Chysauster (Bc) Iron Age village with four pairs of courtyard houses

Falmouth (Fc) *Pendennis* (313388), coastal fort built by Henry VIII in 1543

Glendurgan (Eb) *Glendurgan Gardens*, Mawnan Smith, valley garden with specimen trees and flowering shrubs

Godolphin Cross (Dc) *Godolphin House* (Germoe 2409), part-Tudor house, with a colonnaded front added in the 17th century formerly the home of the Earls of Godolphin

Newlyn East (Fe) *Trerice* (Newquay 5404), an Elizabethan stone manor house with fine plaster ceilings and minstrels' gallery

Newquay (Ff) *Trenance Gardens* (4385), 6 acres of landscaped parkland containing a zoo

Padstow see p. 143

Penzance (Bc) *Trengwainton Gardens*, Heamoor (2 miles north-west of Penzance), contain sub-tropical plants in a series of walled gardens. At *Morrab Gardens* tropical plants growing in the open include acacias, palms, fruit-bearing olive trees and banana trees

Pool (Dd) *East Pool and Agar Mine*, contains an engine

of the type used in Cornish mines during the last century to hoist men and tin ore

Redruth (Dd) *Tolgus Tin Stream Works and Craft Centre* (215171), 2 miles north-west of Redruth on B3300, tin plant producing tin from waste of derelict mines. Visitors may prospect and keep the tin they find

Roche (Gf) *Tregeagle's Dilemma*, 15th-century chapel

St Mawes (Fc) *Castle*, 16th century

St Mawgan (Ff) *Church*, 13th century, has many fine carvings

St Michael's Mount (Cc) A medieval and early 17th-century sea-girt castle (Marazion 710523) that can be reached on foot by a causeway at low tide. Home of the St Levan family

Trelissick Gardens (Fc) 370 acres of wooded parkland (Truro 862090)

Truro (Fd) *Royal Institution of Cornwall* (2205), museum and art gallery; contents include a collection of paintings by the 18th-century Cornish artist John Opie, and the painting by Sir Godfrey Kneller of the 'Loyal Giant', 7 ft 6 in. Anthony Payne, 17th-century bodyguard to the Grenville family. *Truro Cathedral* was completed in 1910 on the site of the 16th-century parish church of St Mary. The walls and wagon roof of the church now form the cathedral's south aisle

AA SERVICE CENTRE: 10 River Street, Truro (Truro 2283). Breakdown service, Truro, 24 hours (Truro 76455)

ST AUSTELL

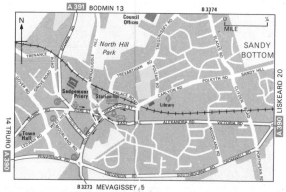

A town plan of NEWQUAY is on p. 142

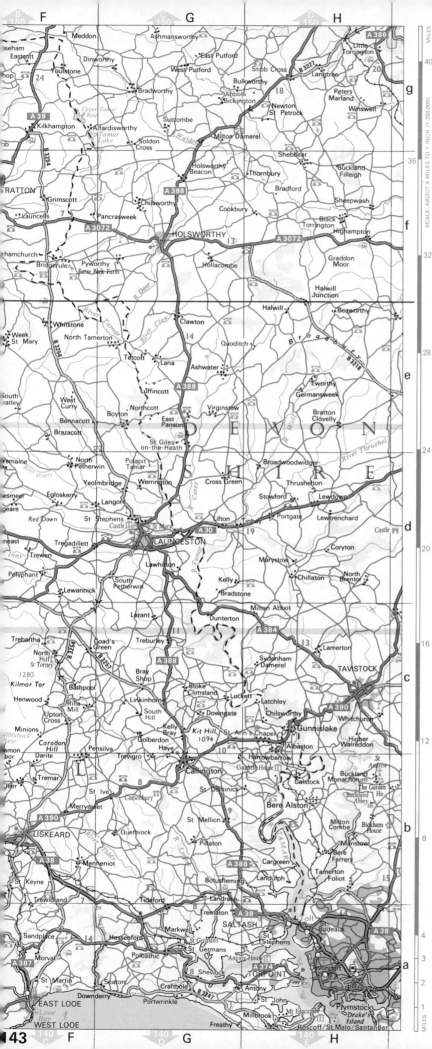

NORTH CORNWALL

Opening times should be confirmed by telephone from the number in brackets. The exchange is given only if it differs from the place name at the beginning of the entry

Map references are shown after each place name

Altarnun (Fd) *Church of St Nonna*, 15th century with carved Norman font. A medieval packhorse bridge is outside the church

Bodmin (Db) *Lanhydrock House* (3320), 2½ miles south-east of Bodmin on B3268, 17th-century house containing a picture gallery with a plaster ceiling depicting scenes from the Old Testament, tapestries and portraits, and a 250-acre wooded park. *St Petroc's Church*, rebuilt in 1469. *St Thomas à Becket's Chapel*, 14th-century ruins

Bolventor (Ec) *Jamaica Inn*, used by Daphne du Maurier as the setting and title of her novel. *Dozmary Pool*, 1½ miles south-east of Bolventor is where, according to tradition, Sir Bedivere flung King Arthur's sword, Excalibur

Buckland Monachorum (Hb) *Church of St Andrew*, 15th to 16th century, Drake family monuments, Perpendicular and Norman fonts. *Buckland Abbey* (Yelverton 3607), 13th-century Cistercian house suppressed by Henry VIII in 1541 and converted by Sir Richard Grenville; it was bought by Sir Francis Drake in 1584. It is now a naval and folk museum

Bude (Ef) *Ebbingford Manor* (2808), part 12th-century manor house with fine Tudor chimneys and a restored Tudor chapel. A museum is in the grounds

Calstock see p. 141

Camelford (Ed) *Slaughter Bridge*, 1 mile to the north, is said to be the scene of King Arthur's last battle against the Saxons

Launceston (Gd) *Castle* (2365), 13th century. *Church of St Mary Magdalene*, 16th century with 14th-century tower. *Lawrence House* (Bodmin 4284), museum with collections of local historical interest

Morwenstow (Eg) *Church of St Morwenna*, part-12th century

Newlyn East see p. 139

Newquay see p. 139

North Hill (Fc) *Church of St Torney*, 15th century, has a granite tower, and 16th and 17th-century tombs

Padstow (Cc) *Church of St Petrock*, part-13th century, built on the site of a monastery sacked by the Danes in the 10th century. The old town stocks are in the church porch

Plymouth see p. 141

Restormel see p. 141

St Mawgan see p. 139

St Neot (Eb) *Church of St Neot*, has 15th and 16th-century stained glass

Saltash see p. 141

Tintagel (Dd) *Castle*, 12th-century ruins on the site of a Celtic monastery. *The Old Post Office* (Bodmin 4284), 14th-century manor house used as letter-receiving office in 19th century, is now a museum. *Church of St Materiana*, part Norman, containing a five-legged Norman font, a fine rood screen and an inscribed stone, probably a Roman milestone

Torpoint see p. 141

PADSTOW

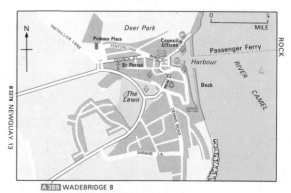

A town plan of PLYMOUTH is on p. 140

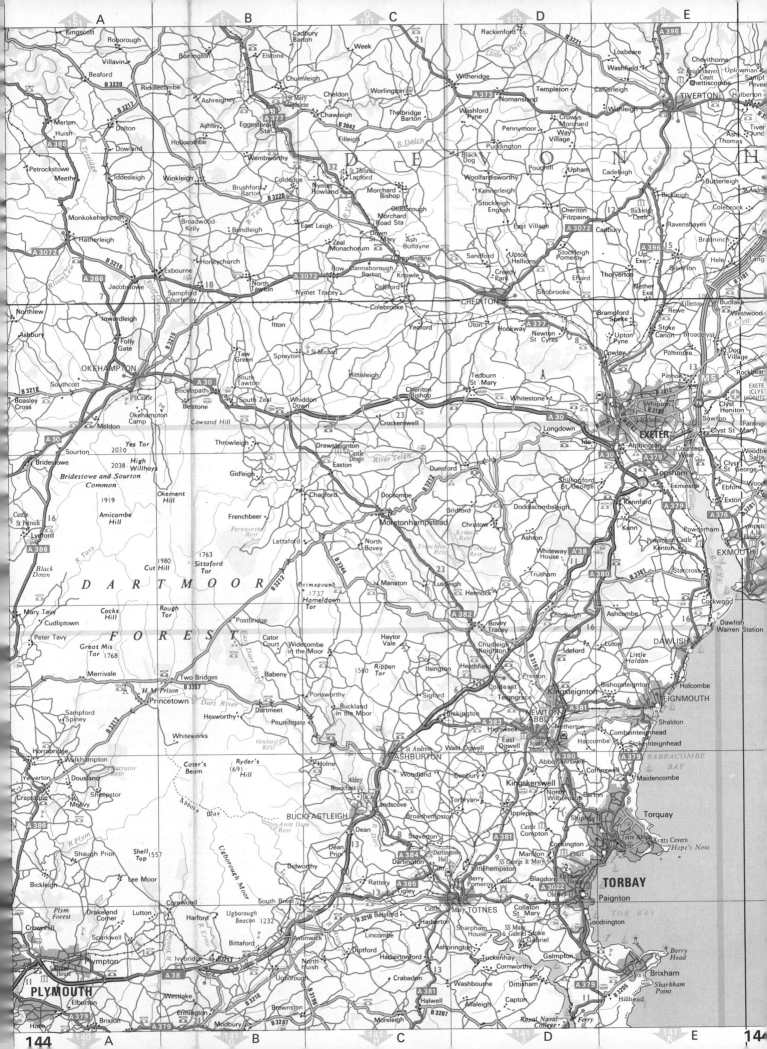

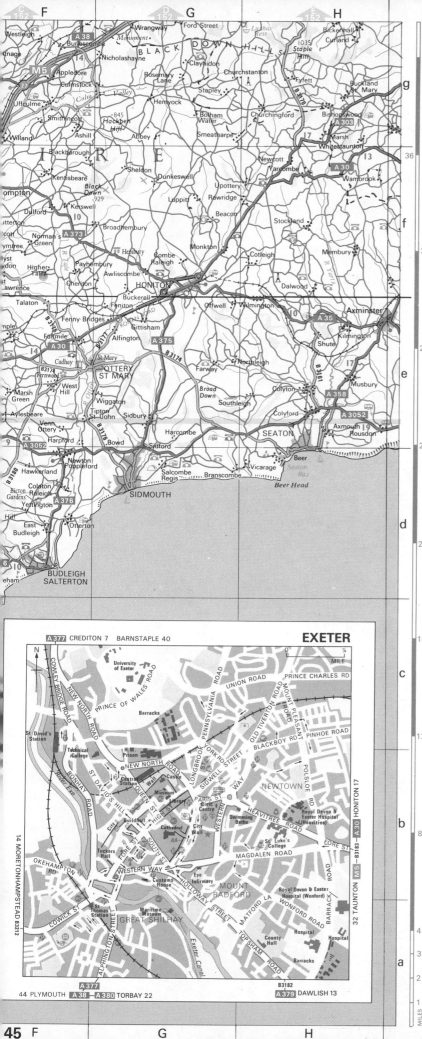

PLACES TO SEE ON
THE DEVON RIVIERA

Opening times should be confirmed by telephone from the number in brackets. The exchange is given only if it differs from the place name at the beginning of the entry

Map references are shown after each place name

Ashburton (Cb) *Museum* (52298). *Church of St Andrew,* 15th century

Berry Pomeroy (Db) *Castle* (Totnes 863397), 11th and 16th-century ruins

Bickleigh (Ef) *Castle* (363), with 11th century chapel and medieval gatehouse

Brixham (Ea) *Aquarium* (2204). *Museum* (4207)

Buckfast see p. 141

Cockington (Db) *Forge* (Torquay 67162), 19th-century cob-and-thatch cottage. *Church of SS George and Mary,* 11th century

Dartmeet see p. 141

Dartmoor National Park see p. 338

East Budleigh (Fd) *Bicton Gardens* (Budleigh Salterton 3881) contain a pine-tree plantation and a narrow-gauge railway

Exeter (Ee) *Cathedral,* part-11th century, rebuilt in 13th–14th centuries, with fine ribbed vault. *Killerton Garden* (Hele 691). *Maritime Museum* (58075). *Rougemont House Museum* (56724), collections of archaeology and local history. *St Nicholas Priory* (56724), 11th-century Benedictine. *Underground passages,* 13th-century aqueducts. *Guildhall* (72979), 14th and 15th century

Exmouth (Ed) *A la Ronde* (5514), 18th-century 16-sided cottage with wedge-shaped rooms radiating from an octagonal hall; built for sisters Mary and Jane Parminter, contrivers of curiosities; exhibits include pictures made from shells and feathers

Hembury (Gf) Iron Age hill fort, built on a Neolithic causewayed camp; the view from the top of the hill is one of the finest in Devon

Lydford (Ad) *Church of St Petrock,* 15th century

Okehampton (Ae) *Castle,* 13th-century ruins. *Okehampton Camp,* an Iron Age hill fort

Paignton (Db) *Zoo and Botanical Gardens* (557479). *Compton Castle* (Kingskerswell 2112), 14th to 16th-century fortified manor house. *Oldway* (550711), 19th-century mansion containing replicas of rooms at Versailles. *Kirkham House,* restored 15th-century manor house

Spreyton (Be) *Church of St Michael,* 15th century

Sticklepath (Be) *Museum of Rural Industry* (352)

Stoke Gabriel see p. 141

Torquay (Eb) *Torre Abbey* (23593), 12th-century ruins with a tithe barn. *Kent's Cavern* (24059), one of the oldest known human dwelling places in Britain, going back 10,000 years. *Natural History Society Museum* (23975)

Totnes see p. 141

AA SERVICE CENTRE: Fanum House, Bedford Street, Exeter, including 24-hour breakdown service (Exeter 32121). Breakdown services: Torquay 25903, 24 hours; Upottery 215, 9 a.m. to 5 p.m.

TOTNES

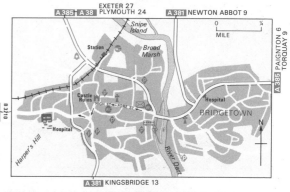

A town plan of **TORQUAY** is on p. 141

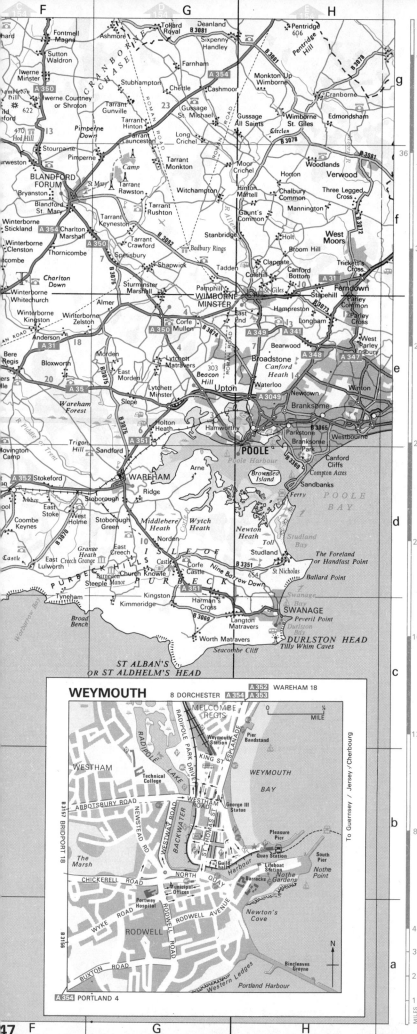

SCALE: ABOUT 4 MILES TO 1 INCH (1:250,000)

PLACES TO SEE IN
SOUTH DORSET

Opening times should be confirmed by telephone from the number in brackets. The exchange is given only if it differs from the place name at the beginning of the entry
Map references are shown after each place name

Abbotsbury (Cd) *Abbey*, 12th-century Benedictine ruins. *Sub-tropical Gardens and Swannery* (Evershot 222). *Abbotsbury Castle*, an Iron Age fort

Athelhampton (Ee) 15th-century house (Puddletown 363) with 10 acres of landscaped and formal gardens

Bournemouth (He) *Russell-Cotes Art Gallery and Museum* (21009), art collections from the 17th century to the present. *Rothesay Museum* (21009)

Bridport (Be) *Museum and Art Gallery* (22116). *Town Hall*, 18th century

Canford Cliffs (Hd) *Compton Acres* (708036), nine separate gardens including a semi-tropical glen, heather dell, and Roman, Japanese and English gardens

Cerne Abbas (Df) *Church of St Mary*, part-13th century. *The Cerne Giant*, a hill figure 180 ft high and 45 ft across the shoulders, is believed to be of Roman-British origin

Chesil Beach (Dc), immense reef of shingle in which pebbles gradually increase in size along 10 mile stretch from west to east

Isle of Portland (Dc) *Light-house*, 19th century, now a bird observatory. *Portland Castle*, 16th-century ruins. *Rufus Castle*, 12th-century ruins

Lulworth (Fd) The cove is a beauty spot. *Stair Hole Chasm* is filled by the sea at high tide. *Durdle Door*, an arch in a limestone promontory, is west of the cove

Lyme Regis (Ae) *Church of St Michael*, 16th century

Maiden Castle (Dd) Neolithic earthworks extended by successive conquerors until it was finally taken by the Romans under Vespasian in AD 43–44

Milton Abbas (Ff) *Abbey Church*, 14th and 15th century

Purse Caundle Manor (Dg) 15th-century manor house (Milborne Port 250400) with great hall and period furniture

Sherborne (Dg) *Abbey*, 15th-century cruciform church with fan vaulting. *Old Castle*, 12th-century ruins. *New Castle* (2072), 16th-century mansion built by Sir Walter Raleigh

Yeovil (Cg) *Church of St John the Baptist*, 14th century. *Montacute House* (Martock 3289), an Elizabethan manor, contains tapestries and heraldic glass

AA SERVICE CENTRE: Fanum House, 47 Richmond Hill, Bournemouth, including 24-hour breakdown service (Bournemouth 25751). Breakdown services: Dorchester 2330, 8 a.m. to 11 p.m.; Yeovil 27744, 24 hours

AA PORT SERVICE CENTRE: Weymouth Quay (Weymouth 786057)

POOLE

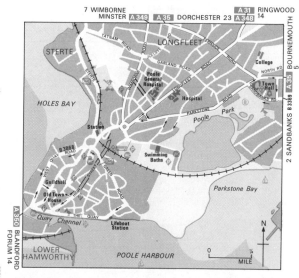

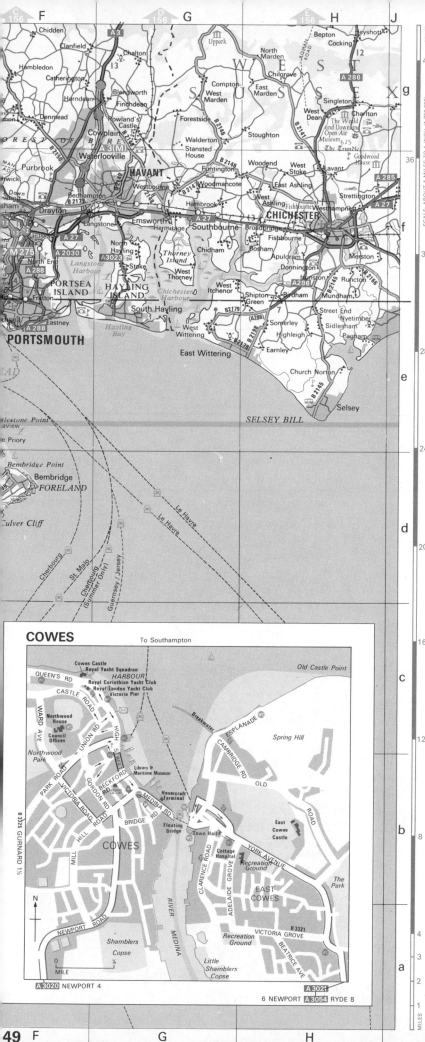

PLACES TO SEE AROUND
THE SOLENT

Opening times should be confirmed by telephone from the number in brackets. The exchange is given only if it differs from the place name at the beginning of the entry
Map references are shown after each place name

Arreton Manor (Ed) 17th century manor house (Newport 528134) contains relics of Charles I and has National Wireless Museum in grounds

Beaulieu (Cf) *Abbey,* 13th century, was destroyed by Henry VIII: its rebuilt gate-house, called Palace House, is the home of Lord Montagu. *National Motor Museum* (612345). *Maritime Museum,* Bucklers Hard (63203). *Church of St Bartholomew,* 13th century, built from Abbey refectory

Carisbrooke Castle (Dd) A Norman castle (Newport 522107) on site of Roman fort.

Chichester (Hf) *Cathedral,* restored after a fire in the 12th century. *City Museum* (784683). *Goodwood House* (527107), 18th century

Christchurch (Ae) *Castle,* 12th-century ruins. *Priory,* 12th and 16th century. *Red House Museum and Art Gallery* (482860), natural history and antiquities. *Place Mill,* Saxon watermill

Eastney (Fe) *Pump House* (Portsmouth 737979), contains 19th-century steam pumps

Godshill (Ed) *All Saints,* a 15th-century church containing a painting of Daniel in the lions' den by Rubens's school

Gosport (Ef) *Submarine Museum* (Portsmouth 22351 ext. 41250)

Osborne House (Ee) A favourite residence of Queen Victoria (Cowes 292511)

Portchester Castle (Ff) 12th-century remains inside the perimeter of a Roman fort

Portsmouth (Fe) *Dickens's Birthplace Museum* (26155) where Dickens was born in 1812. HMS *Victory*, Nelson's flagship, is in HM Dockyard. *The Victory Museum* (22351 ext. 23868) contains a panorama of the Battle of Trafalgar

Sandown (Ed) *Museum of Isle of Wight Geology* (404344)

Singleton (Hg) *The Weald and Downland Open Air Museum* (348), a 35 acre site with re-erected historic buildings from south-east England

Southampton (Cg) *Art Gallery* (23855). *Tudor House* (24216), 16th century with Georgian extensions, now a museum. *Bargate,* 12th-century gateway where merchandise tolls were collected. *Wool House* (23941), 14th-century wool store, now a maritime museum. *God's House Tower Museum* (20007), 15th-century fortification, now an archaeological museum. *Zoological Garden* (556603)

Southsea (Fe) *Cumberland House Museum and Art Gallery* (Portsmouth 732654). *Castle Museum* (Portsmouth 24584). *Cathedral of St Thomas à Becket,* 12th century

AA SERVICE CENTRES: Fanum House, 11 The Avenue, Southampton, including 24-hour breakdown service (Southampton 36811); Fanum House, 47 Richmond Hill, Bournemouth (Bournemouth 25751). Breakdown services: Newport, I.O.W. 522653, 24 hours; Chichester 783111, 9 a.m. to 5 p.m.

AA PORT SERVICE CENTRE: Eastern Docks (inside No. 2 gate, Canute Road), Southampton (Southampton 28304)

ROAD CONDITIONS: Southampton 8021

LYMINGTON

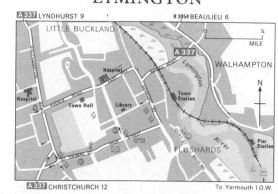

BIDEFORD

APPLEDORE 3
NORTHAM 2
9 BARNSTAPLE A 39

A 386

NORTHAM ROAD
KINGSLEY ROAD
PARK AVENUE
Victoria Park
Art Gallery
NORTHDOWN RD
BELVOIR RD LIME GROVE
NORTH RD
PITT LANE
THE QUAY
RIVER TORRIDGE
INSTOW RD
OLD BARNSTAPLE RD
Hospital
ABBOTSHAM RD
HIGH ST
MILL ST
OLD TOWN
Town Hall
Library
BARNSTAPLE STREET
LONG
EAST-THE-WATER
CLOVELLY RD
MEDDON ST
NEW ROAD
TORRINGTON LA
Hospital
24 STRATTON
54 WADEBRIDGE A 39
HANDY CROSS
N
¼ MILE

18 HOLSWORTHY A 388 — A 386 GREAT TORRINGTON 7
OKEHAMPTON 20

North West Point

LUNDY

H66

Great Shutter Rock · Rat Island

ILFRACOMBE
Holy Trinity
Bull Point
Rockham Bay
Morte Point · Mortehoe · Lee
Woolacombe
B 3343
B 3231
Trimstone
Morte Bay
North Buckland
Baggy Point · Pickwell · Georgeham · Halsin
Croyde Bay
Croyde · Knowle
Saunton · Pippac
Heant Punchar
Braunton
Braunton Burrows
Bideford Bar
Frelington
Appledore · Instow · Bicklet
NORTHAM · Tapeley
Westleigh · Horwoo
BIDEFORD
Woodtown
Alverdisc

BARNSTAPLE
OR
BIDEFORD BAY

HARTLAND POINT · Titchberry
Windbury Point
Stoke · Hartland · Clovelly
Hartland Quay · St Nectan · Abbey
B 3248
B 3237
Clovelly Dykes
Buck's Mills
A 39
Fairy Cross
Westward Ho!
Abbotsham
B 3236
Landcross
Littleham
Weare Giffard
Phillham · Dyke · Buck's Cross
Elmscott
Woolfardisworthy · Parkham · Parkham Ash
Buckland Brewer · Monkleigh
GREAT TORRING
South Hole
Melbury
Fritbelstock
Knaps Longpeak
Welcombe · 24 · Meddon · Ashmansworthy
B 3227
Little Torrington
A 388
Gooseham · Dinworthy · East Putford
Langtree
Morwenstow · Eastcott
West Putford · Stibb Cross · Peters Marland
Higher Sharpnose Point · St Morwen · Shop · Youlstone
Bulkworthy · Winswell
A 386
Woodford · Bradworthy · Abbots Bickington · Newton St Petrock · 20
Lower Sharpnose Point
Upper Tamar Resr.
Sutcombe · 18
Coombe · Tamar Lake
Milton Damerel
Shebbear
Kilkhampton · Alfardisworthy · Soldon Cross
Buckland Filleigh
Petrock
Stibb · B 3254 · R. Waldon · Holsworthy Beacon · Thornbury
BUDE · A 39 · Bradford · Sheepwash
Poughill · STRATTON · Grimscott · Chilsworthy · Cookbury · Black Torrington · Highampton
Bude Haven · Launcells · 7 · Pancrasweek · HOLSWORTHY · 13
BUDE BAY · A 3073 · A 3072 · Hollacombe · Graddon Moor
Marhamchurch · Bridgerule · Pyworthy · Halwill Junction
Widemouth Bay · R. Deer · B 3218 · Halwill · Beaworthy
Coppathorne · 14
Dizzard Point · Whitstone · River Tamar · River Claw · Clawton · Quoditch
Poundstock · North Tamerton · Broadbury
Cambeak · Tregole · A 39 · Week St Mary · Tetcott · Lana · Ashwater · Eworthy · Germansweek
St Gennys · Trewint · Boa Cro
Crackington Haven · North Curry · Luffincott · A 388 · Virginstow · Bratton Clovelly
Wainhouse Corner · Jacobstow · Northcott
Fire Beacon Point · B 3263 · 19 · South Wheatley · West Curry · Boyton · East Panson
Marshgate · Canworthy Water · Bennacott

A   B   C   D

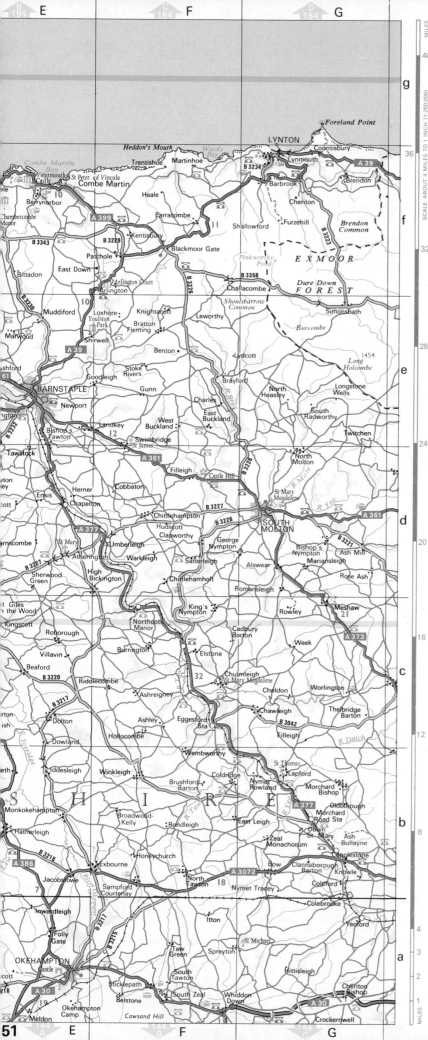

PLACES TO SEE IN
NORTH DEVON

Opening times should be confirmed by telephone from the number in brackets. The exchange is given only if it differs from the place name at the beginning of the entry
Map references are shown after each place name

Arlington Court (Ff) Regency house (Shirwell 296), with original contents; the stables contain 19th-century horse-drawn vehicles

Barnstaple (Ee) *North Devon Athenaeum* (2174), contains geological specimens and local antiquities. *St Anne's Chapel Museum*, local pottery and clocks. *Penrose Almshouses*, 17th century. *Queen Anne's Walk*, 17th-century colonnade

Bideford (Dd) *Burton Art Gallery* (6711)

Braunton (De) *Braunton Tower*, a folly built in the 19th century to celebrate the repeal of the Corn Laws; it makes a good picnic spot

Bude see p. 143

Chulmleigh (Fc) *Church of St Mary Magdalene*, 15th century, with rood screen

Clovelly Dykes (Cd) Prehistoric hill fort consisting of three concentric banks separated by ditches

Combe Martin (Ef) *Church of St Peter ad Vincula*, 13th to 15th century, has a fine rood screen. *Tithe Barn*, 12th century. *The Pack of Cards*, an inn said to have been built by a card-playing enthusiast, has four floors with 13 doors on each floor and a total of 52 windows

Croyde (De) *Gem, Rock and Shell Museum* (Croyde 890407) has demonstrations of cutting and polishing semi-precious stones found on local beaches

Hartland (Bd) *Abbey*, 18th-century mansion on the foundations of a 12th-century Augustinian abbey. The abbey cloisters are incorporated in the mansion

Ilfracombe (Ef) *Chambercombe Manor* (62624), 14th and 15th century, containing Tudor and Jacobean furniture. *Chapel of St Nicholas*, 14th century, used as a lighthouse since 1522. *Church of the Holy Trinity*, 14th and 15th century. *Museum* (63541), natural history and Victoriana

Instow (De) *Tapeley Park Gardens* (860528)

Lapford (Gb) *Church of St Thomas of Canterbury*, 15th century, with a fine carved wooden screen and a varied collection of bench-ends

Marwood (Ee) *Marwood Hill Gardens* (Barnstaple 2528), contain a lake with waterside plantings

Morwenstow see p. 143

Okehampton see p. 145

South Molton (Gd) *Museum* (2501), local history museum with a collection of pewter weights and measures. *Church of St Mary Magdalene*, 15th century, restored in 1865, has a 15th-century carved pulpit

Spreyton see p. 145

Sticklepath see p. 145

Stoke (Bd) *Church of St Nectan*, 14th century, with 128 ft tower built as a landmark for mariners

Swimbridge (Fe) *Church of St James*, 15th century, with a fine wooden font and carved rood screen

AA BREAKDOWN SERVICE: Barnstaple 5691, 24 hours

BARNSTAPLE

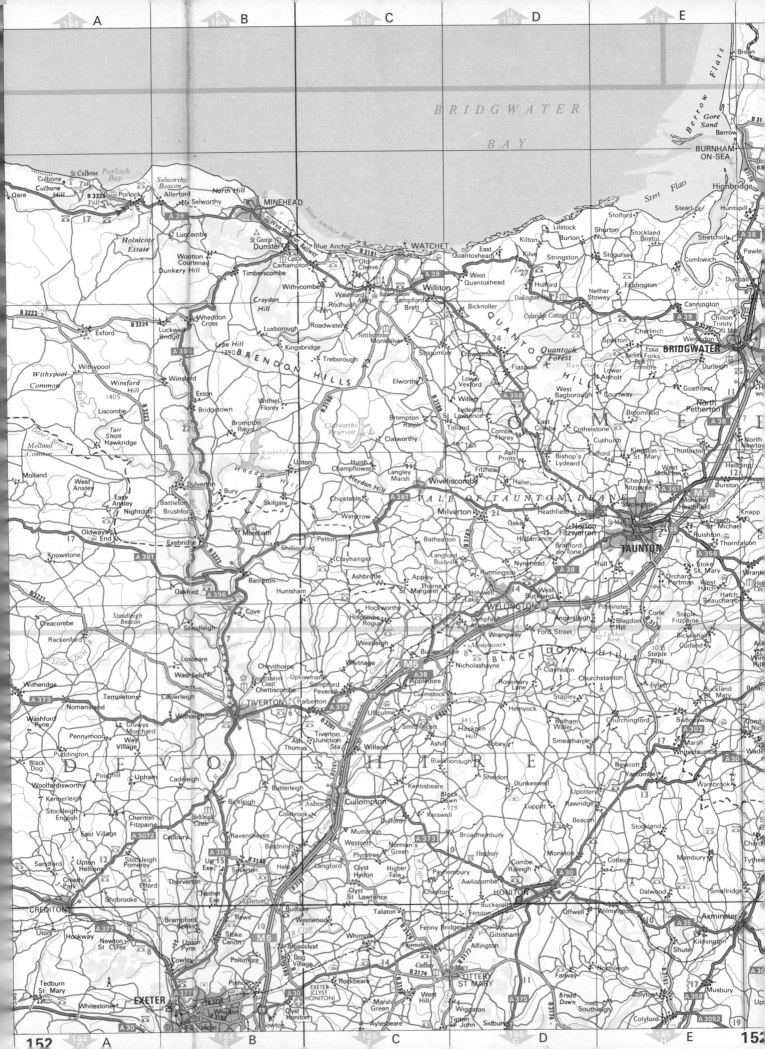

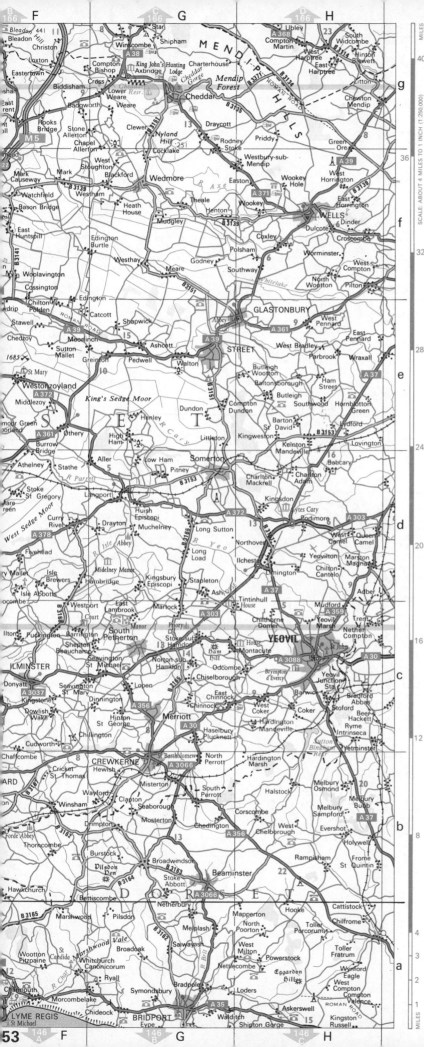

PLACES TO SEE IN
SOMERSET

Opening times should be confirmed by telephone from the number in brackets. The exchange is given only if it differs from the place name at the beginning of the entry
Map references are shown after each place name

Axbridge (Gg) *King John's Hunting Lodge* (732012), early Tudor merchant's house with local museum

Barrington Court (Gc) 16th-century manor house (Ilminster 2242)

Bridgwater (Ee) *Admiral Blake Museum* (56127), contains relics of Robert Blake, Cromwell's admiral, who was born in Bridgwater. *Church of St Mary,* 14th century, with 15th-century pulpit

Cheddar Gorge (Gg) Caves with stalactite and stalagmite formations

Chedzoy (Fe) The site of the Battle of Sedgemoor, where the Duke of Monmouth was defeated by troops of James II in 1685, is 1½ miles south-east of the village

Cleeve Abbey (Cf) 13th-century Cistercian ruins

Cricket St Thomas (Fb) *Wild Life Park* (Winsham 396)

Culbone (Af) *Church of St Culbone,* 15th century: the smallest completed church in England, 12 ft wide 35 ft long

Dunster (Bf) *Castle* (314), built in the 11th century and modified in the 17th and 19th centuries. *Yarn Market,* 17th-century octagonal hall once used for the sale of locally woven cloth. *Church of St George,* part-12th-century cruciform church renovated in the 13th and 15th centuries; it has fine monuments

East Lambrook Manor (Gc) 15th-century house (South Petherton 40328), with 16th-century additions and fine panelling. The cottage-style garden contains rare plants

Exeter see p. 145

Exmoor National Park, see p. 339

Glastonbury (He) *Abbey,* 12th-century Benedictine ruins on the site of 6th to 8th-century churches. *Abbot's Barn,* a 14th-century building with 24 buttresses. *Abbot's Tribunal,* a 15th to 16th-century ecclesiastical court, now a museum, contains pottery found on the site of a pre-Roman village a mile from Glastonbury Tor. *Church of St John the Baptist,* Perpendicular with a 16th-century altar tomb

Lytes Cary (Hd) 14th and 15th-century manor house (Charlton Mackrell 297)

Minehead (Bf) *Quirke's Almshouses,* 17th century

Muchelney (Gd) *Abbey,* ruins of a 12th to 16th-century Benedictine abbey built on Saxon foundations. *Priest's House,* 14th-century thatched residence of the secular priests

Nether Stowey (Df) *Coleridge Cottage* (732662), 18th-century home of Samuel Taylor Coleridge where he wrote 'The Ancient Mariner'; now a museum containing relics of the poet. *Dodington Hall* (Holford 422, by appointment), Elizabethan house with minstrels' gallery

Stoke-sub-Hamdon (Gc) *Priory,* 15th-century chantry house; the Old Hall only is open to the public

Taunton (Ed) *Castle* (73451), 12th and 13th century, now a museum containing relics of natural and local history. *Church of St Mary Magdalene,* 15th and 16th century with double aisles to the nave

Wellington (Dd) *Monument,* an obelisk erected in 1817 in honour of the Duke of Wellington, whose family owned estates in the area

Wells (Hf) *Cathedral,* 12th and 13th century with an astronomical clock in the north transept. *Museum* (73477), with prehistoric cave finds, fossils and minerals

Westonzoyland (Fe) *Church of St Mary,* 14th to 16th century; captured rebels from Monmouth's army at the Battle of Sedgemoor were confined here in 1685

Williton (Cf) *Nettlecombe* (Washford 320), Elizabethan and Georgian manor house (by appointment only)

Winsford (Be) *Tarr Steps,* a stone clapper bridge crosses the River Barle 3 miles south-west of Winsford

Wookey Hole (Hf) *Caves* (Wells 72243), containing multicoloured stalactite formations

AA SERVICE CENTRE: Fanum House, Bedford Street, Exeter, including 24-hour breakdown service (Exeter 32121). Breakdown services: Taunton 3363, 24 hours; Yeovil 27744, 24 hours

A town plan of EXETER is on p. 145

53

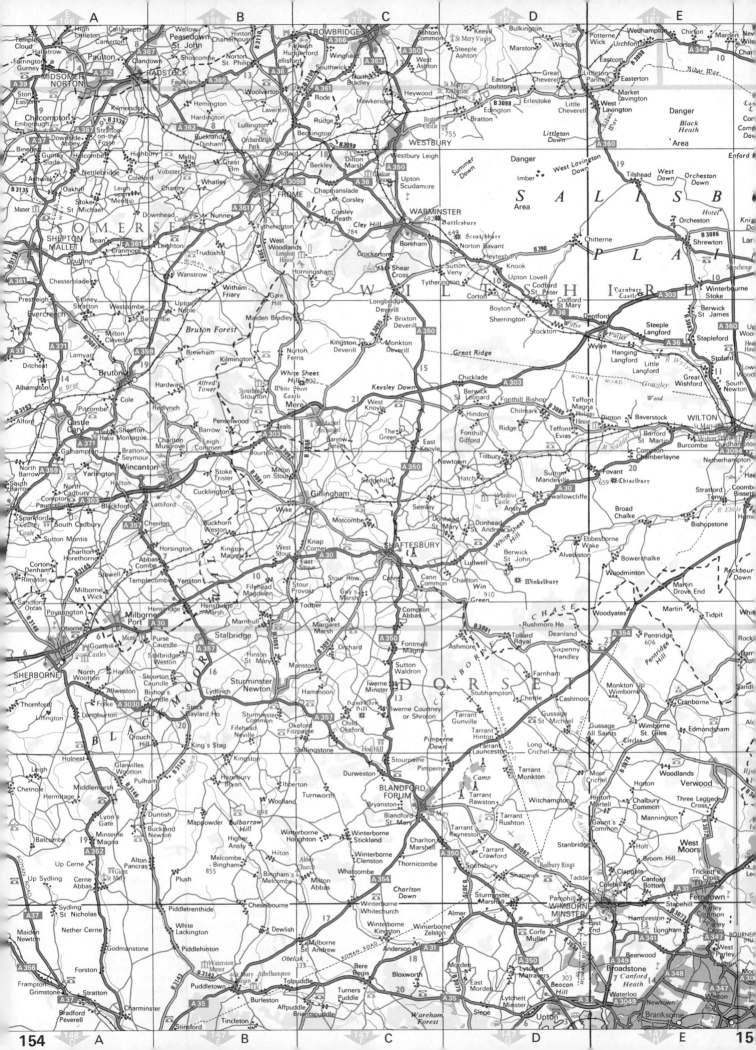

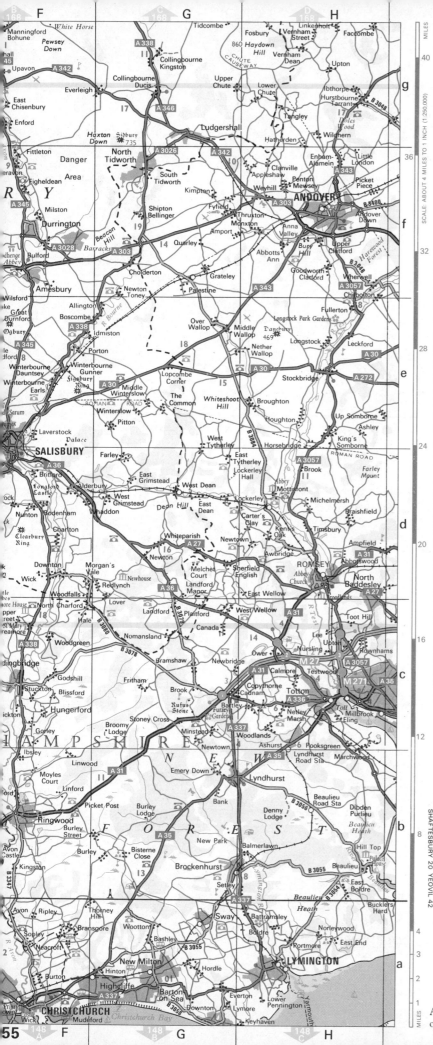

SALISBURY PLAIN

Opening times should be confirmed by telephone from the number in brackets. The exchange is given only if it differs from the place name at the beginning of the entry
Map references are shown after each place name

Athelhampton see p. 147

Beacon Hill (Gf) *Bulford Kiwi*, hill figure cut by New Zealand troops during the First World War

Beaulieu see p. 149

Bournemouth see p. 147

Bratton Castle (Cg) Iron Age hill fort. *Westbury Horse*, a hill figure on Bratton Down carved in the 18th century

Breamore House (Fc) Elizabethan manor house (Breamore 233)

Cerne Abbas see p. 147

Christchurch see p. 149

Durrington (Ff) *Woodhenge*, a Stone Age earthwork

Longleat House (Cf) 16th-century house (Maiden Bradley 328), with 19th-century alterations, has a wild life park

Mere (Ce) *Church of St Michael Archangel*, 12th to 15th century

Milton Abbas see p. 147

Old Sarum (Fe) Site of Sorviodunum, a Roman fortress. Foundations of the Norman cathedral, abandoned in the 13th century when Salisbury Cathedral was built, can still be seen

Purse Caundle Manor see p. 147

Philipps House (De) 19th century (Teffont 208)

Rode (Cg) *Tropical Bird Gardens* (Beckington 326)

Romsey (Hd) *Abbey Church of SS Mary and Ethelfleda*, 10th century, with a Saxon rood screen and carving of the Crucifixion. *Broadlands* (516878), 18th-century Palladian-style home of the late Lord Mountbatten.

Salisbury (Fd) *Cathedral*, 13th century with 14th-century spire. The library contains one of four original copies of Magna Carta. *Church of St Thomas of Canterbury*, 13th and 15th century with 12th-century font. *Museum* (4465), natural and social history collections. *The Old Deanery* (28241). *Poultry Cross*, 14th-century Gothic market cross

Shaftesbury (Cd) *Abbey Ruins Museum* (2910) contains carved stones and tiles from the excavated site of a 9th-century Benedictine nunnery. *Local History Museum* (2157)

Sherborne see p. 147

Stonehenge (Ff) Bronze Age stone circle

Stourhead (Be) 18th-century Palladian-style house (Bourton 224), with gardens containing lakes and temples

Wilton House (Ee) 17th and 19th-century house (Wilton 3115), with State Rooms by Inigo Jones

AA SERVICE CENTRE: Fanum House, 47 Richmond Hill, Bournemouth, including 24-hour breakdown service (Bournemouth 25751). Breakdown service, Salisbury 22246, 8 a.m. to 11 p.m.

ROAD CONDITIONS: Southampton 8021

SALISBURY

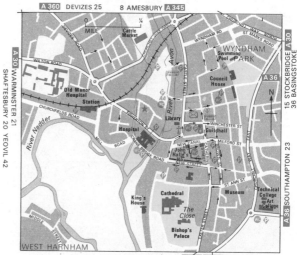

A town plan of BOURNEMOUTH is on p. 96; of LYMINGTON on p. 149

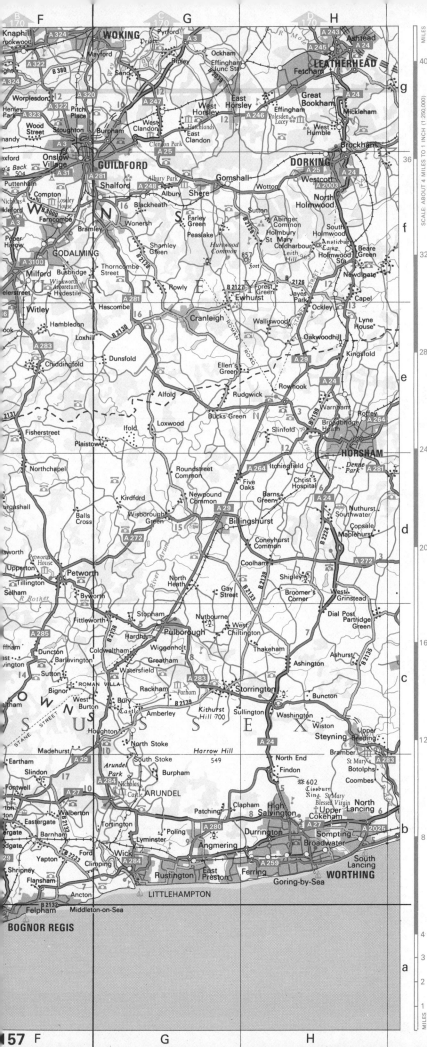

PLACES TO SEE ON
THE DOWNS

Opening times should be confirmed by telephone from the number in brackets. The exchange is given only if it differs from the place name at the beginning of the entry
Map references are shown after each place name

Arundel (Gb) *Castle* (883136), 11th and 12th century, rebuilt in 18th century; it is the seat of the Duke of Norfolk. *Church of St Nicholas*, 14th century

Basingstoke (Cg) *Willis Museum* (65902), watches, clocks, local history and archaeology

Bishops Waltham (Bc) *Palace*, 12th and 14th-century ruins enclosed by a moat. It was originally the palace of the Bishops of Winchester

Clandon Park (Gg) 18th-century mansion (Guildford 222482) with fine plasterwork, furniture and pictures

Farnham (Ef) *Castle* (721194), 11th and 12th century, former seat of the Bishops of Winchester. *Museum* (715094)

Gibbet Hill (Fe) Beauty spot, 900 ft high, overlooking the valley known as the Devil's Punch Bowl

Godalming (Ff) *Charter-house School Museum* (6226), pottery and natural history (open only during term times)

Guildford (Gf) *Chilworth Manor Gardens* (61414), laid out in 17th century on the site of an 11th-century monastery, contain 11th-century stewponds, where the monks kept fish for the kitchens. *Castle Keep*, 11th century. *Cathedral*, 20th-century simplified Gothic-style. In the cobbled High Street are *Abbot's Hospital*, 17th-century almshouses; the 16th-century *Royal Grammar School* (502424), with chained library; *Angel Hotel*, 13th-century posting inn; and *Guildford House* (32133), 17th century, now an art gallery. *Museum* (66551)

Hascombe (Ge) *Hascombe Court* (254), gardens rich in spring flowers and shrubs

Haslemere (Fe) *Educational Museum* (2112), birds, botany, zoology, local industries. *Arnold Dolmetsch Workshop* (51432), where harpsichords, viols and recorders are made

Loseley House (Ff) 16th-century mansion (Guildford 71881) with fine ceilings and tapestries

Petworth (Fd) *Petworth House* (42207), 17th century with 13th-century chapel and fine collection of paintings; the Grinling Gibbons room, named after the Dutch woodcarver and sculptor, contains some of his finest carvings

Polesden Lacey (Hg) Regency villa (Bookham 53401) containing tapestries, furniture and pictures

The Vyne (Cg) 16th-century house (Basingstoke 881337), Tudor panelling

West Humble (Hg) *Box Hill*, a wooded beauty spot; at the top is the grave of Major Peter Labillière, an eccentric who was buried in 1800 head downwards, because he believed the world was topsy-turvy and he wanted to be the right way up at the end. *Chapel*, 12th century, converted barn

Winchester (Ae) *Pilgrim's Hall*, 14th century. *Cathedral*, 11th and 13th century, the longest Gothic church in Europe (556 ft). *Treasury* (Owslebury 213 or Winchester 66242) contains Saxon and Norman finds from recent excavations. *Guildhall Picture Gallery* (68166). *Westgate Museum* (68166) contains medieval weights and measures. *City Museum* (68166), local archaeology. *City Cross*, or Butter Cross, is a four-sided 15th-century Gothic cross. *St Cross Hospital* (51375), 12th-century almshouses

Winkworth Arboretum (Ff), 95 acres of woodland with two lakes

AA SERVICE CENTRE: Fanum House, London Road, Guildford, including 24-hour breakdown service (Guildford 72841). Breakdown services: Sutton Scotney 630, 9 a.m. to 5 p.m.; Basingstoke 56565, 24 hours; Chichester 783111, 9 a.m. to 5 p.m.

A town plan of PORTSMOUTH is on p. 148; of COWES on p. 149; and of SOUTHAMPTON on p. 94

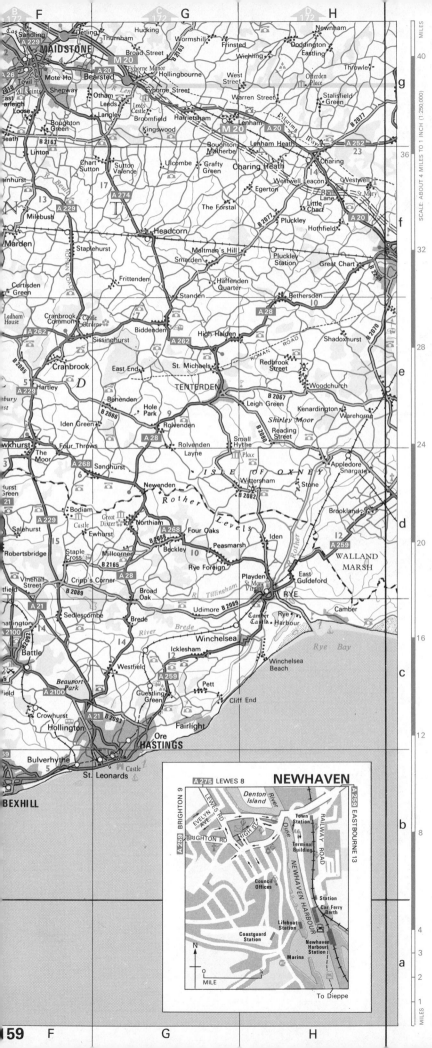

PLACES TO SEE FROM
BRIGHTON TO RYE

Opening times should be confirmed by telephone from the number in brackets. The exchange is given only if it differs from the place name at the beginning of the entry

Map references are shown after each place name

Battle (Fc) *Abbey*, 11th-century ruins on site of the Battle of Hastings, 1066

Bodiam (Fd) *Castle*, moated 14th-century ruins (Staple Cross 436)

Brighton (Bb) *Royal Pavilion* (603005), rebuilt in 1815 for the Prince Regent; the interior, lavishly decorated in Chinese style, contains original furniture and paintings. *Preston Park*, 74 acres of gardens including a scented garden for the blind. *Museum and Art Gallery* (603005). *Booth Museum of British Birds* (552586). *Aquarium and Dolphinarium* (604233)

Burwash (Ed) *Bateman's* (882302), 17th-century home of Rudyard Kipling from 1902 to 1936

Glynde (Cb) *Glynde Place* (337), 16th-century flint and brick house

Hastings (Gc) *Castle*, 11th-century ruins. *St Clement Caves* (422964). *Fishermen's Museum. Museum and Art Gallery* (435952). *Museum of Local History* (425855). *Model Village*, White Rock Gardens

Herstmonceux (Ec) *Castle* (3171), 15th century, restored in 20th century; now the Royal Greenwich Observatory

Leeds Castle (Gg) 12th-century restored castle (Maidstone 65400) surrounded by a lake and parkland

Penshurst (Df) *Penshurst Place* (870307), 14th-century house enlarged in 15th and 16th centuries; it has one of the finest 14th-century halls in England

Pevensey (Eb) *Castle*, 3rd-century Roman fort with 11th-century inner bailey and keep

Royal Tunbridge Wells (De) *The Pantiles*, 17th-century tree-lined walk with colonnade and chalybeate spring

Rye (Hd) *Lamb House* (3753), Georgian mansion, the home of novelist Henry James from 1897 to 1916. *Ypres Tower*, 13th-century fortification, now a museum. *Church of St Mary the Virgin*, 12th-century church rebuilt after the sack of Rye by the French in 1377. *Mermaid Inn*, 15th to 16th century

Sevenoaks (Dg) *Knole*, 15th-century mansion (50608) extended in the 17th century

Westerham (Cg) *Chartwell* (Crockham Hill 368), part-17th-century home of Sir Winston Churchill from 1922 to 1965, with many of his paintings and trophies

AA SERVICE CENTRES: Fanum House, 10 Churchill Square, Brighton (Brighton 23633); 8 Colman House, King Street, Maidstone, including 24-hour breakdown service (Maidstone 55353). Breakdown services: Brighton 695231, 24 hours; Lamberhurst 248, 9 a.m. to 5 p.m.; Crawley 25685, 24 hours
AA PORT SERVICE CENTRE: Newhaven Harbour (Newhaven 4245)
ROAD CONDITIONS: London (01 246 8021)

EASTBOURNE

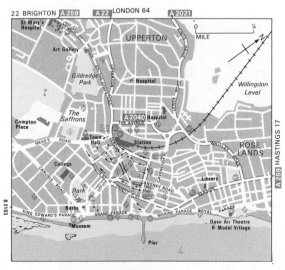

A town plan of BRIGHTON is on p. 96

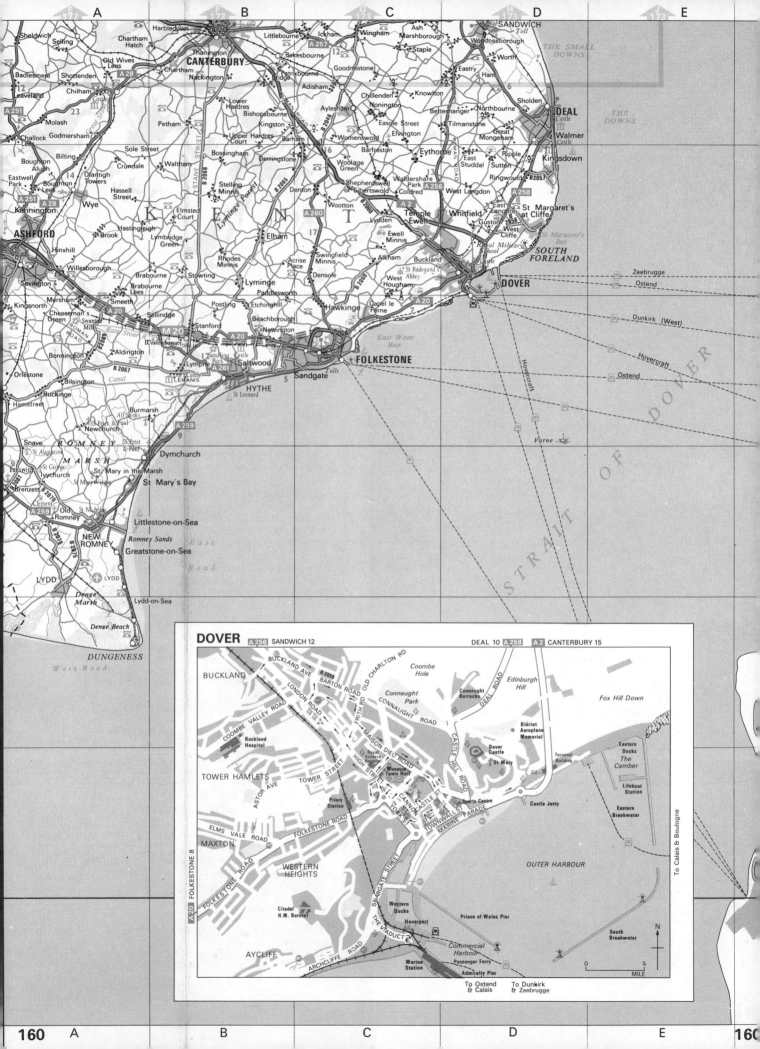

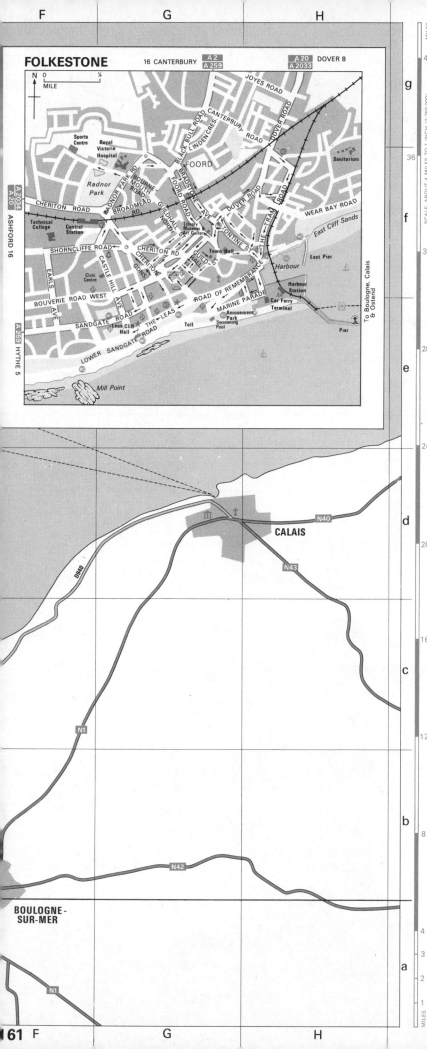

FOLKESTONE

16 CANTERBURY | A 2 / A 259
A 20 / A 2033 | DOVER 8

N 0 ¼
MILE

CALAIS

BOULOGNE-
SUR-MER

PLACES TO SEE IN
KENT

Opening times should be confirmed by telephone from the number in brackets. The exchange is given only if it differs from the place name at the beginning of the entry
Map references are shown after each place name

Canterbury (Bg) *Cathedral,* 12th century, the scene of the murder of Thomas à Becket by four of Henry II's knights in 1170. *St Augustine's Abbey,* 7th to 14th-century ruins with a museum containing finds from excavations. *Church of St Martin,* 6th century or earlier. *Church of St Mildred,* possibly 8th century, reconstructed in the 13th century. *Poor Priests' Hospital,* 13th and 14th century, and *Royal Museum* incorporating the Buffs Regimental Museum (52747). The Westgate, 14th-century fortification. *Greyfriars,* 13th-century Franciscan friary. *Eastbridge Hospital* (68714), 12th to 17th century, now an old people's home

Deal (Dg) *Castle,* 16th century (2762). A plaque on the sea front marks the spot where Julius Caesar landed in 55 BC

Dover (Df) *Castle,* 12th to 13th century, built on the site of a prehistoric fortification. *Church of St Mary in Castro,* a Saxon church near a Roman pharos (lighthouse). *Museum* (201066)

Hythe (Be) *Church of St Leonard,* Norman church rebuilt in the 13th and 14th century. *Museum* (67111)

Sandwich (Dg) *Guildhall* (611160), 16th century with original interior. *Barbican,* 16th century. *Church of St Peter,* part-13th century. The churches of St Clement and St Mary the Virgin were built in the 12th century and restored later

Walmer (Dg) *Castle* (Deal

4115), 16th-century official residence of the Lord Warden of the Cinque Ports. (Hastings, Sandwich, New Romney, Hythe and Dover were the original five ports given royal privileges in exchange for ships and men to defend the country in the 12th century)

Romney Churches The towers and spires of a rich variety of churches, some built by the Normans on the sites of Saxon churches, rise from the flat sheeplands of Romney Marsh. They include: *Brenzett* (Ad) St Eanswith, a 13th-century church with a wooden tower and shingled spire. *Brookland* p. 159 (Hd) St Augustine, 13th century with 12th-century lead font and detached wooden belfry. *Burmarsh* (Be) All Saints, 12th century. *Dymchurch* (Ad) SS Peter and Paul, 12th century. *Fairfield* p. 159 (Hd) St Thomas of Canterbury, part-14th century, altered in the 18th century. *Ivychurch* (Ad) St George, 14th century with battlemented tower. *Newchurch* (Ae) SS Peter and Paul, part-13th century. *Old Romney* (Ad) St Clement, 13th century, built on the site of a Saxon church, has a 14th-century font and an 18th-century minstrels' gallery. *St Mary in the Marsh* (Ad) St Mary the Virgin, part-Norman church rebuilt in the 14th century, has the original pre-Reformation bells. *Snargate* p. 159 (Ha) St Dunstan, 13th century, Perpendicular with battlemented tower. *Snave* (Ad) St Augustine, 14th century

AA PORT SERVICE CENTRES: Eastern Dock Terminal, Dover (Dover 208122); International Hoverport, Dover West (Dover 208122); Folkestone Harbour (Folkestone 58111)

A town plan of CANTERBURY is on p. 100

THE FRENCH COAST

Boulogne-sur-Mer (Fa) *Castle,* 12th century. *Town ramparts,* 13th century. *Basilica of Notre Dame,* 19th century, on the site of a 12th to 15th-century church destroyed during the Revolution; it is the scene of

a pilgrimage in August

Calais (Gd) *Town Hall,* Flemish Renaissance. *The Six Burghers of Calais,* a monument by Auguste Rodin. *Church of Notre Dame,* 12th century. *Tour du Guet,* a 13th-century watchtower

AA AGENTS: G. A. Gregson & Son, Gare Maritime, Boulogne-sur-Mer ((21) 317752); G. A. Gregson & Son, Gare de Transit, Calais ((21) 344 720)

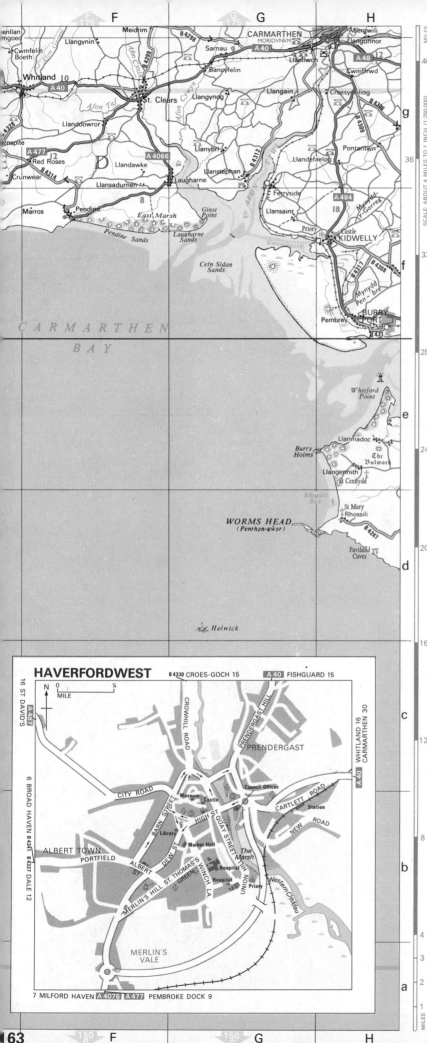

PEMBROKE

Opening times should be confirmed by telephone from the number in brackets. The exchange is given only if it differs from the place name at the beginning of the entry
Map references are shown after each place name

Burry Holms (Ge) A limestone island with an Iron Age earthwork across the middle of it. There are also traces of a medieval monastic cell, believed to have belonged to the 6th-century St Cennydd, whose monastery was at Llangennith (He)

Caldey Island (Ee) *Priory,* 12th-century Benedictine, now occupied by the Cistercians; the stone-vaulted chapel contains a stone with an inscription in ogham, a 5th-century script. Motor launches run regularly from Tenby Harbour. *Watch Tower,* 12th-century circular building with a conical roof, now used as a chapel; standing high on a cliff, it is a good viewpoint

Carew (Df) *Castle,* 11th to 16th-century ruins. *Church of St Mary,* 14th century with a detached chantry chapel in the churchyard. *Carew Cross,* possibly 9th century, is 14 ft high and intricately carved

Carmarthen see p. 175

Haverfordwest (Cg) *Castle,* 12th-century ruins containing the *Pembrokeshire Museum* (3708), with archaeological and art collections. *Church of St Mary,* 13th and 15th century with a fine oak roof

Kidwelly (Hf) *Castle,* preserved 12th-century ruins surrounded by a moat and overlooking the Gwendraeth Fach river. *Priory,* 12th-century Benedictine, the finest example of Decorated style in west Wales

Lamphey (Df) *Palace,* 14th to 16th-century ruins of one of the seven manors of the Bishops of St David's, where the Earl of Essex, ill-fated favourite of Elizabeth I, spent his boyhood: the chapel has a fine east window.

Llangennith (He) *Church of St Cennydd,* 13th century, on the site of a 6th-century monastery founded by St Cennydd and destroyed by the Danes in the 10th century

Llawhaden (Dg) *Castle,* remains of a 14th-century residence of the Bishops of St Davids; the castle was rebuilt from the original 12th-century ring-motte fortification during a lavish spending on bishops' residences

Lydstep (De) A beauty spot

with fine views. *Lydstep Caverns* (Tenby 2402) can be entered only at low tide: the way is signposted along a nature trail

Manorbier (De) *Castle* (394), 12th to 14th century, birthplace of Giraldus Cambrensis, the celebrated 12th-century Welsh scholar. *King's Quoit,* a Neolithic cromlech

Pembroke (Cf) *Castle,* 12th and 13th century, birthplace of Henry VII in 1457; the four-storied keep is roofed with a dome and beneath the castle is a limestone cavern, 70 ft long and 50 ft wide, known as Wogan's Cave, after Sir John Wogan a local squire. *Monkton Priory,* 11th-century Benedictine ruins. *Church of St Mary,* 13th century, restored in the 19th century

Pembrokeshire Coast National Park see p. 341

Penally (Ee) *Church of St Nicholas,* 13th-century stone-vaulted cruciform church with square embattled tower, containing a Celtic cross; palms and semi-tropical plants grow in the churchyard

Rhossili (Hd) *Church of St Mary,* part Norman with a fine ornate south door and lancet windows

St Brides (Ag) Iron Age fort

St Govan's Head (Ce) *Cliffside Chapel,* a 13th-century stone building containing an altar and fitments hewn from stone and a cell cut in the rock, which legend ascribes to a 5th-century hermit

Skokholm Island (Af) A nature reserve; it has colonies of rabbits, some of which are black, shearwaters and puffins

Skomer Island (Af) Also a nature reserve with more than 30 species of birds, including 25,000 pairs of Manx shearwaters, its own race of vole, the Skomer vole, and the comparatively rare grey seal

Tenby (Ef) *Tudor Merchant's House* (2279), 15th century with gabled front and corbelled chimney breast. *Church of St Mary,* 13th and 15th century restored in 19th century. *Town walls,* 14th century. *Castle,* 13th-century ruins. *Museum* (2809) contains a fine collection of sea shells and cave deposits

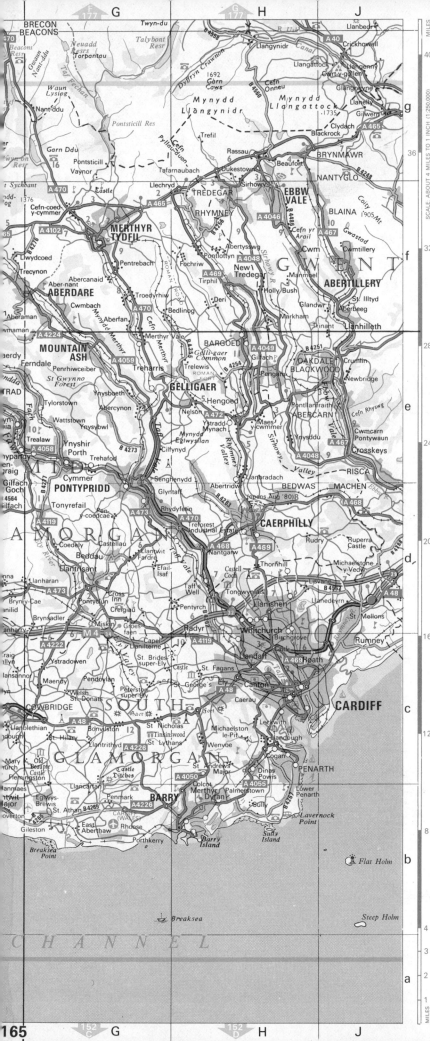

CARDIFF

Opening times should be confirmed by telephone from the number in brackets. The exchange is given only if it differs from the place name at the beginning of the entry
Map references are shown after each place name

Caerphilly (Hd) *Castle,* 13th-century ruins

Cardiff (Hc) *Castle,* 11th-century ruins. *National Museum of Wales* (397951)

Coity (Fd) *Castle,* 12th-century ruins. *Church of St Mary,* 14th century

Ewenny Priory (Fc) 12th to 13th-century Benedictine ruins containing early Christian to 12th-century memorial stones and monuments. The nave and aisle are used as the parish church of St Michael

Llanelli (Be) *Church of St Elliw,* 19th to 20th century with 18th-century monuments. *Parc Howard Museum and Art Gallery* (2029) contains tinplate and pottery exhibits. *Tabernacle,* 19th century with Corinthian columns and pediment

Llanrhidian (Ae) *Weobley Castle* (Cardiff 825111), 13th to 14th century

Merthyr Tydfil (Gf) *Art Gallery and Museum* (3112) containing coins, ceramics and a Welsh kitchen

Mumbles (Cd) *Oystermouth Castle,* preserved 13th-century ruins on the site of a Norman fortification. *Church of All Saints,* part-14th century; Thomas Bowdler who, in 1818, published an expurgated edition of Shakespeare, thus giving rise to the verb 'bowdlerise', is buried in the churchyard. Beauty spots, accessible by car or cliff path, are the bays of Bracelet, Limeslade, Rothersdale, Langland and Caswell

Neath Abbey (De) 12th-century Cistercian ruins

Ogmore Castle (Ec) 12th and 13th-century ruins

Oxwich (Bd) *Church of St Illtyd,* 11th to 12th century with a font said to have been installed by St Illtyd, patron saint of Oxwich. *Castle,* 16th-century fortified manor house on the site of a Norman castle, restored in the 20th century

Penrice (Ad) *Castle,* 13th-century ruins containing a preserved gatehouse

Porteynon (Ad) *Culver Hole,* a cliff cave with the narrow entrance closed by a wall containing windows; local legend says it was a smugglers' den. *Paviland Caves,* 2 miles west, can be reached only at low tide. In 1823 the skeleton of a Stone Age hunter was found in Goat Hole; it is now in the Natural History Museum, London

Reynoldston (Ad) *Arthur's Stone,* a cromlech, or megalithic tomb, said to have been split by King Arthur's sword

St Fagans (Hc) *Castle and Welsh Folk Museum* (Cardiff 569441), 16th-century house within walls of 13th-century castle, containing re-erected old buildings and folk-life exhibits

St Hilary (Gc) *Old Beaupre Castle* (Cardiff 825111), a medieval manor rebuilt in the 16th century, with a fine gatehouse and porch

St Nicholas (Gc) *Tinkinswood Burial Chamber,* a long cairn which, when excavated in 1914, revealed a pit containing animal bones, pottery and the cremated remains of 50 human skeletons from about 2000 BC

Swansea (Ce) *Glynn Vivian Art Gallery* (55006), includes Welsh pottery and porcelain. *Maritime and Industrial Museum* (50351), contains relics of local industries. *Royal Institution of South Wales and University College of Swansea Museum* (53763), contains collections of local antiquarian interest and a library

Vale of Neath (Ef) Beauty spot with waterfalls, streams and limestone gorges. The waterfall of Melin Court at Resolven (Ef) is 80 ft high. At Pont-Nedd-Fechan (Ff) on the River Hepste, the flow of the 50 ft high fall is propelled outwards from its cliff with such force that it is possible to walk behind the arc of water

AA SERVICE CENTRES: 140 Queen Street, Cardiff, including 24-hour breakdown service (Cardiff 394111); 20 Union Street, Swansea (Swansea 55598), 24 hours

ROAD CONDITIONS: Cardiff 8021

A town plan of CARDIFF is on p. 94

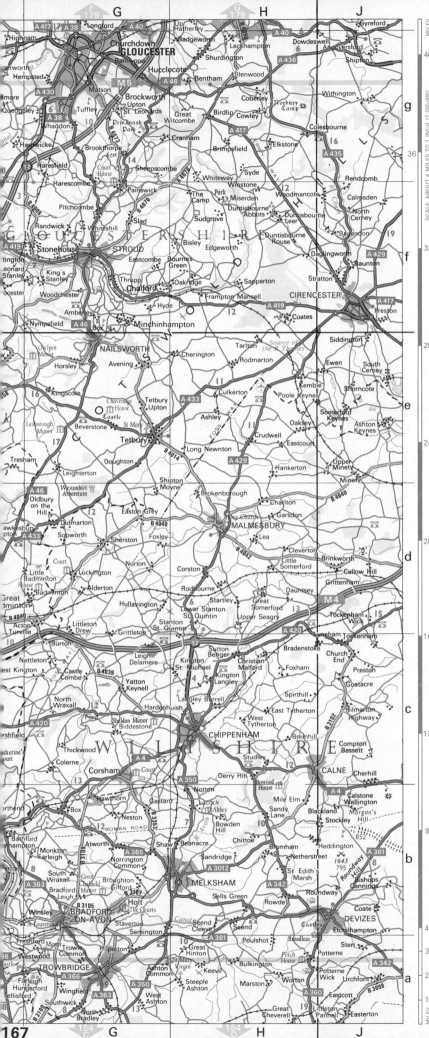

THE SEVERN ESTUARY

Opening times should be confirmed by telephone from the number in brackets. The exchange is given only if it differs from the place name at the beginning of the entry
Map references are shown after each place name

Abergavenny (Bg) Site of the Roman fort of Gobannium. *Castle*, ruins of a 17th-century castle with a museum

Badminton House (Gd) 17th-century Palladian mansion with fine paintings and furnishings

Bath (Fb) *Abbey*, 15th century, Perpendicular style. *Assembly Rooms*, housing *Museum of Costume*, and *Roman Baths and Pump Room* (both 61111). *Pulteney Bridge*, designed by Robert Adam in 1771

Berkeley Castle (Ee) 12th century, oldest inhabited castle in England and the scene of Edward II's murder in 1327

Bradford-on-Avon (Gb) *Barton Tithe Barn*, 14th century. *Church of St Laurence*, one of the finest Saxon churches in Britain. *Bridge*, 14th century, with a pilgrims' chapel which became a lock-up in the 17th century

Bristol (Dc) *Cathedral*, part-12th century. *City Museum and Art Gallery* (299771). *Cabot Tower* (293891), 19th century, gives good views over the city. *Wildlife Park* (500439), at Westbury-on-Trym, 3 miles north of Bristol

Chepstow Castle (De) Remains of an 11th to 13th-century castle (4065)

Claverton (Fb) *Claverton Manor* (Bath 60503), museum of American life

Clevedon Court (Cc) 12th-century manor house (Clevedon 872257)

Clifton (Dc) *Zoo* (Bristol 38951), has fine gardens

Corsham Court. (Gc) Elizabethan mansion (Corsham 712214) with park designed by Capability Brown

Dodington House (Fc) 18th-century Classic-style house (Chipping Sodbury 318899)

Gloucester (Gg) *Cathedral*, 12th century; the east window, 72 ft by 38 ft, is the largest medieval stained-glass window in England. *Folk Life Museum* (26467)

Monmouth (Dg) *Castle*, remains of an 11th-century castle, birthplace in 1387 of Henry V. *Great Castle House* (2935, by appointment), 17th century. *Monmouth Museum* (3519)

Raglan Castle (Cf) Ruins of a 15th-century fortified house (Raglan 228)

Slimbridge (Ff) *Wildfowl Trust* (Cambridge, Glos. 333)

Tintern Abbey (Df) Ruins of a 12th-century Cistercian abbey

AA SERVICE CENTRE: Park Row, Bristol, including 24-hour breakdown service (Bristol 298531). Breakdown services—all 24-hour: Bath 24731; Bristol 298531; Gloucester 23278; Newport (Gwent) 62559

ROAD CONDITIONS: Bristol 8021

WESTON-SUPER-MARE

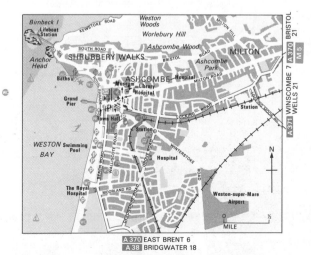

A370 EAST BRENT 6
A38 BRIDGWATER 18

A town plan of BATH is on p. 95; of BRISTOL on p. 95; and of CARDIFF on p. 94

OXFORD AND WILTSHIRE

Opening times should be confirmed by telephone from the number in brackets. The exchange is given only if it differs from the place name at the beginning of the entry
Map references are shown after each place name

Avebury (Bc) Early Bronze Age stone circle. *Alexander Keiller Museum* (250), contains Neolithic and Bronze Age finds from recent excavations. *Avebury Manor* (203), Elizabethan manor house with fine panelling and plasterwork: contains collections of furniture and porcelain; in the formal gardens are a rare animal sanctuary and unusual topiary work. *Church of St James*, 12th-century church on Saxon foundations

Bladon (Eg) *Church of St Martin*, 19th century, on the site of an earlier church: Sir Winston Churchill's simple grave is in the churchyard

Oxford (Ff) *University*, established in the 12th century. Each of the 33 colleges, dating from the 12th to 20th centuries, has an individual charm and interest. All are open to visitors every afternoon (some in the mornings as well). Quarters to be visited vary with each college. *Christ Church*, often referred to as 'The House', was founded by Wolsey in 1525 on the site of a nunnery, but was not given its present name until 1546 when the college chapel also became the cathedral of the diocese: Great Tom, the bell in Wren's Tom Tower, is tolled 101 times every night at 9.05 p.m. to signal the closing of the college gates. The Tower of 15th-century *Magdalen* was used by Charles I as an observation post during the siege of Oxford and today is the central point for Oxford's May Morning celebrations (see p. 58). *Merton* was established in Oxford ten years after its foundation in Surrey in 1264: it still has its original hall, though now much restored, and has a chained library that is older than the Bodleian. A number of colleges are renowned for their lovely gardens, including *St John's*, *Trinity*, *Worcester*, *New College* and *Wadham*. *Ashmolean Museum* (57522), contains Guy Fawkes's lantern and the Alfred Jewel, which is believed to have been made in the 9th century for King Alfred. *Sheldonian Theatre* (41023), 17th-century Wren building, used for university functions. *Bodleian Library* (44675), one of the world's most important libraries, containing about 3 million books and manuscripts. *Radcliffe Camera*, an 18th-century domed Classical building, used as a reading room of the Bodleian, is a prominent landmark, but it is not open to the public. *Christ Church Picture Gallery* (42102). *Christ Church Library* (43957). *Oxford University Museum* (57467)

Silbury Hill (Ab) An enormous man-made mound, believed to be Neolithic, but its origin still baffles archaeologists

West Kennett (Bb) Neolithic long barrow with chambers

Woodstock (Eg) *Blenheim Palace* (811325), Sir John Vanbrugh's masterpiece, built between 1705 and 1722, and presented by Queen Anne to her Captain General, the 1st Duke of Marlborough as a mark of gratitude after his victory over the French and Bavarians in 1704. It was the birthplace of Winston Churchill in 1874 and includes a fine collection of paintings, tapestries and furniture. The gardens are considered the most accomplished work of the eminent 18th-century landscape gardener Lancelot 'Capability' Brown. (See p. 406)

White Horses of Wessex
The hill figures of England and Scotland are unique, and some, such as the Uffington White Horse (Dd), possibly go back to the 1st century BC. The best of these figures are in Wessex. They include white horses at: Milk Hill (Bb), cut in 1812; Broad Town (Ac) 1864; Oldbury (Ab), 1780; Hackpen Hill (Bc), 1838; Marlborough (Bb), 1804; and Pewsey (Ba), 1937. The Old Horse at Pewsey, cut in 1785, is a little below and to the right, but is barely visible.

AA SERVICE CENTRES: 45 Oxford Road, Reading, including 24-hour breakdown service (Reading 581122); 133–4 High Street, Oxford (Oxford 46578), including 24-hour breakdown service (Oxford 40286). Breakdown service: Swindon 21446, 24 hours

A town plan of OXFORD is on p. 98; of READING on p. 97.

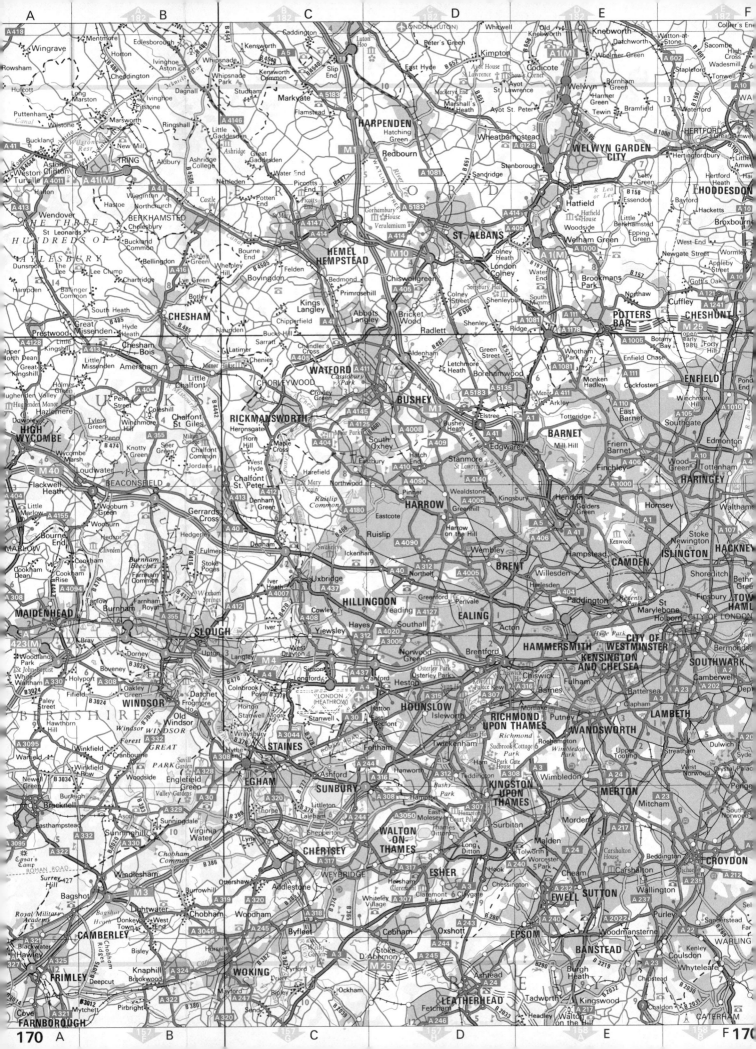

LONDON

Opening times may vary and should be confirmed by telephone from the number given (the London prefix, 01, has been omitted) Map references are shown for places outside Central London

Hampton Court Palace (Db) Riverside palace (977 8441), built by Cardinal Wolsey in 1514, contains fine paintings, tapestries and carving

Hatfield House (Ef) 17th-century Jacobean mansion (Hatfield 62823), containing portraits, furniture, tapestries

Kew Palace (Dc) 17th-century

Dutch-gabled house (940 3321). *The Royal Botanic Gardens* (940 1171) contain rare orchids, ferns and cacti

Windsor Castle (Bc) (Windsor 68286), Norman with Stuart and Regency alterations; the largest inhabited castle in the world, and a royal residence since the 12th century

CENTRAL LONDON. The following places of interest are marked on the maps on pp. 74–77

Art Galleries *National Gallery* (839 3321); *National Portrait Gallery* (930 1552); *Tate Gallery* (821 1313); *Wallace Collection* (935 0687); *Royal Academy of Arts* (734 9052)

Buckingham Palace Principal home of the Queen; Changing the Guard takes place at 11.30 a.m. each day. *Queen's Gallery*, open Tuesday to Saturday from 11 a.m. to 5 p.m., and Sunday 2 p.m. to 5 p.m. *Royal Mews*, where the Queen's horses and coaches are kept; open Wednesday and Thursday, 2 p.m. to 4 p.m.

Cathedrals *St Paul's*, Wren's greatest church, with carvings by Grinling Gibbons and ironwork by Tijou; the crypt and whispering gallery may be visited daily (except Sundays and Holy days) from 11.30 a.m. to 3.30 p.m. *Westminster Roman Catholic Cathedral*, Byzantine-style church with a fine marbled interior. *Westminster Abbey*, founded by Edward the Confessor in the 11th century; the Henry VII chapel has magnificent fan vaulting

Horse Guards Parade Whitehall, Mounting the Guard, Monday to Saturday 11 a.m., Sunday 10 a.m.

Houses of Parliament 19th-century Gothic building. Guided tours from the Victoria Tower entrance 10 a.m. to 4.30 p.m. every Saturday, and on Monday, Tuesday and Thursday in August, and Thursday in September, also each Bank Holiday Monday

and Tuesday. Debates may be heard in the Commons on Monday to Thursday from 4.15 p.m., Friday 11.30 a.m. to 4.30 p.m. and the Lords on Tuesday and Wednesday from 2.30 p.m., Thursday 3 p.m.; join the public queue at St Stephen's entrance, or apply in advance to your local M.P.

Museums *British Museum* (636 1555); *Science Museum* (589 3456); *Victoria and Albert Museum* (589 6371); *Pollock's Toy Museum* (636 3452); *British Piano Museum* (560 8108); *St Bride's Crypt*, Fleet Street (353 1301); *Imperial War Museum* (735 8922); *Madame Tussaud Waxworks* (935 6861) and *Planetarium* (486 1121); *Museum of London* (600 3699)

Ships *HMS Belfast*, Royal Navy cruiser moored opposite the Tower, open daily 11 a.m. to 6 p.m.; *Historic Ship Collection*, St Katharine's Dock, just below Tower Bridge, including Scott's *Royal Research Ship Discovery*, daily 10 a.m. to 5 p.m.

Tower of London (709 0765) Open Monday to Saturday 9.30 a.m. to 5 p.m., Sunday 2 p.m. to 5 p.m., March to October; weekdays only, 9.30 a.m. to 4 p.m., November to Feb. The Crown Jewels are not normally on view in February.
To see the Ceremony of the Keys, when the Chief Warder locks the Tower gates each night at 10 p.m., write to the Governor of the Tower

Zoological Gardens (722 3333)

AA SERVICE CENTRES: Regis House, King William Street, EC4R 9AN (626 9993); 162 Fulham Palace Road, W6 9ES (385 3677); Fanum House, The Broadway, Stanmore (954 7355); Fanum House, 7 High Street, Teddington (977 3200). 24-hour breakdown service (954 7373)

LONDON INFORMATION—Road conditions (246 8021); Children's London (246 8007); Tourists' London (English 246 8041, French 246 8043, German 246 8045, Spanish 246 8047). London Tourist Board, 4 Grosvenor Gardens, SW1 (730 0791)

Plans of LONDON are on pp. 74–77

Opening times should be confirmed by telephone from the number in brackets. The exchange is given only if it differs from the place name at the beginning of the entry
Map references are shown after each place name

Broadstairs (Hb) *Bleak House* (Thanet 62224), known as Fort House when Charles Dickens lived there and wrote 'David Copperfield': it was renamed after the publication in 1853 of 'Bleak House' and part of it is kept as it was in Dickens's day. *Church of St Peter*, part-Norman

Canterbury see p. 161

Chelmsford (Bf) *Cathedral*, part-Perpendicular with a fine south porch and a 15th-century tower topped with an open lantern and an 18th-century spire

Cobham (Ab) *Owletts* (Meopham 814260), 17th-century red-brick house. *Church of St Mary Magdalene*, 13th and 14th century with a fine collection of brasses. *Almshouses*, a 14th-century priests' college suppressed in 1537 by Henry VIII and converted to its present use in the 17th century. *Yeoman's House*, 15th-century yeoman's home. *Cobham Hall* (Shorne 3371), 16th and 17th-century mansion with 18th-century alterations, has fine work by Inigo Jones and the Adam brothers. Now used as a school and open to the public at limited times

Maidstone (Ba) *Allington Castle*, 13th century, restored in the 20th century, is now a Carmelite retreat house. *Church of St Lawrence*, part-12th century. *All Saints Church*, 14th century. *Tyrwhitt-Drake Museum of Carriages* (54497), collection includes a 17th-century Italian gig. *Chillington Manor House* (54497), 16th century, now a museum and art gallery containing a 12th-century Bible and a portable clavichord used by Handel. *The Friars*, Aylesford (77272), restored 13th-century

Carmelite friary noted for the pottery produced by its monks

Ospringe (Db) *Maison Dieu* (Faversham 3751), a 15th-century timber-framed building on the site of a hospital founded by Henry III, is now a museum containing pottery from a Roman cemetery discovered at Ospringe in the 1920's

Reculver (Gb) *Regulbium*, remains of a 3rd-century fort: the towers within its walls belong to a 12th-century church which was destroyed in the 19th century

Rochester (Bb) *Castle*, preserved 11th and 12th-century ruins. *Cathedral*, 12th century, restored in the 19th century. *Guildhall* (Medway 48717), 17th-century red brick on Doric columns; the panelled council room has a fine moulded ceiling. *Restoration House*, 16th-century manor house where Charles II spent the night of May 28, 1660, while on his way to London to reclaim the throne. *Eastgate House* (Medway 44176), Tudor mansion referred to by Dickens in many of his novels, is now a museum containing relics of the author. *Temple Manor*, 13th-century stone building with a vaulted basement, extended in the 17th century

Sandwich see p. 161

St Osyth (Fg) *Priory*, 12th-century Augustinian ruins; the restored 15th-century gatehouse and the gardens are open to the public at limited times. *Church of SS Peter and Paul*, 12th century, with fine 16th-century brick arcades separating the nave from the aisles

AA SERVICE CENTRES: Fanum House, 205 Moulsham Street, Chelmsford, including 24-hour breakdown service (Chelmsford 61711); 8 Colman House, King Street, Maidstone, including 24-hour breakdown service (Maidstone 55353). Breakdown services: Thanet 81226, 24 hours; Faversham 2536, 9 a.m. to 5 p.m.

ROAD CONDITIONS: London (01-246 8021)

A town plan of CANTERBURY is on p. 100; of SOUTHEND-ON-SEA on p. 97

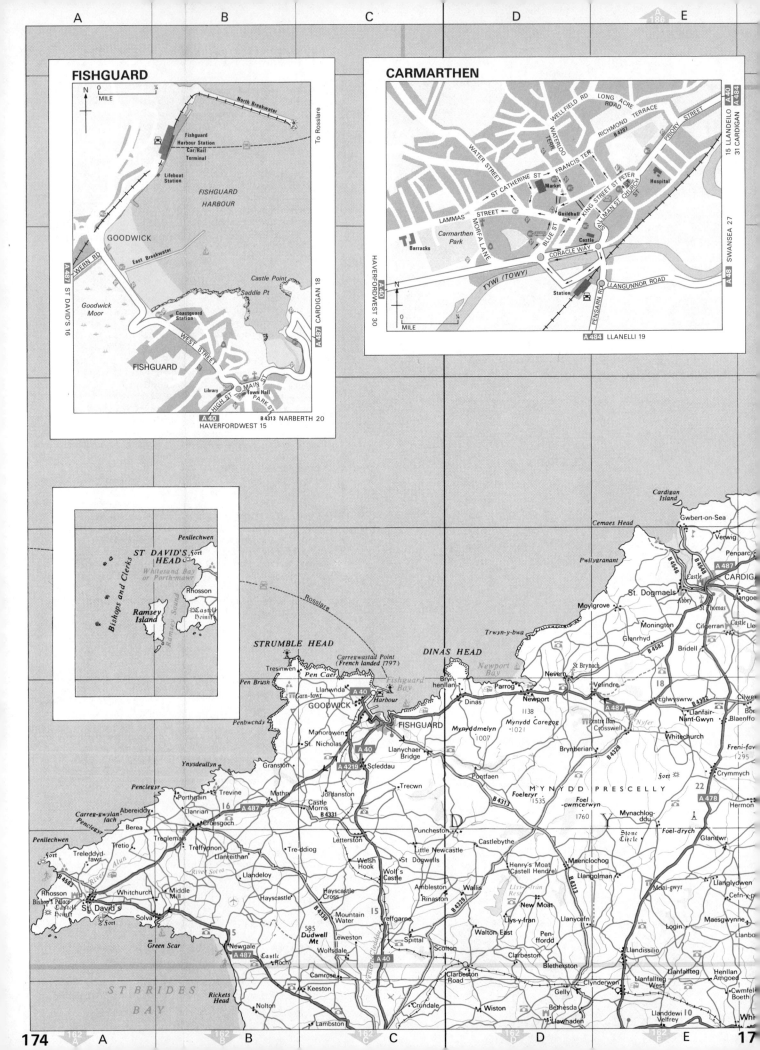

FISHGUARD

N
MILE 0 — ¼

Fishguard Harbour Station
Car/Rail Terminal
North Breakwater
To Rosslare

FISHGUARD HARBOUR

Lifeboat Station

GOODWICK

East Breakwater

Castle Point
Saddle Pt

Goodwick Moor

Coastguard Station

WEST STREET

FISHGUARD

A 487 ST DAVID'S 16
WERN RD
A 487 CARDIGAN 18

Library
HIGH ST
MAIN ST
Town Hall
PARK ST

A 40 HAVERFORDWEST 15
B 4313 NARBERTH 20

CARMARTHEN

WELLFIELD RD
LONG ACRE ROAD
RICHMOND TERRACE
PRIORY STREET
WATERLOO TERR
WATER STREET
ST CATHERINE ST
FRANCIS TER
B 4207
Market
Hospital
KING STREET
ST PETER
ST MAN ST CHURCH ST
Guildhall
LAMMAS STREET
MORFA LANE
BLUE ST
Castle
Barracks
Carmarthen Park
CORACLE WAY
N
MILE 0 — ¼
TYWI (TOWY)
Station
PENSARN RD
LLANGUNNOR ROAD

A 40 HAVERFORDWEST 30
A 40 LLANDEILO 15
A 484 CARDIGAN 31
A 48 SWANSEA 27
A 484 LLANELLI 19

ST DAVID'S HEAD
Penllechwen
Fort
Whitesand Bay or Porth-mawr
Bishops and Clerks
Rhosson
Ramsey Island
Castell Deinif
Ramsey Sound
Rosslare

STRUMBLE HEAD
Tresinwen
Pen Caer
Carregwastad Point (French landed 1797)
Pen Brush
DINAS HEAD
Newport Bay
Cardigan Island
Gwbert-on-Sea
Verwig
Penparc
B 4546
B 4548
A 487
Castle
CARDIGA
St Dogmaels
Abbey
St Thomas
Moylgrove
Cilgerran
Castle
Monington
Glanrhyd
B 4582
Bridell
Trwyn-y-bwa
St Brynach
Nevern
Velindre
18
Eglwyswrw
A 4332
Cilwe
Pwllygranant
Cemaes Head
Penbwchdy
Llanwnda
A 40
Harbour
Fishguard Bay
Brynhenllan
Parrog
Newport
Dinas
Llanfair-Nant-Gwyn
Blaenffo
GOODWICK
FISHGUARD
1138
Mynydd Caregog
1021
Pentre Ifan
Crosswell
Nyfer
Whitechurch
Freni-faw
1295
Manorowen
St. Nicholas
Mynyddmelyn
1007
Brynberian
B 4329
Garn-fawr
Llanychaer Bridge
Granston
A 4219
Scleddau
Pontfaen
MYNYDD PRESCELLY
Fort
Crymmych
Ynysdeullyn
Trecwn
Foeleryr
1535
Foel-cwmcerwyn
1760
22
A 478
Hermon
Penclegyr
Trevine
Mathry
Jordanston
Castle Morris
B 4331
Puncheston
Mynachlog-ddu
Foel-drych
Glandwr
Abereiddy
Llanrian
B 4313
Stone Circle
Porthgain
Croesgoch
16
A 487
Letterston
Castlebythe
Maenclochog
B 4313
Llanglydwen
Carreg-gwylan-fach
Berea
Treglemais
Treffynnon
Tre-ddiog
Little Newcastle
Henry's Moat (Castell Hendre)
Llangolman
Mani-gwyr
Cefn-y-p
Penclegyr
Tretio
Treleddyd-fawr
Llanreithan
Welsh Hook
St Dogwells
Llys-y-fran Resr
Maesgwynne
Penllechwen
Fort
River Alun
Whitchurch
Middle Mill
Llandeloy
Wolf's Castle
Ambleston
Wallis
New Moat
Llanycefn
Login
Llanbo
Rhosson
Bishop's Palace
Castell Deinif
St David's
Fort
Solva
Hayscastle
Hayscastle Cross
B 4330
Rinaston
A 4329
Llandissilio
Llanfallteg
Henllan
Amgoed
Green Scar
Mountain Water
585
Treffgarne
15
Walton East
Penffordd
Llanfallteg West
Cwmfel Boeth
Dudwell Mt
Lewaston
Wolfsdale
Spittal
Scolton
Clynderwen
Llanddewi Velfrey
Camrose
Clarbeston
Gelly
Bethesda
10
Newgale
Castle
Roch
A 487
Keeston
Clarbeston Road
Wiston
Llawhaden
Whi
Rickets Head
Nolton
Lambston
Crundale
A 40
ST BRIDES BAY

174 A 162A B 162B C 162C D 162D E 17

SOUTH CARDIGAN BAY

Opening times should be confirmed by telephone from the number in brackets. The exchange is given only if it differs from the place name at the beginning of the entry
Map references are shown after each place name

Cardigan (Ed) *Castle*, 13th century, the scene of the first recorded Eisteddfod in 1176; it was destroyed by Parliamentary forces in the 17th century

Carmarthen (Hb) Site of the Roman camp Moridunum. *Castle*, 11th-century ruins. *Church of St Peter*, 13th and 14th century with fine stained-glass windows. *Museum* (31691) contains Neolithics from west Wales, Stone Age relics and Roman jewellery. Legend has it that King Arthur's wizard, Merlin, was a Carmarthen man. Henry VII granted the Mayor of Carmarthen permission to have a sword borne before him on ceremonial occasions, a tradition which is still preserved

Cenarth (Fd) Coracles, round boats which are unchanged in design since the time of the Ancient Britons, are made in the village. Until recently they have been used for fishing, but now they are made mainly for races

Cilgerran (Ed) *Castle*, 13th-century ruins; the majestic setting of the castle, overlooking the River Teifi, inspired paintings by Richard Wilson and J. M. W. Turner. Coracle races are held on the River Teifi during August (see p. 62)

Fishguard (Cc) Site of the last invasion of Britain, on February 22, 1797, when French troops and ex-convicts invaded the town. The French, under the command of an American named Tate, were heading for Bristol, where they had hoped to start a peasants' rising, but winds prevented them from sailing up the Bristol Channel and they went ashore in Pembrokeshire. A stone commemorating Jemima Nicholson, the local heroine who rounded up several of the invaders with a pitchfork, is in the churchyard

Henllan (Gd) Beauty spot on the River Teifi, with a single-span bridge over the rapids

Llandyssul (Hd) *Church of St Tyssul*, Norman, restored in the 19th century, with a battlemented tower

Llechryd (Fd) *Bridge*, a 17th-century bridge, with six arches, over the River Teifi

Meini-gwyr (Eb) A Neolithic chambered tomb

Mynydd Prescelly (Dc) A range of hills giving fine views across Wales and containing antiquities including a hill fort and a stone circle; some of the stones used to build Stonehenge were taken from here

Nevern (Dc) *Pentre Ifan Neolithic Burial Chamber*: the capstone, supported on three uprights, is 16 ft long and 7 ft high, with a semicircular forecourt at the south end; it is one of the finest examples of a burial chamber in Britain. *Church of St Brynach*, 11th century, with Perpendicular tower

Newcastle Emlyn (Gd) *Castle*, 13th century, rebuilt in the 15th century; during the Civil War Royalist troops put up such a resistance that Cromwell wrecked the castle after its capture. *Church of the Holy Trinity*, 19th century; the slate used for the interior is from the quarries at Cilgerran (Ed)

St David's (Ab) *Cathedral*, mainly 12th century, contains a stall in which the Queen, a canon of the chapter, sat in 1955. *Bishop's Palace*, 12th-century ruins: legend says that in 1548, Bishop Barlow, before leaving the see, stripped the lead from the roof to provide dowries for his five daughters, all of whom married bishops. *St Mary's College*, 14th-century remnants, including a Perpendicular chapel restored in 1934

St Dogmaels (Ed) *Abbey of St Mary the Virgin*, 12th to 15th-century Benedictine ruins with fine carvings. *Church of St Thomas the Martyr*, 19th-century church on the site of a Celtic monastery, contains an ogham stone, which helped scholars in 1848 to interpret ogham, a 5th-century Gaelic script

Strumble Head (Bd) *Garnfawr*, Iron Age hill fort with remains of hut circles and fortifications. Views of Cardigan Bay from the lighthouse (St Nicholas 258) extend from St David's Head to Bardsey Island

ROAD CONDITIONS: Cardiff 8021

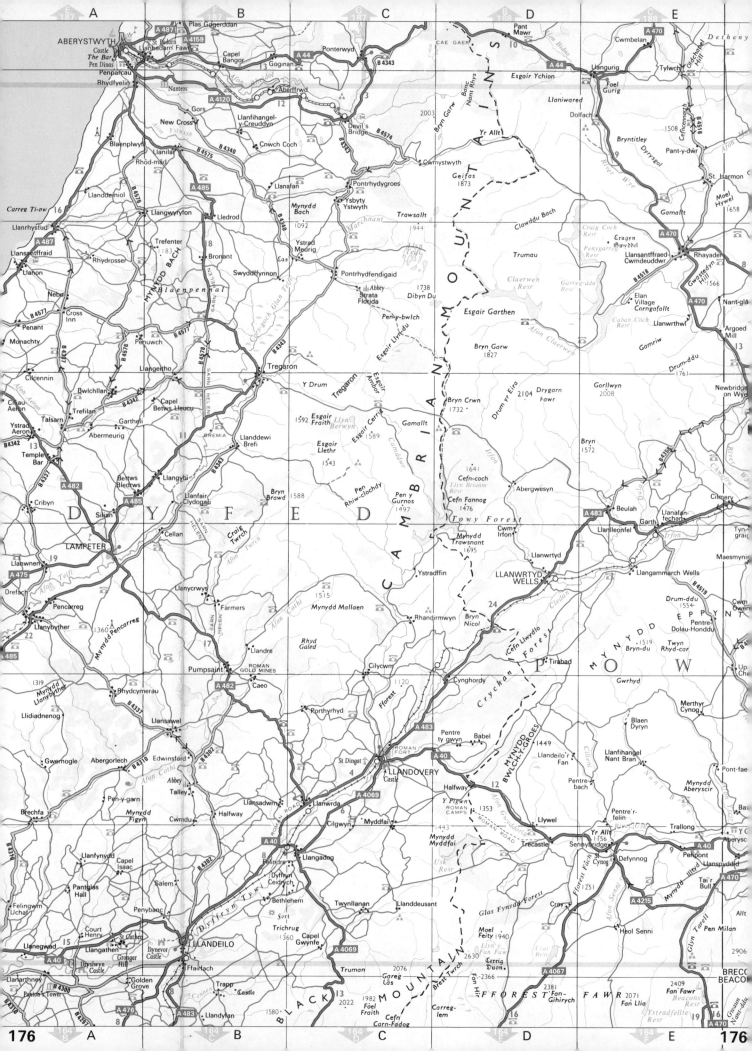

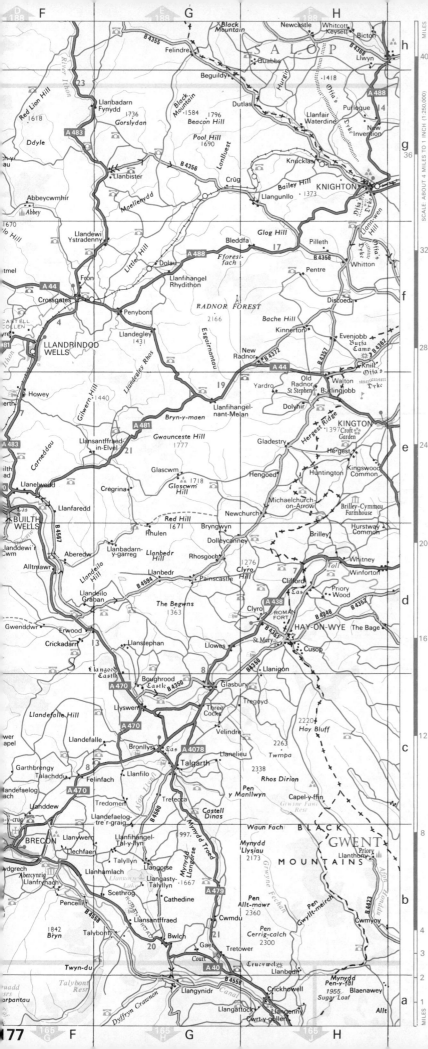

Opening times should be confirmed by telephone from the number in brackets. The exchange is given only if it differs from the place name at the beginning of the entry

Map references are shown after each place name

Abbeycwmhir (Fg) *Abbey*, remains of a 12th-century Cistercian house

Aberystwyth (Ah) *Pen Dinas*, an Iron Age fort. *Castle*, 13th-century ruins on the site of a Norman fortification. Charles I used the castle as a mint, before it surrendered to the Parliamentary forces in 1646 and was left to decay. *National Library of Wales* (3816), receives every newly published book and now contains more than 2 million copies. Its Welsh literary treasures include the manuscript of the Black Book of Carmarthen, one of the earliest works in Welsh, dating from the early 13th century.

Brecon (Fb) *Priory Church of St John the Evangelist*, 12th and 13th century; originally built as a Benedictine abbey, now a cathedral. *Brecknock Museum* (4121). *Church of St Mary*, part-Norman

Brecon Beacons National Park see p. 340

Castell Collen (Ff) A well-preserved Roman fort

Defynnog (Eb) *Church of St Cynog*, 15th century; the ancient font bears the only Runic inscription in any Welsh church; embedded in the tower is a 5th-century pillar inscribed in Latin and ogham

Devil's Bridge (Cg) Beauty spot where three bridges, built one above the other, span the River Mynach. The first bridge was built by monks in 1087, but local legend claims it was built for the impoverished monks by Satan on condition that the first creature to cross should belong to him. A monk foiled the devil, who was expecting a soul, by throwing a bone across, which was pursued by a hungry dog. The second bridge was built in 1708. Both are now spanned by a steel bridge. *Jubilee Arch*, 1½ miles south-east, was built in 1810 to commemorate the Golden Jubilee of George III

Hay-on-Wye (Hd) *Castle*, 12th-century ruins; a Jacobean manor house has been built on the site. *Church of St Mary*, a 12th-century church rebuilt in the 19th century

Llanarthney (Ab) *Paxton's Tower*, a folly built in 1802

by Sir William Paxton, a wealthy banker, as a rebuke to voters who did not elect him as their MP. He won the next election in 1806

Llanddewi Brefi (Be) 6th to 9th-century inscribed stones

Llandovery (Cc) *Castle*, 11th-century ruins. *Llandovery College* (20315); the school chapel contains a painting of the Crucifixion by Graham Sutherland. *Church of St Dingat*, 14th and 15th century, with a Gothic font built round the original Norman one

Llandrindod Wells (Ff) A spa with medicinal springs. *Museum* (2212) contains a craft centre and a collection of bicycles

Llangathen (Ab) *Grongar Hill*, Iron Age hill fort. *Dryslwyn Castle*, Norman ruins. *Church of St Cathen*, 13th century

Llanthony (Hb) *Priory*, 12th-century Augustinian ruins

Old Radnor (He) *Church of St Stephen*, probably 14th century, considered to be one of the finest churches in Wales; the font is formed from what is believed to have been a Bronze Age altar stone

Pen-y-crug (Fc) Iron Age hill fort

Rhayader (Ef) *Elan Valley*, 3½ miles to the west, a beauty spot round a chain of lakes built as reservoirs between 1892 and 1952 and now piping water to Birmingham; the Penygarreg dam, 184 ft high, is the highest gravity dam in Britain

Strata Florida (Cf) *Abbey*, preserved 12th-century Cistercian ruins

Talley Abbey (Bc) 12th century; built by Lord Rhys for the Premonstratensians, an order originating in Prémontré, France

Tretower (Gb) *Castle*, 12th-century tower in the ruins of a Norman castle. *Tretower Court* (Bwlch 730279), 14th-century fortified manor house

Y Gaer (Fb) A Roman fort. Excavations by Sir Mortimer Wheeler in 1925 revealed outlines of streets and various camp buildings; finds of pottery and other objects are in the Brecknock museum

AA BREAKDOWN SERVICES: Aberystwyth 4801, 9 a.m. to 5 p.m.; Brecon 2015, 9 a.m. to 5 p.m.

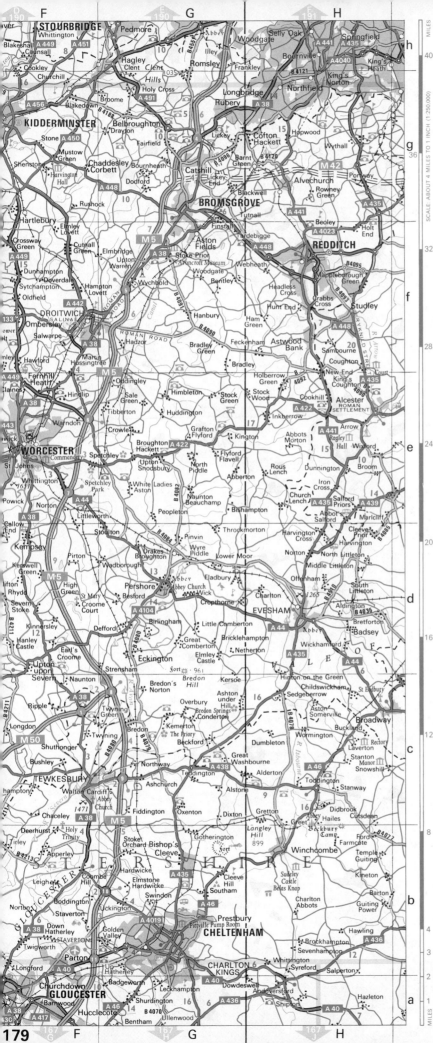

THE SEVERN AND WYE VALLEYS

Opening times should be confirmed by telephone from the number in brackets. The exchange is given only if it differs from the place name at the beginning of the entry

Map references are shown after each place name

Arrow (He) *Ragley Hall* (Alcester 2090), 17th-century seat of the Marquess of Hertford; it has a fine art collection and a park landscaped by Capability Brown

Broadheath (Fe) *Elgar Birthplace Museum* (Worcester 66224)

Broadway (Hc) Village of old cottages and fine gabled houses which is one of the beauty spots of the Cotswolds. *Church of St Eadburgha*, 12th to 17th-century cruciform

Buckland Rectory (Hc) 15th century, one of England's oldest rectories, with a spiral stone staircase and fine stained glass; the two-storied great hall has a timber roof.

Charlton Abbots (Hb) *Belas Knap*, a Neolithic or early Bronze Age long barrow with four side chambers, built about 2000 BC

Cheltenham (Gb) *Pittville Pump Room* (23852), Georgian building with a colonnade and dome. *Prestbury Park*, the centre of National Hunt racing culminating in the Festival meeting in March

Coughton Court (Hf) part-16th century (Alcester 2435), contains the arms of conspirators in the Gunpowder Plot against James I in 1605

Deerhurst (Fb) *Church of St Mary*, part 10th century

Hailes Abbey (Hc) 13th-century Cistercian ruins with a museum on the site

Harvington Hall (Fg) Moated Tudor manor house (Chaddesley Corbett 267), containing priests' hiding places

Little Malvern (Ed) *Little Malvern Court* (Malvern 4580), 14th-century prior's guest hall

Pembridge Castle (Ba) Mainly 13th century with later additions (Skenfrith 226), surrounded by a moat

Ross-on-Wye (Cb) *Market Hall*, 17th-century sandstone building with medallioned windows. *Wilton Bridge*, 16th century with an 18th-century sundial on the parapet. *Church of St Mary*, 13th century, restored in the 19th century; in the churchyard is a rare cross with the inscription 'Plague Ano. Dom. 1637. Burials 315. Libera nos Domine'

Snowshill Manor (Hc) A Tudor manor house (Broadway 2410) with a fine collection of musical instruments and clocks

Sudeley Castle (Hb) 12th century (Winchcombe 602308), was the home of Catherine Parr, sixth wife of Henry VIII, and the headquarters of Charles I during the Civil War; contains a fine collection of paintings, furniture and tapestries; in the grounds are a children's play park and a bird garden.

Tewkesbury (Fc) Site in 1471 of a Yorkist victory during the Wars of the Roses. *Abbey Church of St Mary the Virgin*, Norman and 14th century with fine monuments

Worcester (Fe) *Cathedral*, 11th and 13th century. *Worcester Royal Porcelain Works* and *Dyson Perrins Museum*, containing one of the world's finest collections of Worcester porcelain and bone china, (23221). *City Museum and Art Gallery* (25371). *Tudor House Museum* (25371). *The Greyfriars*, 15th-century half-timbered house. *The Commandery*, 15th-century house on the site of an 11th-century hospital, with a fine Elizabethan staircase. *Guildhall* (23471), Queen Anne building with an Assembly Room containing a portrait of George III by Reynolds. *Spetchley Park* (Spetchley 224), 30 acre garden with wild-fowl and red and fallow deer

AA SERVICE CENTRE: 134 New Street, Birmingham, including 24-hour breakdown service (021 550 4858). Breakdown services: Gloucester 23278, 24 hours; Worcester 51070, 24 hours

ROAD CONDITIONS: Birmingham (021 246 8021); Bristol 8021

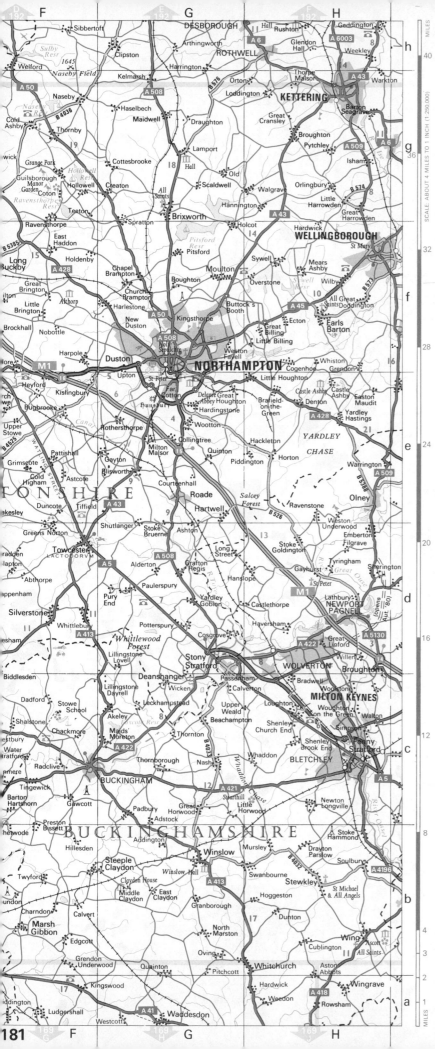

Opening times should be confirmed by telephone from the number in brackets. The exchange is given only if it differs from the place name at the beginning of the entry

Map references are shown after each place name

Charlecote Park (Be) 16th-century house (Stratford-upon-Avon 840277), containing a museum; Shakespeare is said to have been caught poaching deer in the park and to have been summoned before their owner, the magistrate Sir Thomas Lucy, whom he lampooned as Mr Justice Shallow in 'King Henry IV' and the 'Merry Wives of Windsor'

Coventry (Cg) *Cathedral* designed by Sir Basil Spence and consecrated in 1962; the nave contains Graham Sutherland's vast tapestry of 'Christ in Glory'. *Broadgate* contains a statue of Lady Godiva who, in the 11th century, rode naked through the city as part of a bargain with her husband Leofric, Earl of Mercia, to lower oppressive taxes on the town. Statues of the original 'Peeping Tom', the only man to look at Godiva, are in Broadgate, Hertford Street and the Leofric Hotel

Hockley Heath (Ag) *Packwood House* (Lapworth 2024), Tudor, extended in the 17th century, with tapestries and a yew garden depicting Christ and the multitude at the Sermon on the Mount.

Kenilworth (Bg) *Castle*, remains include massive keep, gatehouse and banqueting hall

Northampton (Gf) *Central*

Museum and Art Gallery (34881). *Abington Museum* (31454). *Church of the Holy Sepulchre*, part 12th century, one of the five surviving round churches in England

Stoke Bruerne (Gd) *Waterways Museum* (Roade 862229) covers two centuries of canal history

Stratford-upon-Avon (Ae) *Shakespeare's Birthplace Trust Properties* (4016) include Shakespeare's birthplace, a Tudor house containing Shakespearian relics; Anne Hathaway's Cottage, 15th century; Hall's Croft, Tudor home of Shakespeare's daughter Susanna; Mary Arden's House, Tudor home of Shakespeare's mother; New Place, foundations of Shakespeare's last home, preserved in an Elizabethan setting. *Holy Trinity*, 13th-century church containing a record of Shakespeare's baptism and his tomb. *Royal Shakespeare Theatre Picture Gallery* (296655)

Sulgrave Manor (Ed) Ancestral home of George Washington containing many of his possessions (Sulgrave 205)

Warwick (Bf) *Castle* (45421), 14th century, contains an armoury and a collection of fine paintings. *Doll Museum* (42843). *County Museum* (43431). *St John's House Museum* (43431)

AA SERVICE CENTRE: 19 Cross Cheaping, Coventry, including 24-hour breakdown service (021 550 4858). Breakdown services: Northampton 66241, 24 hours; Leamington Spa 21952, 9 a.m. to 5 p.m.

ROAD CONDITIONS: Birmingham (021 246 8021)

STRATFORD-UPON-AVON

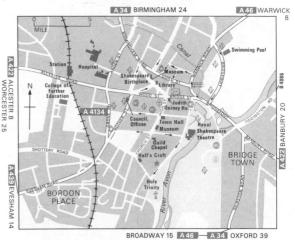

A town plan of COVENTRY is on p. 81; of NORTHAMPTON on p. 103

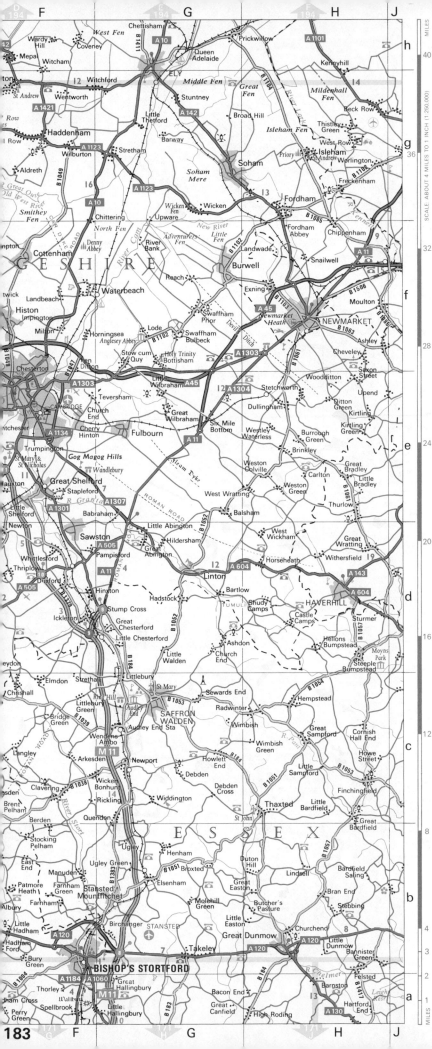

CAMBRIDGE

Opening times should be confirmed by telephone from the number in brackets. The exchange is given only if it differs from the place name at the beginning of the entry

Map references are shown after each place name

Ayot St Lawrence (Ca) *Shaw's Corner* (Stevenage 820307), the home of George Bernard Shaw from 1906 to 1950, containing relics of the author; the study and summer house are left as they were in Shaw's time. *Church of St Lawrence*, 18th-century Grecian style with Roman Classical interior; ruins of the 14th-century church are near by

Bedford (Bd) *Bunyan Collection*, library and exhibition devoted to life and works of the religious author John Bunyan, who lived in Bedford from 1655 until his death in 1688. *Bunyan Meeting*, library and museum contains the author's personal relics. *Elstow Moot Hall* (66889), medieval market hall. *Cecil Higgins Art Gallery* (211222)

Cambridge (Fe) *University*, established in the 13th century; the courtyards, chapels, dining halls and some gardens of the 24 colleges may be visited at most times during daylight: visitors should particularly try to see Rubens's 'Adoration of the Magi' in the chapel of *King's College*; the Old Court of *Corpus Christi*; the President's Lodge of *Queens'*; and the Wren Library of *Trinity*. *Botanic Gardens*, second only to Kew in importance, are open on weekdays from 8 a.m. to 8 p.m. (dusk in winter). *Folk Museum* (355159). *Fitzwilliam Museum* (69501), paintings, antiquities. *University Library* (61441) contain manuscripts dating from the 13th century. *Scott Polar Research Institute* (66499). *Senate House*, 18th-century Classical style, used for university functions

Dunstable (Bb) *Priory*, ruins of a 12th-century Augustinian house, where the annulment of Henry VIII's marriage to his first wife, Catherine of Aragon, was pronounced

Ely (Gh) *Cathedral*, 11th century, on the site of a 7th-century Benedictine abbey

Isleham (Hg) *Priory*, Norman monastic church which has a nave without an aisle. *Church of St Andrew*, 14th century with good panelling and brasses

Knebworth House (Db) 15th-century Tudor mansion (Stevenage 812661) with Gothic-style exterior decoration, containing paintings, furniture and other treasures collected over five centuries

Littlebury (Fc) *Ring Hill Camp*, an Iron Age camp with a wide defensive ditch

Lode (Gf) *Anglesey Abbey* (Cambridge 811200), 13th-century Augustinian abbey restored as a manor house in the 16th century; the Canons' Parlour of the original abbey is the present dining-room; there is a fine collection of paintings and 100 acres of landscaped gardens

Luton (Cb) *Church of St Mary*, 12th to 15th century, with 14th-century octagonal baptistry and black and white chequered stone tower. *Museum and Art Gallery* (36941)

Luton Hoo (Ca) 18th-century mansion (Luton 22955) with Robert Adam exterior, houses a magnificent art collection including Russian Fabergé jewels; the gardens were designed by Capability Brown

Newmarket (Hf) *National Stud*, next to the racecourse, is open to visitors on Sunday afternoons and on the mornings of race days

Saffron Walden (Gc) *Audley End* (22399), 17th-century Jacobean mansion on the site of a Benedictine abbey, with fine Adam work and 18th-century furniture. *Church of St Mary the Virgin*, 15th and 16th-century Perpendicular, with fine carvings

Whipsnade (Ba) *Zoo* (872171), has more than 2000 animals; a steam train takes visitors through the rhino enclosure

Wicken Fen (Gg) 730 acre nature reserve which the National Trust keeps in its natural state; it is largely undrained and abounds with wild duck and other water birds

Wimpole Hall (Ee) 18th century (Arrington 257)

AA SERVICE CENTRE: Janus House, St Andrews Street, Cambridge, including 24-hour breakdown service (Cambridge 312302)

ROAD CONDITIONS: London (01 246 8021)

A town plan of CAMBRIDGE is on p. 98

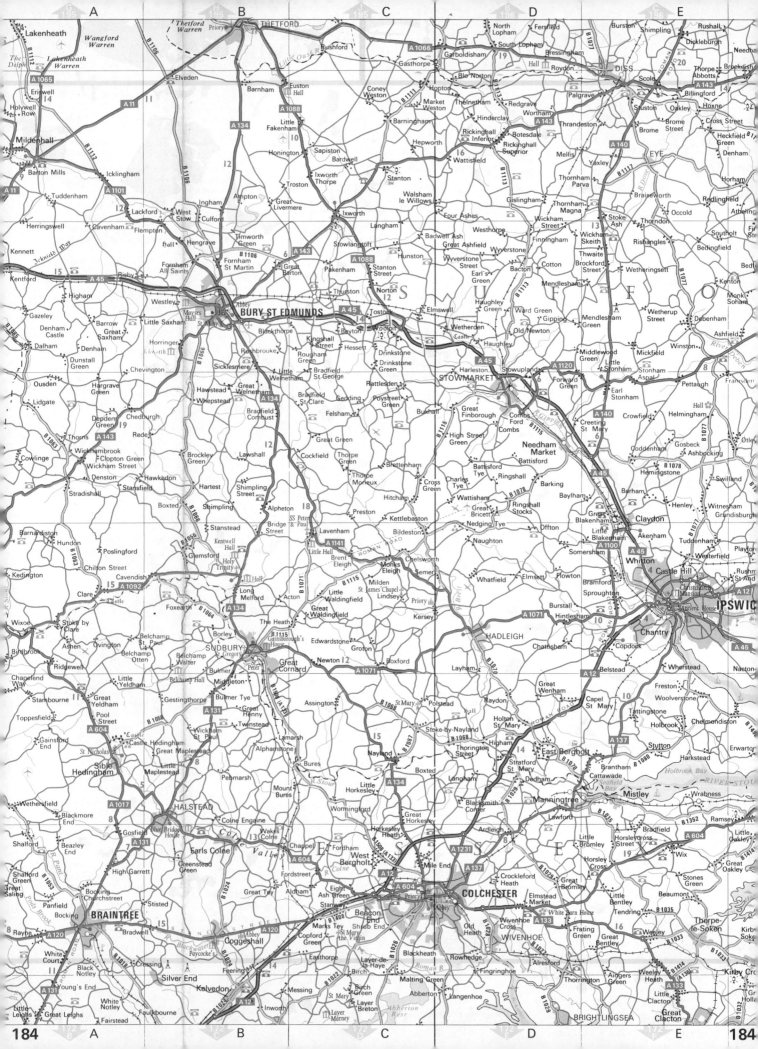

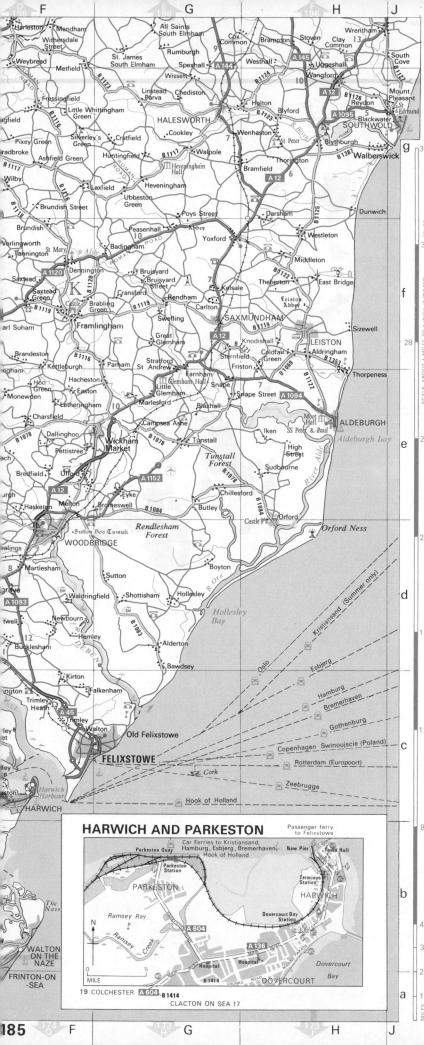

Opening times should be confirmed by telephone from the number in brackets. The exchange is given only if it differs from the place name at the beginning of the entry

Map references are shown after each place name

Aldeburgh (He) *Moot Hall*, 16th century, contains old documents, prints and maps. *Church of SS Peter and Paul*, 16th century with 14th-century tower

Bury St Edmunds 11th and 14th-century Benedictine ruins. *Cathedral Church of St James*, mainly 16th and 19th century. *Church of St Mary*, 15th century. *Angel Corner* (63233), Queen Anne house containing a collection of clocks and watches given by the musician Frederic Gershom-Parkington in memory of a son killed in the Second World War. *Moyses Hall* (63233), 12th-century house now a museum containing local antiquities. *Guildhall*, 13th century, extended in the 19th century. *Athenaeum*, 18th century, with a fine Adam ballroom

Coggeshall (Bb) *Paycocke's* (61305), 16th-century merchant's house with rich panelling and wood carving. *Abbey*, 12th-century ruins

Colchester (Db) *Castle*, 11th century, on the site of a Roman temple; the keep, which is now a museum, is the largest in Europe. *St John's Abbey*, 15th-century Benedictine ruins. *St Botolph's Priory*, 11th-century Augustinian ruins. *Bourne Mill* (72422), 16th-century fishing lodge converted to a mill in the 17th century. The adjoining 16th-century mill house was rebuilt after being severely damaged by an earthquake in 1884. *Minories Art Gallery* (77067)

East Bergholt (Dc) Birthplace of John Constable in 1776. *Flatford*, 1 mile south, is the subject of many of his paintings, including 'Flatford Mill' and 'The Haywain'; the landscape has changed little since Constable's day

Ickworth (Bf) A large 18th-century round house (Horringer 270), containing a fine collection of paintings, silver and furniture

Ipswich (Ed) *Christchurch Mansion* (53246), 16th century, altered in the 17th and 18th centuries, on the site of a 12th-century Augustinian

priory, now contains a fine collection of furniture, paintings and ceramics from Tudor to Victorian times. *Unitarian Meeting House*, 17th century, with a fine pulpit and brass chandelier. *Museum* (213761), archaeology, geology and natural history

Kentwell Hall (Bd) Moated house built in 1564 (Long Melford 207)

Kersey (Cd) Picturesque village with a watersplash (shallow part of a stream which may be crossed) running through the centre. *Priory*, 12th-century Augustinian ruins

Lavenham (Cd) *Church of SS Peter and Paul*, 15th-century Perpendicular with a 14th-century chancel screen. *Guildhall* (646), 16th century

Layer Breton (Ca) *Layer Marney Tower* (Colchester 330202), 1½ miles to the south-west, is a 16th-century gate-house with an eight-storey tower. *Church of St Mary*, 16th century, with Renaissance monuments

Lindsey (Cd) *St James's Chapel*, 13th century, built of flint and stone

Little Glemham (Ge) *Glemham Hall* (Wickham Market 746219), Elizabethan house altered in the 18th century, with a fine staircase and Queen Anne furniture

Melford Hall (Bd) 16th-century mansion (Long Melford 384) with fine collection of Chinese porcelain, pictures and furniture

Orford Castle (He) 12th-century ruins

Sudbury (Bd) *Gainsborough's House* (72958), Tudor with Georgian front, birthplace of Thomas Gainsborough in 1727, now an art centre. *Church of St Peter*, 15th century, with fine painted screens. *Church of St Gregory*, rebuilt in the 14th century on an ancient foundation by Archbishop Simon of Sudbury, the Archbishop of Canterbury murdered in the Peasants' Revolt of 1381; his skull is preserved in the vestry

Thetford see p. 195

AA PORT SERVICE CENTRE: Car Ferry Terminal, Parkeston Quay, Harwich (Harwich 3331)

A town plan of IPSWICH is on p. 102

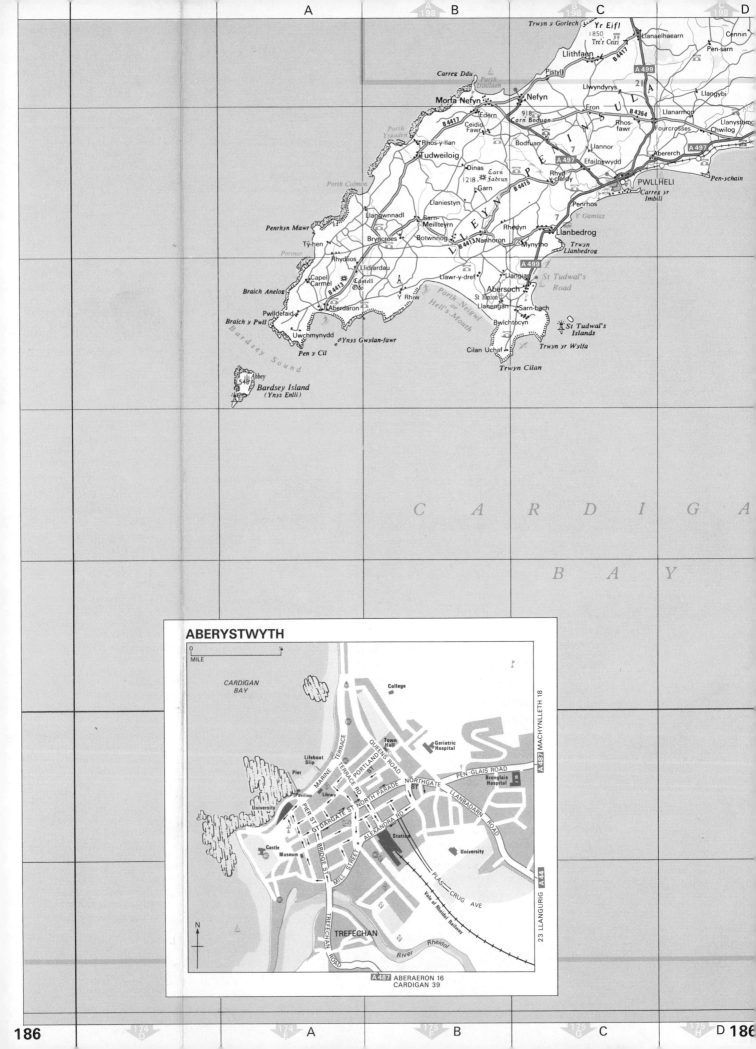

Trwyn y Gorlech   Yr Eifl
1850
Tre'r Ceiri
Llithfaen   Llanaelhaearn
Pistyll   Cennin
B 4417   Pen-sarn
A 499
Carreg Ddu
Porth
Dinllaen   Llwyndyrys   21
Morfa Nefyn   Nefyn   Llangybi
Edern   Fron   B 4354   Llanarmon
B 4417   918   Rhos- Llanystumdwy
Ceidio   Carn Boduan   fawr   Fourcrosses   Chwilog
Fawr   Bodfuan   A 497
Rhos-y-llan   Abererch
Tudweiloig   Llannor   Aberech
Dinas   Efailnewydd   Pen-ychain
1218   Carn   Rhyd-
Sadrun   y-clafdy   PWLLHELI
Garn   B 4415
Llaniestyn   Carreg yr
Penrhos   Imbill
Sarn-   7   Y Gamlas
Penrhyn Mawr   Llangwnnadl   Meilltyrn   Rhedyn
Bryncroes   Botwnnog   Nanhoron   Llanbedrog
Tŷ-hen   B 4413   Mynytho   Trwyn
Portmor   Llanbedrog
Rhydlios   A 499
Lldiardau   Llawr-y-dref   Llangian   St Tudwal's
Capel   Castell   Road
Carmel   Odo   Abersoch
Braich Anelog   B 4413   Y Rhiw   St Tudwal's
Pwlldefaid   Llanengan   Islands
Braich y Pwll   Aberdaron   Porth   Sarn-bach
Neigwl   Bwlchtocyn
Uwchmynydd   or   St Tudwal's
Pen y Cil   Hell's   Islands
Ynys Gwylan-fawr   Mouth   Cilan Uchaf   Trwyn yr Wylfa
Trwyn Cilan
Bardsey Sound
Abbey
548   Bardsey Island
(Ynys Enlli)

C A R D I G A

B A Y

ABERYSTWYTH

0   ½
MILE

CARDIGAN
BAY

College

A 487 MACHYNLLETH 18

Geriatric
Hospital
Lifeboat
Slip   Town
Hall
Pier   Pen-glais road
Pavilion   Bronglais
Library   Northgate   Hospital
University   St
Gt Darkgate St   North Parade   Llanbadarn road
Alexandra rd
Castle   Station
Museum   Mill Street   University
Bridge St   Plas   Crug Ave
A 44
Vale of Rheidol Railway
23 LLANGURIG
N
TREFECHAN   Trefechan road
River   Rheidol

A 487 ABERAERON 16
CARDIGAN 39

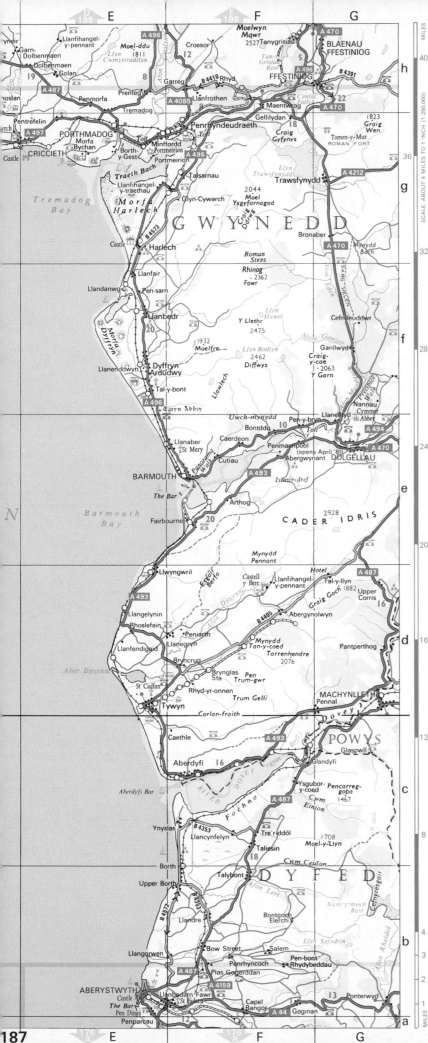

PLACES TO SEE AROUND
CARDIGAN BAY

Opening times should be confirmed by telephone from the number in brackets. The exchange is given only if it differs from the place name at the beginning of the entry
Map references are shown after each place name

Aberystwyth see p. 177

Bardsey Island (Af) *Abbey of St Mary*, remains of a 6th-century abbey founded by St Cadfan. Monks came to Bardsey to refound their Christian community after being expelled from Chester in the 7th century. The community became so large that it is said that '20,000 saints' are buried on the island

Blaenau Ffestiniog see p. 199

Castell y Bere (Fd) Ruins of a 13th-century castle built by Llewelyn the Great as a defence against the English

Criccieth (Eg) *Castle*, 13th-century ruins. A bronze crucifix and sculptured stones excavated on the site are in the National Museum of Wales, Cardiff

Cymmer Abbey (Ge), remains of a 12th-century Cistercian abbey

Ffestiniog (Gh) *Cynfal Falls*, beauty spot; Hugh Lloyd's Pulpit is a column of rock rising from the stream, where a magician in the time of James I is said to have summoned spirits

Dolgellau (Ge) *Bridge*, 17th century. *Precipice Walk*, a nature trail above the Mawddach estuary: the way is marked by red signs, but visitors follow the walk at their own risk

Garn-Dolbenmaen (Dh) *Bryncir Woollen Mills* (236), open 8 a.m. to 5 p.m. Monday to Friday

Glandyfi (Fc) *Cymerau* (230), garden with flowering shrubs, unusual bushes and panoramic views

Harlech Castle (Eg) 13th century, built by Edward I on the site of a Celtic fortress: in 1401 Owen Glendower, the hero of Welsh nationalism, captured the castle, but it fell to Henry of Monmouth, later Henry V, in 1409. It was the last castle to hold out for Charles I in the Civil War

Llanaber (Fe) *Church of St Mary*, 13th century, with Gothic doorway; the most notable example of early English architecture in North Wales. Has a large collection of early Christian monuments

Llanbadarn Fawr (Fb) *Church of St Padarn*, 12th century, on the site of a 6th-century church which was founded by St Padarn and destroyed by the Danes; contains fine Celtic crosses

Llanbedr (Ef) Beauty spot surrounded by hills which are scattered with various standing stones and antiquities. The 16th-century church at Llanddwywe, about 3½ miles south, has an Inigo Jones chapel attached to it, and a circular churchyard which is an early Christian successor to Bronze Age stone circle monuments

Llandanwg (Ef) The 15th-century church contains inscribed stones, probably dating from the 6th century

Llanengan (Bf) *Church of St Einion*, 6th century, with a fine carved screen and sacred vessels from the Abbey of St Mary on Bardsey Island

Machynlleth (Ge) *Pen-yr-Allt*, an Iron Age encampment

Penrhyndeudraeth (Fg) *Beddgelert Pottery*, Cae Ddafydd (Penryn 851); here pomanders are filled with a centuries-old secret recipe

Portmeirion (Eg) Italianate village with campanile, castle and lighthouse, built by the architect Clough Williams-Ellis between the two World Wars. The wild gardens, full of exotic plants, including cypresses and eucalyptus trees, are among the finest in Wales

Rhinog Fawr (Ff) Beauty spot with fine views; the lake, called Du (Black), is said to have been formed, and to be maintained, by dew

Tomen-y-Mur (Gg) Roman fort

Tre'r Ceiri (Ch) Iron Age hut circles; the 5 acre settlement contains huts varying from cell-like structures to circular ones 16 ft across

Tywyn (Ed) *Church of St Cadfan*, Norman, restored in the 19th century, contains the 7th-century Stone of Cadfan, the oldest known monument inscribed in the Welsh language

AA BREAKDOWN SERVICE: Aberystwyth 4801, 9 a.m. to 5 p.m.

A town plan of ABERYSTWYTH is on p. 186

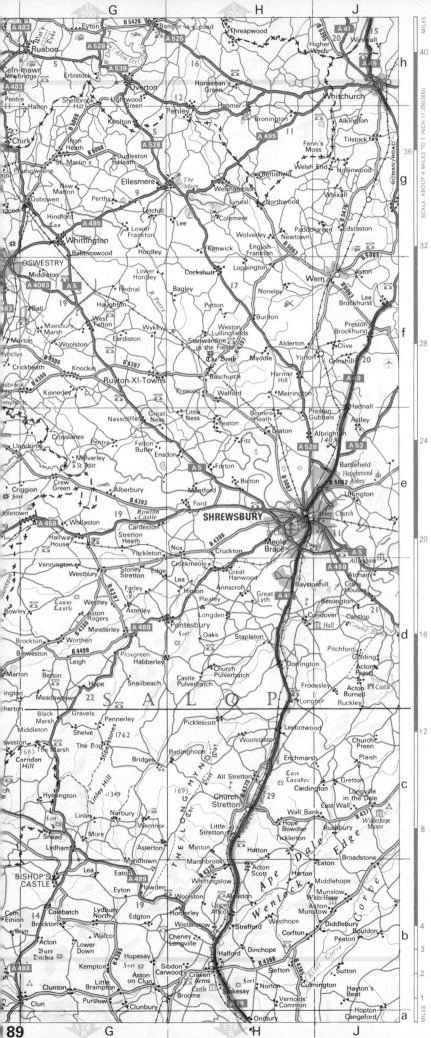

THE WELSH MARCHES

Opening times should be confirmed by telephone from the number in brackets. The exchange is given only if it differs from the place name at the beginning of the entry
Map references are shown after each place name

Acton Burnell (Jd) *Castle*, ruins of a 13th-century fortified manor house on the site of an earlier building

Attingham (Jd) 18th-century mansion (Upton Magna 203), with plasterwork, pictures and fine furniture

Condover Hall (Hd) 16th-century house (Bayston Hill 2320), with fine oak panelling, now a school for the blind with limited access by the public

Haughmond Abbey (Je) The remains of the 12th-century Augustinian abbey include the kitchen, a 14th-century infirmary and a 16th-century abbot's lodging

Llangollen (Fh) Home of the International Music Eisteddfod since 1947. *Bridge,* 12th century with four pointed arches, extended in the 14th century by John Trevor, Bishop of St Asaph, is one of the traditional seven wonders of Wales. *Plas Newydd,* timber-framed home of the 'Ladies of Llangollen', Lady Eleanor Butler and the Honourable Sarah Ponsonby, two 18th-century Irish eccentrics noted for their wit and hospitality. *Castell Dinas Bran,* remains of an 8th-century castle. *Eliseg's Pillar,* a stone monument commemorating a battle fought in AD 603 by Eliseg, a Celtic prince of Powis, against the invading Saxons,

erected in the 9th century by Eliseg's great-grandson

Shrewsbury (He) *Church of St Mary,* Norman to 15th century, with fine stained glass and stone spire. *Abbey Church of the Holy Cross,* 11th century. *Clive House* (54811), 18th-century home of Clive of India, now a museum. *Rowley's House Museum* (54811), 16th-century timbered house containing relics from the Roman site of Viroconium, 5 miles south-east of Shrewsbury.

Stokesay Castle (Hb) 13th-century moated and fortified manor house with an Elizabethan gatehouse. Perfectly preserved, it is one of the finest in Britain

Valle Crucis Abbey (Fh) 13th-century Cistercian; the extensive remains include parts of the church and the 14th-century chapter house and cloister

Welshpool (Fd) *Powis Castle* (2554), 13th century with 16th to 17th-century additions, containing fine plasterwork, murals and tapestries. In the gardens is a 181 ft Douglas fir, which is believed to be the tallest tree in Britain. *Powysland Museum* contains an Iron Age shield

Wilderhope Manor (Jc) 16th-century limestone house (Longville 363) with 17th-century plaster ceilings

AA BREAKDOWN SERVICES: Shrewsbury 53003, 24 hours; Newtown 26103, 9 a.m. to 5 p.m.

ROAD CONDITIONS: Birmingham (021 246 8021)

SHREWSBURY

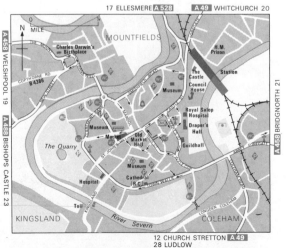

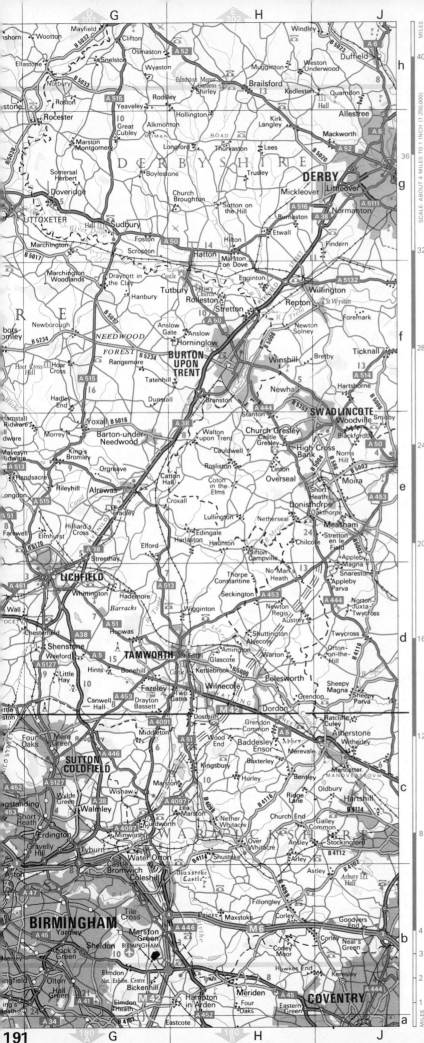

WEST MIDLANDS

Opening times should be confirmed by telephone from the number in brackets. The exchange is given only if it differs from the place name at the beginning of the entry
Map references are shown after each place name

Benthall Hall (Bd) 16th-century stone house (Telford 882659), with fine oak staircase and plaster ceilings

Birmingham (Fb) *Aston Hall* (327 0062), 17th-century Jacobean mansion with fine plasterwork, marble chimney pieces and a panelled long gallery; contains period furniture and paintings. *City Museum and Art Gallery* (235 2834). *Blakesley Hall* (783 2193), 16th-century timber-framed house containing a museum. *Sarehole Mill* (777 6612), restored 18th-century water-powered corn mill. *Barber Institute of Fine Arts* collections of mineralogy (472 0962). *Avery Historical Museum* (558 1112). *Cannon Hill Nature Centre* (472 7775), mainly for children, has a branch museum of natural history. *Geological Sciences Museum* (472 1301)

Blithfield Hall (Ff) Part-Elizabethan house (Dapple Heath 249), with fine carved oak staircase and panelling, containing toy and costume museums

Boscobel (Dd) 17th-century house (Wolverhampton 850244), where Charles II took refuge after the Battle of Worcester in 1651

Chillington Hall (Dd) Georgian House (Brewood 850236), with gardens landscaped by Capability Brown

Hoar Cross (Gf) *Hoar Cross Hall* (224), Elizabethan-style mansion with fine plasterwork, containing one of the largest collections of European and Eastern arms and armour in private ownership, paintings and 17th to 19th-century furniture, and an oak-panelled private chapel

Little Haywood (Ff) *Shugborough* (881388), 17th-century white colonnaded mansion, enlarged in the 18th century, containing fine paintings and furniture

Moseley Old Hall (Ed) Elizabethan house (Wolverhampton 782808) where Charles II sheltered after the Battle of Worcester in 1651, contains his bed, 'hide', and relics relating to his flight; there is a fine collection of period furniture and a 17th-century style garden

Sandon (Ef) *Church of All Saints*, 14th century, with 17th-century wall-paintings which were rediscovered in 1929

Shipton Hall (Ac) Elizabethan manor house (Brockton 225), with stone-walled garden and medieval dovecote

Tamworth (Hd) *Castle* (3561), Norman keep and tower with Tudor and Jacobean additions, containing a museum. *Town Hall* (3561), 18th-century red brick with Jacobean windows. *Church of St Editha*, 14th century with a double spiral staircase in the tower

Weston Park (De) 17th-century mansion (Weston-under-Lizard 207), one of the finest examples of the Restoration period, containing a fine collection of paintings, tapestries and furniture, with gardens and parklands designed by Capability Brown

Wolverhampton (Ec) *Wightwick Manor* (764663), 19th-century Jacobean-style house with fine tapestries, paintings and stained glass. *Church of St Peter,* mainly 15th century, with octagonal font and stone pulpit

Woore (Ch) *Elds Wood*, 3 miles south-east at Willoughbridge, is a disused gravel quarry converted into a woodland garden

AA SERVICE CENTRES: Fanum House, 134 New Street, Birmingham, including 24-hour breakdown service (021 550 4858); 32–38 Stafford Street, Hanley, Stoke-on-Trent, including 24-hour breakdown service (Stoke-on-Trent 25881). Breakdown service, Standeford 790211, 9 a.m. to 5 p.m.

ROAD CONDITIONS: Birmingham (021 246 8021)

A town plan of central BIRMINGHAM is on p. 80; of COVENTRY on p. 81; of WOLVERHAMPTON on p. 80; of DERBY on p. 105. A plan of routes out of BIRMINGHAM and WOLVERHAMPTON is on p. 78

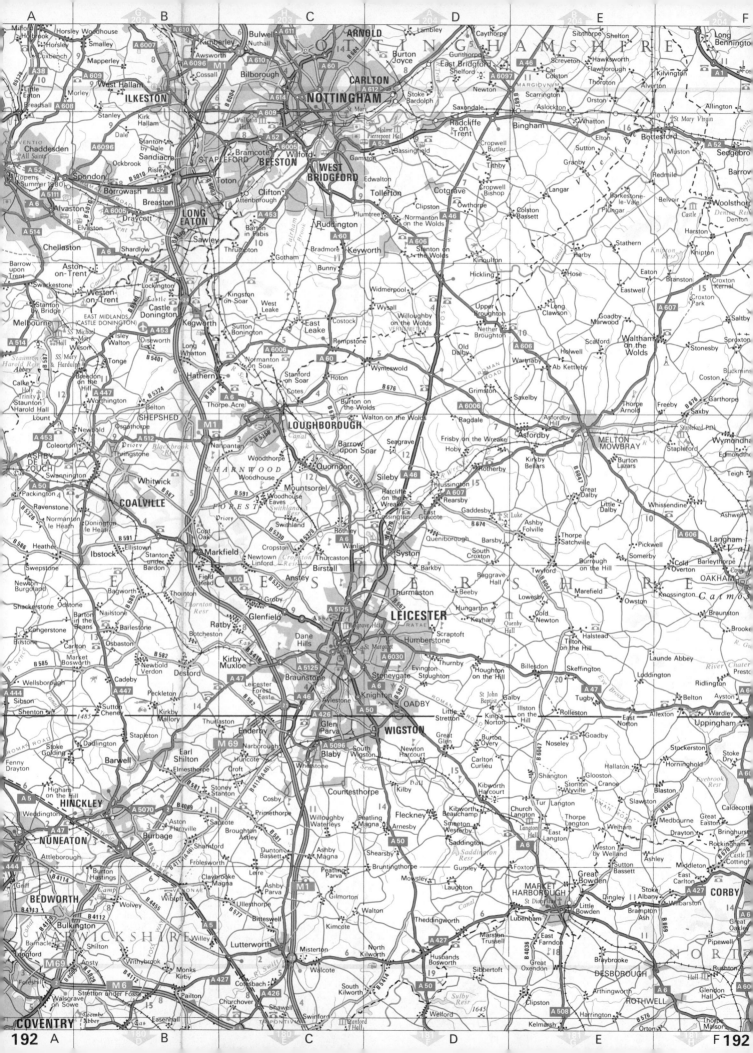

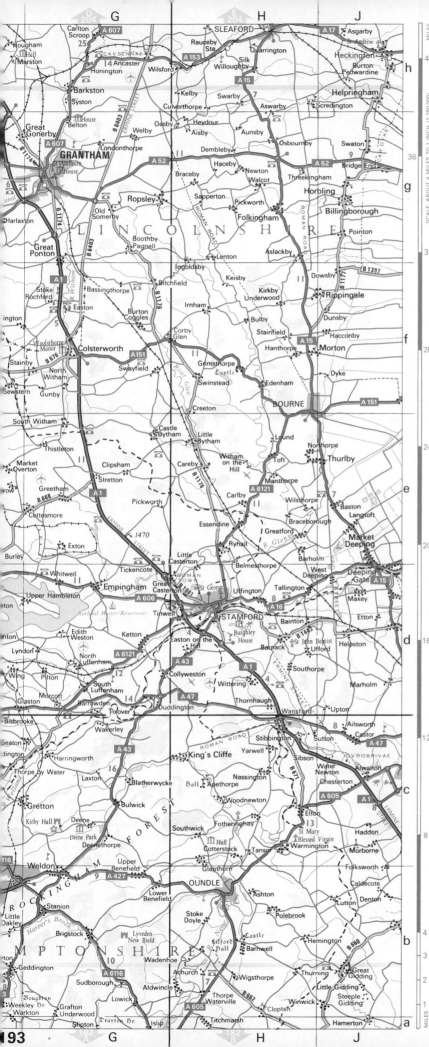

EAST MIDLANDS

*Opening times should be confirmed by telephone from the number
in brackets. The exchange is given only if it differs from the
place name at the beginning of the entry
Map references are shown after each place name*

Belton House (Gg) 17th-century mansion (Grantham 66116), attributed to Christopher Wren, with a fine cedarwood chapel and carvings by Grinling Gibbons, the 17th-century wood carver and sculptor. It is owned by Lord Brownlow, whose father was Lord in Waiting to King Edward VIII, and relics include the only known portrait of the Duke of Windsor as king, painted by Frank Salisbury

Belvoir Castle (Fg) 19th-century home of the Duke of Rutland (Knipton 262), containing fine paintings, furniture, objets d'art and a museum of the 17th/21st Lancers

Burghley House (Hd) Elizabethan home of the Marquess of Exeter (Stamford 52451), with painted ceilings and silver fireplaces, containing fine pictures, furniture and tapestries

Deene Park (Gc) 16th-century house (Bulwick 223), was the home of the Earl of Cardigan, who led the Charge of the Light Brigade in 1854

Grantham (Gg) *Grantham House*, late 14th century with extensive 18th-century alterations (4705). *Church of St Wulfram*, 14th and 15th century, with a beautiful 281 ft spire, six Norman pillars from a church originally on the site, and a 16th-century chained library

Leicester (Dd) *Jewry Wall*, built about AD 125–30, remains of Ratae Coritanorum, the Roman settlement on the site of which Leicester is built. *Church of St Margaret*, 13th to 15th century, with fine Perpendicular tower and chancel. *Belgrave Hall* (666590), a Queen Anne house with 18th and 19th-century furniture. *Museum and Art Gallery* (554100). *Newarke Houses Museum* (554100) contains period costumes, a Victorian street scene, clocks and the history

of the hosiery industry. *Guildhall* (554100), 14th to 15th century, with cells and gibbet irons

Lyveden New Bield (Gb) 17th century, unfinished Renaissance house, built by Sir Thomas Tresham, the 17th-century eccentric in the shape of a cross, with an exterior frieze depicting relics of the Passion. Tresham died before completing the house, which now belongs to the National Trust

Market Harborough (Eb) *Church of St Dionysius*, 13th to 15th century, with fine window tracery. *Grammar School*, 17th-century timber building on wooden pillars

Marston (Fh) *Marston Hall* (Honington 225), 16th-century manor house with fine pictures and furniture; the ancient garden contains a Gothic-style gazebo, a summer house from which to view the scenery

Stamford (Hd) *Church of St George*, 15th century, built by Sir William Bruges, first Garter King of Arms

Stanford Hall (Ca) 17th-century William and Mary house (Swinford 250), with collections of paintings, furniture and costumes, and a museum containing antique kitchen utensils, vintage cars and motor-cycles and a replica of the 1898 flying machine of Percy Pilcher, the pioneer aviator who was killed at Stanford in 1899

Stapleford Park (Fe) 16th-century mansion (Wymondham, Leics. 245), restored and extended in the 17th century, has collections of Staffordshire pottery figures, paintings, tapestries and furniture; the grounds contain a small zoo and a miniature railway

Woolsthorpe Manor (Gf) Birthplace of Sir Isaac Newton in 1642, where he is said to have seen the apple fall from the tree and conceived his theory of gravitation (Grantham 860338)

AA SERVICE CENTRES: 132 Charles Street, Leicester (Leicester 20491); Fanum House, 484 Derby Road, Nottingham (Nottingham 787751). Both have 24-hour breakdown services.

ROAD CONDITIONS: Birmingham (021 246 8021); Sheffield 8021; Manchester (061 246 8021)

A town plan of LEICESTER is on p. 104; of DERBY on p. 105; of NOTTINGHAM on p. 108

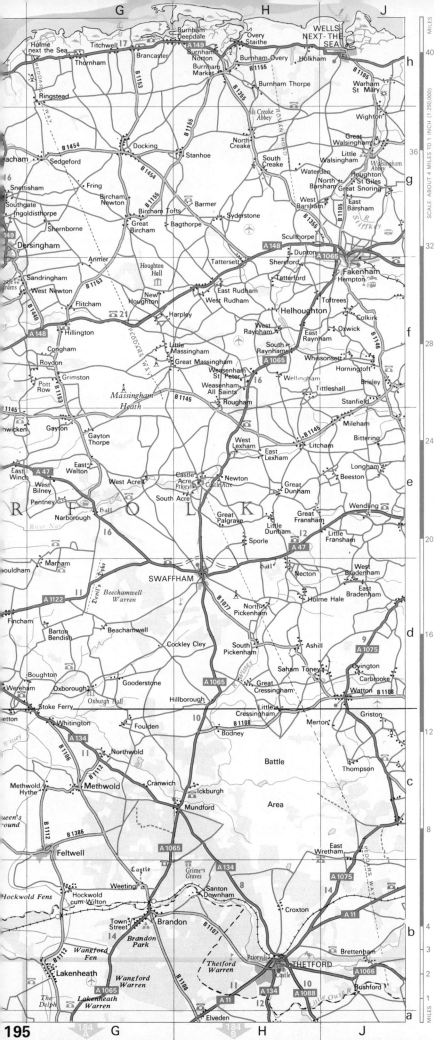

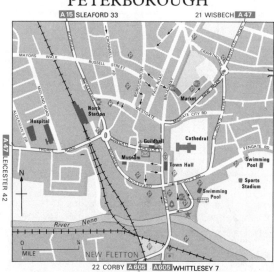

PLACES TO SEE AROUND
THE WASH

Opening times should be confirmed by telephone from the number in brackets. The exchange is given only if it differs from the place name at the beginning of the entry

Map references are shown after each place name

Boston (Ch) *Church of St Botolph*, 14th century, with fine carvings and painted roof, is one of the grandest parish churches in England. *Guildhall* (65954), 15th century, now a museum

Castle Acre (He) *Priory*, 12th-century Cluniac house; the remains include the prior's lodging and chapel, and a 15th-century gatehouse. *Castle*, 13th-century remains and earthworks

Ely see p. 183

Grime's Graves (Hb) Neolithic flint mines. Excavations in 1870 revealed picks made from antlers of red deer and shovels made from the shoulder-blades. Visitors are advised to wear old clothes and to carry a torch

March (Dc) *Church of St Wendreda*, 15th century; the double hammerbeam roof has about 200 angels carved in oak, their wings open in flight instead of being folded back as in most angel roofs

Oxborough (Gd) *Oxburgh Hall* (Gooderstone 258), 15th-century moated house with an 80 ft high gate-tower flanked by octagonal turrets, rising sheer from the moat

Peterborough (Bc) *Cathedral*, one of the finest and least altered of Norman churches, on the site of a 7th-century Benedictine monastery sacked by the Danes in the 9th century; the wooden roof of the nave is richly decorated with fine 13th-century paintings. *Museum and Art Gallery* (43329)

Sandringham (Ff) *Castle* (King's Lynn 2675), 19th-century country residence of the Queen, built by Edward VII. Some rooms, and the grounds, are open to the public only when the Royal Family is not in residence

Spalding (Bf) *Church of SS Mary and Nicholas*, 13th century with double aisles, restored in the 19th century. *Ayscoughfee Hall* (5468), 15th century, containing a collection of British birds

Thetford (Hb) *Priory*, 12th-century Cluniac remains. *Ancient House Museum* (2599), 15th-century timbered house. *Kilverstone Wildlife Park* (5369), with more than 50 acres of parkland

Walsingham (Jg) *Abbey*, 13th and 14th-century Augustinian ruins. The Shrine of Our Lady of Walsingham, built in 1931 on the site of an 11th-century chapel, is the centre of many pilgrimages. The original chapel was built about 1061 by Lady Richeld, the lady of the manor, as the result of a vision. This chapel was destroyed by Henry VIII after his long dispute with the Pope

AA SERVICE CENTRES: Janus House, 46–48 St Andrew's Street, Cambridge (Cambridge 312302); Fanum House, 126 Thorpe Road, Norwich (Norwich 29401). Both have 24-hour breakdown services. Breakdown services: King's Lynn 3731, 24 hours; Boston 63905, 9 a.m. to 5 p.m.

PETERBOROUGH

GREAT YARMOUTH

33 CROMER A149

NEWTOWN
SALISBURY ROAD

N 0   ¼
|____|____|
MILE

BEACONSFIELD ROAD

RIVER BURE

LAWN AVENUE

NORTHGATE STREET

Northgate Hospital

Estcourt Hospital

NORTH DRIVE

North Beach

NELSON ROAD NORTH

B1118

MARINE PARADE N.

North-West Tower

RUNHAM VAUXHALL

ACLE ROAD

A47 NORWICH 20

Vauxhall Station

St Nicholas

Town Wall

A149

HALL QUAY

A149

MARKET PLACE

REGENT ROAD

B1143

Britannia Pier

COBHOLM ISLAND

REGENT RD

St George's Park

NELSON ROAD CENTRAL

TRAFALGAR RD.

Town Hall Museum

St. George's Park

MARINE PARADE

The Beach

YARMOUTH WAY

General Hospital

Maritime Museum

Old Merchant's House

SOUTH QUAY

KING STREET

ST PETER'S ROAD

South-East Tower
Blackfriars Tower

NELSON RD SOUTH

The Jetty

SOUTHTOWN ROAD

RIVER YARE

QUEEN'S ROAD

B1143

KING'S RD.

Wellington Pier

College

SOUTHTOWN

SOUTHGATES ROAD

B1141

MARINE PARADE SOUTH

South Beach

Southtown Common

MAIN CROSS RD.

BECCLES RD HIGH

ROAD

Nelson's Monument

20 BUNGAY A143 A12 LOWESTOFT 9
56 BURY ST EDMUND'S

(left coastal map labels)

Winterton-on-Sea
Hemsby Hole
Newport
Hemsby
Scratby
St Margaret
California
A1064
Mautby
Caister-on-Sea
West Caister
Holy Trinity
West End
A149
YARMOUTH WATER
Old Merchant's Ho.
GREAT YARMOUTH
Burgh Castle
BRANNODVNVM
Bradwell
A143
Belton
Gorleston on Sea
A12
Gorleston Links Halt
Hobland Hall
Hopton
YARMOUTH ROADS
Lound
Blundeston
Somerleyton Hall
Corton
10
A12
Fritton
Somerleyton
Lowestoft End
B1074
Oulton
A1117 A1144
Oulton Broad
LOWESTOFT
Kirkley
A1117
46
B1121
Pakefield
Carlton Colville
Mutford
Gisleham
Rushmere
Kessingland
Henstead
13
Benacre
A12
Wrentham
B1127
Covehithe
South Cove
Scheveningen

PLACES TO SEE IN
NORFOLK

Opening times should be confirmed by telephone from the number in brackets. The exchange is given only if it differs from the place name at the beginning of the entry
Map references are shown after each place name

Blickling (Cf) *Blickling Hall* (Aylsham 3471), 17th-century house, altered in the 18th century, containing fine furniture, pictures and tapestries; in the Peter the Great Room is a tapestry woven in St Petersburg in 1764, representing Peter the Great at the Battle of Poltawa, and given by the Empress Catherine to the Earl of Buckinghamshire, then owner of the house and ambassador to Russia from 1762 to 1765; it is said that Anne Boleyn was born and spent her childhood in an earlier house on the site. *Church of St Andrew*, part Early English, restored in the 19th century by William Butterfield and George Edmund Street, the Gothic Revival architects. Contains an octagonal font, monuments and brasses

Bressingham (Bb) *Bressingham Hall* (386), a steam-engine museum which includes the famous Britannia Class locomotive Pacific No. 70013, 'Oliver Cromwell'; among other exhibits is a roundabout with a steam organ. A miniature railway takes visitors through the extensive gardens

Caister-on-Sea (Ge) 15th-century ruins surrounded by a moat. *Church of the Holy Trinity*, 13th century with a large font, 5 ft high and 3½ ft across

Cromer (Dh) *Zoo* (512947). *Church of SS Peter and Paul*, Perpendicular with a 160 ft high tower

East Dereham (Ae) *Church of St Nicholas*, partly Norman with a detached 16th-century bell tower, on the site of a 7th-century nunnery founded by St Withburga; in the churchyard are St Withburga's Well and the grave of William Cowper, the 18th-century poet

Great Yarmouth (Gd) *Old Merchant's House* (4313), 17th-century house now a museum containing a collection of 17th to 19th-century domestic ironwork. *The Tollhouse*, local history museum. *Art Gallery and Maritime Museum* (2267)

Lowestoft (Gc) *East Anglia Transport Museum* (683398)

Norfolk Broads see p. 336

Norwich (Dd) *Cathedral*, Norman with 15th-century spire. *Castle* (22233), restored 12th-century keep, now a museum and art gallery. *Strangers' Hall* (22233), museum of urban domestic life in the 16th to 19th centuries. *Bridewell Museum of Local Industries and Rural Crafts* (22233). *Church of St Peter Hungate* (22233), 15th century, now a museum of church art. *Church of St Peter Mancroft*, 15th century with hammerbeam roof. *Guildhall* (22233), 15th century

Somerleyton Hall (Fc) 16th-century house, extended in 1844, with Grinling Gibbons carving, pictures and tapestries; the large garden contains a maze

AA SERVICE CENTRE: Fanum House, 126 Thorpe Road, Norwich, including 24-hour breakdown service (Norwich 29401)

LOWESTOFT

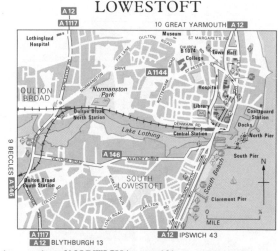

A12
A1117

10 GREAT YARMOUTH A12

Museum
ST MARGARETS RD

Lothingland Hospital

OULTON

FIR LANE

B1074

CHURCH ROAD

Town Hall

College
ST PETER'S

A1144

Hospital

OULTON BROAD

Normanston Park

Normanston Drive

Oulton Broad North Station

Library

DENMARK RD

Central Station

Coastguard Station

North Pier

Lake Lothing

Docks

VICTORIA ROAD

A146

WAVENEY DRIVE

South Pier

Oulton Broad South Station

9 BECCLES

A146

SOUTH LOWESTOFT

South Beach

Claremont Pier

N 0   ¼
MILE

A1117
A12 BLYTHBURGH 13   A12 IPSWICH 43

A town plan of NORWICH is on p. 101

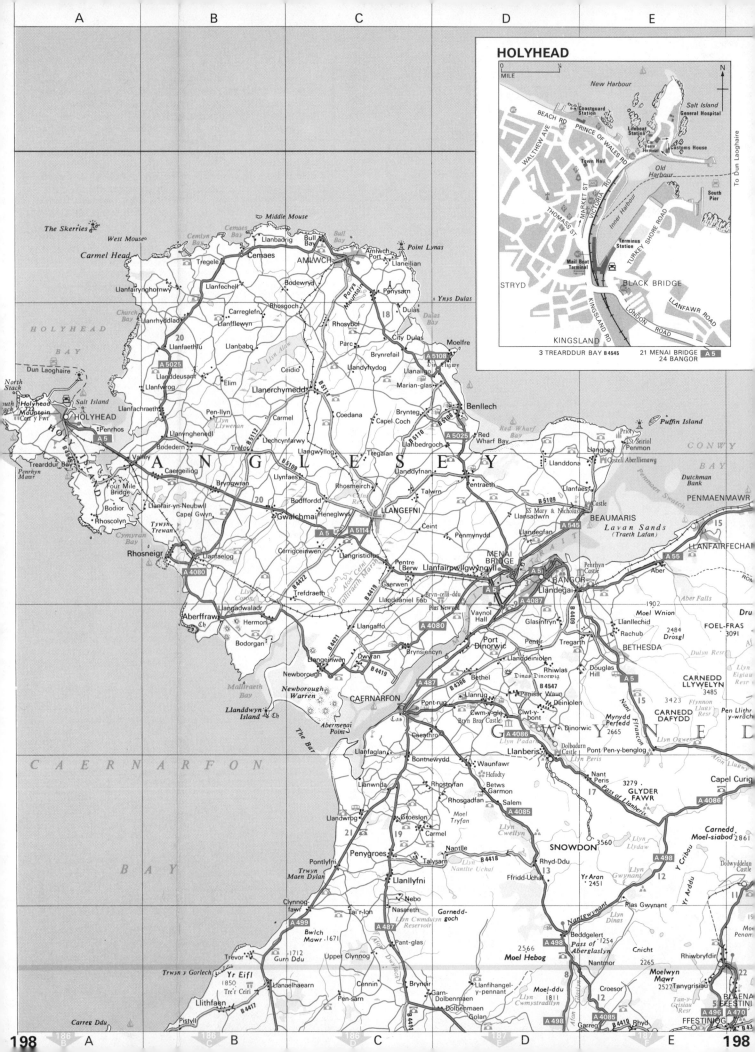

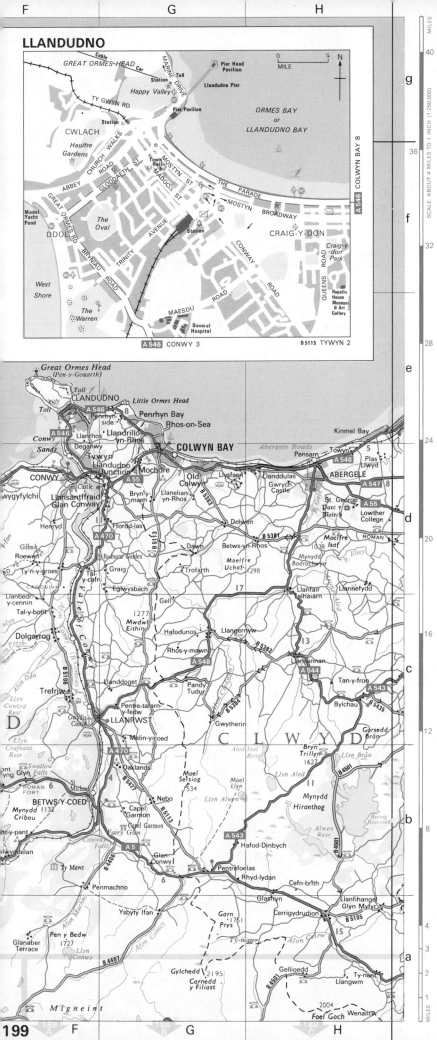

LLANDUDNO

F   G   H

Opening times should be confirmed by telephone from the number in brackets. The exchange is given only if it differs from the place name at the beginning of the entry
Map references are shown after each place name

Bangor (Dd) *Bishop's Garden* contains an example of every flower, shrub and tree mentioned in the Bible that can exist in this climate

Beaumaris (Ed) *Castle*, 13th-century ruins surrounded by a moat. *Church of SS Mary and Nicholas*, 14th-century church with fine choir stalls, contains the stone coffin of Princess Joan, daughter of King John and wife of Llewelyn the Great. *Bull's Head*, 17th-century coaching inn with a large collection of antiques and china. *Tudor Rose*, 15th-century timbered house, with an antique gallery. *Court House*, 17th century. *The Old Jail*, erected in 1829, contains a wooden treadmill

Betws-Y-Coed (Fb) Beauty spot. *Pont-y-Pair*, 15th-century five-arched bridge. *Church of St Michael Archangel*, 14th or 15th-century church now used only for weddings and funerals

Blaenau Ffestiniog (Ea) *Llechwedd Slate Mines*, include a mock 19th-century workface; visitors descend in battery-operated rail cars

Bodnant Garden (Fd) 90 acres of gardens, which are among the finest in Britain, slope down to the River Conwy. They were laid out in 1874 and are renowned for their conifers and rhododendrons (Tynygroes 460)

Bryn-celli-ddu (Dd) Bronze Age burial chamber, excavated in 1865 and 1925–9

Caernarfon Castle (Cc) 13th century (Caernarfon 3094): Prince Charles was invested here as Prince of Wales in 1969

Conwy (Fd) *Castle*, 13th-century ruins (2358). *Plas Mawr* (3413), Elizabethan house, now headquarters of the Royal Cambrian Academy of Art

Holyhead Mountain (Ae) A 720-ft high mass of rock; from the top are fine views of Ireland, Cumberland and the Isle of Man. *Caer y Fwr*, a hill fort, probably Roman. *Hut circles*, 2nd to 4th-century village with round and rectangular huts

Llanfairpwllgwyngyll (Dd) Known locally as Llanfair P.G., this is a shortened version of the longest place-name in Britain, Llanfairpwllgwyngyll-gogerychwyrndrobwll-llantysiliogogogoch, which means 'St Mary's Church in the hollow of the white hazel near a rapid whirlpool and the church of St Tysilio near the red cave': the unabridged name may be seen above two shops and a garage in the village; the nameplate of the railway station is in Penrhyn Castle museum. *Anglesey Column*, monument to the Marquis of Anglesey, the Duke of Wellington's aide, who was wounded at the Battle of Waterloo in 1815; a spiral staircase leads to a platform from which there are fine views of Anglesey and Snowdonia. *Llanfair Gate*, a toll house

Llanrug (Dc) *Bryn Bras Castle* (Llanberis 210), Victorian, with grounds containing woodland and mountain walks, lakes

Llanrwst (Fc) *Gwydir Castle* (640261), Tudor mansion with period furniture; the grounds contain peacocks and tropical birds

Menai Bridge (Dd) Suspension bridge 1000 ft long and 28 ft wide, designed by Thomas Telford, the Scottish engineer, and opened in 1826; from the bridge are fine views of the Menai Strait

Penmon (Ee) *Priory*, 13th to 16th-century Augustinian ruins. *Church of St Seiriol*, 12th-century church, rebuilt in the 15th and 19th centuries; the carved font is the base of an 11th-century cross. *St Seiriol's Well* is believed to have been used by the 6th-century saint for baptising converts. *Cross*, in Deer Park, is 11th century and has Celtic and Scandinavian motifs. *Dovecote*, 17th century. *Castell Aberllienawg*, 11th-century castle ruins

Penrhyn Castle (Ed) 19th century, contains a museum that has collections of dolls and locomotives

Snowdonia National Park see p. 342

AA BREAKDOWN SERVICES: Abergele 824649, 8 a.m. to 11 p.m.; Caernarfon 3935, 9 a.m. to 5 p.m.

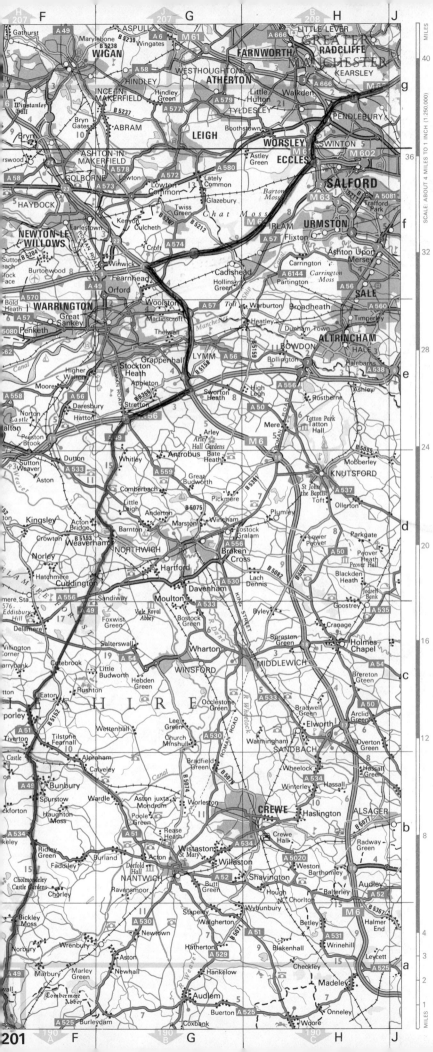

PLACES TO SEE ON
MERSEYSIDE

Opening times should be confirmed by telephone from the number in brackets. The exchange is given only if it differs from the place name at the beginning of the entry
Map references are shown after each place name

Beeston (Fb) *Castle*, 13th-century ruins

Chester (Ec) Remains of Deva, the Roman legionary headquarters founded by Agricola *c.* AD 79, include an amphitheatre and town walls. *Castle*, 13th-century remains containing a military museum. *Grosvenor Museum* (21616), contains antiquities from Deva and a gallery illustrating the Roman army. *Cathedral*, part-11th century, restored in the 19th century, contains beautifully carved 14th-century choir stalls. *Zoo and botanical gardens* (20106). *The Rows*, 13th-century galleried shops in Eastgate, Bridge and Watergate streets. *Leche House*, 16th-century timber building with 17th-century additions. *Bishop Lloyd's House*, 17th-century carved timber house with fine plasterwork and fireplaces and a secret door and stairway

Gresford (Db) *Church of All Saints*, 15th-century Perpendicular; its peal of bells is one of the traditional seven wonders of Wales

Knutsford (Hd) The 'Cranford' of Mrs Gaskell's novel of that name. *Church of St John the Baptist*, 18th-century church where Mrs Gaskell was married

Liverpool (De) *Cathedral of Christ the King*, Roman Catholic cathedral consecrated in 1967; the concrete dome is topped by a stained-glass crown with 16 pinnacles surmounted by ornaments and crosses. *Cathedral Church of Christ*, the Anglican cathedral was begun in 1904 and completed in 1978. *Royal Liver Building*, 20th century; the two main towers are topped by liver birds, the mythical birds from which the city took its name. *Speke Hall* (427 7231), Elizabethan half-timbered house. *Walker Art Gallery* (227 5234). *Sudley Art Gallery and Museum* (724 3245). *Hornby Library* (207 2147) has a permanent exhibition of prints and manuscripts. *Merseyside County Museum* (207 0001). *Bluecoat Chambers* (709 5297), Queen Anne building, now an art centre. *St George's Hall* (709 3752), Victorian Classical-Greek building

Nantwich (Gb) *Churche's Mansion* (65933), Elizabethan merchant's house with oak panelling. *Dorfold Hall* (65245), Jacobean house with panelled rooms and plaster ceilings. *Church of St Mary*, part-14th-century with canopied choir stalls

Northwich (Gd) *Arley Hall Gardens* (Arley 353) contain an avenue of clipped ilex trees and a 16th-century barn converted into a tea-room

Peover Heath (Hd) *Peover Hall* (Lower Peover 2404), Elizabethan gabled house surrounded by a moat. *Church of St Lawrence*, 19th-century church with important earlier side chapels

Ruthin (Bb) *Castle*, 13th-century ruins surrounded by a moat; it was here that Owen Glendower, the Welsh nationalist leader, began his uprising with an attack on the castle in 1400. *Church of St Peter*, 14th century

Tatton Park (He) Georgian house (Knutsford 3155) with fine furniture, pictures, silver, china and glass, and a museum containing sporting trophies and curiosities; in the 50 acre gardens are an orangery and a Shinto temple

Wrexham (Db) *Church of St Giles*, 15th century; the 140 ft ornamental steeple is one of the traditional seven wonders of Wales. *Erddig* (55314), late 17th century, contains much original furniture and a fine collection of porcelain

AA SERVICE CENTRES: Derby Square, Liverpool, including 24-hour breakdown service (051 709 7252); Mercia Square, Frodsham Street, Chester (Chester 20438). Breakdown services: Chester 20438, 7 a.m. to 11 p.m.; St Helens 34189, 9 a.m. to 5 p.m.

ROAD CONDITIONS: Liverpool (051 246 8021)

A town plan of CHESTER is on p. 100; of CENTRAL LIVERPOOL on p. 86. A plan of routes out of LIVERPOOL is on p. 88

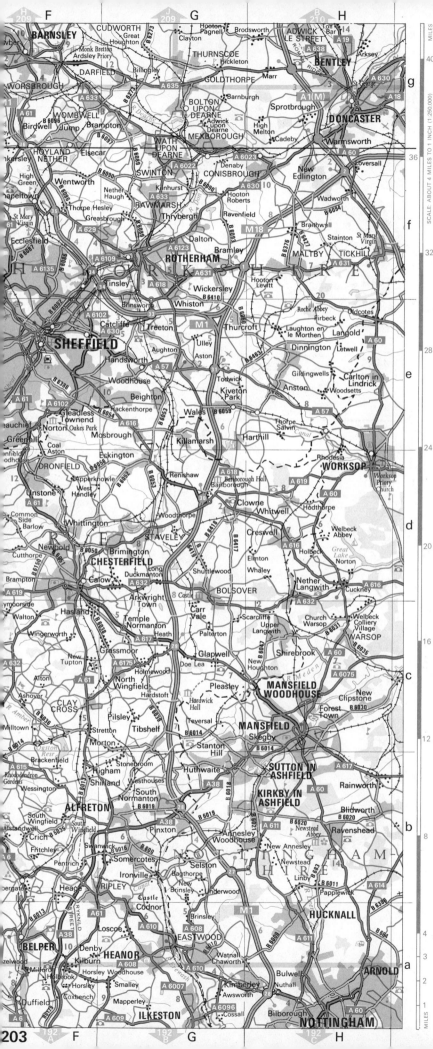

PLACES TO SEE IN
THE PEAK DISTRICT

Opening times should be confirmed by telephone from the number in brackets. The exchange is given only if it differs from the place name at the beginning of the entry
Map references are shown after each place name

Adlington Hall (Be) 15th-century Great Hall (Prestbury 829206) with Elizabethan and Georgian extensions

Bramall Hall (Ae) 15th to 16th-century house with Victorian alterations (061 485 3708), has portraits and tapestries

Capesthorne (Ad) 18th-century house (Chelford 221), attributed to John Wood of Bath, contains pictures, furniture and Americana

Chadderton (Ag) *Foxdenton Hall* (061 624 4886), 18th-century manor house, recently restored

Chatsworth (Ed) 17th-century mansion (Baslow 2204), seat of the Duke of Devonshire and one of the great stately homes; it has fine collections of pictures, books and furniture

Crich (Fb) *Tramway Museum* (Ambergate 2565), 19th and 20th-century trams housed in a disused quarry

Gawsworth (Ac) *Gawsworth Hall* (North Rode 456), 16th-century half-timbered manor house

Haddon Hall (Ec) Part-12th-century greystone house (Bakewell 2855), with battlemented towers and turrets; it is one of the most complete and authentic medieval manors in England and contains tapestries, panelling and carving

Hardwick Hall (Gc) 16th-century house (Chesterfield 850430), one of the finest examples of Elizabethan domestic architecture, contains furniture, tapestries and pictures

Little Moreton Hall (Ab) 16th-century half-timbered house (Congleton 2018) with carved gables and fine plasterwork; a fine example of Elizabethan black-and-white style

Lyme Hall (Be) Elizabethan mansion (Disley 2023) with Palladian exterior, containing period furniture, tapestries and Grinling Gibbons carvings

Manchester (Af) *Cathedral*, mainly 15th century with a 19th-century tower *Town Hall* (236 3377), 19th-century Gothic style with a 280 ft high tower containing a carillon of 23 bells. *Central Library*, rotunda style with a portico of Corinthian columns. *John Rylands Library*, contains early manuscripts and books, and the St Christopher woodcut of 1423, the earliest dated Western print. *Cheetham's Library*, founded in 1653, was the first free public library in Europe. *City Art Gallery* (236 9422). *Heaton Hall* (773 1231), 18th-century house rebuilt in the 19th century, with a fine collection of period furniture, paintings and glass. *Platt Hall* (224 5217), Georgian mansion with fine plasterwork and an overmantle painted by Richard Wilson, now houses the Gallery of English Costume. *Wythenshawe Hall* (998 2331), 16th-century manor house extended in the 17th to 19th centuries, with 17th-century paintings and furniture. *Fletcher Moss Art Gallery* (445 1109), Georgian house containing English watercolours. *Queens Park Art Gallery* (205 2121). *University Museum* (273 3333). *Manchester Ship Canal*, 36 miles long, was opened in 1894 to link the City's textile industry with the sea

Peak District National Park see p. 346

Sheffield (Fe) *Cathedral*, 15th-century Perpendicular cathedral with decorated spire. *Museum* (27226). *Abbeydale Industrial Hamlet* (367731), an 18th-century scythe works. *Shepherd Wheel* (307704), a water-powered grinding shop. *Graves Art Gallery* (734781). *Mappin Art Gallery* (26281)

AA SERVICE CENTRES: St Ann's House, St Ann's Place, Manchester (061 485 6299); Fanum House, Station Road, Cheadle Hulme (061 485 6299); 2 Fargate, Sheffield (Sheffield 28861); 32-38 Stafford Street, Hanley, Stoke-on-Trent 25881). Breakdown services—all 24-hour: 061 485 6299 (Manchester); Sheffield 28861; Stoke-on-Trent 25881

ROAD CONDITIONS: Manchester (061 246 8021)

A town plan of CENTRAL MANCHESTER is on p. 81; of SHEFFIELD on p. 108; of STOKE on p. 104. A plan of routes out of MANCHESTER is on p. 82

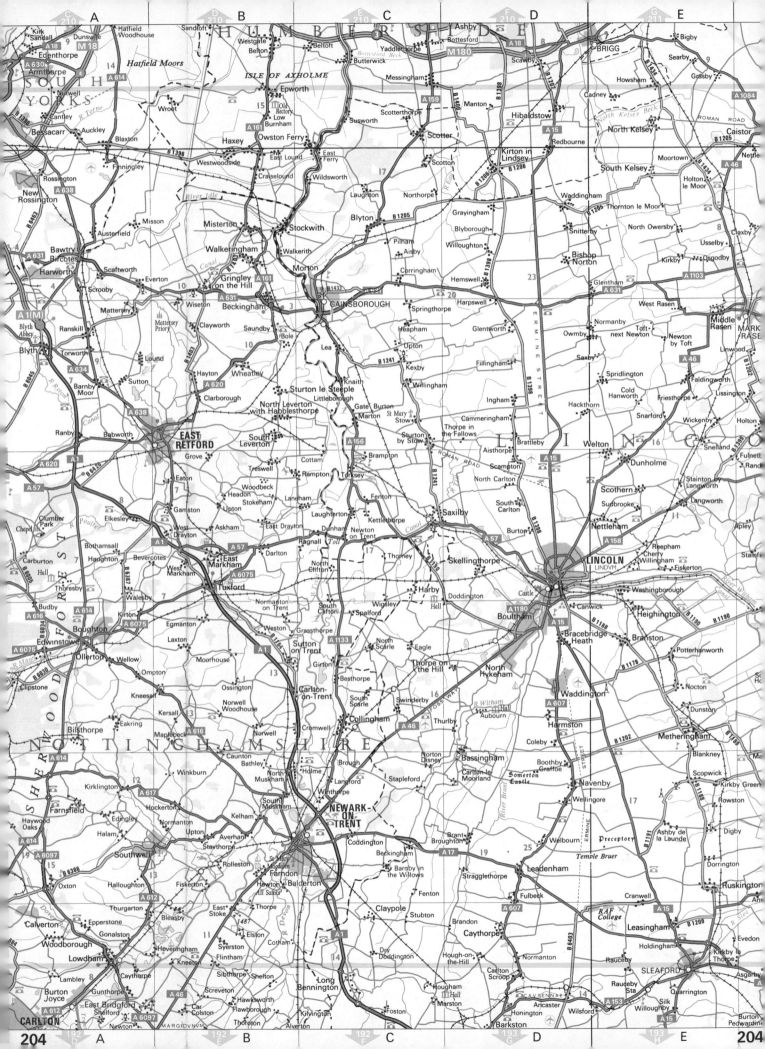

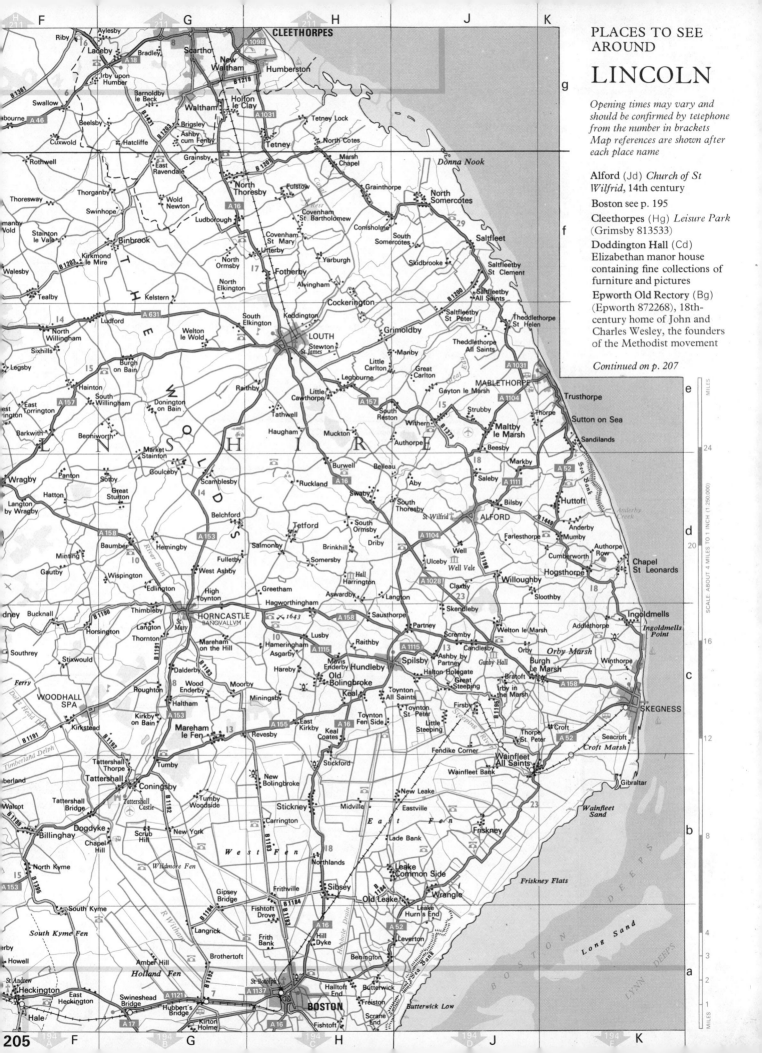

PLACES TO SEE AROUND

LINCOLN

Opening times may vary and should be confirmed by telephone from the number in brackets. Map references are shown after each place name

Alford (Jd) *Church of St Wilfrid*, 14th century

Boston see p. 195

Cleethorpes (Hg) *Leisure Park* (Grimsby 813533)

Doddington Hall (Cd) Elizabethan manor house containing fine collections of furniture and pictures

Epworth Old Rectory (Bg) (Epworth 872268), 18th-century home of John and Charles Wesley, the founders of the Methodist movement

Continued on p. 207

Continued on p. 207

SCALE ABOUT 4 MILES TO 1 INCH (1 250 000)

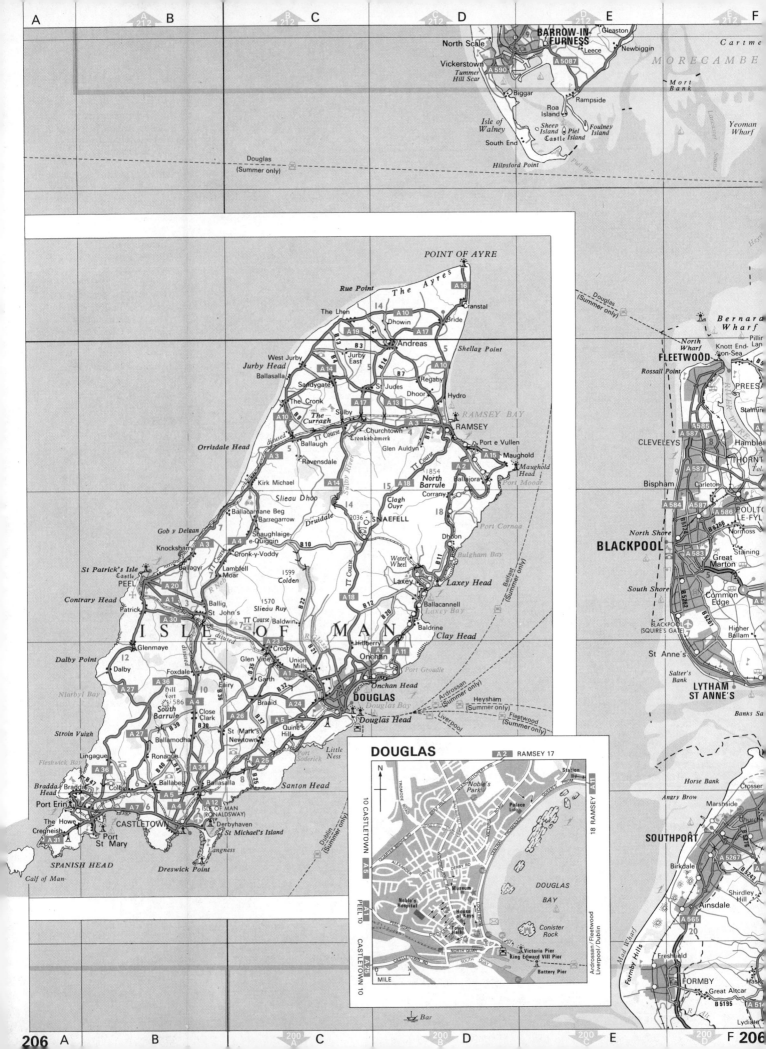

BARROW-IN-FURNESS
North Scale
Gleaston
Leece
Newbiggin
Vickerstown
Tummer Hill Scar
A 590
A 5087
MORECAMBE
Mort Bank
Biggar
Rampside
Isle of Walney
Roa Island
Sheep Island
Piel Castle
Piel Island
Foulney Island
Yeoman Wharf
South End
Hilpsford Point
Piel Bar
Lancaster Sound

Douglas (Summer only)

POINT OF AYRE
The Ayres
Rue Point
A 16
The Lhen
14
Cranstal
A 10
Dhowin
Bride
A 19
B 2
Andreas
A 17
Shellag Point
5
West Jurby
Jurby East
B 3
B 14
B 7
A 10
Jurby Head
A 14
St Judes
Dhoor
Hydro
Ballasalla
Sandygate
Regaby
RAMSEY BAY
The Cronk
A 17
A 13
Solby
A 3
RAMSEY
A 10
The Curragh
disused
Churchtown
Port e Vullen
Orrisdale Head
A 3
5
Ballaugh
Cronksbamerk
Glen Auldyn
B 15
A 15
Maughold
Ravensdale
TT Course
A 2
Maughold Head
Kirk Michael
A 14
1854
Ballajora
Port Mooar
North Barrule
Slieau Dhoo
Clagh Ouyr
Corrany
Druidale
14
15
A 18
18
Ballacarnane Beg
2036
SNAEFELL
Port Cornaa
Barregarrow
Gob y Deigan
7
Dhoon
Shaughlaige-e-Quiggin
B 10
Knocksharry
A 3
A 4
Cronk-y-Voddy
B 11
Bulgham Bay
St Patrick's Isle
Ballagyr
Lambfell Moar
1599
Water Wheel
PEEL
A 20
Colden
Laxey
Laxey Head
A 1
TT Course
Ballacannell
Contrary Head
3
Ballig
1570
B 22
Laxey Bay
Patrick
A 30
St John's
Slieau Ruy
B 12
Baldrine
TT Course
Baldwin
B 20
Clay Head
ISLE OF MAN
A 18
Glenmaye
disused
A 23
Crosby
B 21
Hillberry
A 11
Dalby Point
12
Glen Vine
Union Mills
Onchan
Dalby
Foxdale
Garth
Port Groudle
Narbyl Bay
A 36
hill fort
586
Eairy
A 32
South Barrule
10
Braaid
A 24
Onchan Head
Stroin Vuigh
A 27
Close Clark
A 5
Quine's Hill
DOUGLAS
Fleshwick Bay
B 39
B 30
St Mark's
B 37
Douglas Bay
Lingague
Ballamodha
Newtown
Douglas Head
A 36
Ronague
A 34
A 25
Little Ness
Ardrossan (Summer only)
B 47
Colby
Ballabeg
Ballasalla
B 25
Santon Head
Heysham (Summer only)
Bradda Head
6
8
Fleetwood (Summer only)
Port Erin
A 7
6
A 4
ISLE OF MAN (RONALDSWAY)
Liverpool
The Howe
A 12
Derbyhaven
Cregneish
CASTLETOWN
St Michael's Island
A 31
Port St Mary
Langness
SPANISH HEAD
Dreswick Point
Calf of Man

Dublin (Summer only)

Bernard Wharf
Pillir
North Wharf
FLEETWOOD
PREESA
Knott End-on-Sea
Rossall Point
CLEVELEYS
A 587
A 585
Hamble
THORNT
Bispham
A 587
Carleton
A 584
A 587
A 586
POULTON-LE-FYL
North Shore
A 512
B 5266
Normoss
BLACKPOOL
A 583
Staining
Great Marton
South Shore
B 5262
Common Edge
St Anne's
BLACKPOOL (SQUIRE'S GATE)
7
Higher Ballam
Salter's Bank
LYTHAM ST ANNE'S
Banks Sa
Horse Bank
Angry Brow
Marshside
SOUTHPORT
Birkdale
A 5267
Shirdley Hill
Church
Ainsdale
A 565
FORMBY
Freshfield
20
Formby Hills
Great Altcar
B 5195
Lydiate

DOUGLAS
A 2 RAMSEY 17
N
10 CASTLETOWN
Station
A 11 18 RAMSEY
Noble's Park
Palace Lido
A 5
PEEL 10
Museum
A 1
Noble's Hospital
House of Keys
DOUGLAS BAY
Town Hall
CASTLETOWN 10
A 25
Conister Rock
NORTH QUAY
Victoria Pier
King Edward VIII Pier
Battery Pier
Ardrossan/Fleetwood Liverpool/Dublin
MILE

Bar

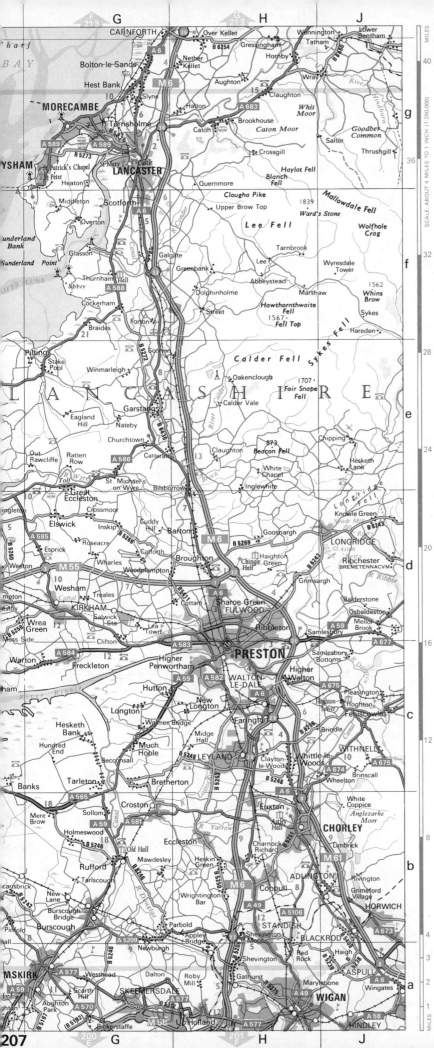

PRESTON AND IN THE ISLE OF MAN

Opening times should be confirmed by telephone from the number in brackets. The exchange is given only if it differs from the place name at the beginning of the entry

Map references are shown after each place name

Astley Hall (Hb) Elizabethan house (Chorley 2166) containing furniture, pottery, tapestries and pictures

Barrow-in-Furness see p. 213

Blackpool (Fd) *Tower* (25252), focal point of autumn illuminations, has a zoo, aquarium and circus hall. *Grundy Art Gallery* (23977)

Calf of Man (Ab) Bird sanctuary containing many species of sea birds. Boats run daily (weather permitting) from Port Erin and Port St Mary

Castletown (Bb) *Nautical Museum* (Douglas 5522) contains what is probably the country's oldest schooner-rigged yacht, the 'Peggy', built in 1791

Cregneish (Ab) *Manx Village Folk Museum* (Douglas 5522)

Douglas (Cc) *Manx Museum* (5522) includes Manx archaeology, folk life and natural history collections; the art gallery contains Manx works of art. *Nobles Park* contains the Manx Cattery, breeding place of the tail-less

Manx cat, a few of which are available for sale

Heysham (Gg) *Church of St Peter*, part-10th-century church with 14th to 17th-century additions, contains a carved gravestone dating probably from the 7th century; in the churchyard is the carved shaft of a 10th-century cross. *St Patrick's Chapel*, believed to be 5th-century Celtic ruins; west of this is a row of six coffins carved out of solid rock

Lancaster (Gg) *Castle*, 12th and 15th-century ruins, partly restored in the 18th and 19th centuries, and now used as a court house and prison. *Priory Church of St Mary*, 15th-century Perpendicular on the site of a Saxon church; the 13th-century carved choir stalls are among the finest in Britain. *Museum* (64637)

Laxey (Dd) *Lady Isabella*, the world's largest water-wheel, $72\frac{1}{2}$ ft across, is capable of raising 250 gallons of water more than 1000 ft in a minute. It was built in 1854 to keep a lead mine free from flooding

AA PORT SERVICE CENTRE: 12b Walpole Avenue, Douglas, Isle of Man (Douglas 5826)

AA BREAKDOWN SERVICES: Blackpool 44947 (24 hours); Southport 36431; Barrow-in-Furness 20665; Carnforth 2036. All 9 a.m. to 5 p.m.

A town plan of BLACKPOOL is on p. 101

LINCOLN (continued from p. 205)

Gainsborough (Ce) *Old Hall* (2669), 15th and 16th-century manor house on the site of an earlier house wrecked by the Lancastrians during the Wars of the Roses. It contains furniture, paintings, period dresses and the original medieval kitchen

Gibraltar (Kb) Nature reserve and bird-watching centre

Horncastle (Gc) Site of the Roman fort of Banovallum. *Church of St Mary*, 13th century, contains relics of the Civil War Battle of Winceby which was fought near by in 1643 (Hc)

Lincoln (Dd) *Cathedral*, 12th century, extended in the 14th century, with triple towers. *Castle*, 12th-century ruins. *Museum* (30401). *Museum of Lincolnshire Life* (28448). *Usher Gallery* (27980), contains antique watches, porcelain and paintings. *Cathedral Library* (21089)

Louth (He) *Church of St James*, 16th century

Theddlethorpe St Helen (Je) National Nature Reserve which includes a specially protected area for the comparatively rare natterjack toad

AA BREAKDOWN SERVICES: Lincoln 22873; Boston 63905; both 9 a.m. to 5 p.m.

A town plan of LINCOLN is on p. 105

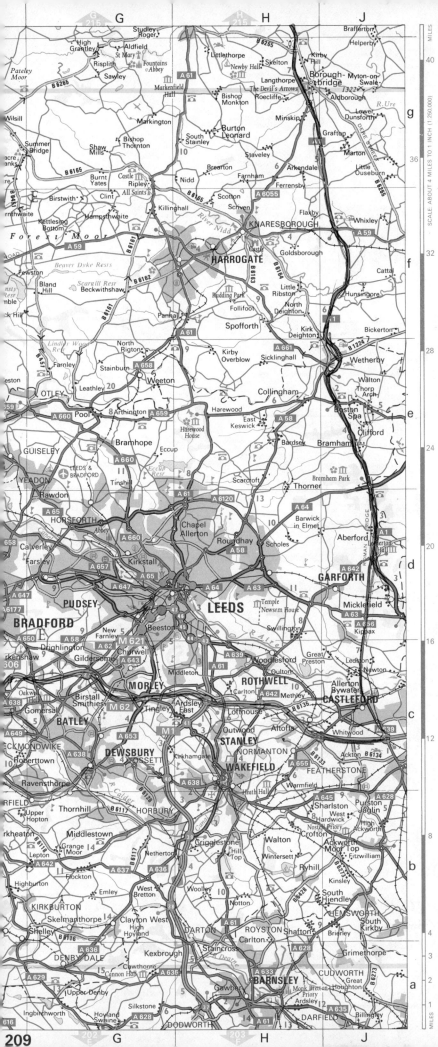

PLACES TO SEE AROUND
THE PENNINES

Opening times should be confirmed by telephone from the number in brackets. The exchange is given only if it differs from the place name at the beginning of the entry
Map references are shown after each place name

Bolton (Ba) *Hall-i'-th'-Wood* (51159), 15th-century half-timbered house, extended in the 16th and 17th centuries and now a folk museum. *Smithills Hall* (41265), 14th and 16th-century timbered house containing Stuart furniture. *Museum and Art Gallery* (22311). *Textile Machinery Museum* (22311) containing inventions which revolutionised the cotton industry, including Crompton's mule, Hargreaves's jenny and Arkwright's water-frame

Bradford (Fd) *Bolling Hall* (23057), 15th to 18th-century house with fine plaster ceilings and heraldic stained glass. *Cathedral*, 15th to 16th-century Perpendicular. *Cartwright Hall* (493313), art gallery and museum. *Industrial Museum* (631756)

Fountains Abbey (Gg) 12th-century Cistercian remains with ornamental gardens laid out in the 18th century

Halifax (Ec) *Shibden Hall* (52246), 15th-century, houses the Folk Museum of West Yorkshire. *Bankfield Museum and Art Gallery* (54823) contains textile machinery, textiles and costumes. *Town Hall*, designed by Sir Charles Barry, the 19th-century architect who designed the Houses of Parliament

Harrogate (Hf) *Harlow Car Gardens*, a 60 acre centre for experimental gardening. *Art Gallery* (502744). *Royal Pump Room Museum* (503340), contains a sulphur well

Harewood House (He) 18th-century Robert Adam house (Harewood 886225), home of the Earl of Harewood, contains fine furniture, china, silver and paintings; the grounds contain one of the best wildlife sanctuaries in the North of England

Haworth (Ed) *Brontë Parsonage Museum* (42323), Georgian home of the Brontë family, is now a

museum containing many relics of the family. *Haworth Station* (43629), museum with extensive collection of standard-gauge locomotives

Knaresborough (Hf) *Castle*, 14th-century ruins. *Mother Shipton's Cave* is where the prophetess was said to have been born in 1488

Leeds (Gd) *Kirkstall Abbey*, 12th-century Cistercian remains; the gatehouse (755821) is now a folk museum. *Museum* (462465). *Town Hall*, Victorian with a columned clock tower more than 200 ft high

Newby Hall (Hg) One of the most famous Adam houses in England (Boroughbridge 2583), containing tapestries and a fine collection of classical statuary

Ripley (Gg) *Castle* (Harrogate 770186), 14th century with 15th-century gatehouse and 16th-century tower, containing fine furniture, paintings, armour and a secret hiding place. *Church of All Saints*, 14th century; in the churchyard is the base of a 2nd-century weeping cross, where penitents used to pray

Ripon see p. 215

Temple Newsam House (Hd) Tudor and Jacobean house (Leeds 647321) containing fine furniture, silver and paintings

Towneley Hall (Cd) 14th-century fortified house (Burnley 24213), altered in the 16th to 19th centuries, containing Tudor and Jacobean furniture, paintings and ceramics; a folk museum is in the grounds

Wakefield (Hc) *Nostell Priory* (863892), 18th-century house with Robert Adam wing, contains important pictures and Chippendale furniture. *Art Gallery* and *Museum* (both 70211)

AA SERVICE CENTRE: 95 The Headrow, Leeds, including 24-hour breakdown service (Leeds 38161). Breakdown services: Bradford 24703, Wakefield 77957, both 24 hours; Blackburn 51369, Harrogate 69545, Huddersfield 20039, Dewsbury 468216, Halifax 57810, all 9 a.m. to 5 p.m.

ROAD CONDITIONS: Leeds 8021

A town plan of BOLTON is on p. 106; of BRADFORD and LEEDS on p. 109; of HALIFAX on p. 110; and of HUDDERSFIELD on p. 111

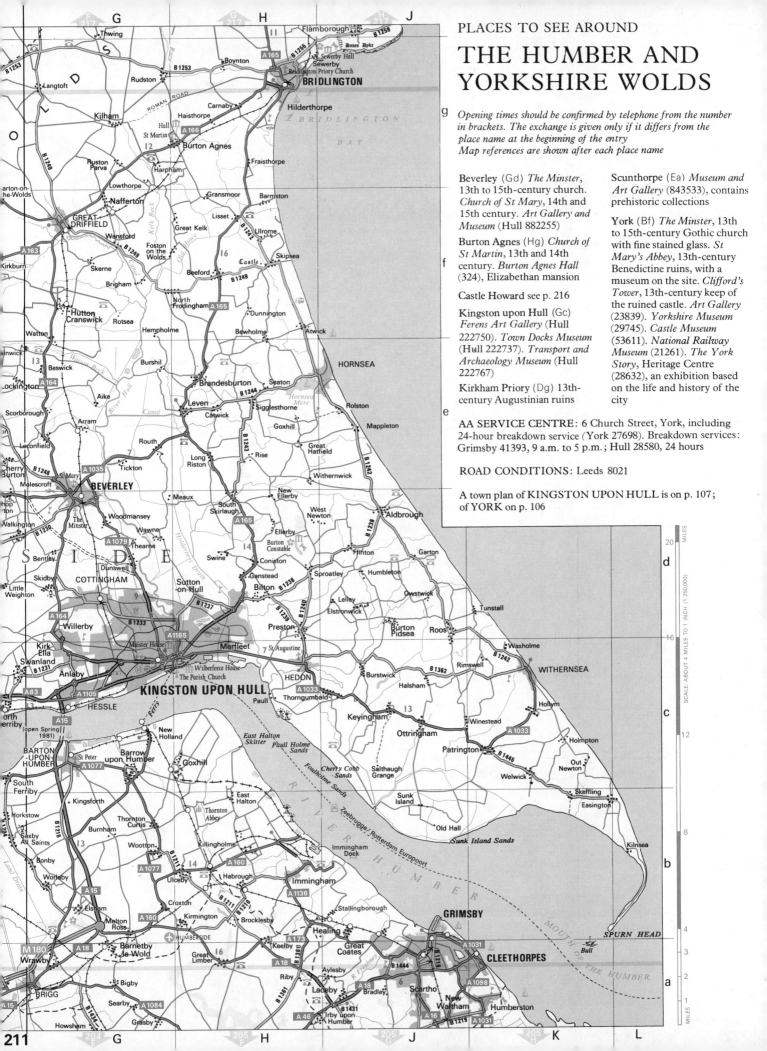

Opening times should be confirmed by telephone from the number in brackets. The exchange is given only if it differs from the place name at the beginning of the entry
Map references are shown after each place name

Beverley (Gd) *The Minster*, 13th to 15th-century church. *Church of St Mary*, 14th and 15th century. *Art Gallery and Museum* (Hull 882255)

Burton Agnes (Hg) *Church of St Martin*, 13th and 14th century. *Burton Agnes Hall* (324), Elizabethan mansion

Castle Howard see p. 216

Kingston upon Hull (Gc) *Ferens Art Gallery* (Hull 222750). *Town Docks Museum* (Hull 222737). *Transport and Archaeology Museum* (Hull 222767)

Kirkham Priory (Dg) 13th-century Augustinian ruins

Scunthorpe (Ea) *Museum and Art Gallery* (843533), contains prehistoric collections

York (Bf) *The Minster*, 13th to 15th-century Gothic church with fine stained glass. *St Mary's Abbey*, 13th-century Benedictine ruins, with a museum on the site. *Clifford's Tower*, 13th-century keep of the ruined castle. *Art Gallery* (23839). *Yorkshire Museum* (29745). *Castle Museum* (53611). *National Railway Museum* (21261). *The York Story*, Heritage Centre (28632), an exhibition based on the life and history of the city

AA SERVICE CENTRE: 6 Church Street, York, including 24-hour breakdown service (York 27698). Breakdown services: Grimsby 41393, 9 a.m. to 5 p.m.; Hull 28580, 24 hours

ROAD CONDITIONS: Leeds 8021

A town plan of KINGSTON UPON HULL is on p. 107; of YORK on p. 106

SCALE ABOUT 4 MILES TO 1 INCH (1:250,000)

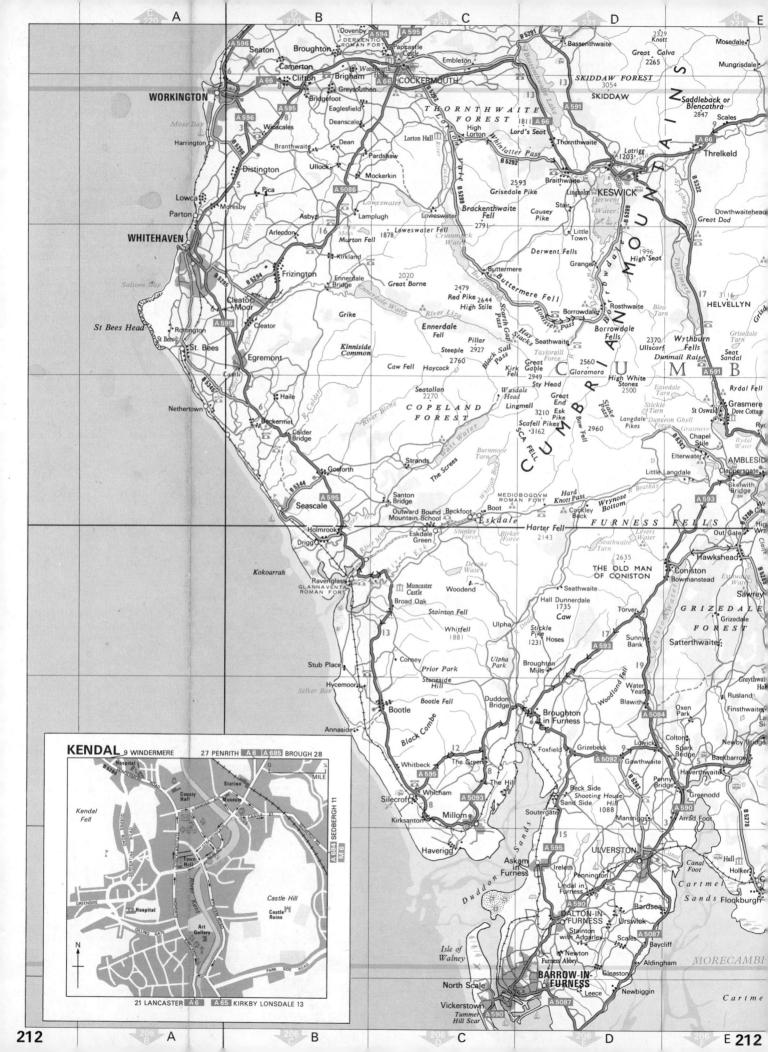

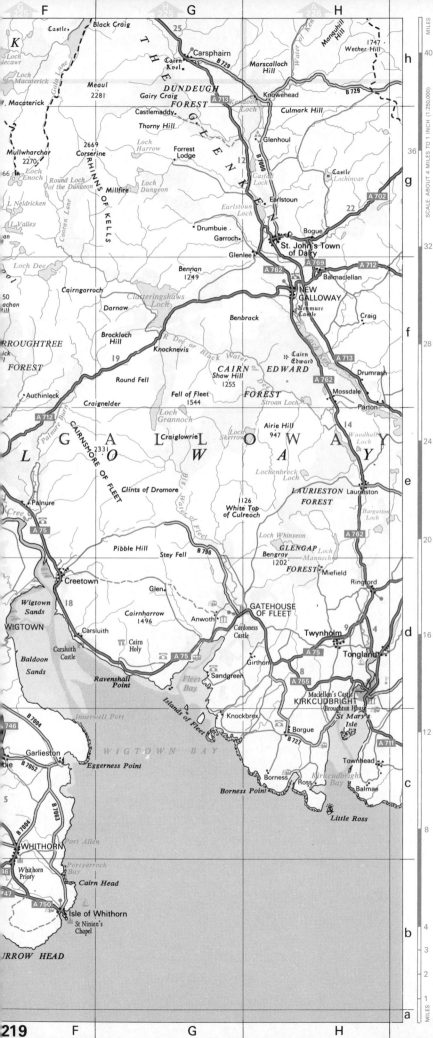

PLACES TO SEE IN
GALLOWAY

Opening times should be confirmed by telephone from the number in brackets. The exchange is given only if it differs from the place name at the beginning of the entry
Map references are shown after each place name

Cairn Holy (Gd) Two Neolithic chambered tombs, which were re-opened for more burials during the Early Bronze Age

Cardoness Castle (Gd) 15th-century tower house (031 229 9321), with a vaulted basement and fine fireplaces

Glenluce (Cd) *Abbey*, 12th-century Cistercian remains. *Castle of Park*, remains of a 16th-century castle

Kirkcudbright (Hd) *Mac-lellan's Castle*, 16th-century ruins. *Broughton House*, 17th-century house, now a museum, contains fine furniture, paintings and a collection of manuscripts and relics of Robert Burns

Kirkmadrine (Bc) An early Christian settlement containing three of the earliest inscribed Christian monuments in Britain, dating from the 5th or 6th century

Lochinch and Castle Kennedy Gardens (Ce) 17th-century gardens (Stranraer 2024), with a fine collection of rare shrubs

Logan Botanic Garden (Cc) Walled gardens (Ardwell 231) containing rare subtropical shrubs and trees

Port Logan Bay (Bc) In the bay is a tidal fish pond, built in the 18th century; it contains tame cod which rise at the summons of a bell to be fed by hand

Port William (Ec) *White Loch of Myrton*, a bird sanctuary

St Ninian's Cave (Fb) Traditionally accepted as the retreat in the 5th century of St Ninian, the first Scotsman to become a Christian missionary. Early Christian crosses are carved on the walls of the cave and the rocks outside

St Ninian's Chapel (Fb) Ruins of a 13th-century church which was thought to have been on the site of a 5th-century chapel built by St Ninian, but recent excavations have failed to establish this. Near the chapel are the earthworks of an Iron Age fort

Stranraer (Be) *Castle*, 16th century. *Wigtown District Museum* (2151)

Whithorn (Fc) *Priory*, ruins of a 12th-century Premonstratensian priory built on the site of the 5th-century 'Candida Casa', or 'White House', founded by St Ninian. The priory museum contains early Christian monuments, including a stone inscribed in the 5th century, in Latin, and crosses which were found in St Ninian's Cave

Wigtown (Fd) *Torhouse Stone Circle*, a Bronze Age circle of 19 stones standing on a low mound. *Baldoon Castle*, 13th-century ruins; the castle was the setting for Sir Walter Scott's novel 'The Bride of Lammermoor'. In 1685, Margaret McLauchlan and Margaret Wilson, two Covenanters (Presbyterians), were tied to stakes at the mouth of the River Bladnoch and drowned by the rising tide after refusing to give up their beliefs. A post marks the site of their martyrdom

STRANRAER

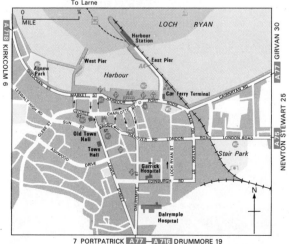

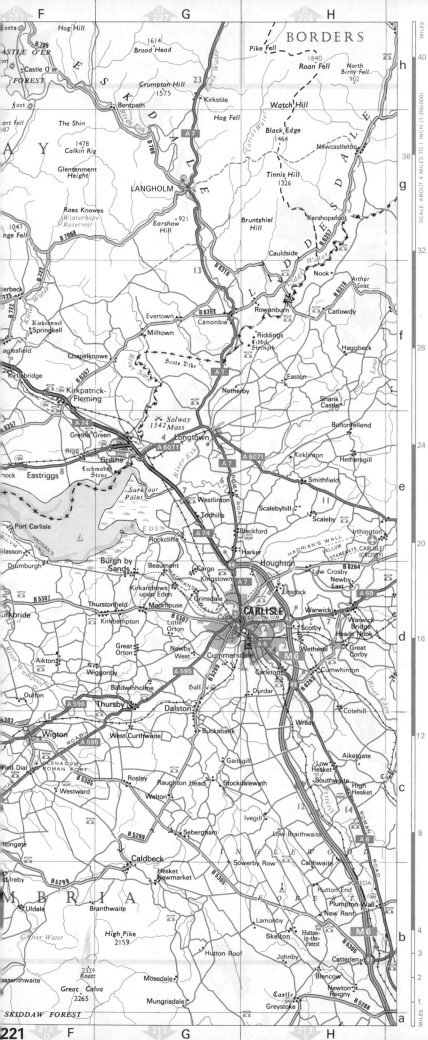

BORDERS

PLACES TO SEE IN
THE SOLWAY FIRTH

Opening times should be confirmed by telephone from the number in brackets. The exchange is given only if it differs from the place name at the beginning of the entry
Map references are shown after each place name

Caerlaverock Castle (De) 13th to 17th-century ruins surrounded by a moat, is one of the finest examples of medieval architecture in Scotland

Carlisle (Hd) *Castle*, 12th to 14th-century ruins; the museum of the Border Regiment is housed in the 12th-century keep. *Cathedral*, 12th to 13th century, has a fine east window

Castle Douglas (Ae) *Threave Castle*, 14th-century ruins of Douglas stronghold. *Threave Gardens* (2575), school for young gardeners open to public. *Threave Wildfowl Refuge* (Bridge of Dee 242), roosting and feeding ground for geese and duck

Cockermouth see p. 213

Dumfries (Cf) *Lincluden College*, a 12th-century Benedictine nunnery which was suppressed in the 14th century and established as a college; the remains are among the finest examples of Decorated architecture in Scotland. *Ruthwell Cross*, probably 7th century, containing a runic inscription of parts of 'The Dream of the Rood', a poem ascribed to Caedmon, the first English Christian poet. *Church of St Michael*, 18th century; in the churchyard is the Mausoleum where Robert Burns, his wife, and five of his children are buried. *Burns House* (5297),

the house where Burns died in 1796; now a museum containing many relics of the poet. *The Globe Inn*, 17th-century inn which Burns frequented; it contains his chair, and two verses which he scratched with his diamond ring on a window pane. *Burns Statue*, a white marble statue erected in 1882 depicting the poet seated on a tree stump with his dog at his feet

Dundrennan Abbey (Ac) 12th-century Cistercian ruins containing many fine monuments; Mary, Queen of Scots spent her last night in Scotland at the abbey, on May 16, 1568

Ecclefechan (Ef) *Carlyle's House* (666), 18th-century house where Thomas Carlyle, the writer and historian, was born in 1795; relics of the author include his correspondence with Goethe, the German poet

Gretna Green (Ge) The *Hall* and the *Smithy* were used for the marriages of runaway lovers for nearly 200 years

Sweetheart Abbey (Ce) 13th-century Cistercian house founded by Dervorgilla, Lady of Galloway, in memory of her husband John Balliol, founder of the Oxford college. It is so named because in 1289 Dervorgilla was buried before the high altar with the 'sweet heart' of her husband resting on her bosom

AA BREAKDOWN SERVICES: Carlisle 24274, 24 hours; Gretna 242, 9 a.m. to 5 p.m.

DUMFRIES

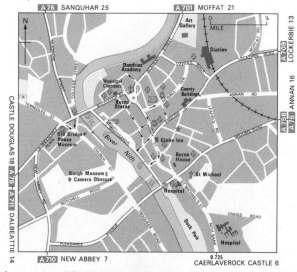

A town plan of CARLISLE is on p. 84

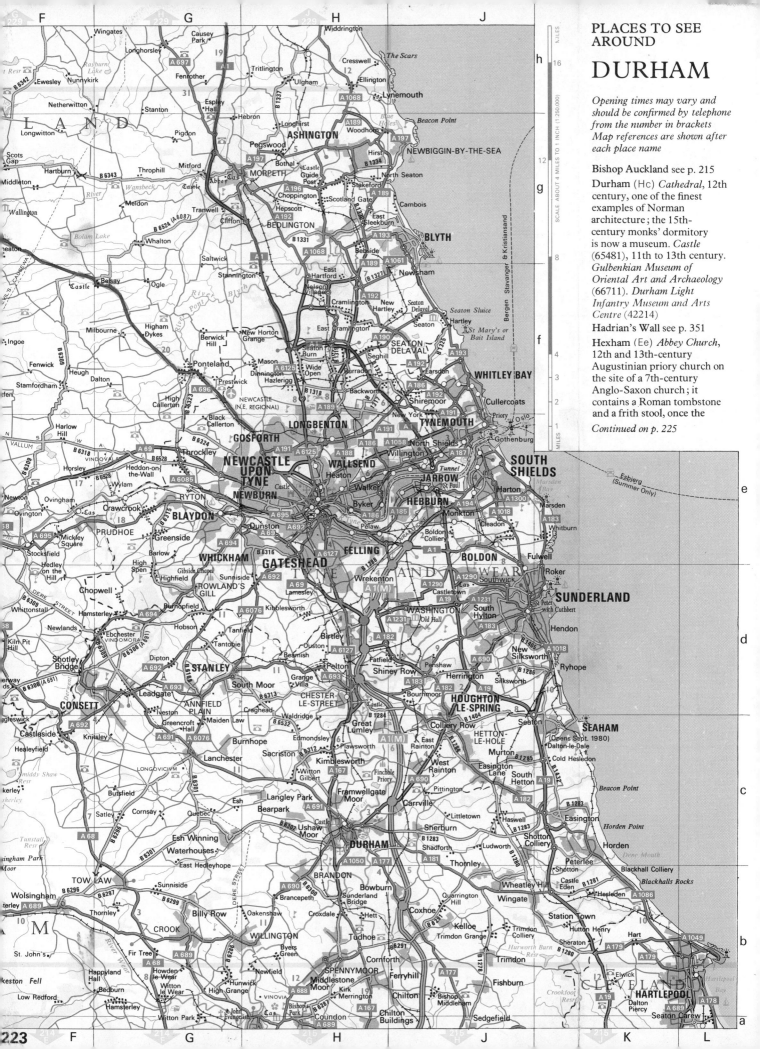

DURHAM

*Opening times may vary and
should be confirmed by telephone
from the number in brackets
Map references are shown after
each place name*

Bishop Auckland see p. 215

Durham (Hc) *Cathedral*, 12th
century, one of the finest
examples of Norman
architecture; the 15th-
century monks' dormitory
is now a museum. *Castle*
(65481), 11th to 13th century.
*Gulbenkian Museum of
Oriental Art and Archaeology*
(66711). *Durham Light
Infantry Museum and Arts
Centre* (42214)

Hadrian's Wall see p. 351

Hexham (Ee) *Abbey Church*,
12th and 13th-century
Augustinian priory church on
the site of a 7th-century
Anglo-Saxon church; it
contains a Roman tombstone
and a frith stool, once the

Continued on p. 225

223

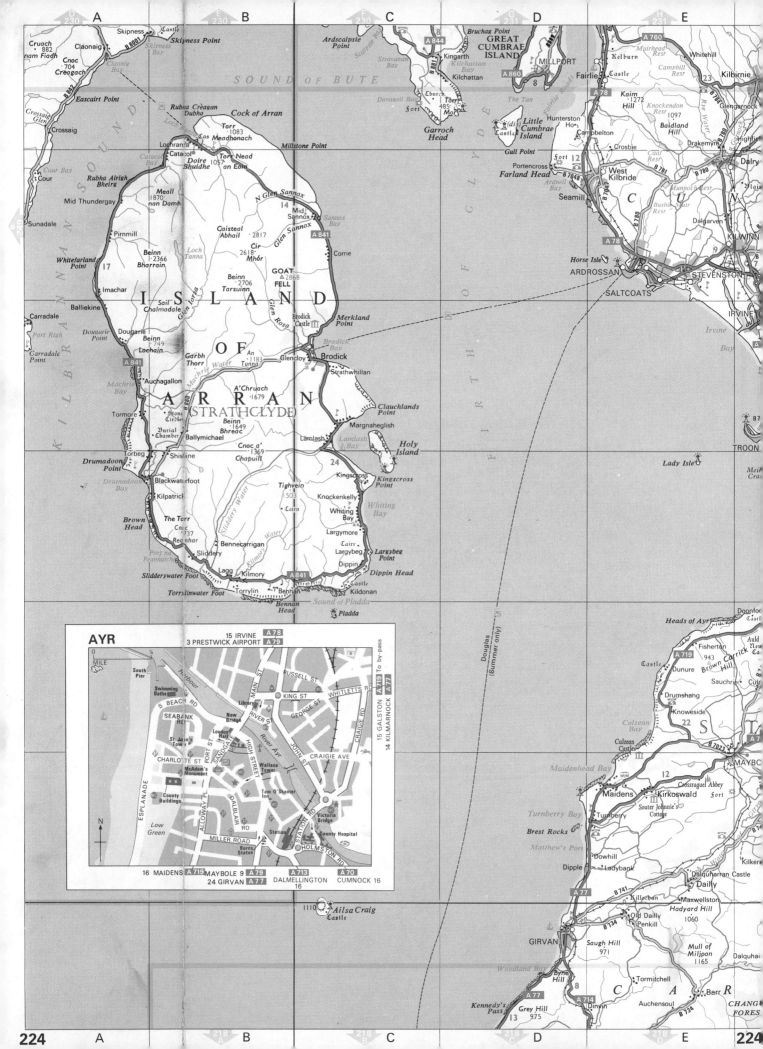

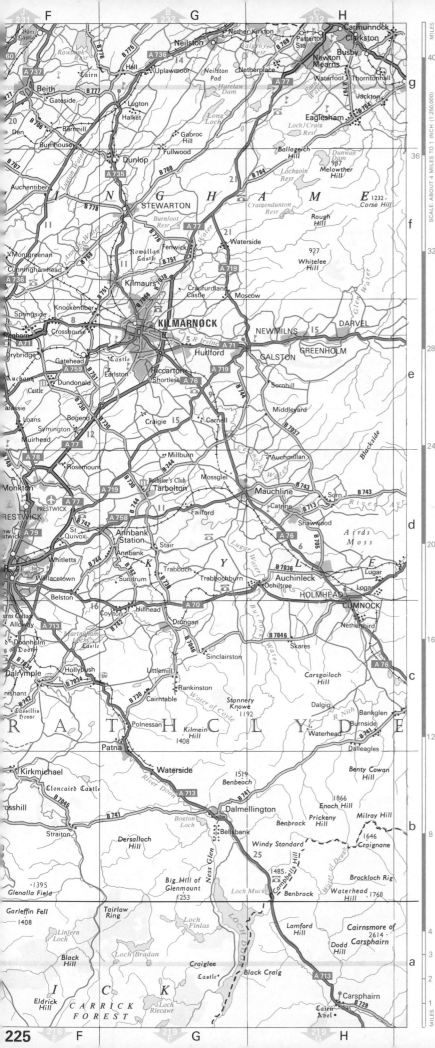

Opening times should be confirmed by telephone from the number in brackets. The exchange is given only if it differs from the place name at the beginning of the entry
Map references are shown after each place name

Alloway (Fc) *Burns Cottage* (41215), 18th-century thatched cottage where Robert Burns was born in 1759; it is now a museum containing relics of the poet. *Auld Kirk*, now ruined, where Burns's Tam o'Shanter saw the witches' orgy. *Auld Brig o' Doon*, 13th-century bridge where Tam escaped from the witches. *Burns Monument*, a Grecian temple with fluted Corinthian columns

Ayr (Fd) *Tam o' Shanter Inn*, the starting place of Tam o' Shanter's ride as described in Burns's poem of that name, is now a museum. *Auld Kirk of Ayr*, built in 1654, has original canopied pulpit

Brodick Castle (Ce) Part-14th-century castle (Brodick 2202), the home of the Duke of Hamilton. It contains fine silver, china and pictures

Crossraguel Abbey (Eb) Ruins of a 13th and 15th-century Cluniac house

Culzean Castle (Eb) An 18th-century Robert Adam house (Kirkoswald 260 or 269). This is one of the finest Adam houses in Scotland

Dundonald Castle (Fe) Ruins of the 14th-century favourite residence of Robert II, the first Stuart king, who rebuilt it from a 13th-century castle; the king died here in 1390

Kilmarnock (Ge) *Burns Monument and Museum* (26401). *Dick Institute Museum* (26401), collections include basket-hilted swords, small arms, and a children's museum

Kirkoswald (Eb) *Souter Johnnie's Cottage*, 18th-century thatched cottage, home of John Davidson, the soutar, or cobbler, on whom Burns modelled Souter Johnnie, in his poem 'Tam o' Shanter'; now a museum

A town plan of AYR is on p. 224

DURHAM *(Continued from p. 223)*

throne of Saxon bishops, and later the centre of an area affording sanctuary to fugitives from civil authority.

Newcastle-upon-Tyne (He) *Castle*, 12th-century ruins; the keep and the 13th-century Black Gate are now museums. *Cathedral Church of St Nicholas*, 14th century with a fine 15th-century lantern tower. *Cathedral Church of St Mary*, 19th century, designed by Augustus Welby Pugin, who designed the decorations for the Houses of Parliament. *Laing Art Gallery and Museum* (26989). *John G. Joicey Museum* (24562)

Northumberland National Park see p. 351

Penrith see p. 213

Rowlands Gill (Gd) *Gibside Chapel*, 18th-century Classical chapel with a three-decker pulpit and box pews; originally a mausoleum, it stands in grounds landscaped by Capability Brown

Seaton Delaval (Jf) *Hall* (481759), 18th-century house, the last and one of the most elegant of Sir John Vanbrugh's masterpieces; it contains antique furniture, pictures and oriental porcelain

Sunderland (Jd) *Museum and Art Gallery* (41235)

Wallington (Fg) 17th-century house (Scots Gap 283), altered in the 18th century, has fine porcelain and needlework collections

AA SERVICE CENTRE: 13 Princess Square, Newcastle upon Tyne, including 24-hour breakdown service (Newcastle upon Tyne 610111). Breakdown services: Durham 62894; Hartlepool 62786; South Shields 567804. All 9 a.m. to 5 p.m.

A town plan of DURHAM is on p. 110; of central NEWCASTLE UPON TYNE on p. 84; of SUNDERLAND on p. 107
A plan of routes out of NEWCASTLE is on p. 84

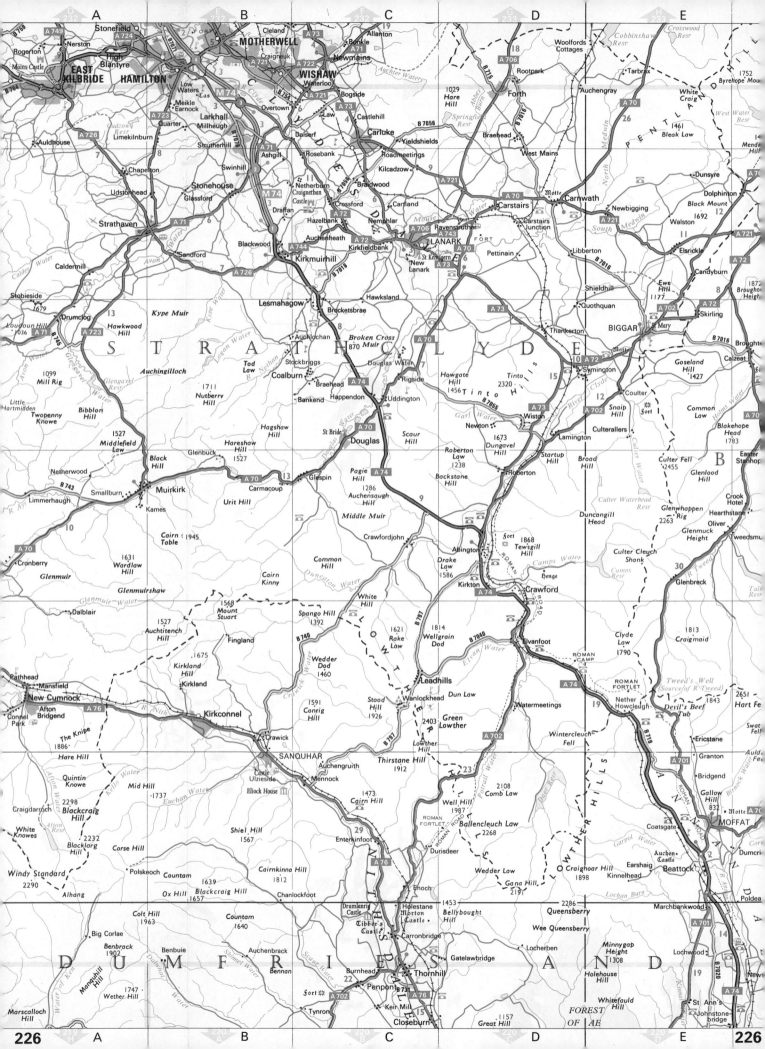

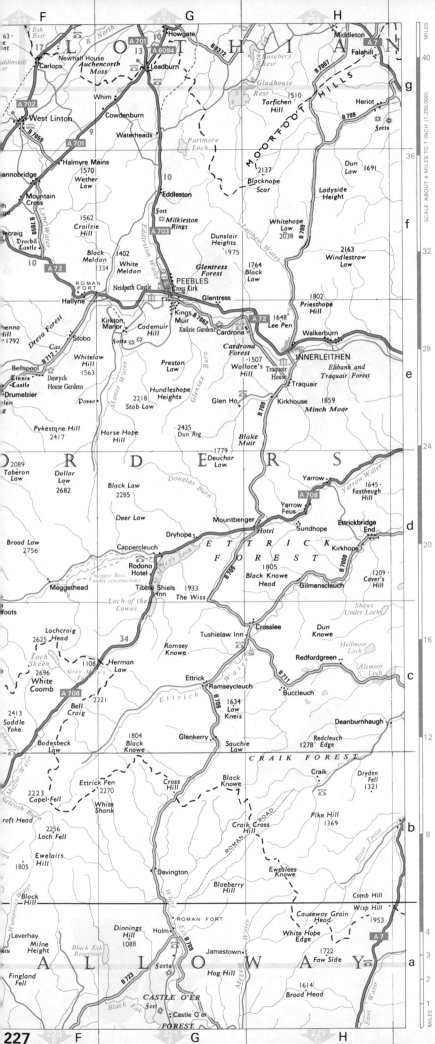

PLACES TO SEE ON
THE LOWLAND HILLS

Opening times should be confirmed by telephone from the number in brackets. The exchange is given only if it differs from the place name at the beginning of the entry
Map references are shown after each place name

Biggar (Ee) *Church of St Mary*, 16th century. *Gladstone Court Museum* (20005), a re-creation of a street containing 19th-century shops

Blantyre (Ag) *David Livingstone Centre* (823140). The tenement house where Livingstone was born in 1813 has been restored as a national memorial to the missionary-explorer. It contains personal relics, working models and tableaux illustrating his African mission

Craignethan Castle (Cf) 15th to 16th-century ruins; chief stronghold of the Hamiltons, supporters of Mary, Queen of Scots during the 16th-century civil wars, the castle was besieged and partly destroyed on James VI's orders in 1579

Douglas (Ce) *Church of St Bride,* 14th-century remains, containing fine monuments; the tower contains a 16th-century clock given by Mary, Queen of Scots and a 17th-century Dutch bell

Dryhope (Gd) *Churchyard of St Mary*, site of a 12th-century church; an open-air service is held here once a year, on the fourth Sunday in July

East Kilbride (Ag) *Mains Castle*, 16th-century ruins

Grey Mare's Tail (Fc) A 200 ft high cascade; one of the highest and most impressive in Scotland, it is on the Tail Burn which flows from Loch Skeen to Moffat Water (Fb). The 2400-acre area surrounding the cascade belongs to the National Trust for Scotland, is rich in wild flowers, and contains a herd of wild goats

Lanark (Cf) *Church of St Kentigern*, 12th-century ruins; one of the church bells, inscribed 'Anno 1100', is said to be one of the oldest in Europe; it now hangs in the Town Steeple

Mennock (Cb) *Eliock House*, part-12th century, birthplace in 1560 of James Crichton, whose unusual character inspired J. M. Barrie to write the play 'The Admirable Crichton'. Crichton, renowned as 'the Marvel of Europe' for his physical and intellectual achievements, was killed in a street brawl in Italy when he was 22

Peebles (Gf) *Cross Kirk*, ruins of a 13th-century church and a 15th to 16th-century Trinitarian friary. *Neidpath Castle* (20333), 14th century with fine views over the River Tweed

Sanquhar (Bb) *Castle*, 15th to 17th-century ruins. *Tolbooth*, a fine example by William Adam of 18th-century Scottish architecture

Stobo (Fe) *Dawyck House Gardens*, woodland garden containing rare trees and shrubs; the larch trees, planted in 1725 on the advice of Linnaeus, the Swedish naturalist, after he had visited the house, are believed to be the oldest in Scotland

Traquair House (He) 12th century (Innerleithen 830323), one of the oldest inhabited houses in Scotland, contains fine collections of silver, glass, tapestries and embroideries; there is an 18th-century library and a priest's room with a secret staircase

LANARK

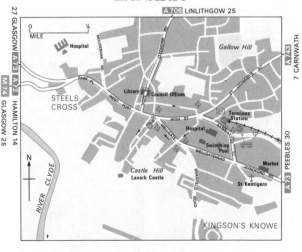

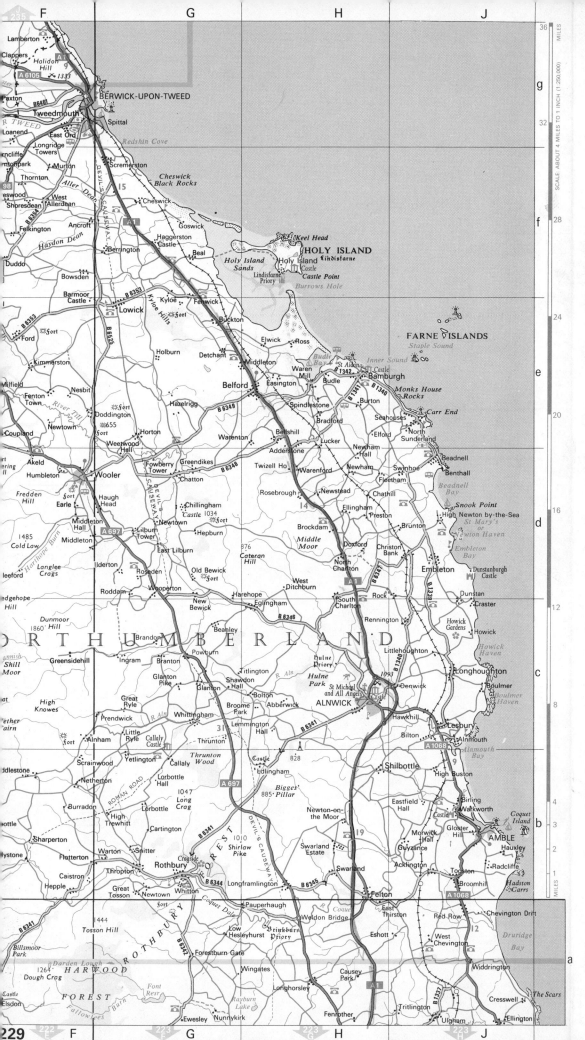

THE BORDER

Opening times may vary and should be confirmed by telephone from the number in brackets Map references are shown after each place name

Abbotsford House (Be) 19th-century mansion (Galashiels 2043), the home of Sir Walter Scott from 1812 to 1832, containing relics of the novelist

Alnwick (Hc) *Castle* (602207), 12th-century castle restored by the 1st Duke of Northumberland in the late 18th century, contains museums of British and Roman antiquities, and of the Northumberland Fusiliers. *Hotspur Tower,* 15th century. *Church of St Michael and All Angels,* 15th century. *Tenantry Column,* a monument to the Duke of Northumberland, erected in 1816 by grateful tenants who had their rents reduced during the agricultural depression; the duke, surprised to find his tenants rich enough to afford such a monument, raised their rents again

Bamburgh (He) *Castle,* 12th century, on the site of a 6th-century fortress, restored in the 18th and 19th centuries. *Church of St Aidan,* 13th to 15th century, with a fine 13th-century crypt; Grace Darling, who rowed out with her father, the Longstone lighthouse keeper, to rescue five people from a wrecked steamer in 1838, is buried in the churchyard. *Grace Darling Museum* contains relics of the rescue

Gordon (Cf) *Mellerstain* (225), 18th-century Adam mansion

Holy Island (Hf) *Lindisfarne Priory,* ruins of an 11th to 12th-century Benedictine house which was built on the site of the Celtic monastery founded by St Aidan in AD 635 and destroyed by the Danes in AD 875. *Holy Island Castle* (Scots Gap 234), built about 1500 and converted into a house by Lutyens in 1902

Jedburgh (Cd) *Abbey,* ruins of a 12th to 13th-century Augustinian abbey built on the site of a 9th-century Celtic church; there is a museum on the site

Newark Castle (Ad) 15th-century ruins

A town plan of BERWICK-UPON-TWEED is on p. 112

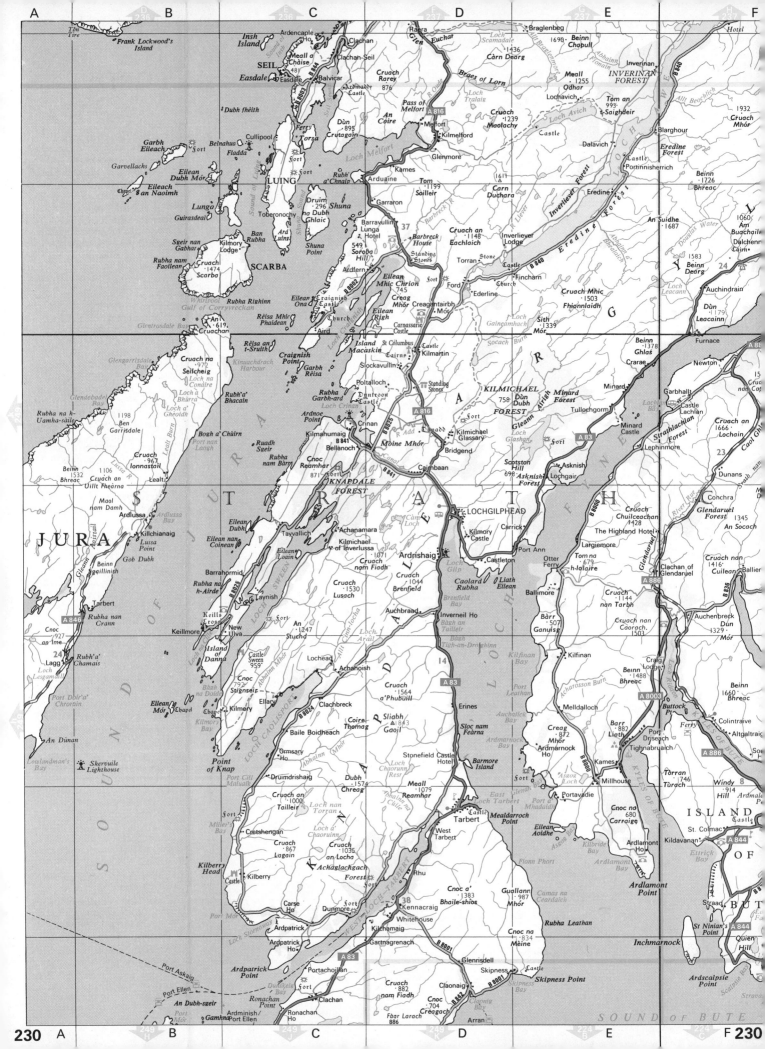

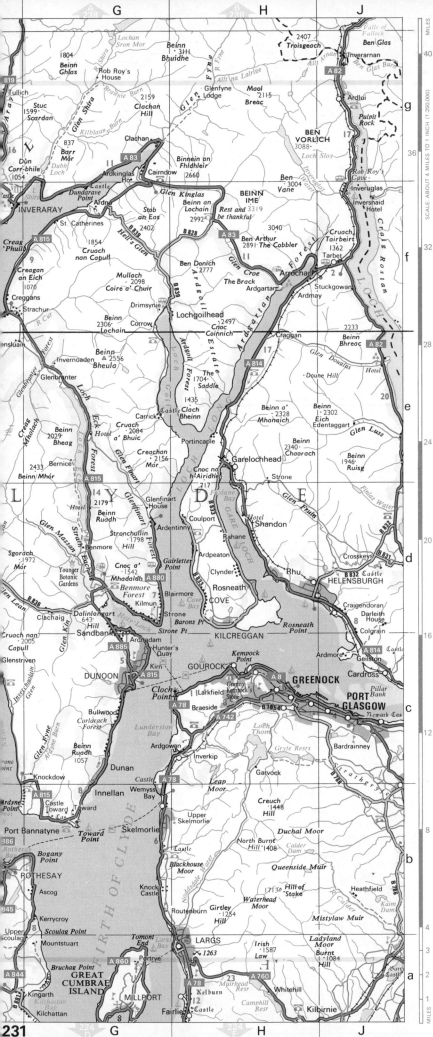

Opening times should be confirmed by telephone from the number in brackets. The exchange is given only if it differs from the place name at the beginning of the entry
Map references are shown after each place name

Beinn Ime (Hf) The highest peak in southern Argyll, 3319 ft; a splendid viewpoint

Ben Arthur (Hf) A mountain peak known as The Cobbler because of the shape of the rocky summit

Benmore Gardens (Gd) Extensive woodland gardens, containing a renowned collection of rhododendrons and a large arboretum

Carnassarie Castle (Df) Ruins of the 16th-century home of John Carswell, the first Protestant Bishop of the Isles; it was captured and part of it burnt as a Campbell possession during the Earl of Argyll's rebellion in the 17th century

Castle Sween (Cc) Probably 12th century, it is believed to be the earliest stone castle in Scotland. It was destroyed in 1647, during the Civil War, by Alexander Macdonald, commander to the Marquess of Montrose, the Scottish general who raised the Highland clansmen in support of the Royalists

Gourock (Hc) *Granny Kempock's Stone,* a 6 ft high monolith, probably prehistoric; it was once regarded with superstition by some local people, particularly fishermen who consulted it to ensure fair winds

Greenock (Hc) *McLean Museum and Art Gallery* (23741), includes relics of James Watt, the pioneer of the steam age, who was born at Greenock in 1736

Kilberry (Cb) *Castle,* 15th century, rebuilt in 1844 after a fire in 1513; in the grounds is a collection of medieval sculptured stones which were gathered from an ancient burial ground

Kilmartin (De) *Glebe Cairn,* one of several Early Bronze Age chambered cairns, or burial places, to the west of the village. When opened in 1804 it was found to contain a beaker and jet beads – typical objects buried with the dead by the Beaker Folk, a nomadic people who roamed Europe 4000 years ago. *Standing Stones,* south of the village, were erected about the same time. *Church of St Columba,* 19th century; in the churchyard are two carved crosses and grave slabs dating from the 16th century

Kilmichael Glassary (De) Bronze Age cup-and-ring marks (carvings composed of a central hollow surrounded by concentric hollow rings) on a natural rock outcrop

Rothesay (Fb) *Castle,* ruins of a 13th-century castle, surrounded by a moat; in 1401 Robert III made Rothesay a royal burgh and his son became the first Duke of Rothesay, a title held now by the Prince of Wales. *Natural History Society Museum*

Seil (Cg) *Clachan Bridge,* an 18th-century single-span bridge believed to have been designed by Thomas Telford, the Scottish engineer, to link the island of Seil with the mainland

ROTHESAY

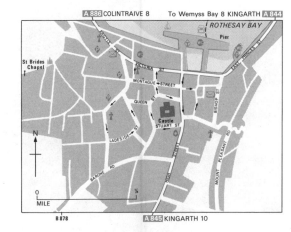

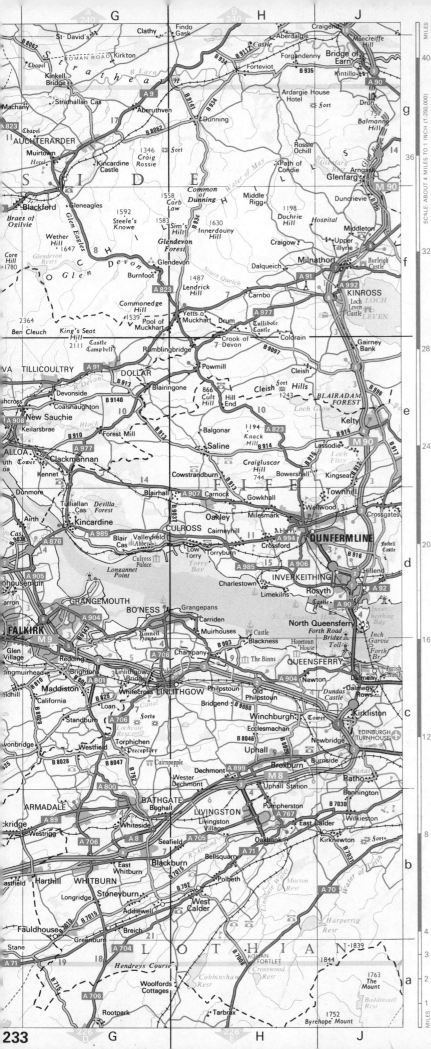

Opening times should be confirmed by telephone from the number in brackets. The exchange is given only if it differs from the place name at the beginning of the entry
Map references are shown after each place name

Blackness Castle (Hd) 15th century, with an oblong tower; a royal castle, it was used in the 17th century as a prison for captured Covenanters, who were fighting to establish Presbyterianism as Scotland's religion

Culross (Gd) *Abbey*, remains of a 13th-century Cistercian monastery; the choir is now used as the parish church. *Culross Palace*, 16th to 17th-century house with a pantiled roof, painted ceilings and walls

Doune Castle (Ef) 14th-century castle (Doune 203); restored in 1883, it is one of the best-preserved medieval fortresses in Scotland

Dunblane (Ef) *Cathedral*, mainly 13th century with a Norman tower

Glasgow (Cb) *Cathedral*, part 12th and 13th-century Gothic church on the site of a 6th-century church built by St Mungo – who was also called St Kentigern – the patron saint of Glasgow. *Botanic Gardens* (334 2422). *Linn Park*, woodland gardens with riverside walks. *Provan Hall*, 15th-century mansion with a walled garden. *Provand's Lordship* (334 1134), the oldest house in Glasgow, built in 1471, now a museum with 17th and 18th-century furniture (closed 1981). *City*

Art Gallery and Museum (334 1134). *Pollok House* (649 7547), 18th-century Adam house containing a fine collection of paintings. *Hagg's Castle* (427 2725), 16th century, now a children's museum. *Transport Museum* (423 8000). *People's Palace* (554 0223), with collections recording the city's rise and development. *Hunterian Museum* (339 8855), Glasgow's first museum, opened in 1807. *Church of St Andrew-by-the-Green*, 18th century. *St Andrew's Cathedral*, 19th-century Gothic Revival. *Calderpark Zoological Gardens* (771 1185)

Hopetoun House (Hc) 18th-century Adam house (031 331 2451) with fine furniture and paintings; there is a deer park and gardens laid out in the style of Versailles

Linlithgow (Gc) *Church of St Michael*, 12th century, rebuilt in the 15th century. *Palace* (2896), 15th century, where Mary, Queen of Scots was born in 1542

The Binns (Hc) 17th-century house (Philpstoun 255) with fine plaster ceilings and a collection of paintings. The Royal Scots Greys were raised here by Tam Dalyell in 1681.

AA SERVICE CENTRE: 269 Argyle Street, Glasgow G2 8DW, including 24-hour breakdown service (041 812 0101)

ROAD CONDITIONS: Glasgow (041 246 8021)

STIRLING

A town plan of CENTRAL GLASGOW is on p. 90. A plan of routes out of Glasgow is on pp. 92–93

FIRTH OF FORTH

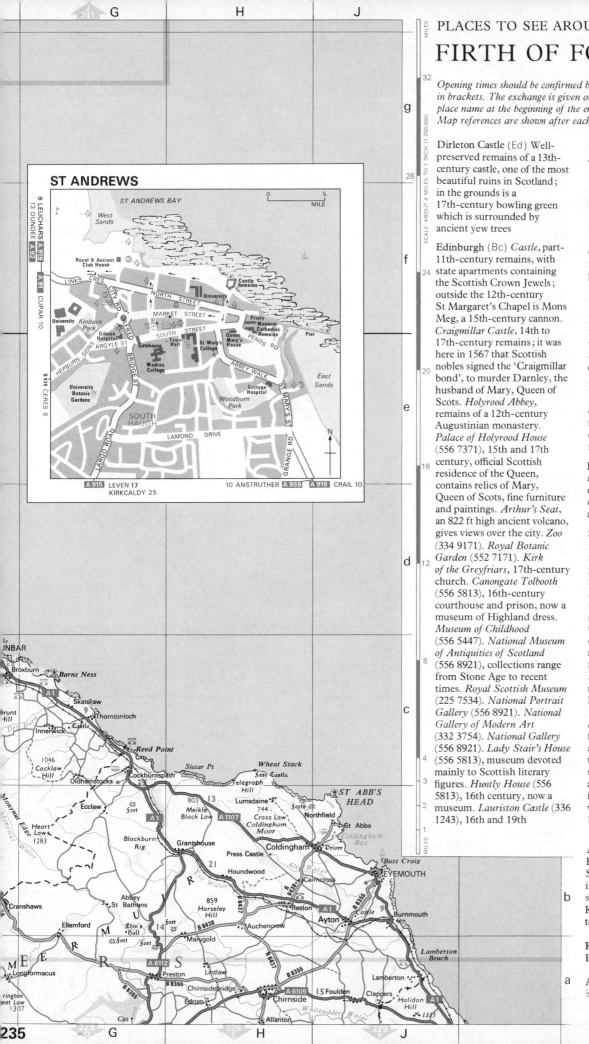

ST ANDREWS

Opening times should be confirmed by telephone from the number in brackets. The exchange is given only if it differs from the place name at the beginning of the entry

Map references are shown after each place name

Dirleton Castle (Ed) Well-preserved remains of a 13th-century castle, one of the most beautiful ruins in Scotland; in the grounds is a 17th-century bowling green which is surrounded by ancient yew trees

Edinburgh (Bc) *Castle*, part-11th-century remains, with state apartments containing the Scottish Crown Jewels; outside the 12th-century St Margaret's Chapel is Mons Meg, a 15th-century cannon. *Craigmillar Castle*, 14th to 17th-century remains; it was here in 1567 that Scottish nobles signed the 'Craigmillar bond', to murder Darnley, the husband of Mary, Queen of Scots. *Holyrood Abbey*, remains of a 12th-century Augustinian monastery. *Palace of Holyrood House* (556 7371), 15th and 17th century, official Scottish residence of the Queen, contains relics of Mary, Queen of Scots, fine furniture and paintings. *Arthur's Seat*, an 822 ft high ancient volcano, gives views over the city. *Zoo* (334 9171). *Royal Botanic Garden* (552 7171). *Kirk of the Greyfriars*, 17th-century church. *Canongate Tolbooth* (556 5813), 16th-century courthouse and prison, now a museum of Highland dress. *Museum of Childhood* (556 5447). *National Museum of Antiquities of Scotland* (556 8921), collections range from Stone Age to recent times. *Royal Scottish Museum* (225 7534). *National Portrait Gallery* (556 8921). *National Gallery of Modern Art* (332 3754). *National Gallery* (556 8921). *Lady Stair's House* (556 5813), museum devoted mainly to Scottish literary figures. *Huntly House* (556 5813), 16th century, now a museum. *Lauriston Castle* (336 1243), 16th and 19th

centuries, now a museum. *John Knox's House* (556 6961). *Gladstone's Land* (226 5658), 17th-century house with fine painted wooden ceilings. *Register House* (556 6585), 18th-century Adam house containing archives of Scotland. *Charlotte Square*, designed by Robert Adam, retains its Georgian lamp-posts, railings and torch extinguishers. *Floral Clock*, 11 ft 10 in. in diameter

Falkland Palace (Bf) Built in the 16th century, the palace was a favourite residence of Scottish kings until the death of James VI in 1625

Haddington (Ec) *Church of St Mary*, ruins of a 15th-century cruciform church; the nave is used as the parish church. *Church of St Martin*, ruins of a Romanesque church

Kellie Castle (Ef) Mainly 16th and 17th century, but part dates from 14th century. Fine example of domestic Lowland architecture (Arncroach 271)

St Andrews (Eg) *Castle*, ruins of the 13th-century archiepiscopal castle of the primate of Scotland. *Priory*, ruins of a 14th-century Augustinian house. *Cathedral*, remains of a 12th and 13th-century church; there is a museum containing Celtic and medieval monuments, glass and pottery found on the site. *Church of St Rule*, or St Regulus, remains of a 12th-century Romanesque church, with a 108 ft high tower. *The Royal and Ancient Golf Club*, founded in 1754, is the ruling authority on the game throughout the world. For a small fee visitors may play on any of the four courses, including the Old Course, where golf was played in the 15th century

AA SERVICE CENTRE: Fanum House, 18–22 Melville Street, Edinburgh, including 24-hour breakdown service (031 225 8464). Kirkcaldy 62371, 9 a.m. to 5 p.m.

ROAD CONDITIONS: Edinburgh (031 246 8021)

A town plan of EDINBURGH is on p. 87

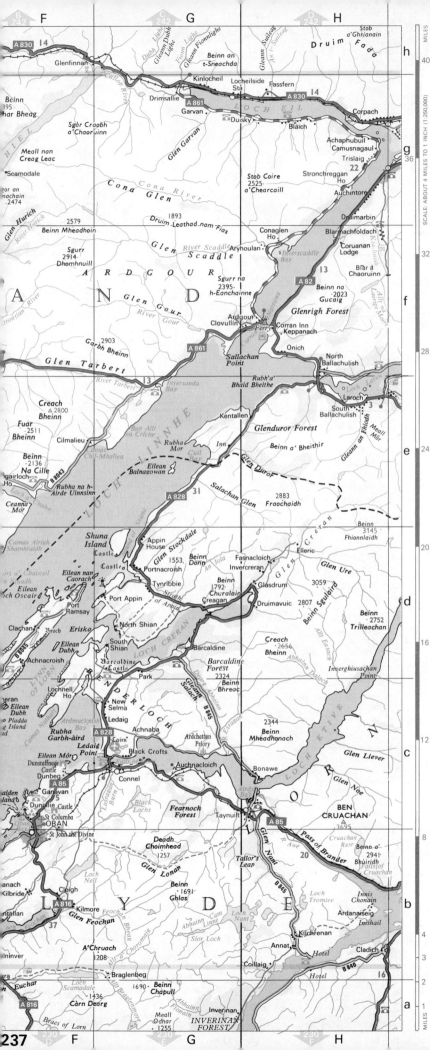

NORTH ARGYLL

*Opening times may vary and should be confirmed by telephone
Map references are shown after each place name*

Ardchattan Priory (Gc)
Ruins of a 13th-century priory which was burnt by Cromwell's army in 1654. A modern mansion has been built on the site

Ardtornish Point (Dd)
Ardtornish Castle, ruins of the 14th seat of the Lord of the Isles

Ben More (Cc) The highest mountain on Mull, 3169 ft; from the top are fine views of Ireland and the Outer Hebrides

Duart Castle (Ec) 13th to 17th-century stone castle, recently restored

Dunstaffnage Castle (Fc)
Remains of a 13th-century castle built on a rock. Near by is a ruined 13th-century chapel

Falls of Lora (Gc) Rapids caused by the outflow cascading over a ledge of rock across the mouth of Loch Etive

Kerrera (Fb) *Horseshoe Bay*, where King Haakon of Norway and his Viking ships gathered before sailing to meet Alexander III of Scotland at the Battle of Largs in 1263. Haakon was defeated and Alexander added the Western Isles, held for centuries by the Norsemen, to his kingdom

Larachbeg (Dd) *Kinlochaline Castle*, half a mile south-east of Larachbeg, stands on a crag at the head of Loch Aline. Built in the 15th century it was breached and burnt by Cromwell's army and restored in 1890

Loch Nell (Fb) A beauty spot.

Serpent's Mound, close to the southern shore, is a relic of early pagan worship; its origin is unknown but when it was opened many years ago cremation urns and flint tools were discovered

Oban (Fb) *Cathedral of St John the Divine*, 19th-century church designed by Augustus Welby Pugin, who modelled much of the decorations of the Houses of Parliament.
Cathedral of St Columba, a granite building designed by Sir Giles Scott. *Dunollie Castle*, ruins of a 12th-century castle with an ivy-covered tower; it stands on an 80 ft high rock. *McCaig's Folly*, a replica of the Colosseum in Rome, begun in 1897 by John Stewart McCaig with the two-fold idea of providing work for local people and creating a museum as a monument to himself and his family; McCaig died before the project was finished. *Pulpit Hill*, a viewpoint with a telescope

Seil see p. 231

Staffa (Ac) A basaltic mass rising out of the ocean and formed by nature into thousands of fantastic shapes. Its most striking feature is a great colonnade of octagonal lava pillars containing huge caverns; the largest of these is Fingal's Cave: 200 ft long, its naturally groined basalt roof, supported by columns of dark-toned lava, is covered with stalactites which reflect a myriad of colours on to its ocean floor

AA BREAKDOWN SERVICE: Oban 2854, 9 a.m. to 5 p.m.

OBAN

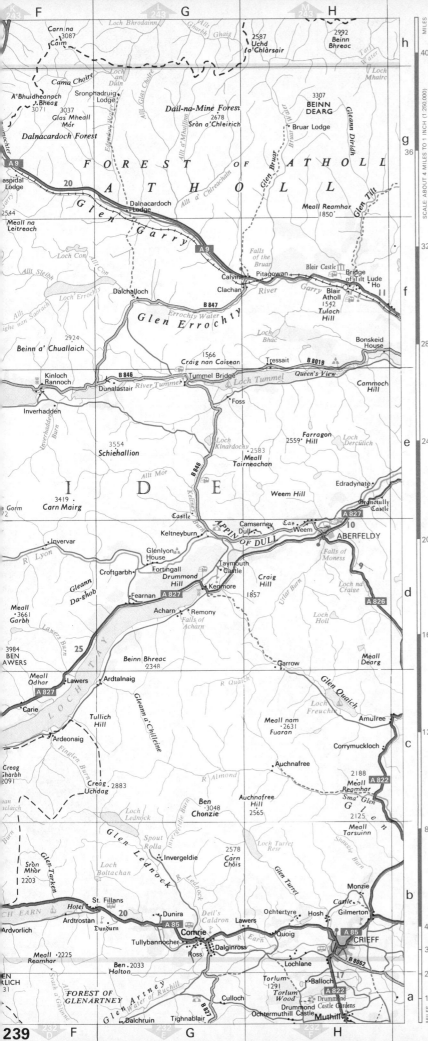

PLACES TO SEE IN
THE GRAMPIANS

Opening times should be confirmed by telephone from the number in brackets. The exchange is given only if it differs from the place name at the beginning of the entry
Map references are shown after each place name

Aberfeldy (Hd) *Bridge*, a five-arched stone bridge over the River Tay, built in 1733 by General George Wade, C-in-C Government troops in Scotland, as part of his scheme to pacify the Highlands after the Jacobite Rising in 1715. It is one of the finest bridges he built in Scotland. He was assisted in the design by Robert Adam

Ben Lawers (Fd) The highest mountain in Perthshire, 3984 ft, noted for its rare alpine plants; a nature trail has been established and from the summit are fine views of the Atlantic and the North Sea

Ben Nevis (Ag) Britain's highest mountain, 4406 ft. A 5 mile path leads to the summit from Achintee Farm, on the eastern bank of the River Nevis, 2½ miles south of Fort William

Blair Castle (Hf) Part-13th-century baronial mansion (Blair Atholl 355), home of the Duke of Atholl; it contains china, lace, paintings, Jacobite relics, and an armoury

Crieff (Hb) *Tolbooth*, 17th century; within an iron railing at the entrance stands an octagonal mercat (market) cross. The old stocks can also be seen at the Tolbooth. Opposite is a red sandstone cross sculptured with runic symbols, probably 12th century. *Bennybeg Smithy*, a forge where visitors can watch ironwork being wrought. *Innerpeffray Library* (2819), founded in 1691 by David Drummond, 3rd Baron Madertie, is one of the oldest libraries in Scotland; among its collection is the pocket Bible carried by

Montrose at his last battle at Carbisdale in 1648

Drummond Castle (Ha) 15th-century castle (Muthill 257), partly demolished by the Jacobites in 1745. The gardens only are open to the public

Fort William (Ag) *West Highland Museum* (2169), collections include folk life, local and natural history and relics of Bonnie Prince Charlie

Glen Coe (Ae) Scene in February 1692 of the treacherous massacre of more than 40 of the Macdonalds by the Campbells. The massacre was ordered by William III because MacIan of Glencoe, the aged chief of the Macdonalds, failed to take the oath of allegiance to the king by New Year's Day. He was five days late in signing because of an unavoidable delay. A monument to MacIan stands near the entrance to the glen. Visitor centre (Ballaculish 307)

Inverlochy Castle (Ag) Preserved ruins of a 13th-century castle with round angle towers. The castle was the scene of Montrose's victory over the Campbells in 1645

Kilchurn Castle (Ab) The remains of a 15th to 17th-century stronghold of the Campbells is one of the finest baronial ruins in Scotland. In 1746 the Campbells, who were then anti-Jacobite, offered the castle as a garrison for Hanoverian troops. The great gale which destroyed the Tay Bridge in 1879 blew the top off one of the castle towers

PITLOCHRY

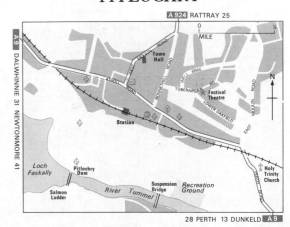

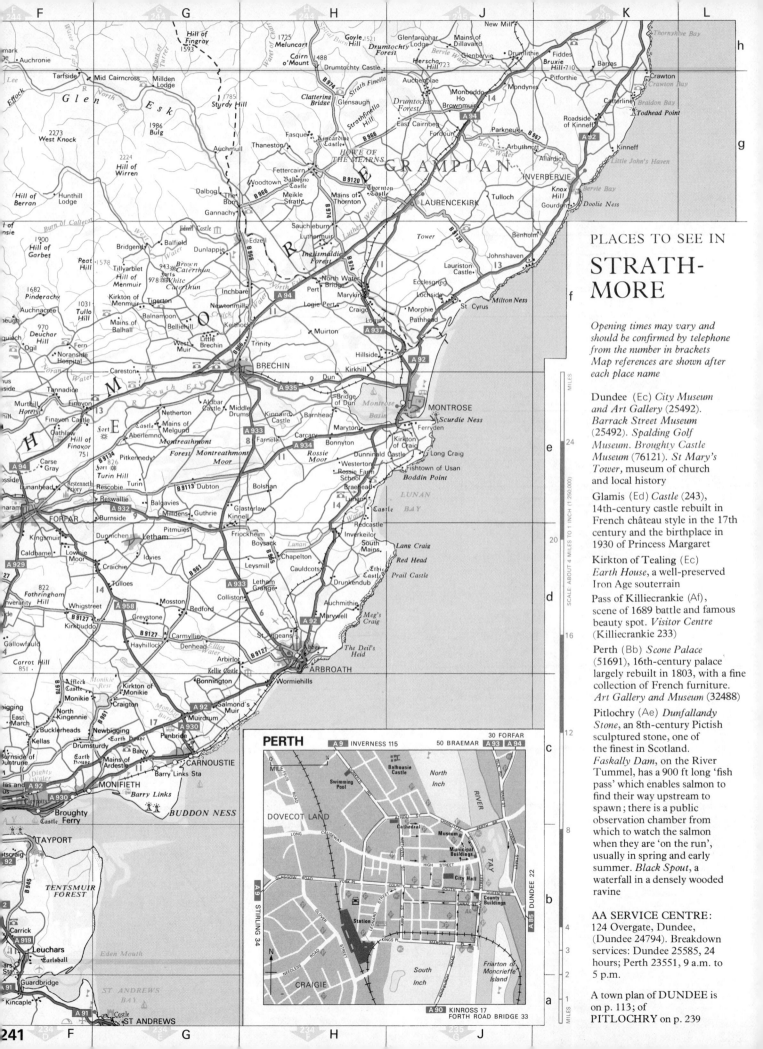

PLACES TO SEE IN
STRATH-MORE

Opening times may vary and should be confirmed by telephone from the number in brackets Map references are shown after each place name

Dundee (Ec) *City Museum and Art Gallery* (25492). *Barrack Street Museum* (25492). *Spalding Golf Museum. Broughty Castle Museum* (76121). *St Mary's Tower*, museum of church and local history

Glamis (Ed) *Castle* (243), 14th-century castle rebuilt in French château style in the 17th century and the birthplace in 1930 of Princess Margaret

Kirkton of Tealing (Ec) *Earth House*, a well-preserved Iron Age souterrain

Pass of Killiecrankie (Af), scene of 1689 battle and famous beauty spot. *Visitor Centre* (Killiecrankie 233)

Perth (Bb) *Scone Palace* (51691), 16th-century palace largely rebuilt in 1803, with a fine collection of French furniture. *Art Gallery and Museum* (32488)

Pitlochry (Ae) *Dunfallandy Stone*, an 8th-century Pictish sculptured stone, one of the finest in Scotland. *Faskally Dam*, on the River Tummel, has a 900 ft long 'fish pass' which enables salmon to find their way upstream to spawn; there is a public observation chamber from which to watch the salmon when they are 'on the run', usually in spring and early summer. *Black Spout*, a waterfall in a densely wooded ravine

AA SERVICE CENTRE:
124 Overgate, Dundee, (Dundee 24794). Breakdown services: Dundee 25585, 24 hours; Perth 23551, 9 a.m. to 5 p.m.

A town plan of DUNDEE is on p. 113; of PITLOCHRY on p. 239

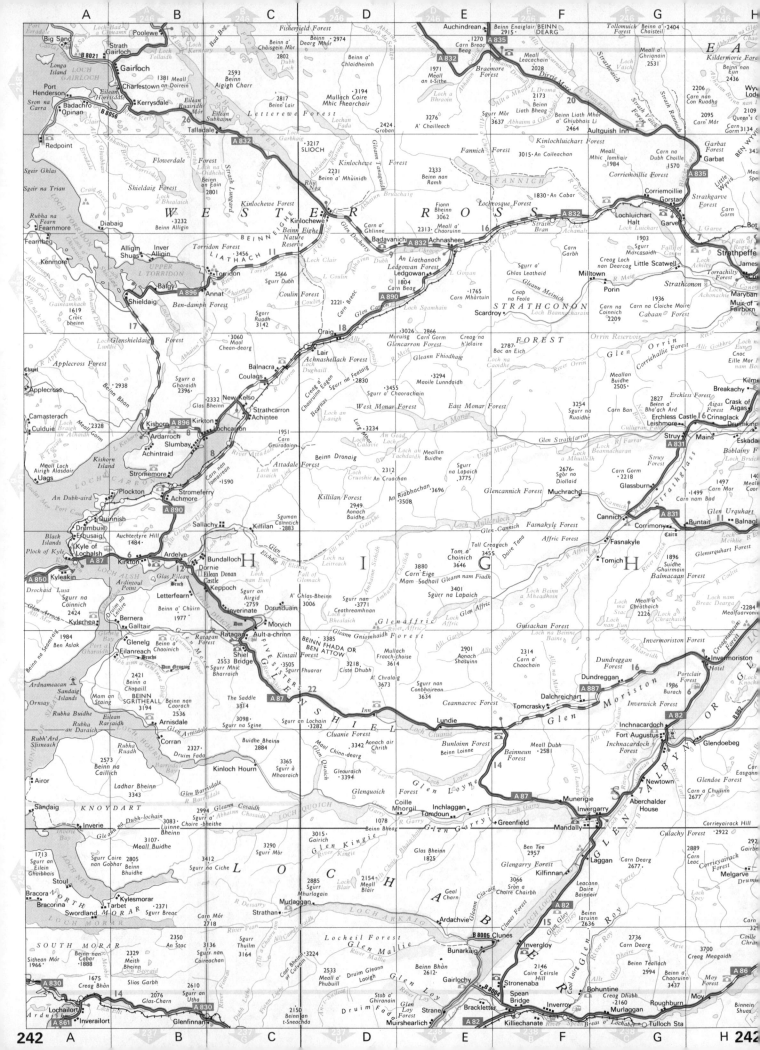

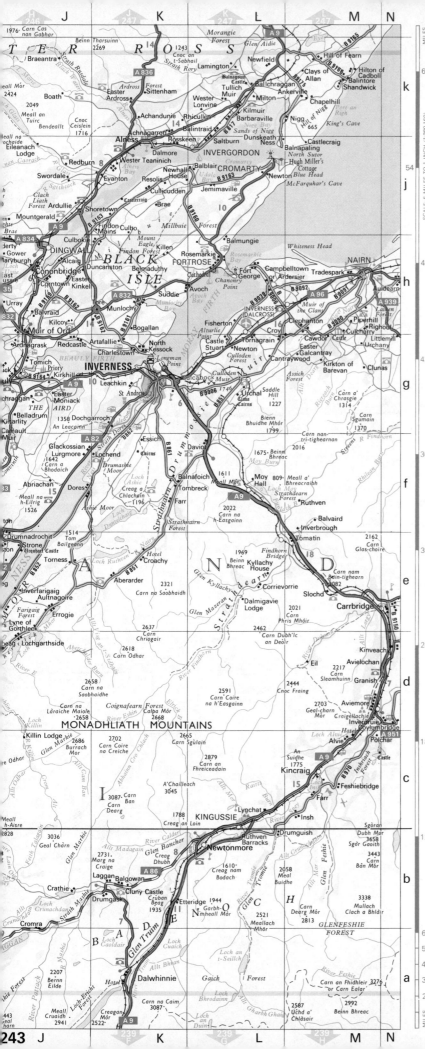

LOCH NESS

Opening times should be confirmed by telephone from the number in brackets. The exchange is given only if it differs from the place name at the beginning of the entry
Map references are shown after each place name

Beauly Priory (Jg) Remains of a 13th-century Cistercian house

Culloden Muir (Lg) Site of the Battle of Culloden in 1746 when the Duke of Cumberland defeated Bonnie Prince Charlie. *Visitor Centre* (Culloden Moor 607)

Eilean Donan Castle (Be) 13th century (Dornie 202)

Inverness (Kg) *St Andrew's Cathedral*, 19th century, has fine carved pillars. *Museum and Art Gallery* (37114). *Craig Phadrig*, a 556 ft high hill; on the summit are the remains of an Iron Age fort. *Boar Stone*, a Pictish sculptured stone, probably 7th or 8th century

AA BREAKDOWN SERVICE: Inverness 33213, 9 a.m. to 5 p.m.

INVERNESS

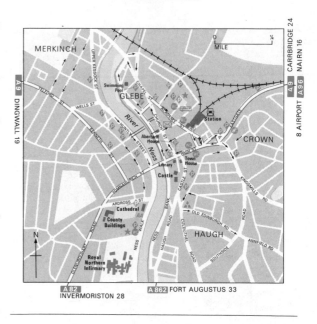

PLACES TO SEE AROUND

ABERDEEN see pp. 244–5

Aberdeen (Lc) *Provost Ross's House* (50291), one of the oldest houses in Aberdeen, being converted into a maritime museum. *Provost Skene's House* (50086), 16th and 17th century. *St Machar's Cathedral*, 13th century. *Art Gallery and Museum* (26333). *University Anthropological and Natural History Museum* (40241)

Balmoral Castle (Db) The Queen's home in Scotland; the grounds only are open daily, except Sunday, from 10 a.m. to 5 p.m. during May to July, if

the Royal Family is not in residence

Braemar Castle (Cb) 17th-century castle (Braemar 219), restored in the 18th century

Crathes Castle (Jb) 16th-century Jacobean castle (Crathes 525), has fine painted ceilings and original furniture

Dunnottar Castle (Ka) Remains of a 14th to 16th-century fortress on a headland 160 ft above the sea

Muchalls Castle (Lb) 17th-century mansion (Newtonhill 30217) with fine fireplaces and plaster ceilings

AA SERVICE CENTRE: Fanum House, 19 Golden Square, Aberdeen (Aberdeen 51231). Breakdown service, Aberdeen 51231, 7 a.m. to 11 p.m.

A town plan of ABERDEEN is on pp. 112–3

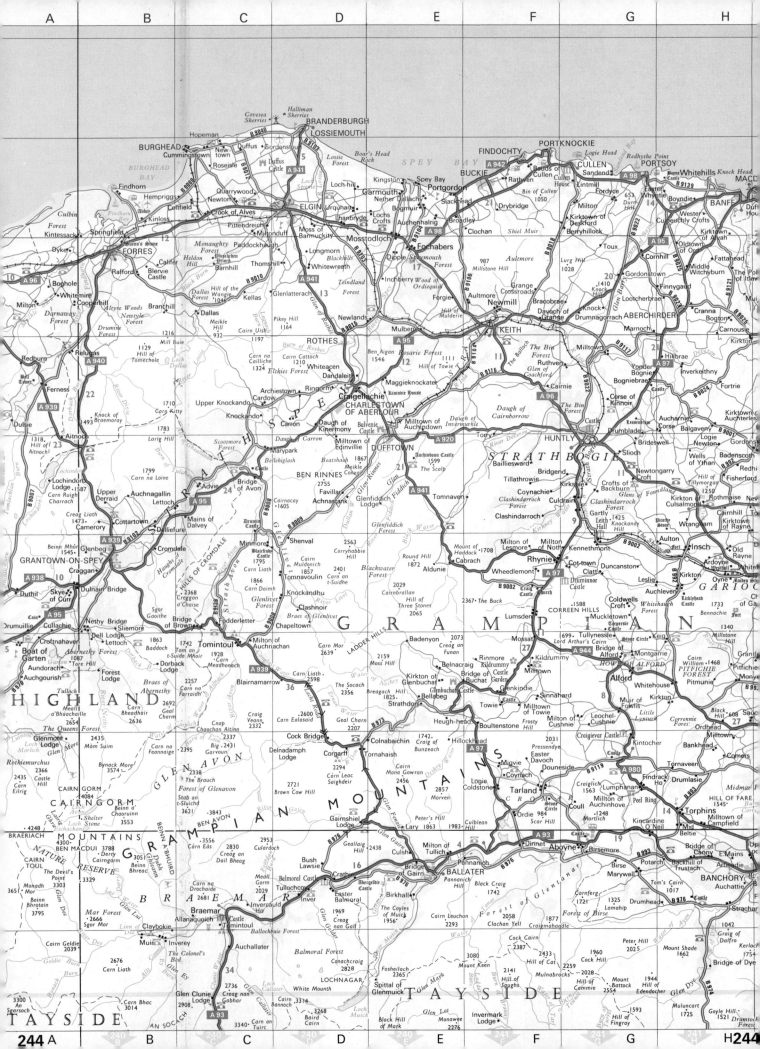

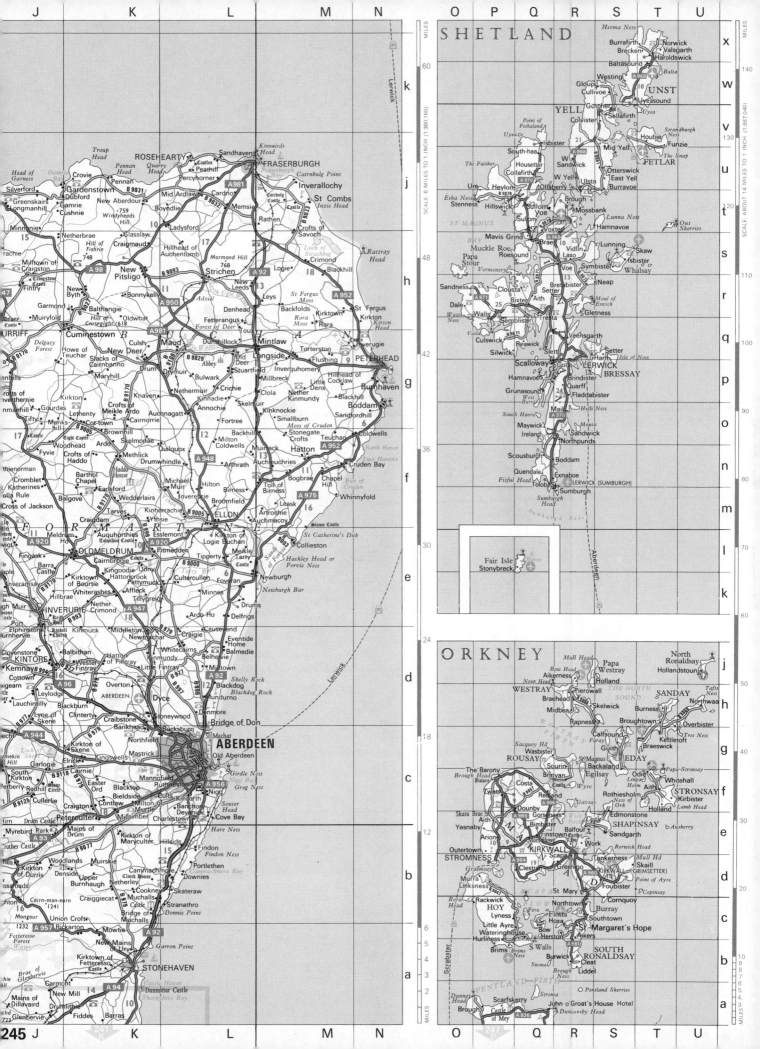

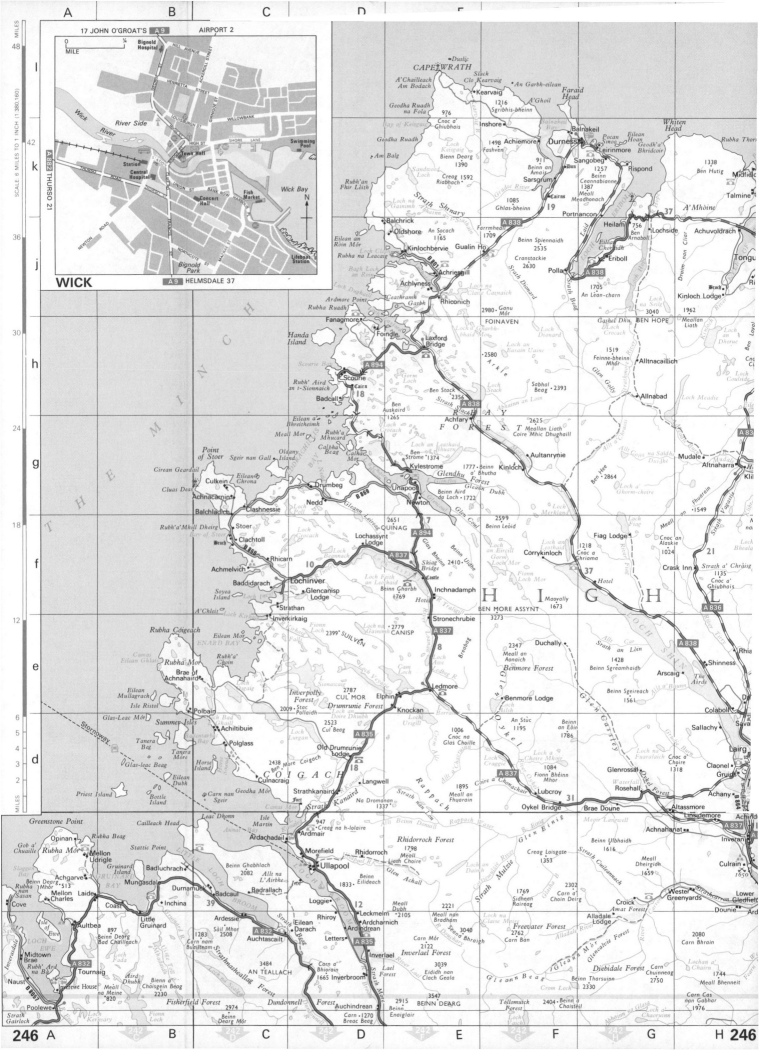

MILES

SCALE 6 MILES TO 1 INCH (1,380,160)

48

42

36

30

24

18

12

6

MILES

l

k

j

h

g

f

e

d

WICK

17 JOHN O'GROAT'S A9
AIRPORT 2
Bignold Hospital
MILE
Wick River Side
THURSO 21
Town Hall
Station
Central Hospital
Concert Hall
Bank Row
Fish Market
Wick Bay
N
Bignold Park
Lifeboat Station
HELMSDALE 37 A9

CAPE WRATH
Duslic
A'Chailleach
Am Bodach
Kearvaig
An Garbh-eilean
A'Ghoil
Faraid Head
Geodha Ruadh na Fola
976
Cnoc a'Ghiubhais
Inshore
Balnakeil
Whiten Head
Geodha Ruadh
1216
Sgribhis-bheinn
Rubha Thor
Bay of Keisgaig
1498
Achiemore
Durness
Leirinmore
Eilean Hoan
Geodh'a'Bhridcair
Loch Keisgaig
Benn Dearg
1390
911
Beinn an Amair
1257
Sangobeg
Sandwood Loch
Creag 1592
Riabhach
Sarsgrum
Beinn Ceannabianne
1387
Meall Meadhonach
Rispond
1338
Ben Hutig
Midfiel
Rubh'an
Fhir Lèith
Cairns
1085
Ghlas-bheinn
Portnancon
19
Talmine
A'Mhòine
Balchrick
Oldshore
An Socach
1165
Farrmheall
1709
Loch
Laid
Heilam
756 Ben
Arnaboll
Lochside
Achuvoldrach
Eilean an
Ròin Mór
Kinlochbervie
Gualin Ho
B 801
A 838
Beinn Spiennaidh
2535
Eilean
Chorbidh
Polla
Eriboll
Drum nan Cliar
Tongu
Rubha na Leacaig
Achriesgill
Cranstackie
2630
A 838
Kinloch Lodge
Ri
Bagh na h Ainn
Achlyness
Rhiconich
2980 Ganu
Mór
3040
1705
An Lèan-charn
Loch na Seilg
Broch
1962
Fanagmore
Rubha Ruadh
Geathramh
Garbh
FOINAVEN
Cashel Dhu
BEN HOPE
Meallan Liath
Rubha Ruadh
Foindle
Laxford Bridge
Beinn an Basain Uaine
Loch Dionard
Loch Crocach
Loch an Dherue
Handa Island
2580
1519
Feinne-bheinn
Mhòr
Alltnacaillich
Loch Coulside
Scourie Bay
A r k l e
Scourie
Cairn
18
Rubh' Aird
an t-Sionnaich
Gorm Loch
Ben Stack
2356
Loch Stack
Sabhal Beag 2393
Allnabad
Loch Meadie
Badcall
Ben
Auskaird
1265
Loch Creach
Achfary
2625
Meallan Liath
Coire Mhic Dhughaill
A 838
Eilean a'
Bhreitheimh
Rubh'a
Mhucard
Calbha
Beag
F O R E S T
Meall Mor
Oldany
Island
Calbha
Mór
Ben
Strome 1374
1777 Beinn
a' Bhutha
Kinloch
Aultanrynie
Mudale
A 83
Point of Stoer
Sgeir nan Gall
Cirean Geardail
Eilean a'
Chrona
Kylestrome
Glendhu
Forest
Gleann Dubh
Ben Hee
2864
Altnaharra
Klii
Cluas Deas
Culkein
Drumbeg
Unapool
Beinn Aird
da Loch 1722
Loch a'
Ghorm-choire
1549
Achnacarnin
Nedd
Newton
Balchladich
Clashnessie
Stoer
2651
QUINAG
7
2599
Beinn Leòid
Loch Merkland
Loch Fiag
Meall
Loch
Rubh'a'Mhill Dheirg
Clachtoll
Loch Poll
809
Loch Crocach
A 894
Glas Bheinn
Fiag Lodge
1218
Cnoc na Alaskie
1024
Strath Vagastie
Broch
Rhicarn
10
Lochassynt
Lodge
2410
Skiag Bridge
Castle
Loch an Eircill
Gorm Loch Mòr
Corrykinloch
1135
Cnoc a'
Ghiubhais
Achmelvich
A 837
Fionn
Loch Mòr
Crask Inn
21
Soyea
Island
Baddidarach
Lochinver
Glencanisp
Lodge
Beinn Gharbh
1769
Inchnadamph
Hotel
37
Hotel
A'Chleit
Loch Kirkaig
Strathan
Inverkirkaig
2779
CANISP
Stronechrubie
H I G H L L
Maovally
1673
A 836
Rubha Còigeach
Fionn Loch
2399 SUILVEN
BEN MORE ASSYNT
3273
Eilean Mòr
Camas
Eilean Ghlais
Rubha Mòr
Rubh'a'
Choin
8
Breabag
2347
Meall an
Aonaich
Duchally
A 838
Brae of
Achnahaird
Cam Loch
Ledmore
Benmore Forest
1428
Arscaig
Shinness
Eilean
Mullagrach
Isle Ristol
Inverpolly
Forest
2787
CUL MOR
Elphin
Benmore Lodge
Beinn Sgreamhaidh
1561
The Airde
Polbain
2009 Stac
Pollaidh
Drumrunie Forest
Knockan
1006
Cnoc na
Glas Choille
Beinn
an Eóin
1786
Colabol
Summer Isles
2523
Cul Beag
A 835
An Stùc
1195
Sallachy
Sava
Tanera
Beg
Old Drumrunie
Lodge
18
Langwell
1084
Fionn Bheinn
Mhor
Glenrossal
1318
Lairg
Tanera
Mòre
Horse Island
2438
Ben More Coigach
Culnacraig
Strathkanaird
1895
Meall an
Fhuarain
Lubcroy
Rosehall
Claonel
Gruids
Achany
Eilean
Dubh
COIGACH
Carn nan
Sgeir
Geodha Mòr
Fort
Na Dromanan
1337
Strath nan Lòn
Oykel Bridge
31
Brae Doune
Altassmore
A 837
Priest Island
Bottle
Island
Camas Mòr
Strath Kanaird
Rappach Water
Oykel
Linsidemore
Achind
Greenstone Point
Cailleach Head
Leac Dhonn
Isle Martin
947
Creag na h-Iolaire
Ardmair
Rhidorroch Forest
Glen Einig
Beinn Ulbhaidh
1616
Achnahanat
Inveran
Opinan
Rubha Beag
Static Point
Ardachadail
Morefield
Rhidorroch
1798
Meall
Liath Choire
Creag Loisgate
1353
Meall
Dheirgidh
1659
Culrain
Gob a'
Chuaille
Rubha Mòr
Mellon
Udrigle
Badluchrach
Beinn Ghabhlach
2082
Ullapool
Beinn
Eilideach
Glen Achall
Strath Mulzie
Loch a'
Daimh
2302
1769
Sidhean Raireag
Croick
Wester
Greenyards
Lower
Gledfiel
Achgarve
Gruinard
Island
Mungasdale
Durnamuck
Badcaul
Badrallach
1833
Meall
Dubh
2221
Meall nan
Bradham
3040
Loch na
Claire Moire
Alladale
Lodge
Dounie
Ard
Beinn Dearg Mhòr 513
Mellon
Charles
Laide
Coast
Inchina
39
Ardessie
Sàil Mhòr 2508
A 832
Eilean
Darach
Rhiroy
12
Leckmelm
Ardcharnich
Carn Mòr
2122
2105
Carn Ban
Inverlael Forest
Freevater Forest
2762
Carn
Chuinneag
2080
Carn Brain
Cove
Aultbea
897
Beinn Dearg
Bad Chailleach
1283
Allt nan
Buailteam
Auchtascailt
Letters
Inverlael
3039
Beinn
nan Clach Geala
3547
1744
Meall Bhenneit
Isle of
Ewe
Midtown
Brae
A 832
Tournaig
Aird
Dubh
Beinn a' Chaisgein Beag
2230
AN TEALLACH
3484
Carn a'
Bhiorain
1665 Inverbroom
Lael
Forest
Gleann Beag
Beinn Tharsuinn
2330
Diebidale Forest
Carn Cas
nan Gabhar
1976
Naust
Rubh' Ard
na Bà
Inverewe House
Poolewe
Fisherfield Forest
2974
Dundonnell Forest
Auchindrean
2915
BEINN DEARG
Tollomuick Forest
2404
Carn a' Chaisteil
Strath
Gairloch
Meall
na Meine
820
Beinn
Dearg Mór
Carn 1270
Breac Beag
Beinn
Enaiglair
Crom Loch

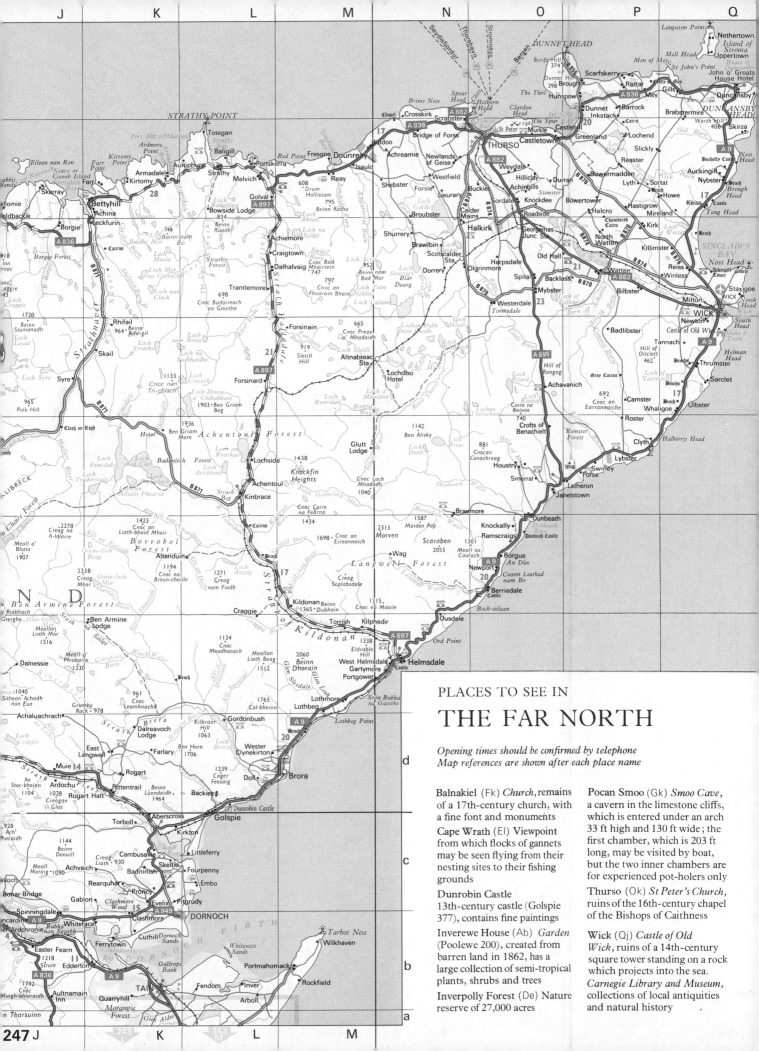

PLACES TO SEE IN

THE FAR NORTH

Opening times should be confirmed by telephone
Map references are shown after each place name

Balnakiel (Fk) *Church*, remains of a 17th-century church, with a fine font and monuments

Cape Wrath (El) *Viewpoint* from which flocks of gannets may be seen flying from their nesting sites to their fishing grounds

Dunrobin Castle 13th-century castle (Golspie 377), contains fine paintings

Inverewe House (Ab) *Garden* (Poolewe 200), created from barren land in 1862, has a large collection of semi-tropical plants, shrubs and trees

Inverpolly Forest (De) Nature reserve of 27,000 acres

Pocan Smoo (Gk) *Smoo Cave*, a cavern in the limestone cliffs, which is entered under an arch 33 ft high and 130 ft wide; the first chamber, which is 203 ft long, may be visited by boat, but the two inner chambers are for experienced pot-holers only

Thurso (Ok) *St Peter's Church*, ruins of the 16th-century chapel of the Bishops of Caithness

Wick (Qj) *Castle of Old Wick*, ruins of a 14th-century square tower standing on a rock which projects into the sea.
Carnegie Library and Museum, collections of local antiquities and natural history

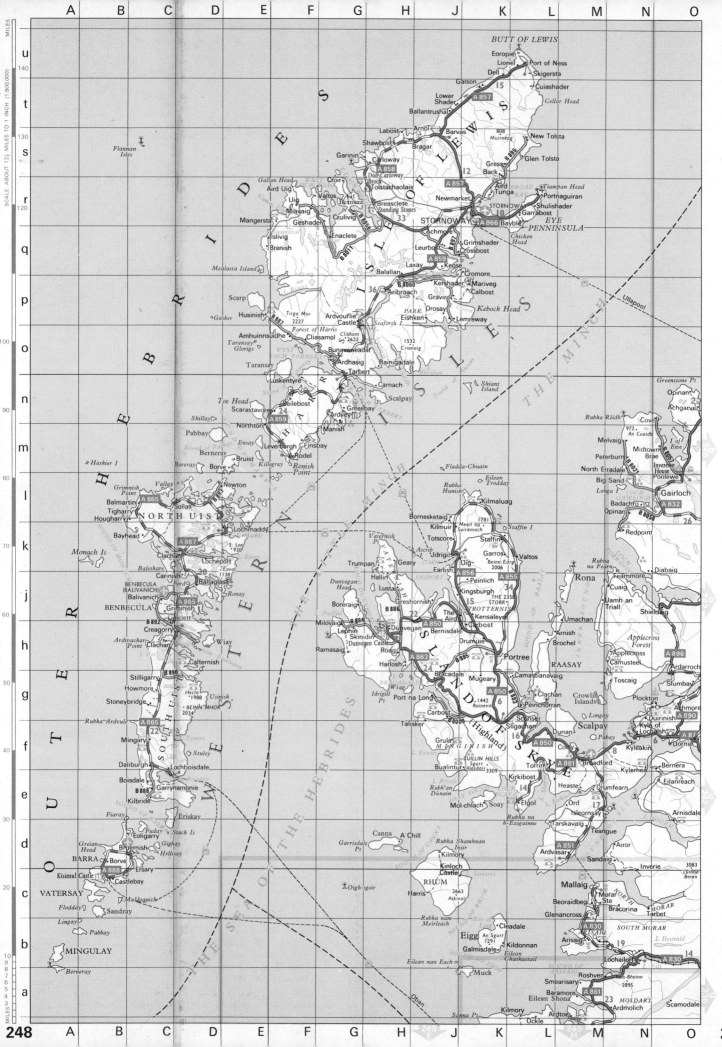

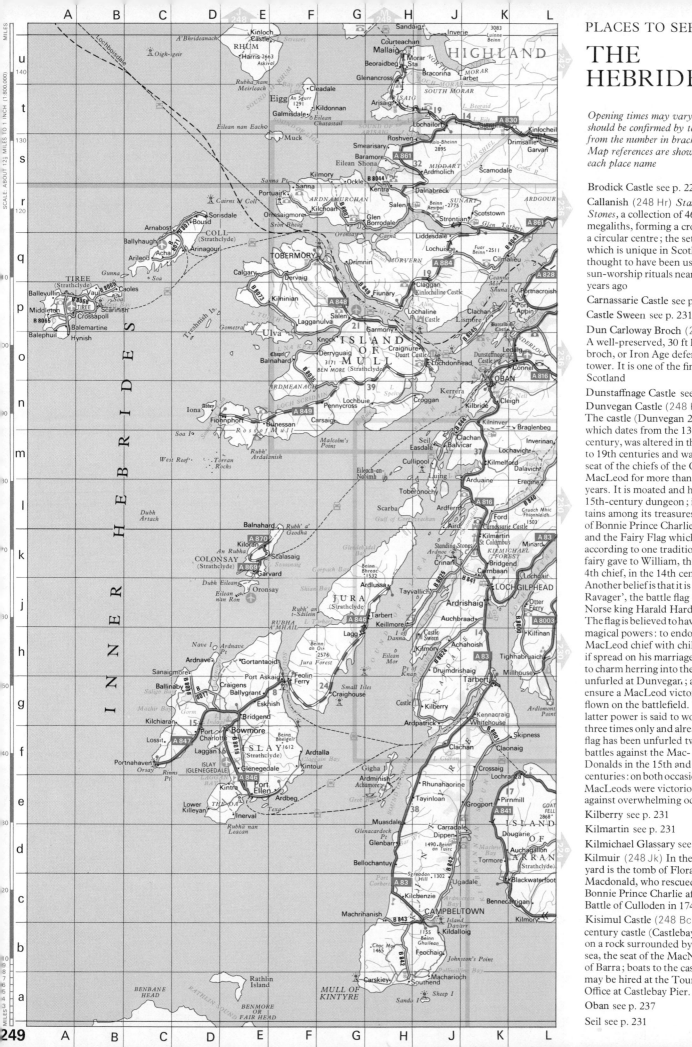

THE HEBRIDES

Opening times may vary and should be confirmed by telephone from the number in brackets Map references are shown after each place name

Brodick Castle see p. 225

Callanish (248 Hr) *Standing Stones*, a collection of 46 megaliths, forming a cross with a circular centre; the setting, which is unique in Scotland, is thought to have been used for sun-worship rituals nearly 4000 years ago

Carnassarie Castle see p. 231

Castle Sween see p. 231

Dun Carloway Broch (248 Gr) A well-preserved, 30 ft high broch, or Iron Age defensive tower. It is one of the finest in Scotland

Dunstaffnage Castle see p. 237

Dunvegan Castle (248 Hh) The castle (Dunvegan 206), which dates from the 13th century, was altered in the 15th to 19th centuries and was the seat of the chiefs of the Clan MacLeod for more than 700 years. It is moated and has a 15th-century dungeon; it contains among its treasures a lock of Bonnie Prince Charlie's hair, and the Fairy Flag which, according to one tradition, a fairy gave to William, the 4th chief, in the 14th century. Another belief is that it is 'Land-Ravager', the battle flag of the Norse king Harald Hardrada. The flag is believed to have three magical powers: to endow the MacLeod chief with children if spread on his marriage bed; to charm herring into the loch if unfurled at Dunvegan; and to ensure a MacLeod victory if flown on the battlefield. The latter power is said to work three times only and already the flag has been unfurled twice in battles against the Mac-Donalds in the 15th and 16th centuries: on both occasions the MacLeods were victorious against overwhelming odds

Kilberry see p. 231

Kilmartin see p. 231

Kilmichael Glassary see p. 231

Kilmuir (248 Jk) In the graveyard is the tomb of Flora Macdonald, who rescued Bonnie Prince Charlie after the Battle of Culloden in 1746

Kisimul Castle (248 Bc) 15th-century castle (Castlebay 300) on a rock surrounded by the sea, the seat of the MacNeils of Barra; boats to the castle may be hired at the Tourist Office at Castlebay Pier.

Oban see p. 237

Seil see p. 231

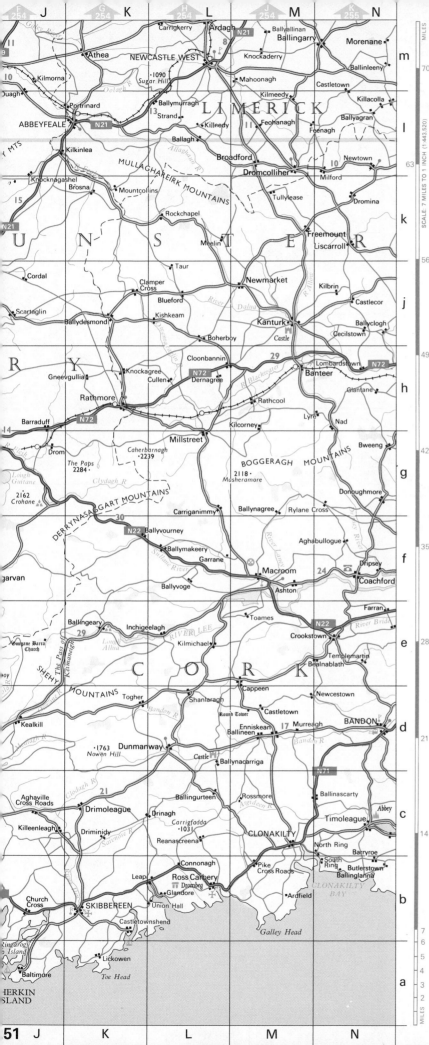

SOUTH-WEST IRELAND

Opening times should be confirmed by telephone from the number in brackets. The exchange is given only if it differs from the place name at the beginning of the entry

Map references are shown after each place name

Ardfert (Fl) *St Brendan's Cathedral*, remains of a 13th-century church containing a 13th or 14th-century effigy of a bishop. *Temple-na-Hoe*, ruins of a 12th-century nave-and-chancel church. *Temple-na-Griffin*, 15th-century ruins: the graveyard contains an ogham stone—an inscription in a 5th-century Gaelic script. *Franciscan Friary*, 13th-century ruins

Ball'inskelligs (Ce) *Abbey*, ruins of a part-13th-century Augustinian priory

Ballydavid (Bj) Fishing village where currachs, boats peculiar to the west coast of Ireland, are built. They are wooden-framed fishing-boats covered with tarred canvas, designed with a high prow to ride Atlantic rollers

Ballynacarriga (Ld) *Castle*, 15th-century ruins

Bantry (Hc) *Bantry House* (78), part-18th-century mansion with a collection of tapestries and art treasures

Castlemaine (Gj) *Killaha Abbey*, a ruined 13th-century Augustinian priory; the remains include a nave-and-chancel church with a fine east window

Gallarus Oratory (Bj) One of the best-preserved early Christian churches in Ireland, 22 ft long, 18 ft broad and 16 ft high. Built of unmortared stone it is completely waterproof after more than a thousand years

Glandore (Lb) *Drombeg Stone Circle*

Glengarriff (Hd) A village in a glen containing woods, Mediterranean plants and flowers

Great Skellig (Ae) A 700 ft high rock, the site of an early Christian monastic settlement. Remains include churches, beehive cells, crosses and two wells. Stone steps cut in the rock lead to the monastery

Ilnacullin, or *Garinish Island* (Hd) Italian-style island garden in Bantry Bay, 1 mile offshore from Glengarriff. It was here that George Bernard Shaw wrote 'St Joan'. Boats are available from Glengarriff

Kanturk Castle (Mj) Ruins of a 17th-century fortified house

Killarney (Hh) *Cathedral of St Mary*, 19th-century limestone cruciform church designed by Augustus Welby Pugin, who designed the decorative detail of the Houses of Parliament

Magharee Islands (El) *Illauntannig Island*, the site of an early Christian monastery believed to have been founded by St Seanach in the 5th or 6th century. Remains include two oratories, three beehive cells and a stone cross, enclosed by a stone cashel, or wall. *Illaunimmil Island* contains a prehistoric chamber tomb and a stone circle. Boats to the islands may be hired at Fahamore (Ek)

Muckross Estate (Hg) National Park comprising most of Killarney's lake district. It includes *Muckross Abbey*, 15th-century Franciscan friary ruins, *Muckross House* (Killarney 31440), a 19th-century mansion now a folk museum, and *Torc Waterfall*, one of the finest falls in Ireland. Jaunting cars—two-wheeled horse-drawn open vehicles with seats back to back—may be hired

Ross Castle (Hg) 14th to 15th-century ruins. A stone spiral staircase leads to the top of the keep, giving views of Killarney lakes

Skibbereen (Kb) *Cathedral*, 19th-century Grecian-style

Staigue Stone Fort (Ee) One of the finest archaeological remains in Ireland, 90 ft in diameter, with several flights of stairs leading to the terraces of its 13 ft thick walls. The fort, which is believed to have been built in the Iron Age, is entered by a sloping doorway about 5 ft high

Timoleague (Nc) *Abbey*, ruins of 14th-century Franciscan friary, which in its day was one of the largest and most important of the religious houses in Ireland

Tralee (Gk) *Church of the Holy Cross*, 19th-century Gothic-style designed by Edward Welby Pugin. The sacristy contains stained glass by Michael Healy of Dublin. *St John's Church*, 19th-century Gothic Revival. *The Court House*, 18th or 19th century

Waterville (De) *Church of St Finan* (on Church Island), 12th-century ruins, contains a beehive cell said to be that of the 6th-century St Finan

CORK (inset)

LIMERICK 63
BLARNEY 5

N20

N8 DUBLIN 161
CAR FERRY TERMINAL

N22 KILLARNEY 54

CORK AIRPORT 4
KINSALE 18

CROSSHAVEN 11

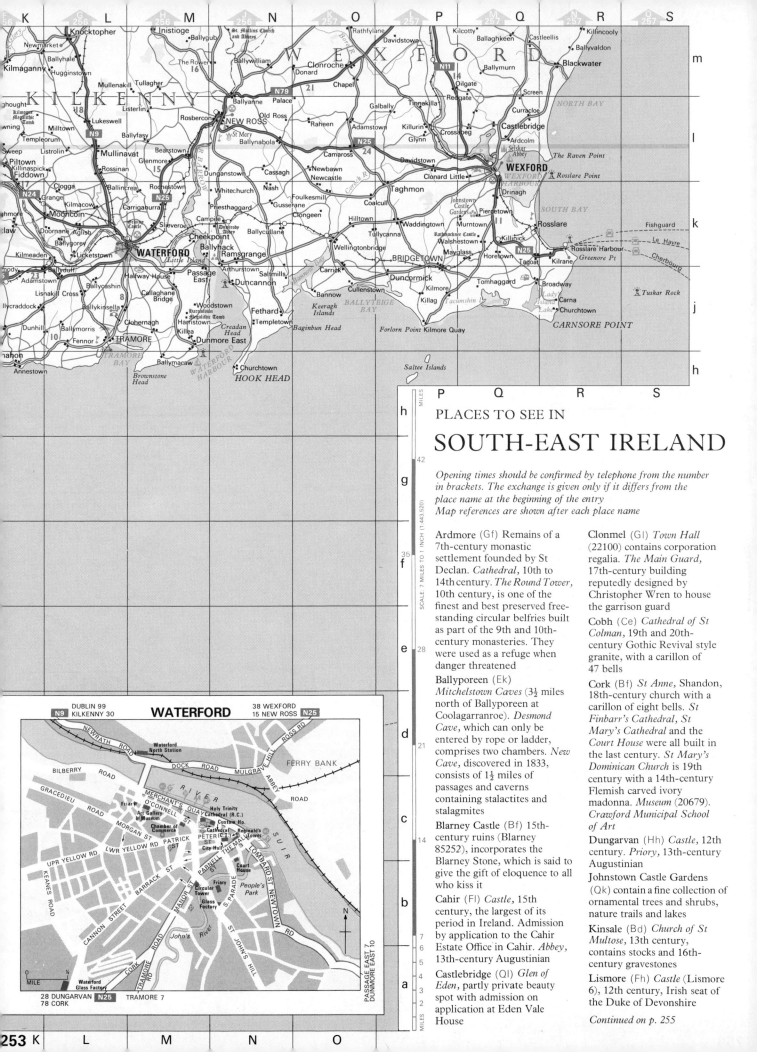

WEXFORD

KILKENNY

PLACES TO SEE IN

SOUTH-EAST IRELAND

Opening times should be confirmed by telephone from the number in brackets. The exchange is given only if it differs from the place name at the beginning of the entry
Map references are shown after each place name

Ardmore (Gf) Remains of a 7th-century monastic settlement founded by St Declan. *Cathedral*, 10th to 14th century. *The Round Tower*, 10th century, is one of the finest and best preserved free-standing circular belfries built as part of the 9th and 10th-century monasteries. They were used as a refuge when danger threatened

Ballyporeen (Ek) *Mitchelstown Caves* (3½ miles north of Ballyporeen at Coolagarranroe). *Desmond Cave*, which can only be entered by rope or ladder, comprises two chambers. *New Cave*, discovered in 1833, consists of 1½ miles of passages and caverns containing stalactites and stalagmites

Blarney Castle (Bf) 15th-century ruins (Blarney 85252), incorporates the Blarney Stone, which is said to give the gift of eloquence to all who kiss it

Cahir (Fl) *Castle*, 15th century, the largest of its period in Ireland. Admission by application to the Cahir Estate Office in Cahir. *Abbey*, 13th-century Augustinian

Castlebridge (Ql) *Glen of Eden*, partly private beauty spot with admission on application at Eden Vale House

Clonmel (Gl) *Town Hall* (22100) contains corporation regalia. *The Main Guard*, 17th-century building reputedly designed by Christopher Wren to house the garrison guard

Cobh (Ce) *Cathedral of St Colman*, 19th and 20th-century Gothic Revival style granite, with a carillon of 47 bells

Cork (Bf) *St Anne*, Shandon, 18th-century church with a carillon of eight bells. *St Finbarr's Cathedral, St Mary's Cathedral* and the *Court House* were all built in the last century. *St Mary's Dominican Church* is 19th century with a 14th-century Flemish carved ivory madonna. *Museum* (20679). *Crawford Municipal School of Art*

Dungarvan (Hh) *Castle*, 12th century. *Priory*, 13th-century Augustinian

Johnstown Castle Gardens (Qk) contain a fine collection of ornamental trees and shrubs, nature trails and lakes

Kinsale (Bd) *Church of St Multose*, 13th century, contains stocks and 16th-century gravestones

Lismore (Fh) *Castle* (Lismore 6), 12th century, Irish seat of the Duke of Devonshire

Continued on p. 255

SCALE 7 MILES TO 1 INCH (1:443,520)

MILES 42 35 28 21 14 7 6 5 4 3 2 MILES

WATERFORD

DUBLIN 99
KILKENNY 30 N9

38 WEXFORD
15 NEW ROSS N25

28 DUNGARVAN N25
78 CORK

TRAMORE 7

PASSAGE EAST 7
DUNMORE EAST 10

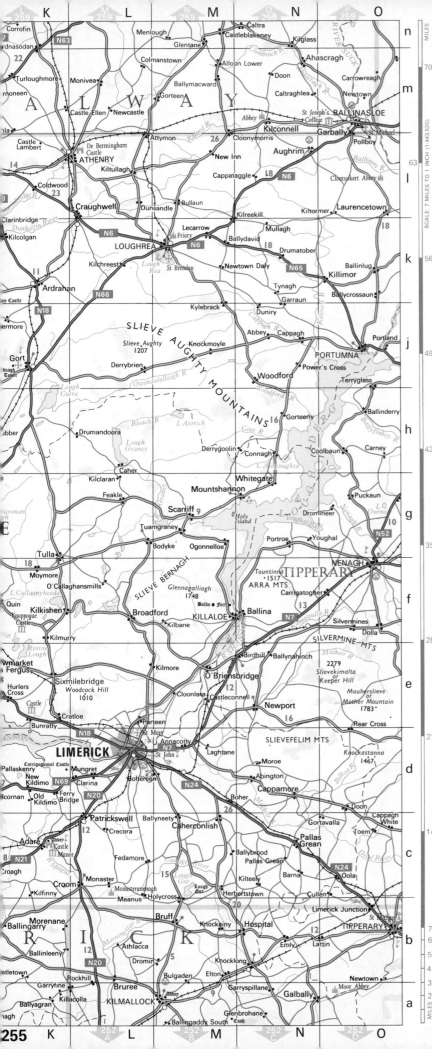

GALWAY TO LIMERICK

Opening times should be confirmed by telephone from the number in brackets. The exchange is given only if it differs from the place name at the beginning of the entry
Map references are shown after each place name

Adare (Kc) *Desmond Castle*, 13th-century castle on the site of an ancient ring fort. *Adare Manor*, 19th-century Tudor-style house; tickets for demesne and gardens are obtainable at the Estate Office

Aran Islands (Dk) The antiquities of Aran include ancient stone forts and early Christian churches and monuments. Daily scheduled flights leave Oranmore Airfield (Jl); boats leave daily during the summer from Galway (Hl). For departure times contact the Galway Tourist Information Office (Galway 63081)

Athenry (Ll) *Dominican Priory*, 13th century, lancet windows. *De Bermingham Castle*, 13th century. *Raford* 18th-century house with a galleried hall

Ballinasloe (Om) *Church of St Michael*, 19th century. *Garbally* (2504), 19th-century mansion, now St Joseph's College: the library contains rare books and manuscripts

Bunratty Castle (Ke) (Shannon 61511), restored 15th-century castle

Clontuskert Abbey (Ol) 15th-century Augustinian priory on the site of a 9th-century monastery. Ancient inscriptions are still legible on tombstones

Ennis (Jf) *Courthouse*, 19th century with an Ionic

portico. *Franciscan Friary*, 13th-century remains; has a vaulted sacristy and fine figure carvings

Galway (Hl) *Salmon Weir Bridge*; salmon may be seen in March or April. *Eyre Square* is landscaped as a memorial to President Kennedy. *Church of St Nicholas*, 14th century. Columbus is said to have prayed here before leaving for America *University College* (7611), 19th-century Tudor-style building with a library containing the Corporation minutes from the 15th to the 19th centuries, and a 17th-century map of the city

Kilconnell (Nm) *Abbey*, remains of a 15th-century Franciscan friary

Limerick (Ld) *Carnegie Library, Museum and Art Gallery* (44686). *St Mary's Cathedral*, 12th century. *St John's Cathedral*, 19th-century Gothic style; the Treasury contains the mitre and crozier of Cornelius O'Dea, a 15th-century Bishop of Limerick

Loughrea (Mk) *Carmelite Friary*, 14th century. *South-Eastern Gate*, 15th century, now a museum. *St Brendan's Cathedral*, 19th century with fine stained-glass windows

Monaster (Lc) *Monasteranenagh*, remains of a 12th-century Cistercian abbey

AA EMERGENCY/NIGHT SERVICES: Galway 64438; Limerick 48241, both 9 a.m. to 5 p.m.

S.E. IRELAND (continued from p. 253)

Tipperary (Dm) *Church of St Michael*, Gothic style

Waterford (Lk) City walls were built by the Danes in the 9th and 10th centuries and Anglo-Normans in the 13th century. *Reginald's Tower*, 12th to 13th-century fortification. *Christ Church Cathedral*, 18th century, on the site of a 12th-century cathedral. *Cathedral of the Holy Trinity*, 18th century with vaulted roof resting on

Corinthian pillars. *Treasury*, contains 15th-century Italian vestments, 17th-century crucifix and chalice. *Municipal Art Museum* (3501)

Wexford (Ql) *Selskar Abbey*, ruins of a 13th-century Augustinian priory. Henry II spent the Lent of 1172 here doing penance for the murder of Thomas à Becket by four of his knights. *Theatre Royal*, 18th century

AA SERVICE CENTRE: 9 Bridge Street, Cork (Cork 505155). Emergency/night services: Cork 505155, 8 a.m. (9 a.m. Sundays) to midnight; Waterford 3765, 9 a.m. to 5 p.m.

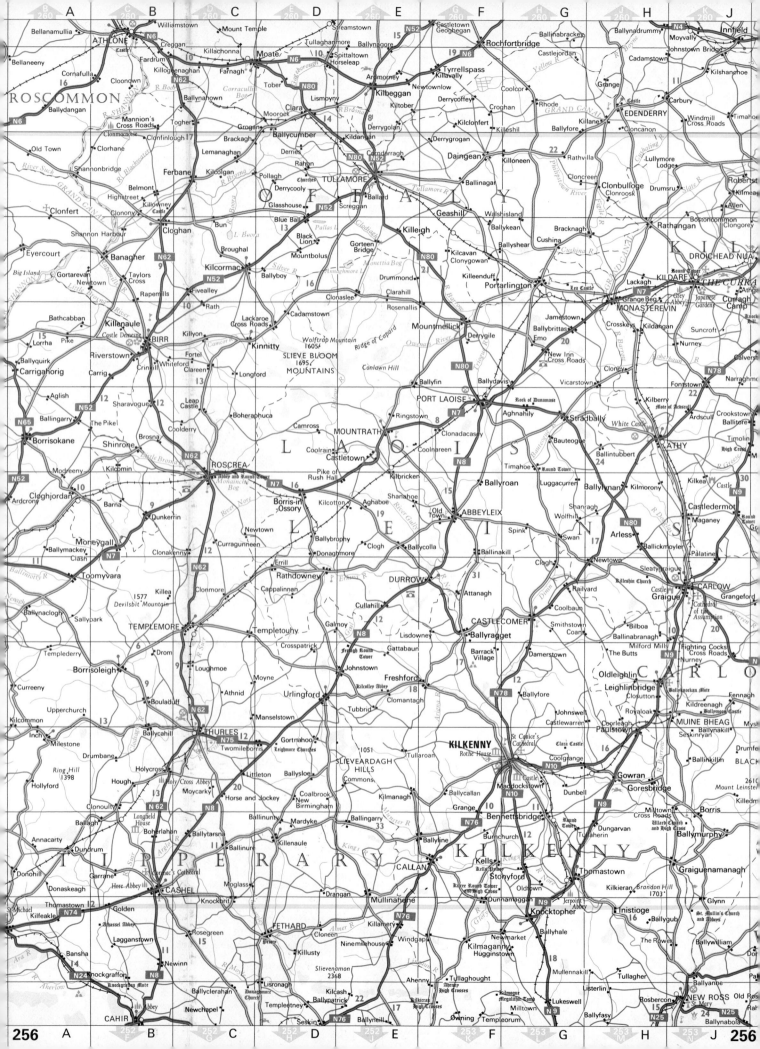

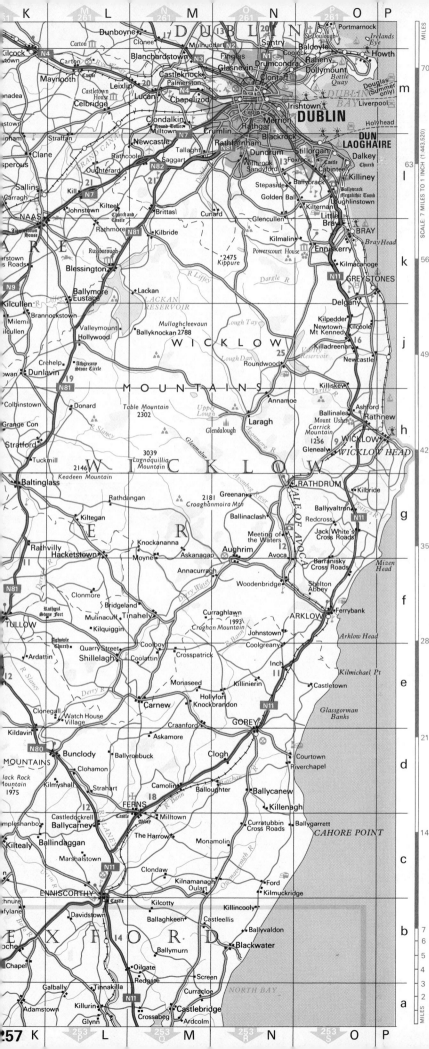

PLACES TO SEE IN
SOUTH LEINSTER

Opening times should be confirmed by telephone from the number in brackets. The exchange is given only if it differs from the place name at the beginning of the entry

Map references are shown after each place name

Abbeyleix (Fg) Site of a 6th-century abbey (31101), with 13th-century Monk's Bridge in the grounds

Ashford (Oh) *Mount Usher* (Wicklow 4116), gardens containing rare trees and shrubs

Athy (Hh) *White Castle*, 16th century. *Dominican Church*, 20th century

Birr (Bj) *Castle Demesne* (56), gardens which include the remains of the Rosse telescope. In the last century this telescope was the largest in the world

Carlow (Jf) *Castle*, 13th century. *Cathedral of the Assumption*, 19th-century Gothic-style cruciform church with a lofty lantern tower

Cashel (Bc) *Hore Abbey*, 13th-century Cistercian. *Cathedral*, 13th century. *St Patrick's Rock*, limestone outcrop containing a 4th to 5th-century fortress. *St Patrick's Cross*, a 12th-century, carved stone cross. *Cormac's Cathedral*, 12th century, contains a carved stone tomb chest

Castledermot (Jg) *Kilkea Castle*, 12th century

Celbridge (Lm) *Castletown House* (Dublin 28 8252), one of the finest Georgian houses in Ireland

Dublin (Nm) *Trinity College* (77 2941), 16th century, contains the Book of Kells, 8th-century illuminated gospels. *National Gallery* (76 7571). *National Museum* (76 5521), antiquities, folklife. *Guinness Museum* (75 6701), contains brewing equipment. *Municipal Gallery of Modern Art* (74 1903). *Christ Church Cathedral*, part-12th century. *St Patrick's Cathedral*, 12th century, where Jonathan Swift, author of 'Gulliver's Travels', was dean from 1713–45. *St Michan's Church*, 17th century, on the site of an 11th-century Danish church, contains the organ which Handel played during a visit; the vaults contain preserved corpses, said to be Crusaders. *Castle* (71 1777), 13th century. *Custom House* (74 2961), 18th century. *The Four Courts*, 18th century, seat of both

Supreme and High Courts. *Royal Hospital* (97 2844), 17th century, built for veteran soldiers; the chapel has a fine stucco ceiling and wood carving. *St Mary's Pro-Cathedral*, 19th-century Grecian-Doric style. *Mansion House* (76 2852), Queen Anne style, residence of Lord Mayors since 1715. *General Post Office* (74 8888), headquarters of Irish Volunteers during the 1916 Rising; the Republic was proclaimed here in 1921. *Chester Beatty Library* (69 2386), contains one of the world's most valuable private collections of Oriental manuscripts and miniatures. *Leinster House* (78 9911), 18th-century mansion, now meeting-place of the Dail and Seanad. *Zoo* (77 1425), Phoenix Park

Glasnevin (Nm) *Botanic Gardens* (Dublin 37 4388), contains 25,000 varieties of plants

Glendalough (Nh) 6th-century monastic settlement of St Kevin

Grange Beg (Hk) A 745 ft high hill with fine views over the Wicklow Mountains; on the top is the *Chair of Kildare*, a limestone outcrop

Kildare (Jk) *Japanese Gardens* and *National Stud* (21251). *Grey Abbey*, remains of a 13th-century Franciscan friary. *Castle*, 15th-century remains

Kilkenny (Gd) *Castle* (21450), 13th century. *St Canice's Cathedral*, 13th century. *Tholsel*, or Town Hall (21076), 18th century. *Rothe House*, 16th-century merchant's house containing period furniture; now a museum

Maynooth (Lm) *Carton* (Dublin 28 6250), Georgian mansion; in the grounds is a cottage faced with seashells

Powerscourt House (Ok) (Dublin 86 3546), 18th-century Italian and Japanese gardens containing a fine waterfall

Thomastown (Gc) *Jerpoint Abbey*, 12th-century Cistercian, one of the best monastic ruins in Ireland

AA SERVICE CENTRE: 23 Suffolk Street, Dublin 2 (Dublin 779481). Emergency/night service, Dublin, 8 a.m. (9 a.m. Sundays) to 1 a.m. (Dublin 779481); Port Laoise, 9 a.m. to 5 p.m. (21692)

A town plan of DUBLIN is on pp. 114–15

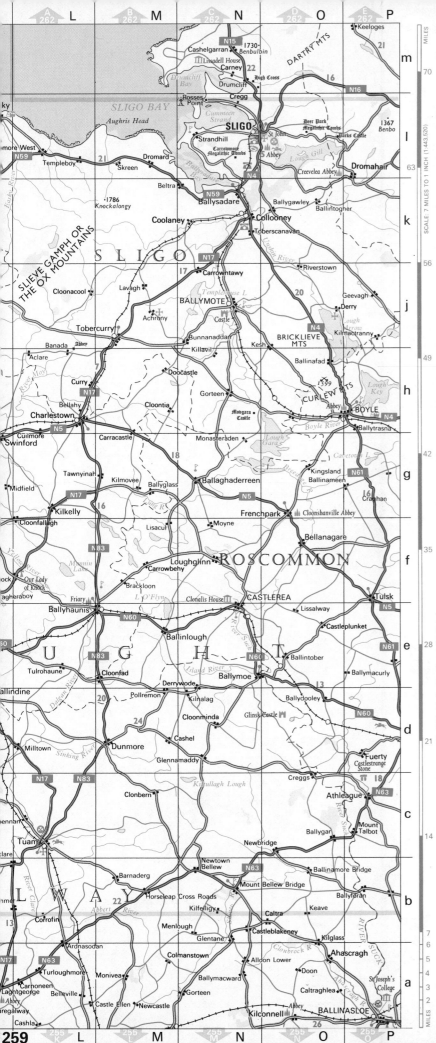

PLACES TO SEE IN
CONNAUGHT

Opening times should be confirmed by telephone from the number in brackets. The exchange is given only if it differs from the place name at the beginning of the entry
Map references are shown after each place name

Athleague (Pc) *Castlestrange Stone*, early Iron Age sculptured granite boulder

Ballyhaunis (Me) 15th-century Augustinian friary

Ballymote (Nj) *Castle*, 14th-century ruins

Benwee Head (Em) *Headland*, 829 ft, with views north-east to Donegal and south to Achill. *The Stags of Broad Haven*, a group of 300 ft high rocks, are 1½ miles offshore to the north-west

Boyle (Ph) *Abbey*, partly preserved 12th-century Cistercian cruciform church

Carney (Nm) *Lissadell House* (Sligo 73150), 19th century with fine furniture and paintings

Creevelea Abbey (Ol) 16th-century Franciscan friary

Croagh Patrick (Ff) Ireland's holy mountain, where St Patrick is said to have fasted during Lent in AD 411. It is the scene of a national pilgrimage on the last Sunday in July

Downpatrick Head (Hm) *Pollnashantinny*, puffing hole with a subterranean channel to the sea

Frenchpark (Og) *Cloonshanville Abbey*, 14th-century Dominican

Kesh (Oj) *Caves*, the entrance is on Keshcorran Hill. Legend claims that Cormac MacAirt, King of Ireland, was reared by a she-wolf in one of the caves

Killala (Jk) *Cathedral*, 17th century, built on the site of a medieval cathedral: only a pointed doorway in the south wall remains of the earlier building. *Round Tower*, near the cathedral, is 84 ft high with a doorway 11 ft from the ground: it is said to be the belfry of an early Celtic church founded in the 5th century by St Patrick. *Rathfran Abbey*, ruins, 2 miles north of Killala, was founded in the 13th century by a Dominican community. Several megalithic tombs and earthworks are near the ruins

Knock (Lf) *Church of Our Lady of Knock*, place of pilgrimage since an apparition was seen in 1879

Moyne Abbey (Jk) Restored ruins of a 15th-century Franciscan friary, with well-preserved cloisters: the church has an imposing tower and tracery in the windows

Murrisk Abbey (Ff) remains of a 15th-century Augustinian friary

Newport (Fg) *Burrishoole Abbey*, remains of a 15th-century Dominican friary

Sligo (Nl) *Abbey*, 13th-century Dominican friary, rebuilt after a fire in the 15th century. *St John's Cathedral*, 19th-century Romanesque. *Museum. City Hall* (2141), 19th-century Italian Renaissance style. *Lough Gill*, beauty spot

Strandhill (Nl) *Carrowmore Megalithic Tombs*

Twelve Pins (Ec) or *Twelve Bens*, a group of quartzite peaks with Benbaun, 2395 ft, at the centre

Westport (Ff) *Westport House* (130), Georgian mansion with Old Masters, Irish silver and glass; in the grounds are ornamental waters formed by the tides of Clew Bay

SLIGO

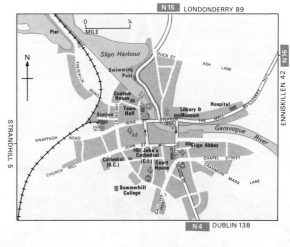

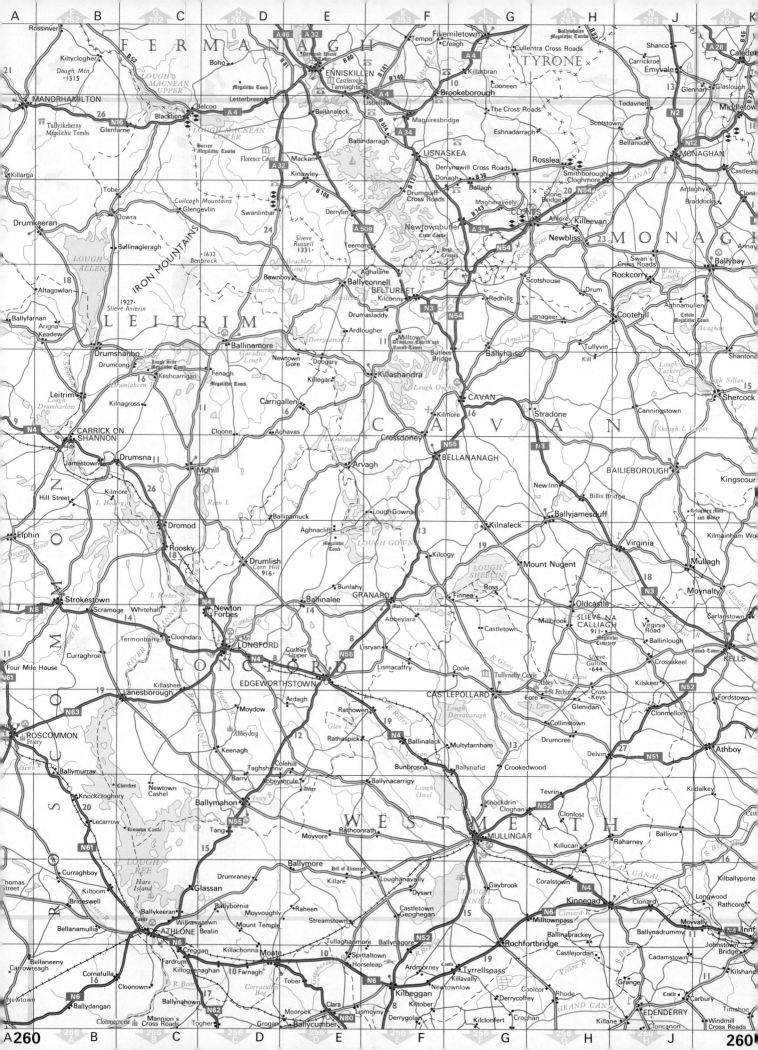

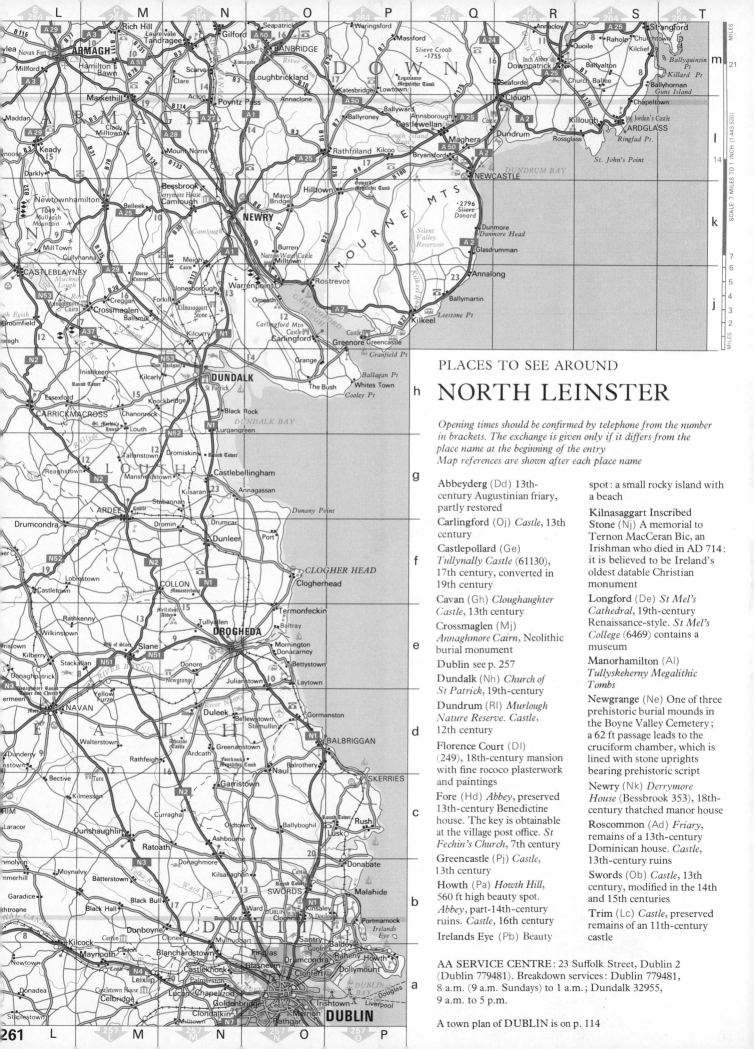

PLACES TO SEE AROUND
NORTH LEINSTER

Opening times should be confirmed by telephone from the number in brackets. The exchange is given only if it differs from the place name at the beginning of the entry
Map references are shown after each place name

Abbeyderg (Dd) 13th-century Augustinian friary, partly restored

Carlingford (Oj) *Castle*, 13th century

Castlepollard (Ge) *Tullynally Castle* (61130), 17th century, converted in 19th century

Cavan (Gh) *Cloughaughter Castle*, 13th century

Crossmaglen (Mj) *Annaghmore Cairn*, Neolithic burial monument

Dublin see p. 257

Dundalk (Nh) *Church of St Patrick*, 19th-century

Dundrum (Rl) *Murlough Nature Reserve. Castle*, 12th century

Florence Court (Dl) (249), 18th-century mansion with fine rococo plasterwork and paintings

Fore (Hd) *Abbey*, preserved 13th-century Benedictine house. The key is obtainable at the village post office. *St Fechin's Church*, 7th century

Greencastle (Pj) *Castle*, 13th century

Howth (Pa) *Howth Hill*, 560 ft high beauty spot. *Abbey*, part-14th-century ruins. *Castle*, 16th century

Irelands Eye (Pb) Beauty spot: a small rocky island with a beach

Kilnasaggart Inscribed Stone (Nj) A memorial to Ternon MacCeran Bic, an Irishman who died in AD 714: it is believed to be Ireland's oldest datable Christian monument

Longford (De) *St Mel's Cathedral*, 19th-century Renaissance-style. *St Mel's College* (6469) contains a museum

Manorhamilton (Al) *Tullyskeherny Megalithic Tombs*

Newgrange (Ne) One of three prehistoric burial mounds in the Boyne Valley Cemetery; a 62 ft passage leads to the cruciform chamber, which is lined with stone uprights bearing prehistoric script

Newry (Nk) *Derrymore House* (Bessbrook 353), 18th-century thatched manor house

Roscommon (Ad) *Friary*, remains of a 13th-century Dominican house. *Castle*, 13th-century ruins

Swords (Ob) *Castle*, 13th century, modified in the 14th and 15th centuries

Trim (Lc) *Castle*, preserved remains of an 11th-century castle

AA SERVICE CENTRE: 23 Suffolk Street, Dublin 2 (Dublin 779481). Breakdown services: Dublin 779481, 8 a.m. (9 a.m. Sundays) to 1 a.m.; Dundalk 32955, 9 a.m. to 5 p.m.

A town plan of DUBLIN is on p. 114

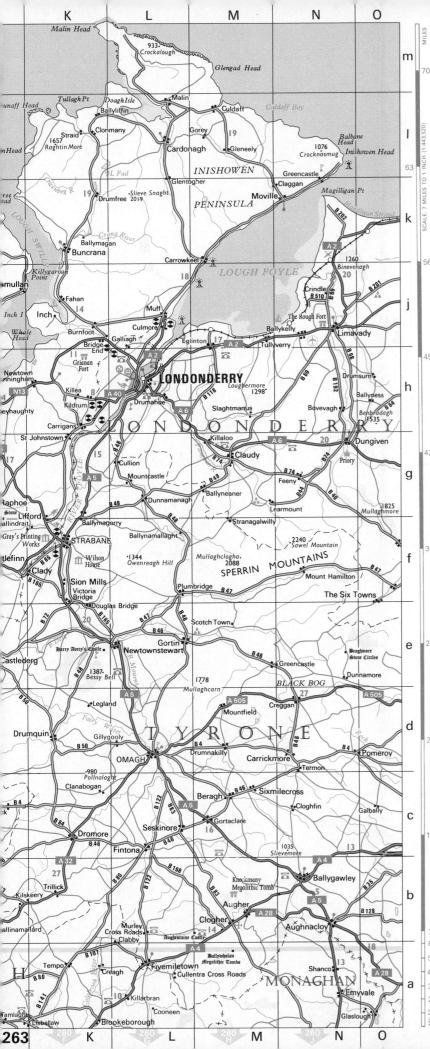

NORTH-WEST IRELAND

Opening times should be confirmed by telephone from the number in brackets. The exchange is given only if it differs from the place name at the beginning of the entry
Map references are shown after each place name

Ballyshannon (Ec) *Kilbarron Castle*, 13th-century ruins

Creevykeel Megalithic Tomb (Db) Megalithic tomb containing four cremated burials, excavated in 1935

Donegal (Fd) *Castle*, ruins of a 16th-century fortified house. *Abbey*, 15th-century Franciscan friary ruins

Dungiven (Ng) *Priory*, 12th-century Augustinian, with a canopied altar tomb

Enniskillen (Ja) *Castlecoole* (2690), 18th-century manor house

Glencolumbkille (Be) Prehistoric fonts and burial ground. Remains of an early Christian monastery

Grianan Fort (Kh) Well-preserved Iron Age circular stone fort

Gweedore (Ej) *National Park*

Irvinestown (Jb) *Old Castle Archdale* (333), ruined 17th-century fortified house

Knockmany (Mb) *Megalithic Tomb*, chambered burial cairn

Letterkenny (Hh) *Conwal Cemetery*, 13th-century graves

Limavady (Nj) *The Rough Fort*, circular earthwork, Gaelic fortified farmstead

Londonderry (Lh) 17th-century city walls, gates, bastions and watch towers

Strabane (Kf) *Gray's Printing Works* (883204) where John Dunlap, printer of American Declaration of Independence, was apprenticed

AA BREAKDOWN SERVICE: Londonderry 43467, 9 a.m. to 5 p.m.

PLACES TO SEE AROUND

ANTRIM see p. 264

Antrim (Ee) *Shanes Castle Railway and Nature Reserve* (3380)

Armagh (Ba) *Navan Fort*, early Iron Age. *County Museum* (524052). *Planetarium* (523689)

Ballycastle (El) *Bonamargy Friary*, 16th-century Franciscan remains

Belfast (Gd) *Botanic Gardens* (661309). *Ulster Museum* (668251). *Ulster Folk Museum* (Hollywood 5411). *City Hall* (20202), 20th-century Renaissance style

Bushmills (Cl) *Dunluce Castle* Ruins of a turreted castle; it was abandoned soon after the kitchen collapsed and slid from the crag into the sea, carrying a number of servants to their deaths in 1639

Carrickfergus (He) *Castle* (63604), 12th century

Cookstown (Bd) *Wellbrook Beetling Mill* (Belfast 669564), 18th-century water-powered linen mill

Dervock (Ck) *Benvarden Safari Park* (474)

Downpatrick (Ha) *Inch Abbey*, 12th-century Cistercian remains. *Castle Ward* (Strangford 204), 18th-century mansion, museum, wildfowl collection

Giant's Causeway (Cl) Rock phenomenon of 38,000 stone columns

Greyabbey (Jc) *Abbey*, 12th-century Cistercian

Killinchy (Jc) *Strangford Lough Wildlife Scheme* (516), has bird observation posts

Moneymore (Be) *Spring Hill* (210), 17th-century manor house

Newtownards (Hd) *Mount Stewart* (Greyabbey 362), 7 miles south-east, has 80 acres of subtropical gardens. *Priory*, 13th-century Dominican

Portadown (Db) *Ardress*, 17th-century manor house with fine plasterwork and a picture gallery

Saintfield (Hb) *Rowallane* (51466), 50 acre garden includes azaleas and magnolias

AA SERVICE CENTRE: Fanum House, 108–110 Great Victoria Street, Belfast (Belfast 26242). Breakdown services: Belfast 44538, 24-hour service; Coleraine 2596, 9 a.m. to 5 p.m.; Craigavon 41576, 9 a.m. to 5 p.m.

ROAD CONDITIONS: Belfast 8021

A town plan of BELFAST is on p. 114

LEISURE MAPS

Where to go and what to do

The ten National Parks in England and Wales cover 5254 square miles. Here, in largely untamed country, are playgrounds for the climber, camper, pony-trekker, angler, bird watcher and naturalist – or anyone who just wants to amble and enjoy some of Britain's most impressive scenery. Details of where to go and what to do in all the National Parks, as well as in six other areas of great scenic beauty in England, Scotland and Ireland, are included. This section begins with a guide to Britain's newest pleasure ground – 3000 miles of canals and waterways.

Scenic splendours of the British Isles

Waterways of Britain

Norfolk Broads and north coast   *Dartmoor and Exmoor*

Brecon, Pembroke and Snowdonia

National Parks in the North

Ireland: South-west and the North

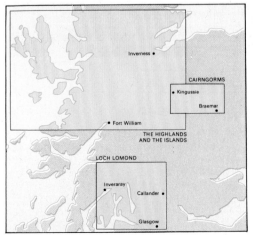

Scotland: Loch Lomond, Cairngorms and Highlands

Contents

INLAND WATERWAYS

Exploring Britain's quiet backwaters

Britain's inland waterway system blossomed with the Industrial Revolution. In the late 18th century when roads were still poor, 6000 miles of navigable rivers and canals became vital arteries between bustling mill and factory towns and the seaports. More canals continued to be opened well into the 19th century, but they were already doomed by the railways, and by 1830 they were declining rapidly.

Now life is returning to these old canals, but the colourful commercial narrow boats and barges have mostly given way to the hired motor-launch, the canoe and the sailing dinghy. On the towpaths once trodden by towing horses, walkers seek the countryside while anglers sit under green umbrellas. The 3000 miles of open canals form Britain's newest pleasure ground.

The attraction of the canals for many people is their loneliness. They seem to follow their own secret routes through the countryside, usually far from the noise of road and rail routes, penetrating right into the unspoilt green heart of the land.

Each canal has its own character whose subtle differences cannot be seen from a distance but only close at hand along the bank. There are towns and villages which owe their existence to them, because they grew up at junctions and wharves. The villages often consist of a warehouse, inn, shop and group of cottages, dating from the early days when the boatmen and bargees lived ashore.

The effect of the railways can still be noticed by the canals. Rail competition forced canal owners to cut their prices, which in turn forced the boatmen to give up their cottages and take their families on their barges for a life afloat. Inns sprang up along the canals for the boat crews and these are still there today.

Exploring by boat is only one way of enjoying the canals, with their villages, humpbacked bridges, aqueducts and secretive tunnels.

Walking and hiking on the towpaths is growing more popular as even minor roads become more crowded with traffic. Every year stretches of towpath are being repaired and opened to the public. On some urban sections there is no right of way, but those on foot are welcome in the rural areas – at their own risk. Walkers are advised to wear stout boots because hedges are often overgrown and banks are eroded by the wash from boats.

Wildlife is abundant along the waterways. The more remote rivers and canals, particularly in the Fens, support many species of birds and wild plants. Some stretches are now designated as Nature Reserves, and conservation associations and local authorities have formed nature trails beside waterways.

For the motorist taking a canal holiday, parking arrangements can usually be made at the yard at which the boat is hired.

Details of alternative routes when canal repairs necessitate diversions can be obtained throughout the 24 hours from the British Waterways Board, Canal phone (01-723 8485).

Away from the roar of traffic – a peaceful stretch through meadows and woods on the Leeds and Liverpool Canal.

How to start planning a holiday afloat

When planning a holiday afloat calculate how far you can travel in the time available on your chosen stretch of waterway. The speed limit on canals is 4 mph and 6–8 mph on rivers. The time taken to get through a lock varies, but ten minutes is average. In practice, six or seven hours cruising a day is comfortable, and one would expect to cover 12–15 miles and six locks in this time. Make allowance for river currents, summer peak traffic and unforeseen delays such as weed clogging the propeller. Canal boats from 2 to 12 berths may be hired and often there is room for a makeshift bunk, so a couple with one child would be comfortable in a 2-berth cruiser.

To obtain a list of hire firms telephone or write to the Inland Waterways Association, 114 Regent's Park Road, London NW1 8UQ. Tel. 01-586 2510 or 2556.

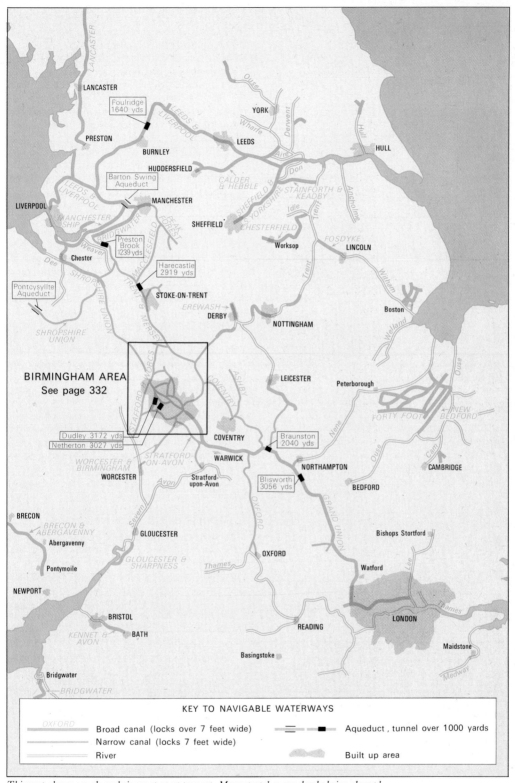

KEY TO NAVIGABLE WATERWAYS

Broad canal (locks over 7 feet wide)   Aqueduct, tunnel over 1000 yards

Narrow canal (locks 7 feet wide)

River   Built up area

This map shows canals and rivers open at present. More stretches are slowly being cleared.

Britain's canals cross under roads, and often run close to them before meandering into the countryside. Choose a stretch of canal from the map above, then plan your route to it from the road map section of this book. Those planning a holiday cruise can choose a circular route to avoid having to return along the same stretch of waterway. Britain's canals are either 'narrow' or 'broad' because they were constructed by different engineers to serve the needs of local industry, and so no standard system was adopted. The determining factor is the width and length of the locks.

Maximum boat sizes are – Narrow canal: length 70 ft, beam, or width, 7 ft. Broad canal: length 55–70 ft (depending on the particular canal), beam 12 ft 6 in. Fens: length 45 ft, beam 10 ft 6 in. Rivers: 55–174 ft, beam 10–19 ft.

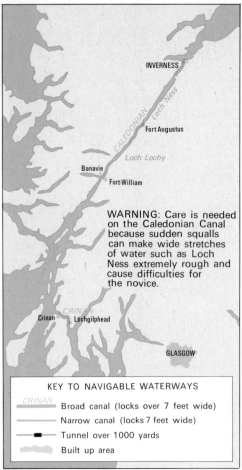

WARNING: Care is needed on the Caledonian Canal because sudden squalls can make wide stretches of water such as Loch Ness extremely rough and cause difficulties for the novice.

KEY TO NAVIGABLE WATERWAYS

——— Broad canal (locks over 7 feet wide)
——— Narrow canal (locks 7 feet wide)
—■— Tunnel over 1000 yards
〰〰 Built up area

Canals linking lochs across Scotland.

Crossing Scotland by canal and loch

The canals, rivers and lochs of Scotland offer a different type of holiday from one on England's narrow canals. Only two Scottish canals, the Crinan and the Caledonian, are now in use, apart from a 30 mile stretch of the old Union Canal which runs west from Edinburgh. Because old bridges are permanently lowered the Union is used only for towpath walks, fishing and canoeing.

The Crinan Canal is a 9 mile short-cut used by sea-going vessels, and has no facilities for hiring pleasure craft. The Caledonian Canal is a 60 mile waterway with 22 miles of canal and 29 locks running right across Scotland, connecting lochs Ness, Oich, Lochy and Linnhe.

The canal runs through dramatic Highland scenery, the boats passing almost within the shadow of Ben Nevis. At three places, Banavie, Fort Augustus and Inverness, the locks are in flights. At Banavie there is a flight of 8 locks, known as Neptune's Staircase, lifting sea-going vessels 64 ft.

There are numerous swing bridges, all manned, crossing the canal, including two railway swing bridges through which commercial traffic usually has priority. The canal passes vessels of 150 ft long by 35 ft beam and 13 ft 6 in. draught.

The canal speed limit is 6 mph, and unrestricted on open waters.

All the locks are large and operated by keepers. They are open, Monday to Saturday, from 6.30 a.m. to 8.30 p.m. in summer but only during daylight hours in winter. Only sea locks are open on Sunday, and passage through them on that day entails an additional charge.

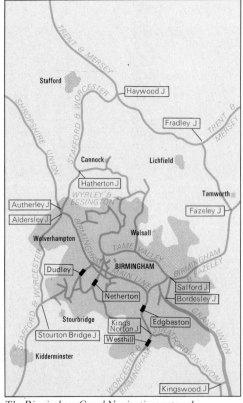

The Birmingham Canal Navigations network.

Grottoes in the Black Country

The largest network of urban waterways in Britain is owned by Birmingham Canal Navigations. Its canals radiate to five main river estuaries. There were once 160 miles of canals. Some stretches have been closed, but more than 100 miles of canal are still navigable.

Although they run through big industrial areas, the canals are remarkably remote, and one can moor in peace and quiet even in the centre of Birmingham. In striking contrast to the industrial sections, there are stretches running through pleasant wooded countryside.

There are more than 120 locks in the network with several impressive lock flights. Among the four tunnels are the 3027 yd long Netherton Tunnel, the last-built canal tunnel in Britain, and the dramatic and cavernous Dudley Tunnel, 3172 yds long, which was restored and reopened in 1973. Much of the tunnel is unlined rock and opens out into large grottoes with branches leading off to now-abandoned underground workings.

Some junctions in the network can be confusing as they are not signposted, but maps are available from The Inland Waterways Association, 114 Regent's Park Road, London NW1. Despite the refuse and factory waste dumped into the canals, the water remains relatively pure and there is some good fishing for bream, roach, perch and pike on some stretches.

How to get through a canal lock

The busiest part of canal cruising is going through locks. These are easy to negotiate if the correct sequence of opening and closing the gates and raising and lowering the water level is followed, as shown below. Every time a lock is used water is drained down the canal, so it is important not to waste water by incorrectly closing gates and paddles.

A lock is a chamber in which a boat can be floated from one level to another. The gates, which are of elm or oak, always point uphill so that water pressure forces them together.

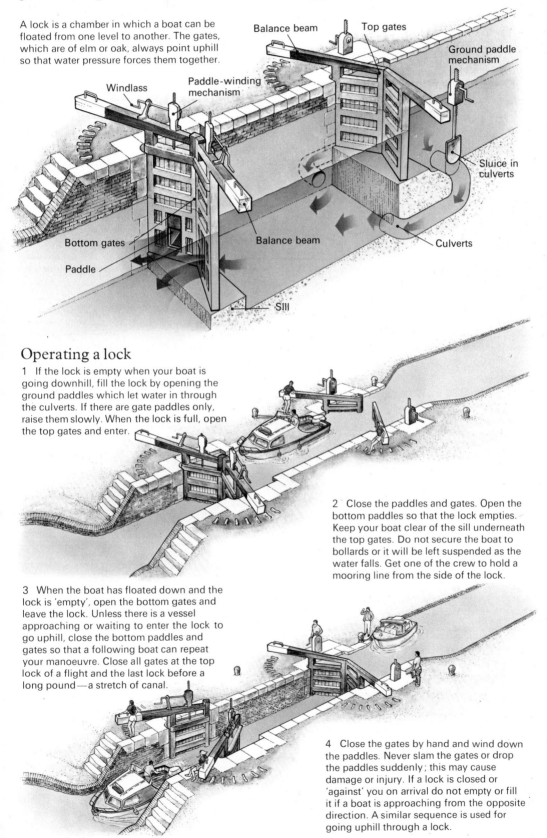

Balance beam
Top gates
Ground paddle mechanism
Windlass
Paddle-winding mechanism
Sluice in culverts
Bottom gates
Balance beam
Culverts
Paddle
Sill

Operating a lock

1 If the lock is empty when your boat is going downhill, fill the lock by opening the ground paddles which let water in through the culverts. If there are gate paddles only, raise them slowly. When the lock is full, open the top gates and enter.

2 Close the paddles and gates. Open the bottom paddles so that the lock empties. Keep your boat clear of the sill underneath the top gates. Do not secure the boat to bollards or it will be left suspended as the water falls. Get one of the crew to hold a mooring line from the side of the lock.

3 When the boat has floated down and the lock is 'empty', open the bottom gates and leave the lock. Unless there is a vessel approaching or waiting to enter the lock to go uphill, close the bottom paddles and gates so that a following boat can repeat your manoeuvre. Close all gates at the top lock of a flight and the last lock before a long pound—a stretch of canal.

4 Close the gates by hand and wind down the paddles. Never slam the gates or drop the paddles suddenly; this may cause damage or injury. If a lock is closed or 'against' you on arrival do not empty or fill it if a boat is approaching from the opposite direction. A similar sequence is used for going uphill through a lock.

333

High above valleys and deep underground

The aqueducts, bridges and tunnels of Britain's canal system are among the most impressive engineering feats of the late 18th and early 19th centuries. All were built by manpower, an army of workmen called navigators – hence the origin of the word 'navvies' – with only the occasional help of horses and steam pumps. One master-piece of engineering which survives is the 1000 ft long Pontcysyllte Aqueduct on the Shropshire Union Canal. Its cast-iron trough perched on slender stone piers carries boats 120 ft up across the Dee Valley. The plans of this bridge by Thomas Telford were greeted with derision by his contemporaries – until it was opened in 1805. Even today the dovetailed joints in the iron trough hardly leak. The

A magnificent three-arched aqueduct carries the Peak Forest Canal 100 ft above the River Goyt at Marple. Beyond is a railway bridge.

The towpath ends at the entrance to most tunnels. A boat was pushed through by 'legging' – two men would lie on boards and push with their feet on the tunnel walls.

longest tunnel, now disused, is at Standedge on the Huddersfield Narrow Canal. It runs for 5456 yds through the Pennines, at times 600 ft below ground.

The last tunnel to be built was the 3027 yd long Netherton Tunnel on the Birmingham Canal Navigations, which was opened in 1858. It was lit throughout by gas and later by electricity. It has a towpath on each side, unlike most tunnels which do not have a towpath at all.

Adding to the beauty of the canal scene are the flowing lines of hundreds of bridges varying from hump-backed stone structures to gracefully curving cast-iron ones. Probably the most attractive are the roving bridges which enabled a barge horse to cross from a towpath on one side of the canal to the other.

A roving bridge was designed to enable a horse to cross the canal without the towrope being detached from the barge. The bridge is used where the towpath crosses from one side of the canal to the other. The horse tows the barge under the bridge, and then walks back over the bridge, trailing the towrope over the parapet.

Beauty by accident and design

Beside the canals and locks are fascinating examples of accidental sculpture. These are the bollards, of wood or metal, used for tying up boats. Some of the wooden bollards have acquired fantastic shapes where ropes have cut into them. It was traditional for bargemen to give their barges individuality by colourful decorations. Names surrounded by flowers were painted on the cabins, and tillers were adorned with whitened rope in nautical tradition. Although rare today, a horse's tail may some-times be seen flowing from a rudder post. This

The scorching and searing of barge mooring ropes running over the woodwork for decades have sculpted canal bollards into weird designs such as these.

334

The waterway code and canal language

One of the pleasures of inland cruising is the freedom to go where you choose, but there are several important 'rules of the road' which must be observed. When meeting another craft pass on the right, except where it would be dangerous. For example, a laden working boat may need the deeper water on the outside of a bend, which will mean your passing on the left. The oncoming vessel will signal two horn blasts for you to do this. Overtake if possible on a straight stretch. Working boats or barges always have priority over pleasure craft; otherwise, priority at locks is on a 'first come, first served' basis, except when the water level in the lock is in favour of a craft seen approaching.

Speed limits are laid down by each waterway authority. Never allow the wash waves to break on the banks. Slow down on bends, and when approaching or passing moored craft, other craft under way, anglers, bridges and tunnels.

The boat should be equipped with a white headlamp for tunnels and night cruising on canals. Full navigation lighting is obligatory on rivers and estuaries. Mooring is possible on most straight stretches but do not moor on bends or near locks and bridges.

Guide to the terms used by watermen

Balance beam Large timber running horizontally from a lock gate. It is used as a lever for opening and closing the gate.

Bridge hole The arch under a canal bridge.

Butty An unpowered narrow boat towed behind a motor boat.

Cut A canal, so called because it is an artificial cut of the land.

Draw To open a sluice or paddle of a lock.

Gates The movable watertight gates at each end of the lock. The gate where the water level is the highest is known as the *top gate*; and where the water is at the lower level, the *bottom gate.*

Keb Long rake kept at locksides for removing debris from the lock.

Lengthman A man employed by a navigation authority to maintain a section of waterway, especially the water levels.

Narrow beam A canal on which the locks do not exceed a width of 7 ft 6 in.

Narrow boat A boat designed for narrow canals. Generally, 70 ft long with a 7 ft beam.

Paddle The sluice for filling or emptying a lock of water. In the North of England a paddle is called a clough (pronounced 'clow'). In Ireland it is a 'rack'.

Pound The stretch of water between two canal locks.

Side pond A small reservoir re-using water to refill a lock instead of letting it run away.

Sill The masonry beneath a lock gate, sometimes projecting several feet from the gate.

Stop gates Wood or metal gates, similar to a lock gate, used to retain a section of a canal during repairs. Also known as planks.

Summit The highest stretch of water on a canal – often fed by a reservoir.

Wheeler or Lock wheeler A person – at one time a cyclist – who travels ahead of the boat to set the locks in readiness.

Winding hole A wide place on the waterway for turning boats. So called as the wind was used to assist in turning.

Windlass The L-shaped crank or handle used for winding the paddles up and down, usually detachable, but sometimes fixed.

Waterway Museums

The Waterways Museum beside the Grand Union Canal at Stoke Bruerne, near Towcester, Northants, houses an important historical collection of waterway relics recording the fascinating canal story of more than two centuries. Inquiries to The Curator (Tel. Roade 862229). The Exeter Maritime Museum on the Exeter Canal has a collection of boats from all parts of the world. Inquiries to The Director, International Sailing Craft Association, The Quay, Exeter (Tel. Exeter 58075).

Stoke Bruerne Waterways Museum

tradition is believed to have begun when a boating family, losing a cherished white horse, pinned its tail astern so that the 'beast's beauty, strength and virtue might go with them forever'.

The intricate flower designs and elaborate printing of barge names gave an individual stamp to the families who spent their lives on canals.

Decorated rudder post of a narrow boat. The entwined bands are called Turk's Head, the vertical piece a Swan's Neck, and the rudder post a Ram's Head.

NORFOLK

Sails on the Broads and wings over the North Coast

The most striking feature of Norfolk is its flatness. From its 'peak', only 329 ft above sea level, ½ mile south-east of Beacon Hill, on the Cromer Ridge, can be seen two differing but characteristic sides of Norfolk which are not repeated anywhere else in Britain.

To the north and west is a 100 mile sweep of coast which includes some of the most important nature reserves in the country.

To the south-east from the Cromer Ridge, can be seen rivers meandering to form part of the Broads, which were formed centuries ago when peat diggings became flooded. Hickling, the largest Broad, is also the shallowest with a maximum depth of 5 ft. There are more than 30 Broads which, together with linked rivers, lakes and man-made waterways, provide about 200 miles of navigable water. The Broads are a fascinating field of study for the naturalist and a playground for the angler, the yachtsman, the canoeist or a family hiring a motor launch from one of the many boatyards on the Broads.

Breydon Water, one of the popular sailing stretches on the Broads.

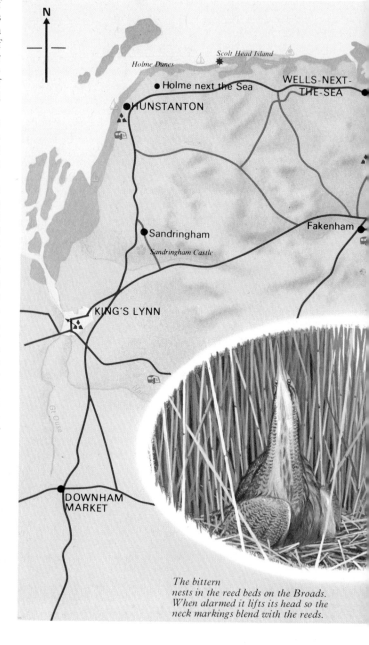

The bittern nests in the reed beds on the Broads. When alarmed it lifts its head so the neck markings blend with the reeds.

Fishing on the Broads

Coarse fishing is excellent on the Broads. Licences for limited periods can be bought at post offices, and annual licences from the Anglian Water Authority, Norfolk and Suffolk Division, Thorpe Road, Norwich.

Finding out more . . .

Inland Waterways Association, 114 Regent's Park Road, London (01-586 2556), publishes an annual holiday guide which includes a list of the many yards hiring out boats.

The British Tourist Authority, 64 St James's Street, London (01-629 9191), also publishes an annual guide to boat hire.

The Anglian Water Authority, Norfolk and Suffolk Division, Thorpe Road, Norwich NR1 1SA (Norwich 615161), issues trout and coarse-fishing licences.

The Broads Society has members on committees of other organisations and authorities to protect the interests of people using the Broads: Miss Pamela Oakes, 63 Whitehall Road, Norwich (Norwich 24642).

Other addresses: Yarmouth Port and Haven Commissioners, 24 South Quay, Great Yarmouth (Gt Yarmouth 55151), for tolls and regulations; Tourist Information Office, Augustine Steward House, Tombland, Norwich (Norwich 20679); British Canoe Union, 45–47 High Street, Addlestone, near Weybridge; Forestry Commission, Government Buildings, Brooklands Avenue, Cambridge (Cambridge 58911), for forest walks.

Berney Arms Mill   Horsey Mill   Thurne Mill

About 700 windmills drained the Fens until 1820 when steam pumps were introduced. These in turn gave way to electric and diesel pumps, but many windmills have been restored and are kept in working order.

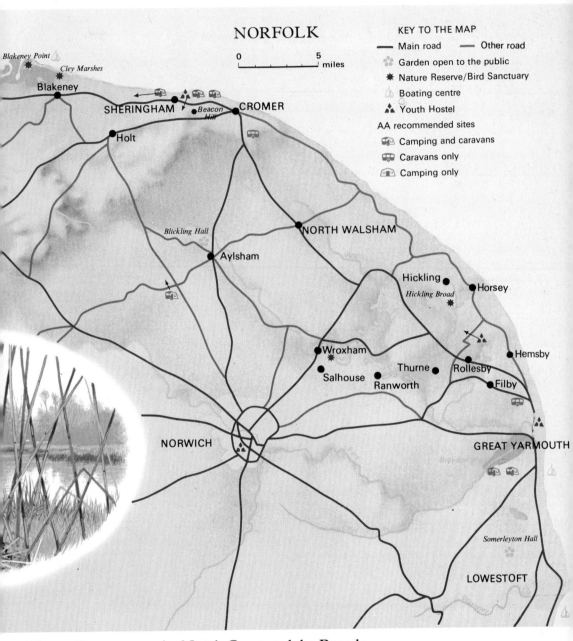

NORFOLK

0   5 miles

KEY TO THE MAP
— Main road   — Other road
- Garden open to the public
- Nature Reserve/Bird Sanctuary
- Boating centre
- Youth Hostel

AA recommended sites
- Camping and caravans
- Caravans only
- Camping only

Blakeney Point
Cley Marshes
Blakeney
SHERINGHAM   Beacon Mill   CROMER
Holt
Blickling Hall   NORTH WALSHAM
Aylsham
Hickling   Horsey
Hickling Broad
Wroxham   Hemsby
Salhouse   Thurne   Rollesby
Ranworth   Filby
NORWICH   GREAT YARMOUTH
Breydon Water
Somerleyton Hall
LOWESTOFT

Nature Reserves on the North Coast and the Broads

Specially built observation posts on the nature reserves along the north coast of Norfolk enable bird watchers to study resident birds and rare migratory visitors from the Continent and Africa.

Hickling Broad: 1361 acres of land and water. The bittern's return to Britain was noted here in 1912 after an absence of about 60 years. Bearded tits, herons and many waders and ducks also nest here.

Cley Marshes: An important reserve for observing passage waders such as the spoonbill and black tern in spring and autumn. Large numbers of wildfowl winter here.

Holme Dunes: The varied habitats attract a succession of migrant waders. Duck winter on the Broadwater and large pools while oyster-catchers and knots feed on the foreshore.

Scolt Head Island: A variety of shore birds nest here. The

sandwich tern colony is one of the largest in Britain. The chicks begin to hatch in July.

Blakeney Point: Large colonies of common and little terns nest here.

Finding out more . . .

Norfolk Naturalists Trust, 72 Cathedral Close, Norwich (Norwich 25540); Nature Conservancy Council, 60 Bracondale, Norwich (Norwich 20558); National Trust, Eastern Regional Office, Blickling Hall, Norwich (Aylsham 3471).

337

DARTMOOR

The bleak grandeur of an ancient mountain range

Dartmoor was part of a mountain range that stretched across Europe 200 million years ago. Gradually the soft peaks were eroded away, leaving granite stumps which were at the base of the mountains. These imposing, weather-carved pieces of granite are the tors that thrust up through the heather and bogs of the moor. Only a few hundred yards from main roads begins a wilderness which has hardly changed since prehistoric times. The people who lived here then left behind them thousands of stone circles dotted about the moor. One of the most spectacular of these settlements is Grimspound, which contains 24 huts surrounded by a stone wall, 4 miles west of Manaton. Later warlike Celts built hill forts such as that at Cranbrook. Wild ponies have roamed Dartmoor for centuries, but a byelaw forbids visitors feeding them so that they do not congregate on the roads and cause accidents.

Haytor . . . a viewpoint over the moors.

Finding out more . . .

Dartmoor National Park Dept., Parke, Bovey Tracey, Devon (Bovey Tracey 832093). Information centres are also open, from Easter to mid-October, at Postbridge, Tavistock, Steps Bridge and New Bridge. Devon Archaeological Society: Norman Shiel, c/o Rougemont House Museum, Castle Street, Exeter. Angling: South-West Water Authority, 3–5 Barnfield Road, Exeter; Duchy of Cornwall Office, Princetown. Youth Hostels Association, Belmont House, Devonport Road, Stoke, Plymouth. Bird-watching: Mrs. H. A. Woodland, Blacksmith's Cottage, West Raddon, Shobrooke, Crediton.

Dartmoor pony . . . a resident for centuries.

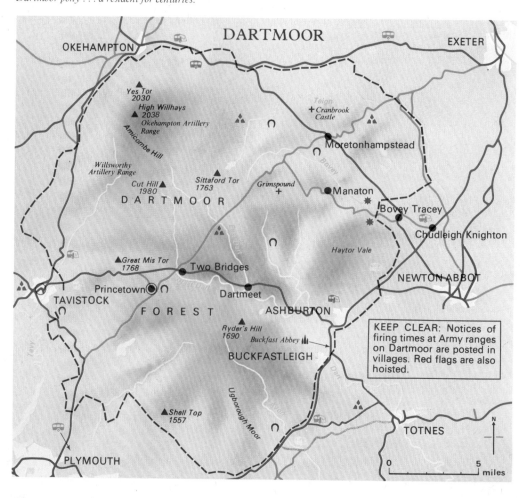

KEEP CLEAR: Notices of firing times at Army ranges on Dartmoor are posted in villages. Red flags are also hoisted.

EXMOOR

Heather-clad hills and a dramatic seascape

The heart of Exmoor is in sharp contrast to Dartmoor's bleak grandeur. Here, instead of granite tors, are rich farmlands, softly rounded hills blanketed with heather, and woods where the last of England's native herds of red deer browse. The drama of Exmoor is along the coast, where densely wooded ravines, cut by fast-flowing rivers, reach to the sea and where the roads plunge alarmingly down steep hills to villages of pink and whitewashed cottages.

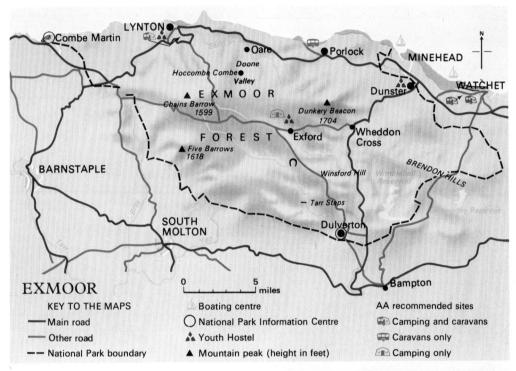

EXMOOR

KEY TO THE MAPS

0 _____ 5 miles

— Main road
— Other road
-- National Park boundary

⛵ Boating centre
◯ National Park Information Centre
▲▲ Youth Hostel
▲ Mountain peak (height in feet)

AA recommended sites
🚐 Camping and caravans
🚐 Caravans only
🚐 Camping only

Finding out more . . .

Exmoor National Park Dept., Exmoor House, Dulverton, TA22 9HL (Dulverton 23665). The following information centres are open only from Easter to September: Lynmouth Parish Hall (Lynton 2509); Beach Car Park, Combe Martin (Combe Martin 3319); County Gate, on A39 between Porlock and Lynmouth (Brendon 321).
Ilfracombe and District Angling Association, 61 High Street, Ilfracombe. Combe Martin Angling Club: B. S. Hill, Homeside, Kentisburyford, Barnstaple.
Pony Trekking: Mrs. D. C. Bassett, Town Farm Riding Stables, W. Anstey, South Molton. Blacklands Riding Stables, Higher Blacklands, Withypool.
Nature Conservancy Council, S.W. Region, Roughmoor, Bishops Hull, Taunton.
National Trust Estate Office, Holnicote, near Minehead (Porlock 862452).

A 180 ft long clapper bridge known as the Tarr Steps crosses the River Barle below Winsford Hill. Some historians claim that it is 3000 years old, but others believe that it was built no earlier than AD 1400.

Oare Church

Visiting the Doone Country

R. D. Blackmore published his novel 'Lorna Doone' in 1869. Since then, admirers of the book have visited the places he describes in his story of robbery and murder said to have been committed by the Doone family in the 17th century. The church where Lorna was supposed to have been shot during her wedding is at Oare (see map above). Two suggested drives around the Doone country, one starting from County Gate and the other from Dulverton, are detailed in free leaflets available from Exmoor National Park Dept., Dulverton TA22 9HL.

BRECON BEACONS

Lonely mountains and tumbling falls

The Brecon Beacons National Park is wild Wales. The Beacons themselves, a 10 mile long mountain range, give an awe-inspiring impression of giant, surging waves about to crash into the valleys. Roads peter out into tracks at the approaches to the highest mountain, 2906 ft Pen y Fan, and the main A470 road gets no nearer than 3 miles to the summit. The waterfalls in the 519 square miles of the Park are as spectacular as the mountains. The Henrhyd Falls, ½ mile north of Coelbren, have a 90 ft drop; while visitors can walk behind the Sgwd yr Eira Falls on the River Hepste, which can be reached from a point 1 mile north of Penderyn on the A4059. For those wishing to enjoy the mountains without too much physical effort, the National Park Authority has built the Mountain Centre on Mynydd Illtyd, near Brecon. It has a car park, picnic spots and a buffet. An easy mountain is the Sugar Loaf, just under 2000 ft, which is approached through the Usk Valley.

The savage beauty of the Beacons.

Caving in the Brecon Beacons

Limestone caves honeycomb the southern fringe of the Brecon Beacons National Park. Some may be explored by beginners, but it is advisable to join a club and be properly equipped. Details from: Cambrian Caving Council, 15 Elm Grove, Aberdare CF44 8DN (Aberdare 87 2585).

Pony trekking in the hills

The foot-sure Welsh pony has helped to make the hills of Wales, particularly the Black Mountains, the most popular trekking area in Britain. Even novices feel safe on Welsh ponies, which can be hired from many local stables.

Only more experienced riders should attempt trail riding. Details from the Pony Trekking and Riding Society of Wales, c/o J. R. Thomas, 32 North Parade, Aberystwyth, Dyfed.

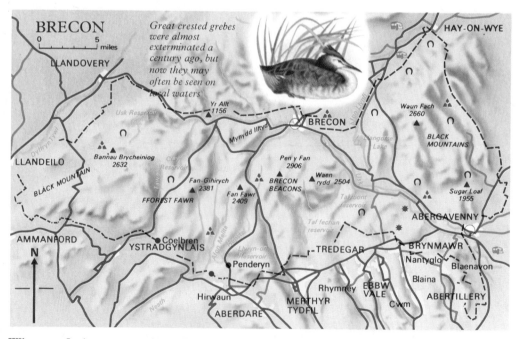

Where to find out more about Brecon . . .

National Park centres: Glamorgan Street, Brecon (Brecon 4437); Monk Street, Abergavenny (Abergavenny 3254); Brecon Beacons Mountain Centre, Libanus, Brecon (Brecon 3366); 8 Broad Street, Llandovery (Llandovery 20693). Postal enquiries to Glamorgan Street, Brecon, only; phone enquiries to Mountain Centre throughout year, to other centres Easter to September only.

Fishing licences: whole area: Welsh National Water Development Authority, Cambrian Way, Brecon, Powys; local waters: Glamorgan River Division, Coychurch Road, Bridgend, Mid Glamorgan; South-West Wales River Division, Penyfai Lane, Llanelli, Dyfed; Usk River Division, The Croft, Goldcroft Common, Caerleon, Newport, Gwent; Wye River Division, 4 St John Street, Hereford.

PEMBROKE

The long path round a spectacular coast

The Pembrokeshire Coast National Park is the smallest and most unusual of Britain's ten national parks. With an area of only 225 square miles, it consists of a strip of coastline a mile or two wide and two regions of great natural beauty inland. One inland section of the park is the inner estuary of the Cleddau and the other is the Prescelly Hills, from which stone was said to have been taken to build Stonehenge. The area is studded with medieval fortifications, including Pembroke Castle, which towers over the coastal path.

A 170 mile path follows the Pembroke coast between St Dogmaels in the north and Amroth in the south. It runs inland for only 9 miles between Freshwater West and Saddle Point.

The path is never far from a road, so motorists not interested in a long walk can park their cars and stroll over small stretches. The path is worth joining anywhere, but particularly attractive is the grand cliff scenery at Strumble Head in the north and the sweeping beaches of St Brides Bay in the south. A detailed route map of the path can be obtained from Pembrokeshire Coast National Park Information Centres (see below).

A headland on the Pembroke path.

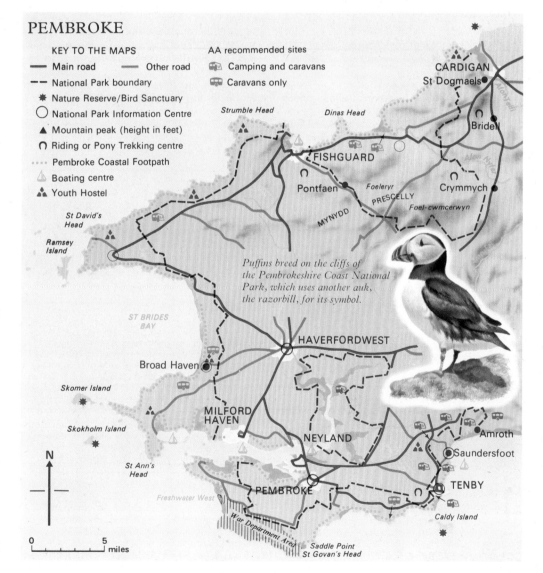

PEMBROKE

KEY TO THE MAPS

— Main road
═══ Other road
–– National Park boundary
✳ Nature Reserve/Bird Sanctuary
○ National Park Information Centre
▲ Mountain peak (height in feet)
∩ Riding or Pony Trekking centre
···· Pembroke Coastal Footpath
⚠ Boating centre
▲▲ Youth Hostel

AA recommended sites
🚐 Camping and caravans
🚐 Caravans only

Puffins breed on the cliffs of the Pembrokeshire Coast National Park, which uses another auk, the razorbill, for its symbol.

CARDIGAN
St Dogmaels
Bridell
Strumble Head   Dinas Head
FISHGUARD
Pontfaen   Foeleryr   Crymmych
PRESCELLY
Foel-cwmcerwyn
MYNYDD
St David's Head
Ramsey Island
ST BRIDES BAY
Broad Haven
HAVERFORDWEST
Skomer Island
MILFORD HAVEN
Skokholm Island
NEYLAND   Amroth
N
St Ann's Head   Saundersfoot
PEMBROKE   TENBY
Freshwater West
War Department Area
Caldy Island
Saddle Point
St Govan's Head
0   5 miles

Where to find out more . . .

All postal enquiries about the Pembrokeshire Coast National Park to Information Service, County Offices, Haverfordwest, Dyfed. Phone enquiries to Haverford-west 3131, ext. 76: summer only Haverfordwest 66141, Pembroke 2148, Tenby 3510, St David's 720392, Broadhaven 412, Saundersfoot 812175.

SNOWDONIA

Peaks of the Princes

The Welsh call the five mountain ranges that make up Snowdonia Eryri – the Home of the Eagles. At the heart is Snowdon itself, at 3560 ft the highest mountain south of Scotland. There are six marked pathways and a mountain railway to the summit, yet this remains a true mountain, rugged, complex, grand in outline – and capable of killing those who go unwarily in mist or snow.

From its summit on a clear day the climber can get some idea of the enormous extent of the Snowdonia National Park. To the north are the ranges of the Glyders and Carneddau. To the south-west is Moel Hebog and its associated tops. East and south are Moel Siabod above the village of Capel Curig and Moelwyn. Still further south, are the Rhinogs, running down to the Mawddach Estuary, and beyond the estuary is Cader Idris. Even this tally does not exhaust the ranges and complexes of mountains lying within the 840 square miles of the National Park.

The borders of the Park roughly coincide with those of the realm of Gwynedd, whose rulers were Princes of Wales until the English conquered the area in the 13th century. At Harlech is the massive castle, roofless yet dominating, which Edward I built to control his conquest.

The Carneddau range is full of romantic names. Carnedd itself means cairn, a heap of stones or memorial, so the two chief mountains – Carnedd Dafydd and Carnedd Llywelyn – are the Cairns of David and Llewellyn, the last two Princes of Wales before the English conquest. But Welsh names can spell danger too. One of the Carneddau mountains is called Pen Llithrig-y-Wrâch, the Witch's Slide. In the Glyder range

Snowdon rises majestically over Llyn Llydaw.

is Twll Ddu, the Black Hole, also known as the Devil's Kitchen where a stream from Llyn-y-Cwn (Lake of the Dogs) falls into a dramatic chasm.

The beauty and romance of these mountains can be tasted – but only tasted – from the roads through the Park. A drive over the Llanberis Pass or along the windings of the Mawddach Estuary from Barmouth to Dolgellau reveals some of the scenic glory of Britain.

But sooner or later the tourist must explore a little way at least on foot. A good place to start is the Coed y Brenin, a stretch of rolling countryside just north of Dolgellau, which has been planted with conifers by the Forestry Commission. Then the more adventurous will find their way out of the low woodlands and up on to the flanks of mountains.

Chugging up from Tywyn on the Talyllyn line.

Snowdonia's little trains

Six narrow-gauge railways run through Snowdonia National Park. The Festiniog Railway, with a gauge of only 1 ft 11 in., climbs from Porthmadog to Tanygrisiau with views of the Snowdon Mountain range, Harlech Castle and the sea. On the Talyllyn line trains run from Tywyn to Nant Gwernol. The Llanberis Railway runs along the side of Llyn Padarn near Mount Snowdon. On the Snowdon Mountain Line trains climb 3560 ft to the summit. The Fairbourne Railway runs alongside beaches between Barmouth and Fairbourne, and the Bala Lake Railway from Llanuwchllyn skirts the lake.

Where to find out more about Snowdonia

Snowdonia National Park Information Office, Yr Hen Ysgol, Maentwrog, Blaenau Ffestiniog (Maentwrog 274). National Park information and exhibition centres (no postal enquiries): The Wharf, Aberdyfi (Aberdyfi 321); Old British High School, High Street, Bala (Bala 520367); Isallt, High Street, Blaenau Ffestiniog (Blaenau Ffestiniog 360); The Bridge, Dolgellau (Dolgellau 422888); High Street, Harlech (Harlech 658); Royal Oak Stables, Betwys-y-coed; Visitor Centre, Plas Tanybwlch.

Horse riding: Apply for a permit for riding in forest parks off roads or bridleways from the Forest Office, Gwydyr Uchaf, Llanrwst (Llanrwst 640578).

Fishing: Licences can be obtained from sub-post-offices and fishing tackle dealers. Information from Gwynedd River Division, Bron Castell, Bangor (Bangor 52881) or the Federation of Gwynedd Anglers, Llwyn, Blaenau Ffestiniog.

Nature Conservancy Council, Penrhos Road, Bangor (Bangor 4001).

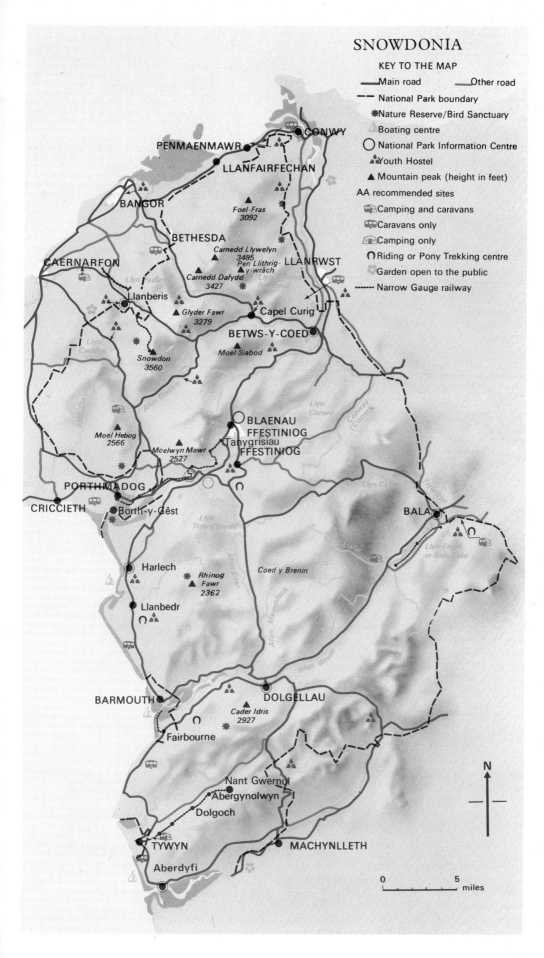

SNOWDONIA

KEY TO THE MAP

— Main road   ○— Other road

– – – National Park boundary

✳ Nature Reserve/Bird Sanctuary

△ Boating centre

○ National Park Information Centre

▴ Youth Hostel

▲ Mountain peak (height in feet)

AA recommended sites

🚐 Camping and caravans

🚐 Caravans only

🚐 Camping only

∩ Riding or Pony Trekking centre

∩ Garden open to the public

· · · · · Narrow Gauge railway

CONWY

PENMAENMAWR

LLANFAIRFECHAN

BANGOR

Foel-Fras
3092

BETHESDA

Carnedd Llywelyn
3485
Pen Llithrig-
y-wrâch

LLANRWST

CAERNARFON

Carnedd Dafydd
3427

Llanberis

Glyder Fawr
3279

Capel Curig

BETWS-Y-COED

Llyn Padarn

Llyn Cwellyn

Snowdon
3560

Moel Siabod

Llyn
Conwy

Conway
(Conwy)

Afon Dyli

Afon Glaslyn

Moel Hebog
2566

○ BLAENAU
FFESTINIOG
Tanygrisiau
FFESTINIOG

Moelwyn Mawr
2527

Llyn Celyn

Tryweryn

PORTHMADOG

CRICCIETH

Borth-y-Gêst

○ ∩

BALA

Llyn
Trawsfynydd

Llyn Tegid
or Bala Lake

Harlech

Rhinog
Fawr
2362

Coed y Brenin

Afon Eden

Afon Mawddach

Llanbedr

BARMOUTH

Afon Wnion

DOLGELLAU

Cader Idris
2927

Fairbourne

Nant Gwernol

Abergynolwyn

Dolgoch

TYWYN

MACHYNLLETH

Aberdyfi

N

0   5
└─────────┘ miles

THE LAKE DISTRICT

A national park 'discovered' by the poets

Volcanic upheavals 450 million years ago helped to make the spectacular scenery of one of Britain's finest natural playgrounds – the Lake District. Climbers now scale the weathered volcanic peaks, walkers take the gentler climbs, while boats sail on four of the eight major lakes formed when Ice Age glaciers melted 10,000 years ago.

The Lake District was 'discovered' in the 18th century when romantic and picturesque scenery became fashionable. The poet Thomas Gray was one of the first visitors, followed by Wordsworth, Coleridge and Southey, who became known as the Lake Poets (see p. 212). The railways made the Lakes popular in the last century and recently the M6 has opened the area to a summertime flood of visitors from the south of England, Wales, the Midlands, the north-west of England and Scotland. In the peak holiday rush of July and August accommodation is difficult to find and main roads are crowded. The Lake District is a national park, the biggest of the ten in England and Wales, covering nearly 900 square miles. Its heart is a knot of mountains which includes Scafell Pike, the highest summit in England (3210 ft), Great Gable, Allen Crag, Glaramara, the Langdale Pikes, Fairfield and Helvellyn.

From this centre the dales, dropping down to the lakes, radiate like spokes of a wheel. To the south are Langdale, with Elter Water in it and the valley of the Rothay flowing down to Grasmere, Rydal Water and Windermere. To the north is Borrowdale, a mixture of water, woods and crags with the River Derwent flowing on from Derwent Water to Bassenthwaite, the northernmost lake.

To the west Honister Pass leads out of Borrowdale and down to Buttermere and Crummock Water. The spoke south of that central knot is remote Wasdale with Wast Water and Eskdale. From Eskdale a miniature railway runs down to the coast. To the east lie Ullswater and Hawes Water beyond. To the north, outside of the wheel, is 'back o' Skidda', which was John Peel's hunting ground.

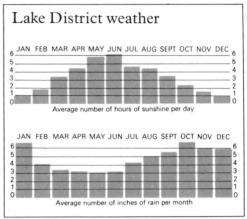

Lake District weather

JAN FEB MAR APR MAY JUN JUL AUG SEPT OCT NOV DEC

Average number of hours of sunshine per day

JAN FEB MAR APR MAY JUN JUL AUG SEPT OCT NOV DEC

Average number of inches of rain per month

Buzzards over the peaks

Buzzard

Raven

The buzzard and the raven, which almost became extinct in inland regions in the last century, are now thriving and multiplying in the Lake District. Buzzards, which can be distinguished from other hawks by their broad rounded wings and rounded tails, now nest in lowland woods as well as on the fells. Ravens are larger than the carrion crow and have wedge-shaped tails. The Lake District is rich in other bird life: wheatears, skylarks and ring ouzels can be seen on the fells, pied flycatchers, redstarts and tree pipits near woods, and dippers, wagtails and whooper swans by the lakes.

Traces of Lakeland's ancient peoples

The first known settlers in the Lake District were a Stone Age people who, nearly 8000 years ago, fashioned tools and polished axes from flint or stone. A 96 ft by 44 ft cairn, where people of this time buried their dead, can be seen between Ennerdale and Wasdale. Two great stone circles, at Castlerigg, 1 mile east of Keswick, and Swinside, 3 miles west of Broughton in Furness, were set up by Bronze Age peoples c. 1800 BC. Their purpose is unknown, although smaller circles found in the Lake District marked burial places. Of Roman remains Hardknott Castle is the most impressive. It was built in Hadrian's time, soon after

The great stone circle at Castlerigg.

AD 120. A circular building with walls up to 5 ft high and a three-roomed bathhouse are surviving buildings. A levelled space near the camp is believed to have been a parade ground.

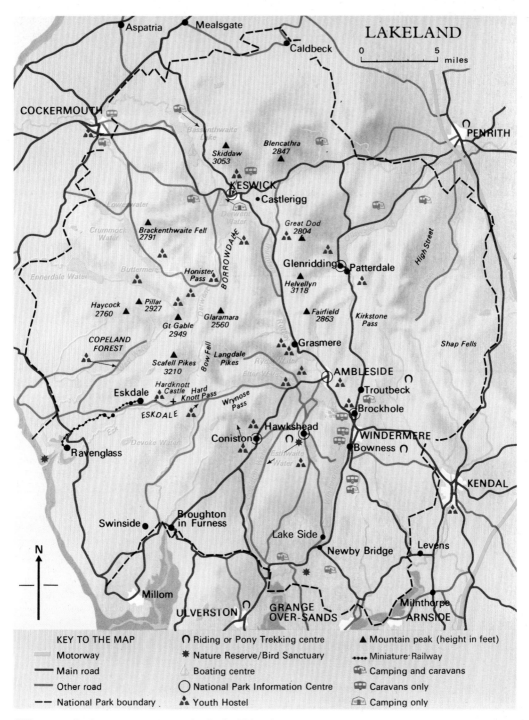

Where to find out more about the Lake District

The Lake District National Park Information Service, Brockhole, Windermere LA23 1LJ, gives general information, by post only, about the park and advises on places to visit. Vehicles of the Park Ranger Service, bearing the symbol based on a view of Wastwater, tour the park, and wardens will answer general queries about the area.

The Cumbria Naturalists' Trust, Rydal Road, Ambleside (Ambleside 2476), gives information about nature reserves.

Nature trails: guide books can be obtained at National Park Information Centres at Bowness Bay; Old Courthouse, Ambleside; Seatoller Barn, Borrowdale; Moot Hall, Keswick; Hawkshead; Coniston; Glenridding; Pooley Bridge; Waterhead; and Brockhole, Windermere.

National Trust Information Centres at Ambleside, Grasmere, Hawkshead and Keswick.

Forestry Commission Information Centres at Grizedale (Satterthwaite 272); Kendal (Kendal 22587); Keswick (Keswick 73915); and Visitor Centre at Whinlatter Pass, Keswick.

Fishing: A North West Water Authority (Liverpool Road, Great Sankey, Warrington WA5 3LW) licence and several permits are required to fish at random in the National Park.

Yachting: Bassenthwaite Sailing Club (Bassenthwaite Lake 341); Royal Windermere Yacht Club (Windermere 3106).

Gliding: Lakes Gliding Club, Walney (Barrow-in-Furness 41458).

WALKING IN SAFETY – see p. 351.

THE PEAK DISTRICT

On wild moorland and in sheltered dales

Great cities hug the Peak District on all sides. Within 50 miles of the National Park lives one-third of Britain's population. Yet here are open spaces – adventurous country with peat moors to tramp across, precipitous ridges to climb and limestone caves to explore.

The area is riddled with caves. Where nature has not burrowed, man has dug for lead, copper or fluorspar, a flux used in the steel industry. Sir Arthur Conan Doyle said of the Peak District: 'All this country is hollow. Could you strike it with some gigantic hammer, it would boom like a drum or possibly cave in altogether.'

The Peak District is the southern tip of the Pennines, the mountain spine of England.

Beside the roads, giant circles of the hard, dark grey rock called millstone grit mark the boundary of the 542 square mile Peak District National Park. Millstone grit is the dominant stone of the northern Peak – the Dark Peak as it is named, after the colour of the grit. Further south is the limestone plateau called the White Peak, from the colour of the stone which thrusts up through the grass. People have lived here for at least 4000 years. Among relics of these settlers are the earthwork at Arbor Low ('low' is a local word for barrow or burial place) built c. 1700 BC, and Mam Tor, an Iron Age hill fort 1½ miles west of Castleton, which is the start of a 3 mile ridge walk to Lose Hill.

Stalactites bristle from the roof of the Dream Cave, in the Treak Cliff Cavern at Castleton.

Caverns under the Pennines

Magnificent groupings of floodlit stalactites and stalagmites can be seen in four limestone caverns open to the public at Castleton. A fast-flowing stream leads into Peak Cavern, which has a number of natural rock chambers including Roger's Rain House, where water continually runs down the walls, and the Orchestral Chamber, where sounds echo strangely. A fairy-tale grotto is floodlit in Treak Cliff Cavern, while water drops spectacularly into the Bottomless Pit in Speedwell Cavern. Blue John Cavern is named after a type of fluorspar which is found there and made into jewellery.

Some caves should be explored only by experienced potholers. Apply for information to: Derbyshire Caving Association, 3 Greenway, Hulland Ward, Derby DE6 3FE.

Where nature takes over the old railways

Two walking and riding trails follow former railway tracks in the Peak District National Park. One, the 13 mile Tissington Trail, is along the route of the Ashbourne-Buxton line, and the other, the 10 mile High Peak Trail, runs along the old Cromford-Buxton railway. They join at Parsley Hay. The old railway banks are rich in wildlife. After the tracks were laid in the last century the sides were left bare, and hawthorn, elder and dog rose, their seeds scattered by the birds, quickly established themselves.

The trails cross some of the loveliest country in the Peak District – past weather-worn villages, woodland glades and curious rock formations, such as those at Harboro' Rocks. Railway enthusiasts will be interested in features such as the 400 yd Hopton Incline on the High Peak Trail. This has a gradient of 1 in 14, and was the steepest worked by locomotives in Britain. Only walkers, cyclists and pony trekkers are allowed on the trails. Access points where motorists can park their cars include:

High Peak Trail Black Rocks Picnic Site: from Cromford Hill (B5036 Cromford to Wirksworth road). Middleton Top Engine House: from

Middleton-by-Wirksworth via road to Ashbourne.

Tissington Trail Mapleton Lane, Ashbourne: from Ashbourne on road to Mapleton village. Tissington: from Tissington village. Alsop en le Dale: adjoins A515 opposite the road to Milldale. Hartington: off B5054, 1½ miles northeast of Hartington village.

Cycles can be hired during the summer months from centres at Parsley Hay, Middleton Top and Ashbourne.

A former steep railway incline which is now part of the 10 mile nature walk, the High Peak Trail.

HEN CLOUD, a dark, forbidding outcrop 3½ miles north of Leek.

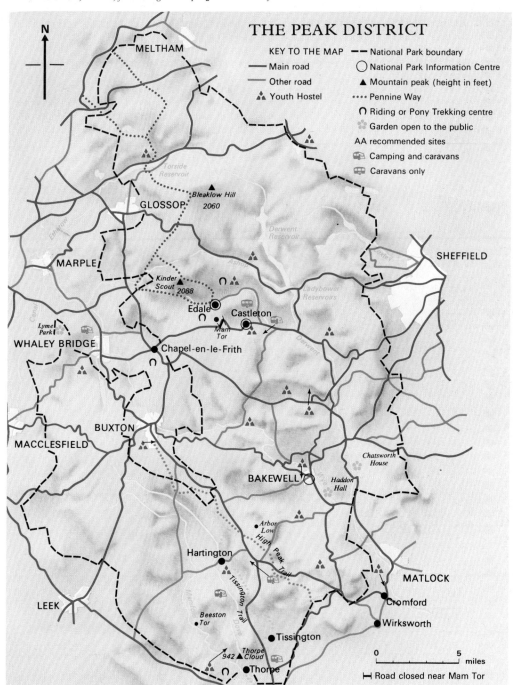

Where to find out more about the Peak District

Peak National Park Office, Baslow Road, Bakewell, Derbyshire DE4 1AE (Bakewell 2881). National Park information centres: Edale (Hope Valley 70207); Castleton (Hope Valley 20679); Bakewell (Bakewell 3227). Tourist information centres: Buxton 5106; Matlock 55082; Chesterfield 32047.

Ramblers' Association, Matlock and Bakewell Group: P. Salisbury, Pentland, The Yeld, Bakewell DE4 1FH (Bakewell 2892).

WALKING IN SAFETY – see p. 351.

347

YORKSHIRE DALES

Untamed moors and snug villages

Serene dales, savage fells and wide stretches of moorland comprise much of the 680 square miles of the Yorkshire Dales National Park. Villages built of stone cluster in the dales under the untamed fells, or hills. Many towns compete for the title 'Gateway to the Dales', but Skipton (the name means sheep town) probably has the best claim. It leads into Upper Airedale and Upper Wharfedale, where the hills are lower and the valleys broader than in most other parts of the park. Malham Beck, which eventually joins up with three other waters to form the River Aire, rises at Malham Cove, just

north of Malham village. Two miles to the north is Malham Tarn, an inviting lake in summer, but a wild, grey sheet of coldness in winter. A mile north-east of the village is Gordale Scar, a deep gorge with overhanging cliffs and a superb waterfall. Three other fine falls can be seen at Aysgarth, in Wensleydale.

Swaledale is the most northerly and remote of the dales in the park. The most spectacular crossing from Wensleydale to Swaledale is by the Butter Tubs Pass, so-called after the giant fissures beside the road which local people thought were shaped like flutings of butter tubs.

Drystone walls crisscross the moorlands below Ingleborough Hill – a view from Chapel le Dale.

Danger in old mine workings

For centuries lead has been mined in the Yorkshire Dales, and many dangerous shafts and tunnels remain. Small waste tips indicate the whereabouts of mining areas and pit shafts can often be suspected if a circle of grass is greener than the surrounding area – caused by better drainage near the shaft. Do not be tempted, even in a storm, to enter derelict buildings. The tops of shafts, particularly on Grassington Moor, are often in a 'house' – a small square building.

AVOID mining areas in fog or stormy weather.
DO NOT go near shafts, throw stones down them or climb on shaft walls.
NEVER explore a tunnel.

How drystone walls were built

Medieval open fields began to be enclosed (divided by walls or hedges) about 400 years ago. Builders, using local stone, evolved distinct regional styles. In Yorkshire the walls are drystone, which means that they are built without mortar binding the stones. Two outer walls taper towards the top with an in-filling of small stones.

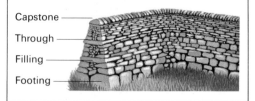

Capstone
Through
Filling
Footing

Where to find out more about the Yorkshire Dales

National Park Officer (Information Service), Colvend, Hebden Road, Grassington, Skipton, North Yorkshire BD23 5LB. National Park centres, open from April to October and at certain weekends during winter, are at Malham (Airton 363), Hawes (Hawes 450), Clapham (Clapham 419), Sedbergh (Sedbergh 20125), Aysgarth Falls (Aysgarth 424), and Grassington (Grassington 752748).

Fishing: Details from Northern Angler's Handbook, Dalesman Publishing·Co., Clapham via Lancaster, North Yorkshire.
Field Studies Council Centre, Malham Tarn House, via Settle.
Rambling: Mrs K. Richards, 78 Regent Avenue, Harrogate (Harrogate 58771).
National Park Cave and Fell Centre: Whernside Cave and Fell Centre, Dent (Dent 213).

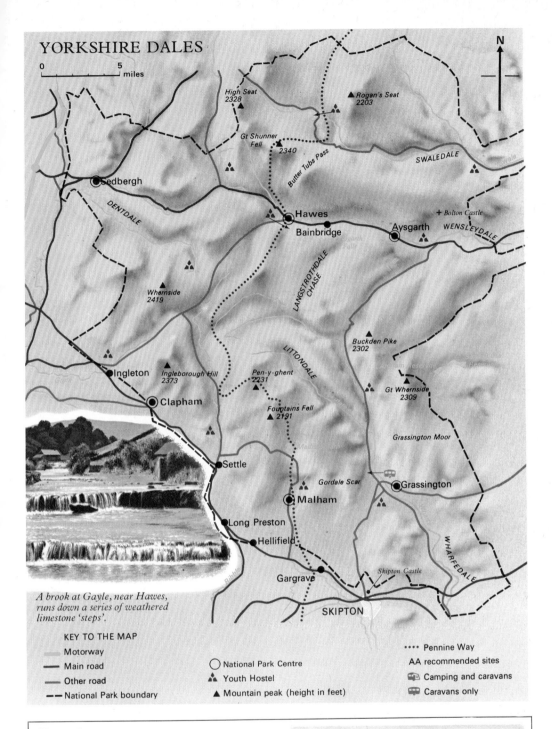

YORKSHIRE DALES

N

0   5 miles

High Seat
2328

▲ Rogan's Seat
2203

Gt Shunner
Fell
2340

Butter Tubs Pass

SWALEDALE

Sedbergh

DENTDALE

Hawes

Bainbridge

+ Bolton Castle

Aysgarth

WENSLEYDALE

Whernside
2419

LANGSTROTHDALE
CHASE

Buckden Pike
2302

Ingleton

Ingleborough Hill
2373

LITTONDALE

Pen-y-ghent
2231

Gt Whernside
2309

Clapham

Fountains Fell
2191

Grassington Moor

Settle

Gordale Scar

Grassington

Malham

WHARFEDALE

Long Preston

Hellifield

Skipton Castle

Gargrave

SKIPTON

A brook at Gayle, near Hawes, runs down a series of weathered limestone 'steps'.

KEY TO THE MAP

    Motorway
— Main road
— Other road
– – National Park boundary

◯ National Park Centre
▲ Youth Hostel
▲ Mountain peak (height in feet)

•••• Pennine Way
AA recommended sites
🚐 Camping and caravans
🚐 Caravans only

Sheep that never stray

A Dales farmer grazes his sheep on a 'heaf', an allocated area of the open moorland. By long practice and careful shepherding the individual flocks have been taught not to stray from their part of the moor. In September the shepherds show off their skills and those of their dogs, usually collies, at the Upper Wharfedale Agricultural Society show. In these sheepdog trials a shepherd, by whistling, guides his dogs to round up a number of sheep. In one test the dogs drive the sheep from a pen, along a marked route and into a circle. In another test the dogs have to drive the sheep through a course of hurdles to a pen.
Swaledale, a hardy sheep with a curly fleece, and Wensleydale, which have long, curly wool, are among the breeds seen at the show.

NORTH YORK MOORS

Walks amid the heather

Purple heather glows on the North York Moors from mid-summer into autumn before the hills again take on a sombre dark brown cloak. Then spring bursts again when a 5 mile stretch of riverside in Farndale is splashed yellow with daffodils. This is walking country, and anybody who completes the 40 mile Lyke Wake Walk from Osmotherley to Ravenscar in 24 hours is presented with a coffin-shaped badge by the Lyke Wake Club. Part of this walk is along the 93-mile Cleveland Way, which makes a horseshoe turn round the National Park.

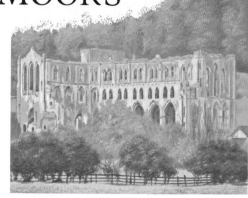

RIEVAULX ABBEY, majestic 12th-century ruins rising among the woods in the National Park.

A stretch of Wade's Causeway near Hunt House.

The way Romans built their roads

Wade's Causeway is part of a road built by the Romans across the moors from camps at Cawthorn to the River Esk near Grosmont. The section near Hunt House, one of the best preserved stretches of Roman road in Britain, shows how the 16 ft wide road was built with flat stones laid on gravel and completed with side gutters and culverts.

Where to find out more about the North York Moors

North York Moors National Park centres: The Old Vicarage, Bondgate, Helmsley YO6 5BP (Helmsley 70657); Danby Lodge, Danby, Whitby YO21 2NB (Castleton 654); Sutton Bank, Thirsk YO7 2EK (Thirsk 597426); Pickering Station (Pickering 72508), Danby Lodge and Sutton Bank, Easter—October.

Fishing: permits are issued by the Yorkshire Water Authority, W. Riding House, 67 Albion Street, Leeds LS1 5AA (Leeds 448201).
Nature Reserves: for permission to visit any reserve apply to the Yorkshire Naturalists' Trust, 20 Castlegate, York YO1 1RP (York 59570).

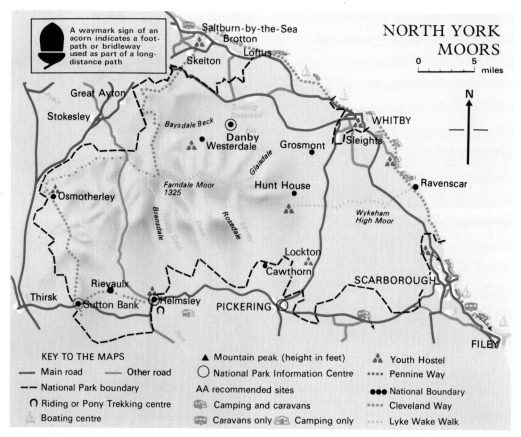

A waymark sign of an acorn indicates a foot-path or bridleway used as part of a long-distance path

NORTH YORK MOORS

0 — 5 miles

N

Saltburn-by-the-Sea
Brotton
Loftus
Skelton
Great Ayton
Stokesley
Scaling Reservoir
Baysdale Beck
Danby
Westerdale
Grosmont
Sleights
WHITBY
Farndale Moor 1325
Hunt House
Osmotherley
Bransdale
Rosedale
Wykeham High Moor
Ravenscar
Lockton
Cawthorn
Rievaulx
Thirsk
Sutton Bank
Helmsley
PICKERING
SCARBOROUGH
FILEY

KEY TO THE MAPS

—— Main road	—— Other road	▲ Mountain peak (height in feet)	▲▲ Youth Hostel
--- National Park boundary		○ National Park Information Centre	•••• Pennine Way
∩ Riding or Pony Trekking centre		AA recommended sites	●●● National Boundary
⚠ Boating centre		🚐 Camping and caravans	····· Cleveland Way
		🚐 Caravans only 🚐 Camping only	····· Lyke Wake Walk

NORTHUMBERLAND

A secluded corner of England

The Northumberland National Park, stretching from Hadrian's Wall north to the Cheviot Hills on the Scottish border, is one of the few parts of England where the invasion of industry and modern building has been completely repulsed. Even the roads fade away before reaching the tops of the rounded hills. Only narrow river valleys of great beauty, such as Coquetdale and Breamish Valley, penetrate into the heart of the hills. A long-distance footpath is the Pennine Way, which runs 250 miles up the spine of England from Derbyshire into Scotland.

Walking in safety

A sudden change in weather may bring danger to walkers on the moors, but hazards can be reduced by taking simple precautions. Wear walking boots, thick socks, a windproof anorak, thick trousers, warm underwear and a jumper. Carry waterproofs and spare clothing. The equipment should include a map, compass, watch, rucksack, torch and spare batteries, whistle, first-aid kit, 2p and 10p pieces for telephoning, food, a polythene survival bag and pencil and paper.

For the inexperienced in bad weather the minimum party for safety is five. If one is hurt, two can stay with him and two can get help. In planning a route allow a pace of 2 mph and complete the walk before dusk. In an emergency, note the map reference and find the nearest phone box. Dial 999 and ask for the police. Stay by the box until help arrives.

If hopelessly lost at night, stop and find shelter out of the wind. Put on spare clothing and get into the polythene bag and have something to eat. Make the standard distress call. This is six long flashes with a torch or six long blasts on a whistle.

Keep signalling after getting an answer, to guide rescuers. If there is no reply, wait for daylight.

Twelve miles of Hadrian's Wall, one of the most spectacular relics of Roman Britain, run through Northumberland National Park. The wall, begun c. AD 120 by order of the Emperor Hadrian, stretched 73 miles from Wallsend, near Newcastle upon Tyne to Bowness, on the Solway Firth. This section is near Hexham.

Finding out more . . .

National Park Officer, Eastburn, South Park, Hexham NE46 1BS (Hexham 605555).

Rambling: W. G. Stothard, 14 Mill Hill Road, East Denton, Newcastle upon Tyne (Newcastle 674859).

Fishing: Northumbrian Anglers' Federation, J. Hardey, c/o Hardey Bros., Alnwick.

Rod licences: Northumbrian Water Authority, Regent Centre, Gosforth (Gosforth 843151).

LOCH LOMOND

From the bonnie banks to the Trossachs

The dramatic contrasts in the scenery of Loch Lomond and the Trossachs are due to the Highland Boundary Fault, a geological slip running across Scotland from Kintyre in the south-west to Stonehaven in the north-east. Here the Highlands meet the Lowlands. To the north and west are mountains, waterfalls and forests; to the south and east, rounded hills and gentle farmland.

The fault runs through Loch Lomond just north of Balmaha, and the islands in the fault zone – Inchmurrin, Inchcailloch, Crainch and Torrinch – look like huge stepping stones. The loch, 21 miles long and Britain's largest inland stretch of water, has about 30 islands; five are part of a national nature reserve.

To the east is the Trossachs, a name now loosely used to describe the romantic area set around Lochs Katrine, Achray and Venachar and dominated by Ben Venue, 2386 ft. Sir Walter Scott brought the area fame and started a rush of tourists early in the 19th century with

The noble peaks of Ben More and Stob Binnein.

his poem 'The Lady of the Lake' and his historical novel *Rob Roy*.

The Trossachs ('the bristly country') is, in fact, the name of a wild, wooded glen about a mile long between Lochs Achray and Katrine. Once it was a tortuous pass through which Highland raiders drove Lowland cattle. Now there is an easy road, but the glen has kept much of its rugged splendour.

There are about 30 islands within the shores of Loch Lomond.

Loch Lomond Nature Reserve

Loch Lomond Nature Reserve consists of five islands plus part of the nearby mainland at the south-east corner of the loch. Inchcailloch, with its viewpoint, picnic area and more than two miles of woodland paths, is the best of the islands to visit. No permit is necessary for small family parties, but larger groups should apply for permission well in advance to the Nature Conservancy Council, The Castle, Loch Lomond Park, Balloch, Dunbarton G83 8LX.

Permission from the Senior Warden, 22 Muirpark Way, Drymen, by Glasgow G63 0DX (Drymen 428), is required to visit the Mainland Reserve, which is noted for its wintering wildfowl, particularly greylag and Greenland white-fronted geese, and the different waders recorded during spring and autumn migration. The reserve was established in 1961 to conserve the oak woodlands, and has a wide variety of trees, shrubs, ferns and flowering plants.

The land of Rob Roy

The Trossachs became a base in the 16th and 17th centuries for the wild MacGregor outlaws, who lived by robbery and cattle stealing. The most notorious son of the clan was Rob Roy – Robert MacGregor or Campbell (1671–1734) – who was born at Glengyle at the head of Loch Katrine. Sir Walter Scott's novel *Rob Roy* romanticised him into a kind of

Robin Hood, but the real Rob Roy was a daring raider, kidnapper, blackmailer and extorter of protection money. The Government had to establish a garrison at Inversnaid to keep law and order because of him and his like. Rob and his wife, Mary, and two of their sons are buried in the churchyard overlooked by the Braes o'Balquhidder.

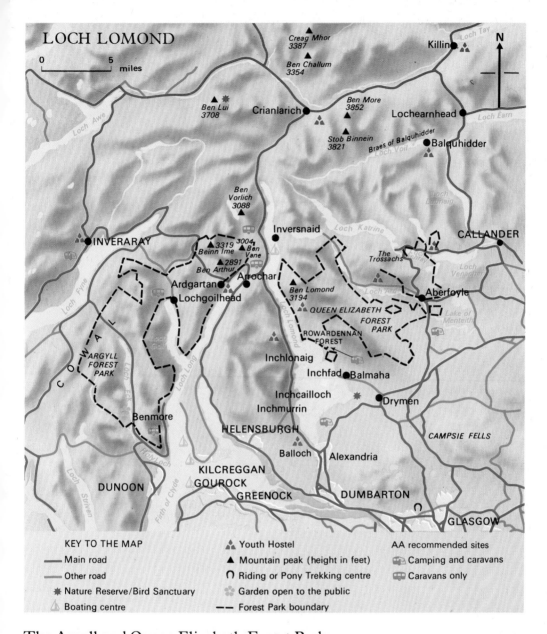

LOCH LOMOND

0   5   miles

KEY TO THE MAP

— Main road

— Other road

✴ Nature Reserve/Bird Sanctuary

⚠ Boating centre

♠ Youth Hostel

▲ Mountain peak (height in feet)

∩ Riding or Pony Trekking centre

✿ Garden open to the public

— — Forest Park boundary

AA recommended sites

🚍 Camping and caravans

🚍 Caravans only

The Argyll and Queen Elizabeth Forest Parks

The forest parks of Argyll and Queen Elizabeth, which are run by the Forestry Commission, are ideal for camping, hiking, fishing, canoeing and hill climbing. Tourists can wander among the birch, rowan, spruce, pine, larch, fir, oak and beech, and sometimes see red and roe deer or the occasional golden eagle and wildcat.

Queen Elizabeth Forest Park, between the eastern shore of Loch Lomond and the Trossachs, takes in the Achray, Loch Ard and Rowardennan Forests which climb the slopes of Ben Venue and Ben Lomond. Aberfoyle is a good centre for touring the 65 square miles of the forest park.

The Argyll Forest Park, stretching from the western shore of Loch Lomond to Loch Fyne and down the Cowal Peninsula, has six forests much broken up by peaks and sea lochs.

Ardgartan, near Arrochar at the head of Loch Long, is the main centre for climbing Ben Arthur ('The Cobbler'), 2891 ft, Beinn Ime, 3319 ft, and Ben Vane, 3004 ft.

Where to find out more about Loch Lomond and the Trossachs

Information centres (some open only during the summer months): The Square, Aberfeldy (Aberfeldy 276); Main Street, Aberfoyle (Aberfoyle 352); Ardgartan (Arrochar 388); Leny Road, Callander (Callander 30342); James Square, Crieff (Crieff 2578); 5 Waverley Bridge, Edinburgh (031-332 2433); George Square, Glasgow (041-221 7371); Inveraray 2063; Killin 254; Lochgilphead 2344; Dumbarton Road, Stirling (Stirling 5019).

Fishing: Loch Lomond permits are obtainable from R. A. Clement and Co., 224 Ingram Street, Glasgow G1 1HH. Day permits are also obtainable from the various boat hirers around the loch.

Full list of where to get other permits for fishing from the Scottish Tourist Board, 23 Ravelston Terrace, Edinburgh EH4 3EU (031 332 2433).

Scottish Wildlife Trust, 8 Dublin Street, Edinburgh EH1 3PP (031 557 1525).

353

THE CAIRNGORMS

Scotland's ski playground

The Cairngorms – the name means 'blue hills' – form the highest mountain mass in Britain. Four peaks rise higher than 4000 ft and at least a dozen top 3000 ft. In the last Ice Age, which ended 10,000 years ago, these granite mountains withstood the glaciers that tore out this landscape of wild beauty from the original plateau.

In a winter of good snow the slopes of Cairn Gorm itself are loud with the calls of skiers. Snow sometimes lies from November to late May and even June. Although the Cairngorms are most popular at Christmas and New Year the powder snow, which is best for ski-ing,

falls mainly in February and March. A chair-lift in Coire Cas takes them to within 400 ft of the summit of the 4084 ft high mountain. When the skiers have gone the chair-lift carries up summer visitors for views over the mountains.

In Aviemore there is a large all-the-year holiday centre with shops, restaurants, hotels, a theatre, a concert hall, a swimming pool and ice rinks.

For those who prefer to enjoy the mountains, the whole of the Glen More Forest Park offers unparalleled walks; and anglers will find some of the best salmon fishing in Britain in the Spey and its tributaries.

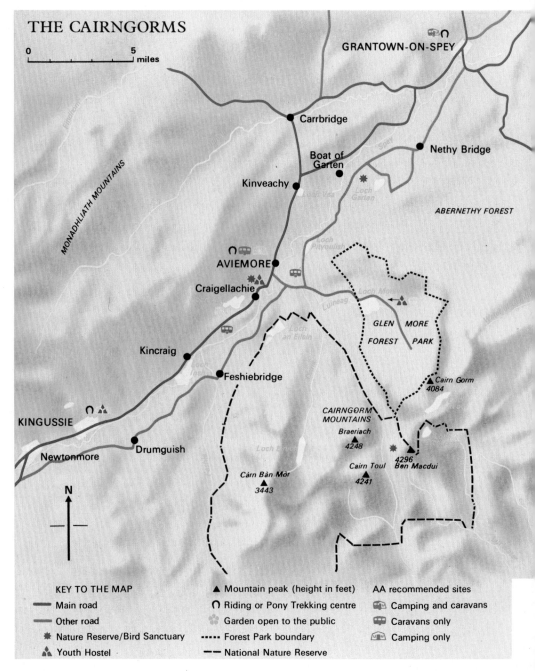

THE CAIRNGORMS

0 — 5 miles

GRANTOWN-ON-SPEY

MONADHLIATH MOUNTAINS

Carrbridge

Boat of Garten

Nethy Bridge

Kinveachy

ABERNETHY FOREST

AVIEMORE

Craigellachie

GLEN MORE FOREST PARK

Kincraig

Feshiebridge

Cairn Gorm 4084

CAIRNGORM MOUNTAINS

KINGUSSIE

Braeriach 4248

Newtonmore   Drumguish

4296 Ben Macdui

Càrn Bàn Mòr 3443

Cairn Toul 4241

N

KEY TO THE MAP

— Main road
— Other road
✳ Nature Reserve/Bird Sanctuary
⛺ Youth Hostel

▲ Mountain peak (height in feet)
∩ Riding or Pony Trekking centre
✤ Garden open to the public
····· Forest Park boundary
—— National Nature Reserve

AA recommended sites
Camping and caravans
Caravans only
Camping only

Skiers set off up the slopes of Cairn Gorm. Car parks 2000 ft up give access to chair-lifts and tows capable of lifting 5000 people an hour.

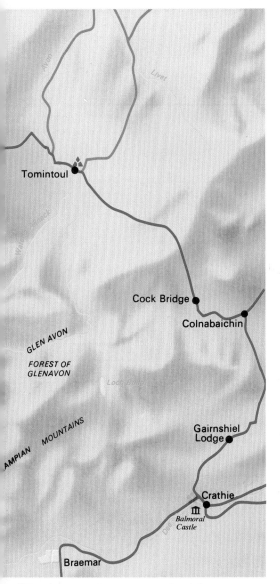

Walks through the Forest Park

Glen More is one of Scotland's five Forest Parks, which have been opened as leisure grounds. The others are the Argyll Park, Glen Trool in Galloway, the Queen Elizabeth Forest Park in the Trossachs, and the Border Park, which stretches from Roxburghshire across into England. Camping and picnic areas are set aside in all the parks.

The Glen More Forest Park lies in a magnificent setting around Loch Morlich. Among the trees in the 20 square miles of forest are Scots pine, lodgepole pine, Sitka and Norway spruces and some European and Japanese larch. There are also a few Scots (or Caledonian) pines. This species formed the primeval forest which covered much of Scotland. Some are 200 years old.

Three nature trails, the Loch an Eilein, the Achlean and the Craigellachie, run through the forest. Red and roe deer, otters, badgers, stoats, squirrels and the occasional wildcat may be glimpsed on these trails.

In Glen More there is a herd of reindeer, an animal extinct in Scotland for 800 years, but re-introduced from Swedish Lapland in the 1950's. A guide from Reindeer House, above Glenmore camp site, takes visitors on a tour to see the herd every morning at 11.

Among the nesting birds that may be seen are the golden eagle, merlin, dotterel, greenshank, capercaillie, ptarmigan, crested tit and snow bunting.

The ospreys return

Every year more than 20,000 bird-lovers look through a telescope to watch ospreys nesting in the Abernethy Forest near Loch Garten. A pair nested there in the mid-1950's – the first ospreys to return after an absence of nearly 50 years. Each year since, at least one pair rears its young in a nesting area guarded by the Royal Society for the Protection of Birds.

The osprey . . . a guarded visitor.

Danger on the mountainsides

Much of the Cairngorms is remote and blizzards can strike at any time. Listen to radio weather forecasts before setting out for a walk or climb.

WALK IN SAFETY – see p. 351.

Find out more . . .

Scottish Tourist Board, 23 Ravelston Terrace, Edinburgh (031-332 2433). Highlands and Islands Development Board, Bridge House, Bank Street, Inverness (Inverness 34171). National Trust for Scotland, 5 Charlotte Square, Edinburgh (031-226 5922). Highland Wildlife Park, Kincraig, Kingussie (Kincraig 270). For information on Glen More Forest Park: Forestry Commission, 231 Corstorphine Road, Edinburgh (031-334 0303).

355

HIGHLANDS AND ISLANDS

Scenic grandeur on the roads to Skye

The Highlands and Islands of Scotland cover about one-fifth of Britain's land surface—but fewer than one in fifty of the population live there. This is a lonely land in which wild sea lochs gouge deeply into the land and icy streams tumble through wooded glens. A drive to one of the ferries for Skye goes through spectacular scenery whichever road is taken. The traditional Road to the Isles starts at Fort William at the south-west end of the Great Glen. The road runs by Loch Eil to the head of Loch Shiel and the Glenfinnan Monument, marking where Bonnie Prince Charlie raised the Jacobite standard 1745; then west with views of the isles of Eigg, Muck and Rhum; and north-west past Loch Morar to Mallaig and the ferry to Skye, landing at Armadale.

A second scenic route runs to Kyle of Lochalsh from the Great Glen, either up the glen from Fort William to Invergarry or down from Inverness to Invermoriston; west by Loch Cluanie, Cluanie Forest, the towering Five Sisters and Loch Duich; and on to Kyle for the short ferry trip to Kyleakin.

A third road runs to Kyle by the north-west route from Inverness; by Beauly and Loch Garve, west by Loch Luichart to Achasheen; follows the River Carron and the southern shore of Loch Carron to Stromeferry; then south, picking up the Kyle road by Loch Alsh.

The untamed beauty of Skye

The Isle of Skye, the largest of the Inner Hebrides, attracts climbers from all over the world to face the rocky, rugged challenge of the Cuillin Hills. But the untamed beauty of its scenery is enough by itself to bring thousands of less energetic tourists over the sea on its ferries every year.

Skye scenery can be obscured by dank mist and cloud, and appear suddenly in sparkling light. Then its peaks and edges of the corries (hollows in the mountain sides) are etched out in breath-taking majesty.

The road to Dunvegan and the castle of the Clan MacLeod's chiefs carry banners saying 'This is the Faery Isle'. Legends persist of beautiful warrior queens, Little Folk dwelling in hillocks and fearsome water horses living in the island's deep lochans (little lochs).

Skye is a land of volcanic rock thrown up 70 million years ago, then carved and scarred by the glaciers of the Ice Age. About 8000 people live on this grotesquely shaped island—roughly 50 miles long by 30 miles wide. It is an island of peaty, purple moorland and green valleys with a backcloth of the rounded Red Hills outlying the jagged Black Cuillins.

For non-climbers here is an island to be explored on foot or by car. Dr Samuel Johnson and James Boswell 'discovered' it in 1776—and they did no climbing.

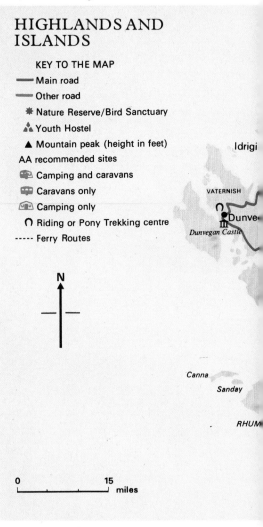

HIGHLANDS AND ISLANDS

KEY TO THE MAP

— Main road
— Other road
✳ Nature Reserve/Bird Sanctuary
⚑ Youth Hostel
▲ Mountain peak (height in feet)
AA recommended sites
🚐 Camping and caravans
🚐 Caravans only
🚐 Camping only
∩ Riding or Pony Trekking centre
----- Ferry Routes

N

Idrigi
VATERNISH
Dunve
Dunvegan Castle

Canna
Sanday

RHUM

0   15   miles

Eilean Donan Castle, a MacKenzie stronghold dating from 1220, was reduced to a ruin in 1719 by an English man-o'-war to subdue a Jacobite garrison. It was rebuilt, at a cost of £230,000, between 1912 and 1932 by the MacRae family, who held Eilean Donan as hereditary constables for the MacKenzies.

Ferry services to Skye

Mallaig–Armadale 5 return sailings weekdays May to September. Advance booking essential. In winter, services are restricted and no cars are carried. Details from: Caledonian MacBrayne, The Pier, Gourock, 0475 33755.

Kyle of Lochalsh–Kyleakin Frequent weekday service with some reductions on Sundays. No reservations.

Glenelg–Kylerhea Frequent weekday service June to mid-September. No reservations.

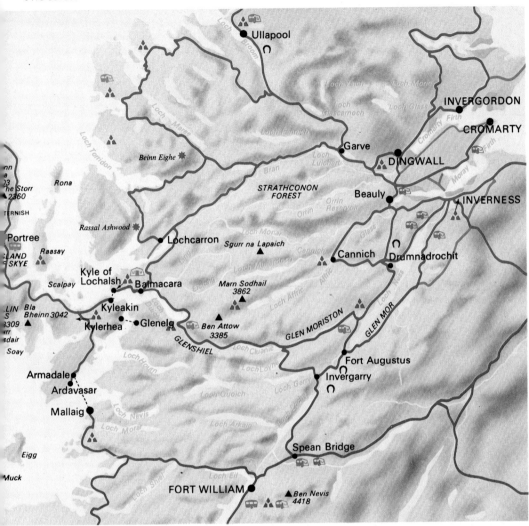

Fishing in Scotland

Scotland is renowned for its salmon rivers and trout streams. The sea lochs and bays of Skye and the mainland provide ideal fishing for sea trout, pollock, cod, halibut, haddock, hake, mackerel and whiting. The deeply shelving coast enables most to be caught from the shore. Details of all types of fishing are given in *Scotland for Fishing* and *Scotland for Sea Angling*, two books published by the Scottish Tourist Board, 23 Ravelston Terrace, Edinburgh (031 332 2433). The Highlands and Islands Development Board publishes a free leaflet on sea angling.

The best season for sea trout is August–September.

Where to find out more about the Roads to the Isles

Information centres: Pier Esplanade, Dunoon (Dunoon 3785); Argyll Square, Oban (Oban 3122); Travel Centre, Fort William (Fort William 3581); Meall House, Portree (Portree 2137); South Beach Street, Stornoway (Stornoway 3088); Achtercairn, Gairloch (Gairloch 2130); Kyle of Lochalsh (Kyle 4276); Lochgilphead 2344; The Pier, Campbeltown (Campbeltown 2056); Inverness 34353.
Highlands and Islands Development Board, Bridge House, Bank Street, Inverness (Inverness 34171).
National Trust for Scotland, 5 Charlotte Square, Edinburgh (031-226 5922).
Forestry Commission, 21 Church Street, Inverness (Inverness 32811).

SOUTH-WEST IRELAND

From Killarney's lakes to the Atlantic coast

The south-west corner of Ireland is a land of mountain fingers clawing at the Atlantic above drowned valleys. The roads are narrow and winding and, even at the height of the tourist season, are surprisingly free of traffic. A donkey cart carrying milk to the dairy, or a horse-drawn caravan, are often the only vehicles seen on long stretches of road. The cart and the caravan symbolise the pace of life. This is a country and a coast whose scenery should be savoured leisurely. One of the most magnificent scenic routes is the Ring of Kerry, a 110 mile circular drive starting from Killarney or Kenmare with views over the Atlantic and of the Caha and Slieve Miskish mountains. In the heart of the region are the lakes of Killarney, extolled by poets, painters and writers. The three biggest

lakes occupy a broad valley stretching between the mountains. Trees and rhododendrons rise from the water's edge, giving a reflected picture of greens, browns and blues.

Finding out more . . .

This sign, seen in all large towns in Ireland, indicates tourist information offices which give details of accommodation, caravan and camping sites, sporting facilities, and a calendar of local events and festivals.

Apply for brochures to the Irish Tourist Board, 150 New Bond Street, London (01 493 3201). The main information centre in south-west Ireland is Monument Buildings, Grand Parade, Cork.

Macgillycuddy's Reeks, the mountains round Killarney seen from Lady's View.

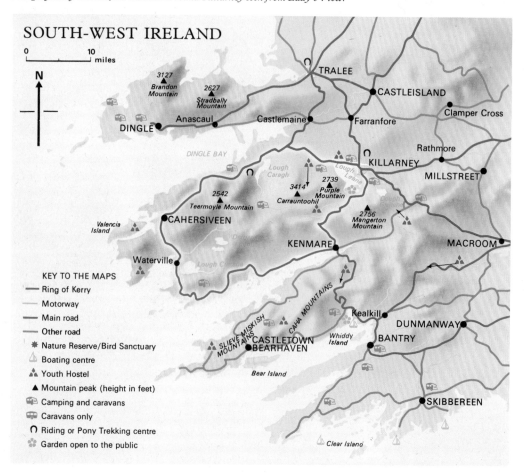

SOUTH-WEST IRELAND

0   10 miles

N

3127 ▲ Brandon Mountain
2627 ▲ Stradbally Mountain
TRALEE
CASTLEISLAND
Clamper Cross
DINGLE   Anascaul   Castlemaine   Farranfore
Rathmore
DINGLE BAY
Lough Caragh
Lough Leane
KILLARNEY
MILLSTREET
2542 ▲ Teermoyle Mountain
3414 ▲ Carrauntoohil
2739 ▲ Purple Mountain
Valencia Island
CAHERSIVEEN
2756 ▲ Mangerton Mountain
KENMARE
MACROOM
Waterville
Lough C_____
CAHA MOUNTAINS
Kealkill
DUNMANWAY
SLIEVE MISKISH MOUNTAINS
CASTLETOWN BEARHAVEN
Whiddy Island
BANTRY
Bear Island
SKIBBEREEN
Clear Island

KEY TO THE MAPS
— Ring of Kerry
— Motorway
— Main road
— Other road
✱ Nature Reserve/Bird Sanctuary
△ Boating centre
▲ Youth Hostel
▲ Mountain peak (height in feet)
🚐 Camping and caravans
🚐 Caravans only
∩ Riding or Pony Trekking centre
❀ Garden open to the public

THE NORTH OF IRELAND

Green pastures and craggy headlands

The north and north-west of Ireland is a land of sharp contrasts. Lush green pastures give way to bleak mountains, craggy cliffs – in places towering 2000 ft out of the sea – and miles of sandy beaches.

There is breathtaking coastal scenery from the east, where the Mountains of Mourne sweep down to the sea, round the north past the Giant's Causeway to the cliffs of Donegal.

On these fierce cliffs and headlands are safe and unspoilt breeding grounds of great colonies of seabirds, including roseate terns, storm petrels, black guillemots, razorbills, puffins and fulmars. The heart of the country is a land of lakes – County Fermanagh alone has more than 1000 of them.

The landscape around Sligo is stamped with the imagery of the poet W. B. Yeats who spent his boyhood in Sligo and later wrote about the countryside around. He is buried in Drumcliff churchyard. Yeats loved the strangely shaped hills 'where the wandering water gushes'. Dotting the landscape are megalithic tombs, the ruins of early Christian monasteries and crumbling medieval castles bearing witness to 6000 years of Irish history.

Fishing in streams and lakes

Ireland is an anglers' paradise – with clear streams feeding or draining great loughs, some of which are 30 miles long. The game fisherman will find salmon and trout, and there is a great variety of coarse fishing. For information about licences and permits write to The Irish Tourist Board, Angling Information Service, Baggot Street Bridge, Dublin 2, and the Northern Ireland Tourist Board, River House, 48 High Street, Belfast.

The Giant's Causeway

The freakish masonry of the Giant's Causeway is one of the most spectacular geological phenomena in the British Isles. The Causeway and the cliffs above were formed from lava which erupted during a volcanic outburst 60 million years ago.

The Causeway's 38,000 basalt columns are stacked together in such regular shapes that they seem to have been cut by hand. They were formed from lava which, as it contracted, shrank and then fractured into columns. The foreshore and cliffs of the north Antrim coast are made up of these columns. They are mostly six-sided and stand almost vertically.

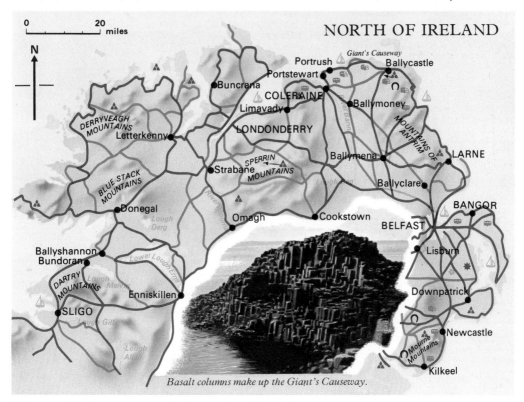

Basalt columns make up the Giant's Causeway.

Where to find out more about the north of Ireland

Tourist offices in towns all over Northern Ireland give information on accommodation, caravan and camping sites, sporting facilities and local activities. Detailed brochures containing lists of addresses and telephone numbers for any area can be obtained from the main tourist offices in Britain. Northern Ireland Tourist Board offices in England and Scotland: 11 Berkeley Street, London (01 493 0601); PO Box 26, Sutton Coldfield, Warwickshire (021 353 7604); 121 West George Street, Glasgow (041 221 5115). For Donegal: Irish Tourist Board, 150 New Bond Street, London (01 493 3201).

THE SEASHORE

Life at the sea's edge

Around the 7000 mile coast of the British Isles a narrow strip of land amounting to about 600,000 acres is regularly covered and exposed by the rising and falling tides. This frontier with the sea is only a small part of the total land mass, but it includes amazingly rich and varied communities of animals and plants.

The character of the shore at any particular place is the result of a complex interaction between the sea and land, and the balance between the destructive and constructive forces of the ocean. Outcrops of hard rock may withstand the pounding of the waves and form high cliffs or craggy rock shores. Softer material is worn away by the action of the sea and weather and is carried along the coast by currents to be deposited as the water movement diminishes. Pebbles are left by the waves to form steeply sloping shingle beaches which are virtually devoid of life. Any organism which settles on this type of shore would be crushed between the stones as they are ground together by the waves. In more sheltered areas smaller stones and grains of sand are deposited, forming deep, wide beaches, while in estuaries rivers dump fine particles of silt to make mud-flats.

These different types of shore provide environments for plants and animals as distinct as those of meadow and woodland, and mountain and valley, on land. Conditions also vary at different levels on a single shore, depending on the period of exposure to the drying effects of wind and sun.

WOOD BORERS
Pieces of wood lying on the shore are often riddled with holes. Tunnels about $\frac{1}{4}$ in. across have been bored by shipworms, molluscs whose shells are adapted for boring. Smaller holes are made by the gribble, a $\frac{1}{8}$ in. long crustacean found in large numbers – 400 to the cubic inch. They tunnel into jetty piles at water level until the piles collapse.

OYSTERCATCHER
This wader is found all round Britain's coasts. It feeds on all kinds of shellfish.

SCALLOP
Lives offshore on sandy bottoms. A scallop moves swiftly by 'clapping' its valves rapidly together.

COMMON WHELK
A carnivorous mollusc, living mainly offshore. Its shell is often 4 in. long.

TROPICAL BEANS
Cacoon beans from the West Indies and brown beans from tropical America, both 2 in. across, are deposited in south-west England by the Gulf Stream.

LITTLE PIDDOCK
A rock borer which excavates by scraping with two rows of fine teeth. One piddock has been known to bore straight through another when their tunnels cross.

VIOLET SEA SNAIL
Often found on the shore, but lives in the open sea on a 'raft' of air bubbles. It feeds on jellyfish.

Sea shells

Sea shells, the protective external skeletons of a large group of soft-bodied animals known as molluscs, can be found on most shores. More than 800 species occur in the seas around the British Isles. Most of them live offshore, either on the sea-bed or burrowing beneath it. Their shells are often washed ashore by the tide when the animals have died. The most common group of molluscs are the gastropods, which usually have a single shell, and the bivalves which have two pieces hinged together to form one shell. Gastropods – the most common is the limpet – are usually active but bivalves stay in one place, obtaining food by filtering water or sifting sand.

The strand line

The strip of shore just at the upper limits of high-water mark is the strand line. It is usually marked by quantities of rotting seaweed torn from its rocky anchorages by the sea and cast high and dry on the beach.

This is the habitat of the sand-hoppers – small crustaceans that scavenge beneath the vegetation. They may jump several feet in the air when disturbed. Sandhoppers often occur in immense numbers and rise in clouds if anyone approaches. The remains of plants and animals, such as the shells of crabs, sea urchins and molluscs, lie scattered among the debris.

Most of these strand-line objects come from deeper water immediately offshore, but some, including the seeds of exotic plants, such as tropical beans from the West Indies, are carried thousands of miles to our shores.

STING WINKLE
A 2 in. high whelk which preys on barnacles, mussels and oysters. A pest on oyster beds, often found near low-water mark but more usually in deep water.

HORNWRACK
Despite its plant-like appearance, hornwrack is not a seaweed but the remains of an animal which lives in colonies offshore. It has flat, sandy-coloured 'leaves' up to about 6 in. long with minute honeycomb markings.

CUTTLE BONE
The internal shell of the cuttlefish. It is a white, oval, chalky 'bone' up to 6 in. long and $\frac{1}{2}$–1 in. thick.

MERMAID'S PURSE
The egg cases of dogfish, skates and rays. The cases are horny packets about 6 in. long.

MERMAID'S PURSE

BLUE-RAYED LIMPET
A dull brown shell up to 1 in. long with lines of bright blue spots. This limpet grazes on the large kelp seaweed. Young specimens have yellow-brown translucent shells with bright blue stripes.

RAZOR SHELL
Empty razor shells, up to 7 in. long, are cast up by the sea when the animal dies. The living creatures are rarely seen, as they burrow at low tide.

WHELK EGG CASES
The egg cases of the common whelk are pale, sponge-like masses of empty cells often as large as a football. Until the young hatch out these cases are anchored to rocks or the sea-bed.

361

Rocky shore

The pounding of the waves on a rocky shore, and the rhythmic and sometimes violent movement of the tides, make life hazardous for plants and animals compared with the stable world of deep water. Yet an astonishing variety live in this world of ebb and flow. Except where the coast

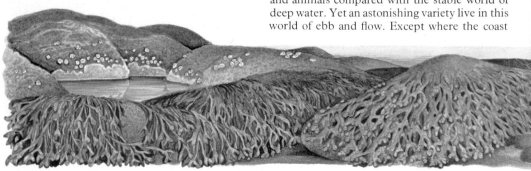

Upper shore: an exposed area where marine life is scarce

The most difficult region for marine animals and plants to live in is the upper shore, because it is covered by the sea for only a short time each day, even when tides are high.

ACORN BARNACLE
A group of prolific barnacles found on rocky shores – reaching densities of 30,000 to a square yard. The two most common and smallest, at $\frac{1}{2}$ in. across, are *Balanus balanoides*, found on northern shores, and *Chthamalus stellatus*, common in the south.

CHANNELLED WRACK
Found at the highest levels on the shore, where it is exposed most of the time. During neap tides it often becomes dried out and blackened and turns brittle, but when submerged regains its olive-green colour.

SEA LETTUCE
The most conspicuous green seaweed, frequently forming large masses on almost any part of the shore. Young plants are pale green and found attached to stones.

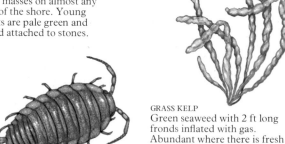

GRASS KELP
Green seaweed with 2 ft long fronds inflated with gas. Abundant where there is fresh water high on the shore. Often bleached white in summer.

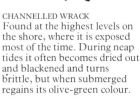

FLAT WRACK
This seaweed is readily identified by its flattened fronds, which are fairly short, each with a prominent mid-rib. It has no air bladders.

SEA SLATER
A greenish-grey woodlouse, often more than 1 in. long, which is abundant around harbour walls, under stones and seaweed high on the shore. It has antennae about two-thirds its body length.

SMALL PERIWINKLE
Less than $\frac{1}{4}$ in. high, this is found high on the shore, often in rock crevices, but usually in exposed places. It is brown to dark blue.

ROUGH PERIWINKLE
This is larger than the small periwinkle – up to $\frac{1}{2}$ in. high. Its shell is usually dark brown but ranges from red to black. It is also found on the top of the middle shore.

PURPLE LAVER
Similar to the sea lettuce, but purplish-red or brown with flat-lobed fronds up to 10 in. long. Found at most levels, attached to stones. Used in Wales to make laver bread.

is exposed to the full force of Atlantic rollers, life is more abundant here than on any other type of shore.

The twice-daily rise and fall of the tide produces three distinct separations of zones among sea-weeds and animals: the upper shore, which is dry except for a short time at high tide; the middle shore, which is continuously covered and uncovered by the sea; and the lower shore which is exposed for only a short time each day at low tide. The lowest shore is uncovered only by neap, or low, tides.

Middle shore: where life is abundant as the tide ebbs and flows

This region is between high-water mark and low-water mark, and so is exposed and submerged twice a day. More life exists here than on any other part of the shore.

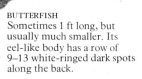

BUTTERFISH
Sometimes 1 ft long, but usually much smaller. Its eel-like body has a row of 9–13 white-ringed dark spots along the back.

BLADDER WRACK
Seaweed with gas-filled swellings often arranged in pairs, on either side of a prominent mid-rib. It usually dominates the main part of the middle shore.

BEADLET ANEMONE
One of the most common anemones, $\frac{1}{2}$–$1\frac{1}{2}$ in. high, usually green or yellow. On uncovered rocks it contracts into a flat-topped jelly mass.

SHANNY
Up to 5 in. long, found in shallow pools. It has strong jaws for biting barnacles off rocks.

ROCK GOBY
Up to 4 in. long, most common of the ten species of goby found in rock pools in Britain. Rare in Scotland.

FLAT PERIWINKLE
Usually less than $\frac{1}{2}$ in. high. Its colour ranges from yellow through green and red to brown. Common on seaweed.

CORAL WEED
Tufted growths, up to 5 in. long, fringing middle-shore rock pools. The plants are hard and brittle to the touch, being heavily impregnated with lime.

CLADOPHORA RUPESTRIS
These are erect tufts of green seaweed with slender fronds up to 6 in. Often in rock pools.

COMMON PERIWINKLE
Up to 1 in. high, with a sharply pointed shell compared with the rounded shell of the flat periwinkle.

COMMON LIMPET
At high water they feed on rock vegetation, but move no more than 3 ft. returning as the tide ebbs.

KNOTTED WRACK
Similar to bladder wrack, but growing in sheltered places. This plant also has bladders, but they occur singly and fill the whole width of the rounded frond. Blackens when dry.

SPIROBIS
Small, curled, chalky tubes, less than $\frac{1}{4}$ in. across, which look like snails but are the tubes of tiny worms.

SHORE CRAB
The most common British crab, up to 4 in. across; usually dark green, but often with lighter markings.

363

Rocky shore

The ebbing tide leaves miniature seas among the rocks, trapping in them a rich variety of plant and animal life. Hiding among the seaweed and under stones can be found crabs,

Lower shore : where a rich and wide variety of life abounds

This region is submerged most of the time during normal tides and, because there is little exposure to air, it provides a home for a greater variety of marine life than other parts of the shore.

SERRATED WRACK
A seaweed found clinging to rocks, so named because of the saw-toothed margins on its wide, flat fronds.

COMMON PRAWN
Up to 4 in. long, found in pools and among seaweed at the edge of the sea on the south and west coasts.

HERMIT CRAB
A soft-skinned crab which uses an empty shell for protection. It withdraws rapidly when disturbed. Large hermits usually live in whelk shells and often carry an anemone on them.

KEELWORM
A worm producing irregular chalky tubes up to 6 in. long. Found on stones and shells from shallow to deeper water. Under water, the worm's crown of red and white barred tentacles may emerge.

BROAD-CLAWED PORCELAIN CRAB
This differs from other crabs in apparently having only three pairs of legs apart from the claws, the fourth pair being much reduced and folded. Grey to red-brown.

PLUMOSE ANEMONE
One of the most attractive sea anemones, up to 5 in. tall with numerous tentacles. Found on rock overhangs and pier piles.

VELVET SWIMMING CRAB
A pugnacious crab which adopts a threatening posture when disturbed. The back legs are broad and flattened to form swimming paddles.

COMMON MUSSEL
Up to 4 in. long, it often forms dense beds, each mussel attached to rock by tough threads. Also found on muddy shores where there are stones.

AMPHIPODS
Abundant under stones on the middle and lower shore, where they wriggle on their sides when exposed.

COMMON STARFISH
The largest starfish, up to 20 in. across, but usually smaller. Feeds on molluscs ; lives on mussel beds.

miniature sea

shannies and rock gobies, and clinging to the rocks, limpets and beadlet anemones.
Life is precarious in these rock pools. Sun and rain can change the amount of salt in the water by evaporation and dilution. If the pool becomes too fresh some animals become bloated and die. If it becomes too briny, they lose fluid and shrivel to death.

Lowest shore: where the sea only rarely retreats from tangled weed

The area uncovered only by the lowest spring tides. A few animals and some weeds – kelps or tangles – which usually extend into depths of 100 ft or more, commonly occur here.

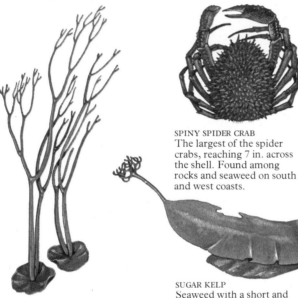

EDIBLE CRAB
It lives mostly offshore, and only small ones are found between tide-marks. It grows to 10 in. across, and the edge of its shell resembles a pie crust.

SPINY SPIDER CRAB
The largest of the spider crabs, reaching 7 in. across the shell. Found among rocks and seaweed on south and west coasts.

SUGAR KELP
Seaweed with a short and slender stem carrying a wavy-edged frond which is often 10 ft or more long.

COMMON SEA URCHIN
Usually 4–6 in. across, and more common below low-tide mark. The empty shells, usually without spines, are often found on the beach.

THONG WEED
Often grows near low-water level. It has leathery, disc-like, dark brown fronds and long slender reproductive bodies, up to 8 ft long, growing from the centre.

DEVIL'S APRON
From the same family as the sugar kelp, but with a stem flattening into a broad frond split into a number of fingers 6 ft long. Found on rocks.

BRITTLE STAR
Up to 7 in. across the arms. Found under stones or among weed. Fragile, and may throw off its arms in pieces.

SQUAT LOBSTER
Usually about 2 in. long. Common under stones, particularly in April and May. Carries its tail tucked under the body.

STAR ASCIDIAN
Lives in groups of 3–12 surrounding a large central opening, the jelly-like colony forming an encrustation 6 in. or more across. Found on stones and other submerged objects.

365

Sandy or muddy shore

A sandy beach or mud-flats at low tide appear barren and devoid of life, apart from a scattering of birds along the water's edge. Even weeds, which need an anchorage, are absent. Yet there is teeming life beneath the surface, and in the shallow lagoons left by the retreating tide. Most

Sandy shore: where beach dwellers keep on the move

Two groups of animals live on a sandy shore; those that move in and out with the tide, such as the plaice, sand goby and lesser weaver, and those which burrow below the surface when the sand is exposed, such as worms, cockles and shrimps. Because of this continuous migration,

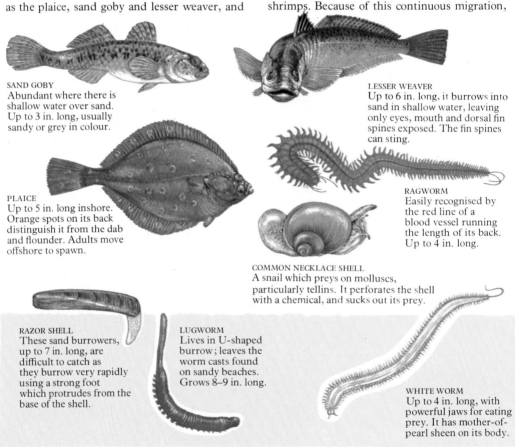

SAND GOBY
Abundant where there is shallow water over sand. Up to 3 in. long, usually sandy or grey in colour.

LESSER WEAVER
Up to 6 in. long, it burrows into sand in shallow water, leaving only eyes, mouth and dorsal fin spines exposed. The fin spines can sting.

PLAICE
Up to 5 in. long inshore. Orange spots on its back distinguish it from the dab and flounder. Adults move offshore to spawn.

RAGWORM
Easily recognised by the red line of a blood vessel running the length of its back. Up to 4 in. long.

COMMON NECKLACE SHELL
A snail which preys on molluscs, particularly tellins. It perforates the shell with a chemical, and sucks out its prey.

RAZOR SHELL
These sand burrowers, up to 7 in. long, are difficult to catch as they burrow very rapidly using a strong foot which protrudes from the base of the shell.

LUGWORM
Lives in U-shaped burrow; leaves the worm casts found on sandy beaches. Grows 8–9 in. long.

WHITE WORM
Up to 4 in. long, with powerful jaws for eating prey. It has mother-of-pearl sheen on its body.

Muddy shore

As the amount of mud increases, animal life becomes more restricted until only a few highly specialised forms are found in the clogging environment of a sticky mud-flat.

LAVER SPIRAL SHELL
Tiny snail, less than ½ in. long. Found in immense numbers.

GAPER
Bivalve with 5 in. shell, lies below muddy sand.

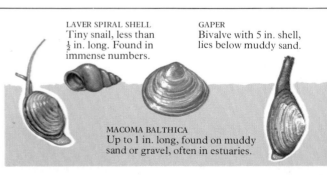

SCROBICULARIA PLANA
Common on soft mud, shell 2 in. long; usually stays below surface.

MACOMA BALTHICA
Up to 1 in. long, found on muddy sand or gravel, often in estuaries.

of the creatures that live on the beach are burrowers; they retreat beneath the surface to escape the pounding of the breakers and to avoid being dried out by the wind and sun.
In sheltered places, such as small enclosed bays or the mouths of estuaries where the force of the sea is reduced, fine material is deposited and sand is gradually replaced by mud. Every gradation of mixture may be found and there is generally no sharp distinction between the animals found in sand and mud although some animals, such as the lugworm, need to live in mud.

the division of life zones so sharply etched on a rocky shore is much less distinct. The main problem for the animals is finding food. They do this in one of several ways: by filtering suspended matter from the water, by collecting food particles from the sand's surface, by swallowing sand and then straining nourishment from it, or by preying on other sand dwellers.

GREATER SAND EEL
These eels, up to 12 in. long, swim in shoals offshore, sometimes moving into shallow water. They burrow into sand with their shovel-shaped jaws.

COMMON (BROWN) SHRIMP
Up to 3 in. long, common in shallow water at low tide. Spends the day burrowing below the sand, emerging at night to feed. Changes colour to match different types of sand.

HEART URCHIN
Common near low-tide mark. It grows up to 3½ in. long, and is roughly heart shaped with spines. The urchin burrows 3–6 in. under the sand.

MASKED CRAB
Usually lives below low-water mark, but sometimes found at lower level of sandy shore. It burrows backwards into the sand, breathing through a tube formed by its antennae.

EDIBLE COCKLE
Found in large numbers, with its shell buried 1 in. or so deep. It feeds with two 'siphons' through the sand at high water.

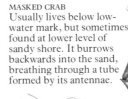

THIN TELLIN
Abundant from mid-tide level to the lowest shore and often occurs in dense beds of 1000 to 1 sq yd. Uses long 'siphons' for feeding.

SAND MASON
This worm constructs a flexible tube of sand grains through which it protrudes its tentacles to feed. At low tide it withdraws 1 ft or more under the sand.

SLIPPER LIMPET
Prolific in creeks and estuaries. A pest on oyster beds where it lives in groups.

SEA MOUSE
Massive worm with body 6 in. long and 2 in. wide, covered with fine bristles and hair.

PEACOCK WORM
A 4–10 in. long worm which makes muddy tubes. Its bright tentacles emerge under water.

COROPHIUM VOLUTATOR
Small crustacean ⅓ in. long. Lives in U-shaped burrows, emerging to forage for food.

367

PEBBLES ON THE BEACH

Rock fragments smoothed by wind and wave

Pebble beaches are constantly changing because of the action of tides and currents. Each pebble starts as a rock fragment which falls from a cliff or is swept into a stream or river, joining other rocks which are ground and smoothed by currents and surging waves into the familiar rounded pebble. This erosion on the beach never ceases, and eventually the pebble is reduced to grains of wind-blown sand.

Pebbles on the beaches have been formed from the rocks of nearby cliffs, from rocks miles inland and even from rocks which do not naturally occur in these islands. At the end of the Ice Age, 10,000 years ago, melting ice scooped up rocks and moved them hundreds of miles. For example, blocks of larvikite, a distinctive volcanic rock, were carried by icebergs from Norway to the Yorkshire coast where it occurs in boulder clay.

This movement of rocks and pebbles still goes on. River currents carry them from inland to the beaches, while the phenomenon known as 'longshore drift' – the movement of the sea along the coast – relentlessly sweeps them from one beach to the next.

Seaweed, such as bladder wrack, also plays a part in this constant change. This seaweed has air bladders which make it buoyant. It anchors itself to rocks and strong tides may sweep it along the coast, dragging its rock anchor with it.

Man, too, has helped this movement of rocks. Ships carrying shingle as ballast from as far away as Australia have been wrecked off the British coast, throwing pebbles from the other side of the world on our beaches.

For these reasons, pebble beaches make ideal sites for finding geological specimens. Almost every type of rock can be found in sizes small enough to carry away to make up a collection or to be polished for home-made jewellery.

Some of the most common pebbles that are found round the coasts of Britain

GRANITE A hard rock composed of quartz, feldspar and mica, varying in colour from grey to pink. The mica in granite gives it its characteristic sparkle, while feldspar adds the pink tint. Granite is an igneous rock – one formed by the cooling of molten material. It is rough and hard to the touch, but is attractive when smoothed and polished. Granite pebbles are found mostly around the coasts of Cornwall, Wales and eastern Scotland.

SANDSTONE A rock composed of sand grains held together by a natural cement of clay, iron or limestone. It once formed the bed of ancient seas and oceans. Upheavals of the earth's crust thrust up mountain ranges from the ocean floors and the endless cycle of weathering is returning the sandstone to the sea. Mineral oxide often stains it with colourful tints of blue, red, yellow and green.

BASALT Solidified lava which looks like dark glass. The pebbles are widespread, especially on the west coast of Scotland, and spectacular formations of this iron-black rock are seen in the Giant's Causeway in County Antrim and at Fingal's Cave on the island of Staffa. Unworked basalt is not as attractive as granite, but it can look magnificent when smoothed and polished. Basalt was formed by the eruption of molten lava which cooled and hardened very quickly on contact with the air.

LIMESTONE The pebbles are opaque, dull white to yellow, and often colourfully stained. They consist largely of calcite and will effervesce strongly in weak acid. Limestone which has been subjected to great geological heat and pressure becomes marble.

SHALE Formed when fine-grained clays were subjected to great heat and pressure. Shale pebbles are characteristically flat and usually grey or dark blue. If the rock splits at right angles to its bedding plane it becomes the familiar roofing material, slate.

FLINT One of the most common pebbles on the beach, found in a variety of shades, including black, grey and brown. Flint is composed of silica, derived from the bodies of extinct sea creatures, which has been coloured by iron or sandstone impurities.

Semi-precious pebbles

There are no truly precious stones on Britain's beaches, but there are enormous numbers of attractive pebbles, such as amethyst, agate, jasper and serpentine, which are called semi-precious. A stroll along any shingle beach will reveal colourful pebbles to take home. The best beaches to find these stones are:

1. The Cornish peninsula – agate, citrine, carnelian, chalcedony, amethyst, serpentine, rock crystal.
2. North Wales coast – agate, jasper, serpentine.
3. Norfolk and Suffolk coasts – agate, carnelian, citrine, amber, chalcedony.
4. Fifeshire coast – agate, amethyst, smoky quartz.
5. East coast of Scotland – smoky quartz, serpentine, jasper, amethyst, agate.
6. West coast of Ireland – amethyst, carnelian, chalcedony and jasper.

Areas where semi-precious stones may be found

Agate — Rock crystal — Amber — Citrine — Carnelian — Jet — Chalcedony

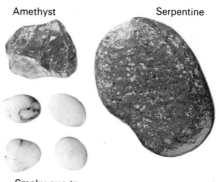

Amethyst — Serpentine — Smoky quartz

A selection of semi-precious stones

AGATE A range of stones with a strong, defined banding and wide colour range – pink, red, yellow, white, brown and blue.

ROCK CRYSTAL Clear quartz, which is easily confused with glass. Test for rock crystal by striking two pieces together in the dark. There should be an orange spark and a smell of burning.

AMBER A pale yellow to dark red 'rock' formed from fossilised tree resin. It floats in salt water and has been carried by currents from the Baltic to the east coast of England.

CITRINE A lemon-yellow to golden quartz, like amethyst. This stone is similar to topaz and is often sold as Scotch topaz or fake topaz – fetching a higher price than yellow quartz.

CHALCEDONY A translucent quartz with a waxy lustre; milky white, blue or grey.

CARNELIAN Red variety of chalcedony. The pebble seems to glow when held up to a strong light.

JET A hard, intensely black, fossilised wood similar to coal but much harder. It is now rare, and the only likely collecting area is around Whitby, Yorkshire. At first sight jet can be confused with coal, as pebbles of sea-coal are common on this coast, particularly on Durham beaches a few miles north. A test for jet is to balance its weight against a piece of glass of similar size. Jet will be lighter.

AMETHYST A coloured variety of rock crystal. It is purple to pink with a white banding.

SMOKY QUARTZ Also known as Cairngorm from the granite mountains from which they were first extracted. It has been carried by streams and rivers to Scottish beaches, and by longshore drift to the eastern coast of England. The stone is a deep yellow to brown, and is a familiar jewel for Highland dress.

SERPENTINE An opaque, usually red or green rock, whose surface has a soapy feel. The cliffs of the Lizard, Cornwall, are composed of serpentine.

Making the most of your finds

Lapidary – the art of making jewellery from pebbles – is a fast-growing hobby. The pebbles can be smoothed and polished in a home tumble polisher. The finished stones can then be mounted as jewellery. Most seaside resorts with good pebble beaches have rock shops which sell pebble-collecting maps and equipment.

Among lapidary clubs are: Mid-Cornwall Rocks and Minerals Club, 37 Whitestone Crescent, Bodmin, Cornwall; Anglo-Continental Minerals Society, 97 Hodford Road, London NW11; West of Scotland Minerals and Lapidary Society, 4 Millwood Street, Glasgow G41 33X.

369

FRESHWATER LIFE

Ponds and sluggish rivers

Complex communities live in ponds, lakes and rivers. Here, easily observed, is a great variety of life—amphibians, surface-skimming insects, beetles, carnivorous larvae and some of the 34 kinds of freshwater fish found in Britain. Still or slow-moving water offers them a relatively stable environment. The temperature of the water is fairly constant, while rooted plants provide food and shelter.

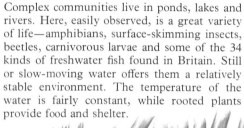

Frog

12 weeks

Toad

Spawn

5 weeks

Newt

Two worlds of the amphibians

NEWT 4 in. For most of the year the newt stays on land. It hibernates in winter, and in spring takes to the water to reproduce.

TOAD 3 in. The warty-skinned toad feeds on insects, worms and slugs. It spawns in spring, leaves the pond in summer, hibernates from October, and returns to breed the next spring.

FROG 3 in. The smooth-skinned frog has much the same diet as the toad. The female lays as many as 2000–3000 eggs while the male, lying on her back, fertilises them. Tadpoles develop in eight days but comparatively few escape their many predators to become adult frogs. Those tadpoles surviving lose their tails and develop legs in 12–14 weeks to become $\frac{1}{2}$ in. long frogs. They mature in three years.

Fish lurking among the weeds

PIKE 16–25 in. The ferocious pike lies among weeds waiting to capture fish, birds, frogs and newts. It spawns in spring.

CARP 20 in. Moving in small shoals the carp feeds on bottom-living animals and plants. It spawns May–July and can live up to 40 years.

BREAM 12–20 in. A deep-bodied fish, the bream has slimy skin and a small head. It feeds on animals on the river bed and spawns April–June.

EEL 18–30 in. The eel lies in weed beds by day and eats bottom-living animals by night. It migrates to the sea to breed.

TENCH 12 in. The tench lives buried in mud or among weeds where it feeds on bottom-living animals. It has slimy skin with tiny scales and spawns May–July.

ROACH 7 in. The roach feeds on algae, insects, crustaceans and snails. It spawns April–May, attaching its eggs to water plants.

PERCH 6–12 in. The perch feeds on crustaceans, insects and fish. It spawns in April and May, attaching its eggs to water plants.

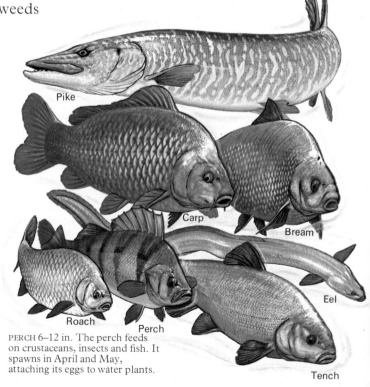

Pike

Carp

Bream

Roach

Perch

Eel

Tench

Insects on the surface

DAMSELFLY 1½ in. This slender fly hovers by the waterside to catch insects. The larva, which lives on the mud or among weeds, swims with serpentine movements, and eats small invertebrates.

CADDIS FLY 1 in. Emerges swiftly from the water for mating, and during its life of a few hours it eats little or nothing. Its moth-like wings are covered with fine hairs.

DRAGONFLY 3 in. The brilliantly coloured dragonfly feeds on insects, locating its prey with multi-faceted eyes. The larva or nymph lives deep in ponds, and breathes by pumping water back and forth over gills in its rectum. It feeds on invertebrates and tadpoles, catching them in its hooked lower jaw.

ALDER FLY 1 in. This fly is found resting or crawling on trees or walls near water in May and June. It can be recognised by the way it folds its black-veined wings into a roof-like ridge.

POND SKATER ½ in. Since its wings are poorly formed or do not develop at all, the pond skater must slide or jump over the surface of the water. It feeds on the dead insects it finds under banks.

WHIRLIGIG BEETLE ¼ in. This beetle swims in circles and has divided eyes enabling it to see upwards and downwards at the same time.

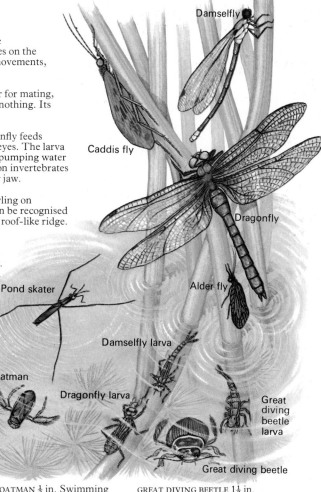

Damselfly

Caddis fly

Dragonfly

Alder fly

Pond skater

Damselfly larva

Water boatman

Dragonfly larva

Great diving beetle larva

Whirligig beetle

Water scorpion

Great diving beetle

WATER SCORPION 1½ in. A dark brown bug, resembling a leaf, which seizes its prey—insects and small animals—in its front legs.

WATER BOATMAN ½ in. Swimming on its keeled back, using oar-like legs, the water boatman feeds on insects, tadpoles and tiny fish.

GREAT DIVING BEETLE 1½ in. Carrying its own air bubble this beetle dives to catch snails and tadpoles. It can also fly strongly.

Creatures living on the bottom mud

SWAN MUSSEL 6 in. Burrowing through mud, the mussel extracts oxygen and food from the water passing through its shell valves.

HORSE LEECH 6 in. When extended this leech can swim or move on the bottom mud using its suckers. It feeds on worms, snails, insects and tadpoles.

TUBIFEX WORM 1½ in. Also known as the sludge worm, it lives head down in a tube feeding on organic matter in mud. It uses its tail as a gill to obtain oxygen.

RAM'S HORN SNAIL 1 in. across. This snail, with a vertically coiled brown shell, hibernates in mud. It lives on decayed animal matter.

STICKLEBACK 2 in. In spring the three-spined male stickleback develops a brilliant red throat and builds a nest. It entices the female inside to lay her eggs, then guards them until they hatch.

POND SNAIL 2 in. across. This snail grazes on algae and takes in surface air with a primitive lung.

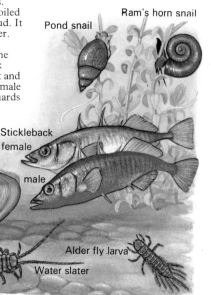

Ram's horn snail

Pond snail

Stickleback female

Swan mussel

male

Horse leech

Caddis larva

Alder fly larva

Water slater

Tubifex worm

CADDIS LARVA ¾ in. In still water the larva builds a protective case of vegetable matter. It feeds on algae and decaying material.

WATER SLATER ½ in. A scavenging, louse-like creature, the slater crawls about in the mud, eating decaying organic matter.

ALDER FLY LARVA 1 in. This larva preys on the larvae of other insects, seizing them in its powerful jaws. It has jointed gills on its body.

Fast-flowing rivers

Animals in fast-flowing streams have had to adapt themselves to different conditions from those living in sluggish rivers. Since plants cannot take root in turbulent water, most animals must live on the stony bed, feeding on algae or smaller animals. Many use suckers to anchor themselves to stones while some, such as stonefly larvae, have a flattened, streamlined shape so that water flows over them instead of sweeping them away.

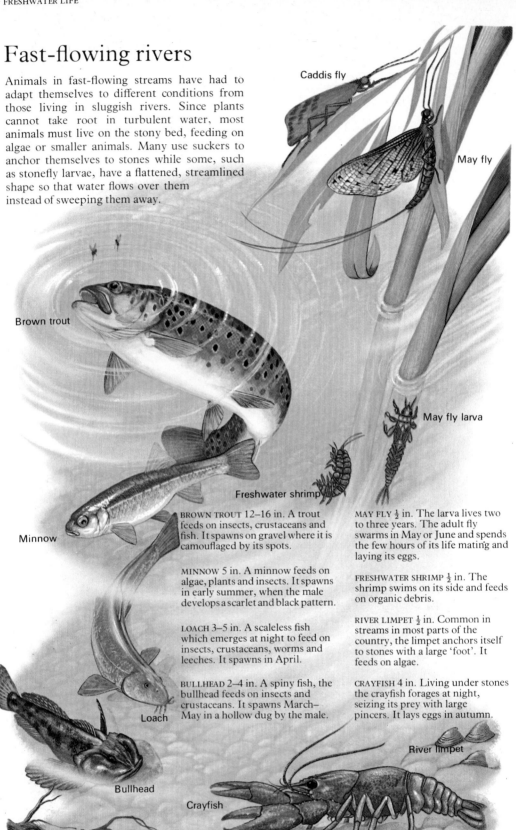

Caddis fly

May fly

May fly larva

Brown trout

Freshwater shrimp

Minnow

Loach

Bullhead

River limpet

Crayfish

Stonefly larva

Blackfly larva

Caddis larva

BROWN TROUT 12–16 in. A trout feeds on insects, crustaceans and fish. It spawns on gravel where it is camouflaged by its spots.

MINNOW 5 in. A minnow feeds on algae, plants and insects. It spawns in early summer, when the male develops a scarlet and black pattern.

LOACH 3–5 in. A scaleless fish which emerges at night to feed on insects, crustaceans, worms and leeches. It spawns in April.

BULLHEAD 2–4 in. A spiny fish, the bullhead feeds on insects and crustaceans. It spawns March–May in a hollow dug by the male.

MAY FLY $\frac{1}{2}$ in. The larva lives two to three years. The adult fly swarms in May or June and spends the few hours of its life mating and laying its eggs.

FRESHWATER SHRIMP $\frac{1}{2}$ in. The shrimp swims on its side and feeds on organic debris.

RIVER LIMPET $\frac{1}{2}$ in. Common in streams in most parts of the country, the limpet anchors itself to stones with a large 'foot'. It feeds on algae.

CRAYFISH 4 in. Living under stones the crayfish forages at night, seizing its prey with large pincers. It lays eggs in autumn.

CADDIS LARVA $\frac{3}{4}$ in. The larva throws out a silken net, leaving it open upstream to catch minute animals and plants.

STONEFLY LARVA 1 in. Found among stones and gravel, the larva lives on small invertebrates which it grabs in its strong claws.

BLACKFLY LARVA $\frac{1}{2}$ in. The larva attaches itself with hooks in its tail. If dislodged it throws out a silk safety line so it can return.

PLANTS AND FLOWERS

Wildlife sanctuaries by the roadside

Roads criss-cross hills and valleys, flood-plains and fens, woodlands and moors—and each roadside bank provides a refuge for the plant life of the region.

Along downland roads in Sussex, for example, the blue-violet round-headed rampion is common, yet only a few miles from the chalk hills it never occurs. Near heath or moorland roads bell-heather thrives, but it cannot take root in anything other than well-drained acid soils.

Because roads run through such varying countryside, about 70 per cent of the native and naturalised species of plants in Britain can be found somewhere within a few yards of the roadside.

Some conservationists lament that rare or local plants might disappear during the building of motorways. But this is not always the case. The vast embankments which border many miles of motorway eventually become habitats for wildlife, and they are soon colonised by species from the surrounding countryside. Such sites are often difficult to get to on foot and in effect become wildlife sanctuaries.

Already several rare species of plants are known to have established themselves on motorway embankments, and in a few places local naturalists have planted native plants from endangered sites near by.

A threat to wildlife, however, is the practice of moor burning. This is common in Scotland where it is called 'muirburn'. Upland areas of heather and purple moor grass are burnt in spring every few years to improve the quality of the grazing. Fortunately, moor burning is unlawful between April 11 and November 1.

The species shown in the next few pages are only a small sample of Britain's varied plant life. They are not necessarily all common, but are grouped in the particular habitat where they most often grow. They are also grouped according to their height and flowering time.

Hedges—1000 years of living history

The 550,000 miles of hedgerows which stretch across the fields and hills of Britain provide a home for a richer and wider variety of plant and animal life than any other part of the land.

The trees, shrubs, wild flowers and grasses in the hedges make a home for the birds, insects and small mammals that once lived on the fringes of the forests which covered most of the country. Today, the hedgerows connect small woods, like highways across open country, enabling animal and insect life to move between patches of woodland.

The open land of England was enclosed with hedges by Acts of Parliament, particularly in the 18th century. Hedges were planted to divide land used for cattle grazing and crop growing because they were cheaper to build than walls or fences. These hedges were usually of hawthorn with elm trees planted at intervals.

Some hedges, however, existed centuries earlier. The Saxons planted them as boundaries between estates, and some of these 1000-year-old hedges exist today. The practice developed slowly through the Middle Ages, until the major enclosure movements—for sheep under the Tudors 400 years ago, and for crop growing in the late 18th century.

Botanists have found they can date hedges by counting the number of different species of shrub growing in them. As a rough guide, hedges have one species of shrub for every 100 years of the hedge's existence in each 30 yd stretch. For instance, a Saxon hedge, 1000 years old, has ten different species of shrub in every 30 yd stretch. Tudor hedges, about 400 years old, have three or four woody species every 30 yds. The dating process has been confirmed by studying existing hedges marked on Saxon and Tudor documents. This has provided local historians and naturalists with an invaluable guide to the history of the countryside—each hedge being a living document. Sadly, some of these 'documents' are being destroyed before there is time for naturalists to 'read' them.

For nearly 25 years up to 1970 an average of 4500 miles of hedges were uprooted and destroyed by farmers each year, the heaviest loss being in eastern England. This was done so that giant cultivating machines could be used more economically. Since then, however, the rate of removal has declined to less than 2000 miles a year, but this still poses a threat to some animal and plant life.

When a hedge is removed a sanctuary for wildlife is lost. A well-tended hawthorn hedge contains a much larger variety of animal and plant life than a natural hawthorn thicket where little light penetrates.

Among the animals which live in hedgerows are mice, rabbits, voles, badgers and foxes, while the list of insects runs into thousands. Dozens of different birds live in hedgerows. Of the 91 land species which breed in lowland Britain, 65 of them do so in hedges.

The richest variety of life is provided by the plants. About 30 woody species can be found growing as part of the hedge itself, the most common being ash, elm, field maple, hawthorn, hazel, holly, oak, privet, rose and sycamore.

Another 500 species of flowering plants have been found growing in the hedge bottom. Most of them are common and were growing at woodland edges before Neolithic farmers first cleared the forests about 5000 years ago.

Hedgerows and woodland margins

Since the 18th century all but a small part of the enormous mileage of British hedgerows has been planted deliberately, either from wild seedlings or from nursery-raised stocks, usually hawthorn. As the years pass, other species

HORSE CHESTNUT 80 ft. White flowers with pink spots, May–June.

HAZEL 18 ft. Male catkins yellow, Jan.–Apr. *Also* in thickets.

WAYFARING TREE 10 ft. Cream-white flowers, May–June.

SPINDLE TREE Shrub, 10 ft. Green flowers, May–June. *Also* in open woods.

BLACK BRYONY Yellow-green flowers, May–July. *Also* in thickets.

HAWTHORN 25 ft. White, red or pink flowers, May–June. *Also* in woods.

BLACKBERRY White or pink flowers, May–Sept. *Also* in thickets.

Plants growing up to 3 ft

BARREN STRAWBERRY White flowers, Feb.–May. Fruit dry, colourless.

JACK-BY-THE-HEDGE White flowers, Apr.–June. *Also* roadsides.

1 English elm 2 Elder 3 Honeysuckle 4 Guelder rose
5 Bush vetch 6 Jack-by-the-hedge 7 Red campion

appear in the hedgerow from wind-blown and bird-sown seed. Most of the trees, shrubs and plants that eventually make up a mature hedgerow are of scrub or woodland origin. The conditions of shelter, light and humidity in hedgerows closely resemble those in woodland margins and, while no wild flower is confined to hedgerows, many species are characteristic, particularly the climbers such as honeysuckle, dog rose and black bryony.

GOAT WILLOW 30 ft. Fluffy yellow catkins before leaves, Mar.–Apr.

FIELD MAPLE 30 ft. Pale green flowers, May–June. *Also* scrub.

WILD CHERRY 60 ft. White flowers, Apr.–May. *Also* hill scrub.

SYCAMORE 90 ft. Yellow-green flowers, Apr.–June. *Also* parks.

ENGLISH ELM 90 ft. Reddish flowers, Feb.–Mar. *Also* in parks and gardens.

LOMBARDY POPLAR 100 ft. Reddish catkins, Apr. Always planted.

EVERGREEN OAK 80 ft. Male catkins yellow, May. Often planted.

COMMON LIME 80 ft. Yellow-white flowers, July. *Also* in parks.

DOG ROSE Pink or white flowers, May–Sept. *Also* in scrub.

ELDER 25 ft. Cream-white flowers, June–July. *Also* in scrub.

HONEYSUCKLE Cream-white flowers, flushed purple, June–Sept.

TRAVELLER'S JOY Green-white flowers, July–Sept. *Also* in thickets.

GUELDER ROSE 15 ft. White flowers, June–July. *Also* in scrub.

COMMON PRIVET Shrub, 8 ft. White flowers, June–July. *Also* in scrub.

BITTERSWEET Purple and yellow flowers, June–Sept. *Also* near the sea.

HOP Climber, 20 ft. Yellow-green flowers, July–Aug.

WILD STRAWBERRY White flowers, Apr.–July. *Also* grassland.

RED CAMPION Bright pink flowers, May–Sept. *Also* cliffs.

GREATER CELANDINE Yellow flowers, May–July. *Also* below walls.

BUSH VETCH Pale purple flowers, May–Aug. *Also* in scrub.

AGRIMONY Yellow flowers, June–Sept. *Also* by roadsides.

Woodlands and thickets

The forests that once covered most of the British Isles have been steadily cleared by man since prehistoric times. Remnants of these ancient woodlands show how tree species, if allowed to spread naturally, vary according to the type of

SPURGE LAUREL Evergreen, 4 ft. Yellow-green flowers, Feb.–Apr.

IVY Evergreen climber, 90 ft. Green flowers, Sept.–Nov. *Also* walls.

Plants growing up to 2 ft

BLUEBELL Violet-blue flowers, Apr.–June. *Also* hedgerows.

EARLY PURPLE ORCHID Purple-crimson flowers, Apr.–June.

Plants growing up to 1 ft

LESSER CELANDINE Glossy yellow flowers, Mar.–May. Also near water.

WOOD ANEMONE White or pink flowers, Mar.–May. *Also* grassland.

DAFFODIL Pale and darker yellow, Feb.–Apr. Often planted.

RAMSONS White flowers, Apr.–June. Has a strong garlic smell.

PRIMROSE Pale yellow flowers, Dec.–May. *Also* hedgerows, grassland.

COMMON VIOLET Pale to deep blue-violet flowers, Apr.–June.

1 Oak   2 Holly   3 Wych elm   4 Norway maple   5 Spurge laurel
6 Wood avens   7 Golden rod   8 Herb Robert
9 Early purple orchid   10 Fly agaric   11 Wood anemone
12 Primrose   13 Common violet   14 Devil's boletus

soil, the degree of moisture and height of the land. In moister areas, common oak is dominant, sometimes mixed with hornbeam. Better drained and alkaline soils on the slopes of hills support beech and ash, while birch and Scots pine are typical trees on acid soils. A wide variety of plants grow in woodlands, many of which bloom in the early spring before the leaves cut out the light. Typical of these are wood anemone, primrose and bluebell.

SWEET CHESTNUT 80 ft. Yellow-white catkins, July. Widely planted.

BOX Evergreen, 20 ft. White-green, petal-less flowers, Mar.–Apr.

CRAB APPLE 30 ft. White and pink flowers, May. *Also* hedges and scrub.

YEW Evergreen, 60 ft. Male flowering cones, yellow-white, Mar.–Apr.

COW-WHEAT Yellow-white flowers, May–Oct. *Also* on heaths.

ENCHANTER'S NIGHTSHADE White or pinkish flowers, June–Aug.

WOOD AVENS Yellow flowers, June–Aug. *Also* in hedges.

GOLDEN ROD Yellow flowers, July–Sept. *Also* in hedgerows.

YELLOW PIMPERNEL Yellow flowers, May–Sept. *Also* hedgerows.

WOOD BLEWITT Edible and tasty, Sept.–Dec. Often in beechwoods.

BLUSHER Edible, but can easily be confused with poisonous fungi, July–Dec.

FLY AGARIC Poisonous, but rarely fatal, Aug.–Nov. Pine and beechwoods.

HERB ROBERT Bright pink or white flowers, May–Sept. *Also* hedgerows.

WOOD MUSHROOM Edible, smells of aniseed, Aug.–Nov. Coniferous woods.

DEVIL'S BOLETUS Poisonous, but not fatal, July–Oct. Turns blue when bruised.

DEATH CAP Deadly poisonous, July–Nov. Mainly on chalky soils.

CEP Edible and very tasty. Found July–Nov., mostly in beechwoods.

CHANTARELLE Edible, Aug.–Nov. Especially beechwoods. *Also* on heaths.

SICKENER Inedible, causes sickness if eaten raw, Aug.–Nov. Under conifers.

YELLOW-STAINING MUSHROOM Poisonous, but not fatal, Aug.–Nov.

☠ Indicates poisonous

377

Cultivated ground and waste land

The wild plants on cultivated land are weeds to the farmer and gardener, whose only thought is to eradicate them. To the naturalist these weeds are of great interest, and form a group of plants which may occur only on cultivated land, their

WELD Green-yellow flowers, June–Aug. *Also* banks and roadsides.

COMMON ST JOHN'S WORT Yellow flowers, June–Sept. *Also* woods.

Plants growing up to 2 ft

CHARLOCK Bright yellow flowers, May–Aug. *Also* roadsides.

WHITE CAMPION White flowers, May–Sept. *Also* hedges and roadsides.

Plants growing up to 1 ft

GROUNDSEL Green and yellow flowers, Jan.–Dec. *Also* walls, roadsides.

RED DEADNETTLE Red or pink-purple flowers, Feb.–Nov. *Also* roadsides.

COMMON CHICKWEED Dull, white flowers, Jan.–Dec. *Also* roadsides.

DANDELION Yellow flowers, Feb.–Nov. *Also* grassland and roadsides.

BUXBAUM'S SPEEDWELL Sky-blue or blue and white flowers, Feb.–Nov.

COLTSFOOT Yellow flowers, Mar.–Apr. *Also* grassland and banks.

1 Common St John's wort   2 Evening primrose
3 Bladder campion   4 Red deadnettle   5 Fumitory
6 Charlock   7 White campion   8 Buxbaum's speedwell
9 Dandelion   10 Scarlet pimpernel

original homeland being unknown. Some weeds are garden plants, run wild, their seeds having been brought to their present sites by wind and birds. Others have been carried accidentally on imported goods, such as raw wool. Weeds have their uses to farmers and gardeners as soil indicators. For example, scarlet pimpernel and white campion are more likely to be found on chalky or limestone soils; whereas sheep's sorrel denotes an acid, often sandy soil.

EVENING PRIMROSE Yellow flowers, opening at dusk, June–Sept.

COMMON RAGWORT Yellow flowers, June–Oct. *Also* grassland.

HEMP NETTLE Pink-purple or white flowers, July–Sept. *Also* heaths.

HEDGE WOUNDWORT Claret-red flowers, July–Sept. *Also* woods.

BLADDER CAMPION Dull, white flowers, June–Sept. *Also* grassland.

YARROW White flowers, June–Sept. Common in grassland and by roads.

STINKING MAYWEED White flowers with yellow centre, July–Sept.

CANADIAN FLEABANE White to lavender flowers with yellow centre, Aug.–Oct.

DAISY White or pink flowers with yellow centre, Mar.–Nov. *Also* short grass.

SAND SPURREY Pink flowers, May–Sept. *Also* sandy or gravelly places.

CREEPING CINQUEFOIL Yellow flowers, June–Sept. *Also* roadsides.

RESTHARROW Pink flowers, June–Sept. *Also* grassy places and roadsides.

BLACK MEDICK Bright yellow flowers, Apr.–Sept. *Also* roadsides.

SUN SPURGE Green-yellow 'flowers' which are modified leaves, May–Oct.

BINDWEED White or pink flowers, June–Sept. *Also* hedgerows, grassland.

PINEAPPLE MAYWEED Dull, green-yellow flowers, June–Sept.

DOVE'S-FOOT CRANESBILL Rose-purple or white flowers, Apr.–Oct.

FUMITORY Pink, blackish-red flowers. May–Oct. *Also* by roadsides.

SCARLET PIMPERNEL Red or pink flowers, rarely blue, June–Sept. *Also* on dunes.

PALE PERSICARIA Green-white flowers, June–Oct. *Also* roadsides.

379

Meadows and grassy hills

Grassland is the predominant vegetation in the British Isles, but it was not always so. In prehistoric times forest covered most of the land. Then came man who for centuries felled vast tracts of trees for fuel, building homes and ships,

WHITEBEAM 35 ft. Cream-white flowers, May–June. *Also* woods, thickets.

BIRCH 70 ft. Yellow male catkins, Apr.–May. *Also* woods and heathland.

Plants growing up to 2 ft

YELLOW RATTLE Yellow flowers with violet 'teeth', May–Sept.

COMMON VETCH Purple flowers, May–Sept. *Also* hedgerows.

RED CLOVER Rose-purple flowers, May–Sept. *Also* roadsides.

OX-EYE DAISY White flowers with yellow centre, May–Sept. *Also* roadsides.

Plants growing up to 1 ft

GERMANDER SPEEDWELL Deep sky-blue flowers with white eye, Mar.–July.

SORREL Pale green or red-tinted flowers, May–June. *Also* woods and roadsides.

PASQUE FLOWER Violet-purple flowers, Apr.–May. *Also* grown in gardens.

MOUSE-EAR HAWKWEED Pale yellow flowers, May–June. *Also* roadsides.

1 Birch 2 Beech 3 Whitebeam 4 Field scabious
5 Ox-eye daisy 6 Meadow buttercup 7 Knapweed
8 Selfheal 9 Carline thistle 10 Germander speedwell
11 White clover 12 Shaggy ink cap 13 Common puff ball

and to create pasture for his animals. Grassland is essentially artificial and maintained only by grazing or mowing for hay. Left unattended the land would soon revert to scrub, then woodland. Many broad-leaved plants growing in grassland would die out if trees returned. Certain species prefer particular situations. Meadow buttercup thrives in moist low-lying areas, while the bulbous buttercup is more common on the drier chalk and limestone hillsides.

ASH 75 ft. Flower clusters before leaves, Apr.–May. *Also* woods, hedgerows.

LARCH 150 ft. Pink flowering cones, Mar.–Apr. Mainly planted for timber.

NORWAY SPRUCE 120 ft. Yellow flower cones, May–June. Mainly planted.

BEECH 100 ft. Tiny flowers in stalked clusters, Apr.–May. Prefers lime soil.

SALAD BURNET Green or purple-tinged flowers, May–Aug.

GOAT'S-BEARD Yellow flowers, June–July. *Also* found by roadsides.

KNAPWEED Red-purple flowers, June–Sept. *Also* roadsides and in scrub.

MARJORAM Rose-purple flowers, July–Sept. *Also* hedgebanks and scrub.

MEADOW BUTTERCUP Bright yellow flowers, May–Oct. *Also* roadsides.

LUCERNE Blue-purple flowers, June–Aug. *Also* waste land.

FIELD SCABIOUS Blue-lilac, pink or white flowers, July–Sept. *Also* roadsides.

VERVAIN Pale lilac flowers, July–Sept. *Also* roadsides and below walls.

HOARY PLANTAIN White flowers with lilac anthers, May–Aug. Hoary leaves.

KIDNEY-VETCH Yellow or red flowers, June–Sept. Common near sea.

WHITE CLOVER White flowers with green veins, June–Sept. *Also* roadsides.

COMMON PUFF BALL Edible when young, July–Oct. *Also* in mixed woods.

SELFHEAL Violet, pink or white flowers, June–Sept. *Also* woods, waste ground.

FELWORT Blue-purple flowers, July–Oct. *Also* on dunes.

HAREBELL Blue, sometimes white, flowers, July–Sept. *Also* dunes, thickets.

SHAGGY INK CAP Tasty when young, May–Nov. *Also* by roadsides.

381

Lowlands, uplands, heaths and bogs

Heaths and moors, whether in the lowlands or the highlands, are dominated by heather. The underlying soil is always acid and often peaty. Bogs are areas of wet, acid peat where rainfall is high and the drainage is poor.

MOUNTAIN ASH 45 ft. Flowers cream, May–June. *Also* heaths.

BOG MYRTLE Shrub, 6 ft. Red catkins, Apr.–May. *Also* in fens.

FOXGLOVE Rose-purple or white flowers, June–Sept. *Also* woods, roadsides.

SNEEZEWORT White flowers with green centres, July–Sept. *Also* grassland.

Plants growing up to 1 ft

BILBERRY Green-pink flowers, Apr.–June. *Also* in woods.

RAGGED ROBIN Rose-red flowers, May–June. *Also* fens, woods.

CRANBERRY Pink flowers, June–Aug. Usually in wet places.

BOG PIMPERNEL Pink or white flowers, June–Sept. *Also* grassland.

CROSS-LEAVED HEATHER Pink to white flowers, July–Sept.

LOUSEWORT Pink flowers, Apr.–July. *Also* found in marshes.

BUTTERWORT Violet flowers, May–July. Traps and eats insects.

SUNDEW White flowers, June–Aug. Traps and eats insects.

TORMENTIL Yellow flowers, June–Sept. *Also* in woods.

BELL HEATHER Pink to crimson-purple flowers, July–Sept.

COMMON COTTON GRASS Slaty-silver flowers, May–June.

MILKWORT Blue, pink or white flowers, May–Sept.

COMMON EYEBRIGHT White or purple flowers, June–Sept.

BOG ASPHODEL Yellow flowers, July–Sept. *Also* in mountains.

LING Purplish-pink, sometimes white, flowers, July–Sept.

1 Mountain ash 2 Bell heather 3 Sneezewort
4 Lousewort 5 Ling 6 Foxglove
7 Butterwort 8 Sundew

Rocky slopes, dry walls, dunes and seaside

Few species of plants grow on rocky slopes, dry walls or dunes, because of the shortage of water. Among those that survive are the very few truly succulent plants in Britain, biting stonecrop and navelwort, which have swollen leaves.

SCOTS PINE Evergreen, 100 ft. Yellow-flowering male cones, May–June.

SEA BUCKTHORN Spiny shrub, 10 ft. Greenish flowers, Mar.–Apr.

RASPBERRY Shrub, 6 ft. White flowers, June–Aug. *Also* woods.

PELLITORY-OF-THE-WALL Tiny green flowers in clusters, June–Oct.

JUNIPER Shrub, 20 ft. Yellow-flowering cones, May–June

RED VALERIAN Red, pink or white flowers, June–Sept. *Also* on banks.

VIPER'S BUGLOSS Bright blue flowers, June–Sept. Near sea.

SEA HOLLY Metallic-blue flowers, July–Aug. Sand dunes.

Plants growing up to 1 ft

WHITLOW GRASS White flowers, Mar.–June. *Also* dry banks.

BITING STONECROP Bright yellow flowers, June–July.

SEA ROCKET Purple, lilac or white flowers, June–Aug. Dunes.

STORKSBILL Rose-purple flowers, June–Sept. *Also* fields.

COMMON ROCK ROSE Bright yellow flowers, June–Sept.

WALL RUE Evergreen fern, brown spores ripen June–Oct.

MAIDENHAIR SPLEEN-WORT Fern, spores ripen May–Oct.

NAVELWORT White-green flowers, June–Sept. *Also* hedgebanks.

IVY-LEAVED TOADFLAX Lilac flowers with yellow spots. May–Sept.

1 Scots pine 2 Viper's bugloss 3 Storksbill
4 Ivy-leaved toadflax 5 Maidenhair spleenwort
6 Biting stonecrop 7 Common rock rose 8 Wall rue

383

Waterside and grassy banks

There is a distinct group of plants which needs abundant moisture. These plants are rarely found far from lakes, ponds, rivers or streams and they either grow completely submerged or live beside the water's edge. Several species of tree are found only in such places, particularly alder and several kinds of willow. Among herbaceous plants that root in water are watercress, great spearwort, water crowfoot and amphibious bistort; while growing in wet soil are king-cup, yellow flag and meadowsweet. On banks above a ditch or a sunken road, where the soil drains well but does not dry out, are found plants such as comfrey and teasel.

1 Alder   2 White willow   3 Meadowsweet   4 Tansy
5 Marsh marigold   6 Cuckoo flower   7 Great spearwort
8 Water plantain   9 Water crowfoot
10 Greater stitchwort   11 Marsh orchid

MARSH VALERIAN Pale pink flowers, May–July. *Also* wet meadows, bogs.

WATER PLANTAIN White to pale lilac flowers, June–Aug. *Also* in ditches.

Plants growing up to 3 ft

YELLOW FLAG Orange-yellow flowers, May–July. *Also* grows in meadows.

COMFREY Blue-purple to white flowers, June–Aug. *Also* roadsides.

Plants growing up to 2 ft

MARSH MARIGOLD Golden-yellow flowers, Mar.–July. *Also* wet meadows.

GREATER STITCHWORT White flowers, Apr.–June. *Also* in woods.

CUCKOO FLOWER Pale to deep lilac flowers, Apr.–June. *Also* damp grassland.

WATER CROWFOOT White flowers, May–June. Usually lives in water.

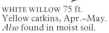

BLACK POPLAR 100 ft. Red catkins during Apr. *Also* in woods and on hills.

WEEPING WILLOW 50 ft. Yellowish catkins with young leaves, Apr.–May.

WHITE WILLOW 75 ft. Yellow catkins, Apr.–May. *Also* found in moist soil.

ALDER 50 ft. Red catkins, Feb.–Apr. Cone-like fruits in autumn.

GREAT MULLEIN Yellow flowers, June–Aug. *Also* roadsides, waste land.

GREAT SPEARWORT Glossy yellow flowers, June–Sept. *Also* in ditches.

TEASEL Rose-purple to white flowers, July–Aug. *Also* in ditches, hedges.

FLOWERING RUSH Pink flowers with darker veins, July–Sept.

MEADOWSWEET Cream-white flowers, June–Sept. *Also* ditches and fens.

YELLOW LOOSESTRIFE Yellow flowers, July–Aug. *Also* found in fens.

TANSY Golden-yellow flowers, July–Sept. *Also* roadsides, waste ground.

HIMALAYAN BALSAM Pale to deep rose-purple flowers, July–Oct.

MARSH ORCHID Dark-purple to mauve flowers, May–June.

MARSH CINQUEFOIL Deep red-purple flowers, May–July.

WATER AVENS Purple and pink flowers, May–Sept.

SKULL-CAP Violet-blue flowers, June–Sept. *Also* wet meadows.

FROGBIT Flowers have crumpled white petals, July–Aug.

BOG BEAN Pink and white flowers, May–July. *Also* ditches.

WATERCRESS White flowers, May–Oct. *Also* found in ditches.

SILVERWEED Yellow flowers, June–Aug. *Also* damp pastures.

GIPSY-WORT White flowers with purple dots, June–Sept.

AMPHIBIOUS BISTORT Pink flowers, July–Sept. Water or land.

IDENTIFYING BIRDS

Where to find residents and visitors

More than 220 species of birds are found in Britain. Some stay all the year; others are migrants arriving either in spring to breed or in autumn to escape the harsh north European winter; while some migrants stop only to feed and rest during long journeys. Man has modelled Britain's landscape and birds have had to adapt to his changes. Birds which once nested on forest fringes are now found in hedgerows, and some former cliff-dwellers nest on the 'cliff-faces' of buildings. The birds illustrated are placed in the habitats where they are most often found, although many of them may move from one environment to another.

Salt-marsh and estuary

Though lacking good cover and nest sites, the muddy channels and pools of salt-marsh and estuary provide a rich source of insects and sea organisms all the year for large numbers of birds, such as the shelduck. In winter, when food is scarce elsewhere, these all-the-year residents are joined by large flocks of water birds, including white-fronted geese, grey plovers and knots migrating from the far north. Others, such as the whimbrel, stop only to feed during their migrations north in spring and south in autumn.

DUNLIN 7 in. Small, mud-probing shore bird. Some stay all the year but many only winter here.

SHELDUCK 24 in. Feeds on bare mud-flats. Resident, nesting in a burrow further inland.

Spoonbill   Barnacle goose   Brent goose   White-fronted goose   Wigeon

BRENT GOOSE 23 in. Winter visitor. Grazes eel grass that grows only on large tidal flats.

WHITE-FRONTED GOOSE 28 in. Winter visitor from the Arctic. It grazes grass meadows and the saltings of larger inlets.

SPOONBILL 34 in. Occasional summer visitor to south and east. Feeds in shallow brackish water.

BARNACLE GOOSE 25 in. Winter visitor. Prefers grazing on drier turf. Has a yapping call.

WIGEON 18 in. Winter visitor. Noisy flocks feed on turf and mud. Drake has a loud whistle.

WHIMBREL 16 in. Spring and autumn visitor. Probes deep mud for food. Repetitive whistle.

AVOCET 17 in. Scarce summer visitor to south and east. Swings bill through shallow water to feed.

REDSHANK 11 in. Resident wader on muddy shores. It bobs up and down when anxious.

KNOT 10 in. Winter visitor. Stout grey wader. Large flocks feed on mud-banks and estuaries.

GREY PLOVER 11 in. Winter visitor. Feeds on mud-flats. Unsociable, with plaintive two-note whistle.

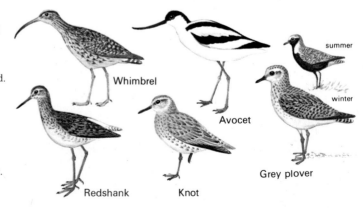

Whimbrel   Avocet   Redshank   Knot   Grey plover

Seashore and cliffs

For many birds the seashore is an uneasy resting place which attracts them only because it borders the rich feeding grounds of the sea and tide-edge. Birds of the open sea such as the fulmar are suspicious of land, but they are forced to cliff edges to breed in summer, while on the beaches colonies of tern are nesting. In winter the cliffs are almost deserted and small waders, such as sanderlings, have the beaches to themselves to hunt for food.

(juveniles)

Herring gull

Ringed plover

Common gull

HERRING GULL 24 in. Cliff-nesting resident. Scavenges on shores and rubbish dumps.

COMMON GULL 16 in. Nests inland, visits shores to feed. Some are residents, others winter abroad.

RINGED PLOVER 7 in. Resident of shores, feeding on tiny creatures. Nests on stones or sand.

Common scoter

Turnstone

Sanderling

Oystercatcher

Common tern

Little tern

F

M

Eider duck

winter

summer

Snow bunting

EIDER DUCK 23 in. Resident bird of rocky inshore waters. Dives for crabs and other shellfish.

SNOW BUNTING 7 in. Strong-flying winter visitor. Feeds on seeds of shore plants. Tinkling call.

OYSTERCATCHER 17 in. Noisy resident which prises open shellfish with its chisel bill.

SANDERLING 8 in. Winter visitor. It races along the tide-edge, snatching up tiny sea animals.

TURNSTONE 9 in. Usually a winter visitor. Flips over stones or weeds with its bill to find food.

COMMON SCOTER 19 in. Offshore winter visitor. Flocks dive in deep water for shellfish.

COMMON TERN 14 in. Summer visitor. It breeds in colonies on beaches and salt-marshes, and plunges into the water after fish.

LITTLE TERN 9 in. Summer visitor. Smallest of the terns. Nests in small noisy groups on beaches.

Sea cliffs

FULMAR 19 in. Cliff-nesting resident. Straight winged, graceful flyer, but clumsy on land.

SHAG 30 in. Cliff-nesting, sea-fishing resident. Slimmer and darker than the cormorant.

CORMORANT 36 in. Common resident. Nests in colonies on cliffs and rocks. Dives to catch fish.

GREAT BLACK-BACKED GULL 29 in. Goose-sized resident gull with deep call. Nests on cliffs.

ROCK PIPIT 7 in. Small, drab, rock-haunting resident, which nests in crevices and eats insects.

GUILLEMOT 17 in. Resident which feeds at sea. Nests in close-packed colonies. Lays eggs on rock.

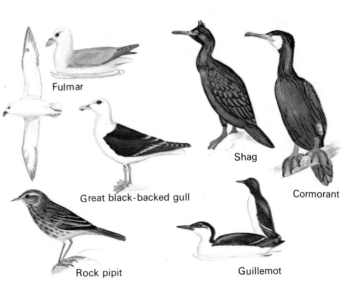

Fulmar

Great black-backed gull

Shag

Cormorant

Rock pipit

Guillemot

387

Freshwater margins

Many waders and small song-birds feed on the insects and minute water animals that inhabit marshes and the edges of lakes, ponds and rivers. Bitterns prey on frogs and fish, and other species, such as the reed bunting, eat the seeds of the plants that grow there. Nests are usually built a little above the damp ground – in waterside bushes or other vegetation. Small birds often roost among the reeds and some, such as the bearded tit, nest in them.

Heron

Grey wagtail

Yellow wagtail

GREY WAGTAIL 7 in. Resident by fast-running streams. It snatches insects from the air.

YELLOW WAGTAIL 7 in. Summer visitor to waterside grasslands. It nests on the ground.

HERON 36 in. Large, slow-flying, resident wading bird. Snatches prey with a sudden dart of its head.

WATER RAIL 11 in. Rarely seen resident of lush waterside vegetation. Discordant cry.

SNIPE 11 in. Marsh resident which probes mud for worms. It nests in hollow on ground. Flight erratic.

COMMON SANDPIPER 8 in. Summer visitor to watersides. Constantly bobs head up and down.

BITTERN 30 in. Rare resident of reed beds. Feeds on eels and fish. Booming cry.

BLACK-TAILED GODWIT 16 in. Scarce resident but common winter visitor to mud-flats. Noisy.

RUFF 11 in. Rare, boldly patterned summer visitor. Builds nest in hollow, sometimes by water.

Water rail

Snipe

Common sandpiper

Bittern

Black-tailed godwit

males in summer

M

F

Ruff

Reed warbler

Dipper

Reed bunting

M

F

Bearded tit

Osprey

Sedge warbler

Sand martin

Marsh harrier

REED WARBLER 5 in. Reed-loving summer visitor that slings nest between reeds. Musical song.

DIPPER 7 in. Resident. It walks along the bottom of fast-running streams, searching for food.

REED BUNTING 6 in. Resident waterside nester. Its song is a succession of squeaky chirps.

BEARDED TIT 7 in. Rare reedbed resident that nests low among the reeds. Twanging calls.

SEDGE WARBLER 5 in. Furtive but noisy summer visitor. Nests in thick waterside vegetation.

SAND MARTIN 5 in. Summer visitor. It breeds in holes scooped in sandbanks, and roosts in reeds.

OSPREY 22 in. Summer visitor. The only fishing hawk. It snatches fish from near the surface.

MARSH HARRIER 21 in. Gliding, long-winged resident hawk that hunts waterfowl and frogs.

Kingfisher

KINGFISHER 7 in. Resident that dives after fish. It nests in a hole in a bank.

Lakes, rivers and reservoirs

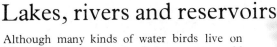

Mute swan

Although many kinds of water birds live on lakes, rivers and reservoirs they appear to avoid conflict because each concentrates on a particular kind of food or feeding area. Grebes, divers and certain ducks, for example, take different sizes of fish. Other birds either graze on shore or snatch insects in flight. Ducks eating the same kind of plants and tiny animals choose their own feeding grounds, staying in weedy margins, dabbling near the shore or diving in deep water.

Mallard

MUTE SWAN 60 in. A familiar and graceful resident, aggressive and intolerant of other birds.

MALLARD 23 in. Resident and a visitor. It is an ancestor of domestic breeds of ducks.

MOORHEN 13 in. A resident living in all waters. It is shy in the wild but often tame in parks.

Moorhen

Goldeneye

Teal

Tufted duck

GOLDENEYE 18 in. Winter visitor. A squat diving duck, preferring clear, flowing waters.

TEAL 14 in. A small resident duck, feeding along the overgrown margins of waters.

TUFTED DUCK 17 in. A resident or visitor to still waters, it dives for weed and small fish.

GADWALL 20 in. Rare resident. A surface-feeding dabbler of shallow lakes and pools.

SHOVELLER 20 in. This resident feeds on the surface, straining food from the water with its bill.

POCHARD 18 in. A resident and winter visitor, this diving duck likes large, open waters.

DABCHICK 11 in. A small resident which dives constantly for small fish. It has a trilling call.

COOT 15 in. A resident with lobed feet. Aggressive and noisy, it likes open stretches of water.

Gadwall

Shoveller

Pochard

summer   winter

Dabchick

Coot

SMEW 16 in. A rare visitor in winter, it is the smallest of the thin-billed fish-eating ducks.

CANADA GOOSE 38 in. A resident. This bird, introduced from abroad, thrives in lakes and rivers.

GOOSANDER 26 in. Resident. Largest of the fish-eating ducks. It nests along northern rivers.

Smew

Canada goose

winter

summer

Great crested grebe

Goosander

GREAT CRESTED GREBE 19 in. Fish-hunting bird of still waters. Its nest is a floating pile of weeds.

RED-BREASTED MERGANSER 23 in. Fish-eating resident duck. It catches fish under water.

RED-THROATED DIVER 22 in. Nests in Scotland in summer, winters in south. Fishes under water.

Red-breasted merganser

summer   winter

Red-throated diver

389

Mountains, moor and heath

Only the hardiest birds can survive the harsh winters on mountains and moors. Some are specialists such as the red grouse which feeds on heather and has the stamina to keep treading for long spells to avoid being buried in drifting snow. Other all-the-year residents are scavengers or predators, but most species come only in summer to nest on ledges. Heaths attract insect-eating birds, such as the whinchat, or seed-eaters, such as the linnet. Many of the birds sheltering in the scrub are summer visitors that move to warmer areas in winter.

Ring ouzel

Meadow pipit

RING OUZEL 10 in. This melodious mountain blackbird nests on rocky slopes in summer.

MEADOW PIPIT 6 in. An inconspicuous resident of grass slopes, where it nests. It has a squeaky call.

Raven

Twite

Hooded crow

Curlew

Red grouse

Merlin

Short-eared owl

Golden eagle

RAVEN 25 in. Large resident scavenger of mountain regions, nesting on crag ledges.

TWITE 5 in. A small and drab finch that nests on the ground and winters in the lowlands.

HOODED CROW 19 in. A cunning and cautious scavanger, nesting on rock ledges and small trees.

CURLEW 22 in. Moorland-nesting wader with melodious bubbling calls. It winters on estuaries.

RED GROUSE 14 in. A resident moorland gamebird, that nests and feeds on heather.

MERLIN 12 in. This small falcon preys on other birds and nests on the ground or in old crows' nests.

SHORT-EARED OWL 15 in. Nests on ground. This long-winged bird flies by day and feeds on mice.

GOLDEN EAGLE 33 in. Nests in rocks or trees. Our largest bird of prey eats hares, birds or carrion.

Heathland

STONECHAT 5 in. A bold, bright resident of bushy places, which nests on or close to the ground.

LINNET 5 in. Soft-twittering, sociable resident, nesting in low bushes and sparse cover.

WHITETHROAT 6 in. A skulking summer visitor which lives in bushes, and nests near the ground.

WHINCHAT 5 in. A ground-nesting summer visitor to heaths and moors. It feeds on insects.

CUCKOO 13 in. A summer visitor which leaves its egg for other birds to hatch and rear.

WHEATEAR 6 in. Identified by its white rump, this summer visitor nests on wasteland and rocks.

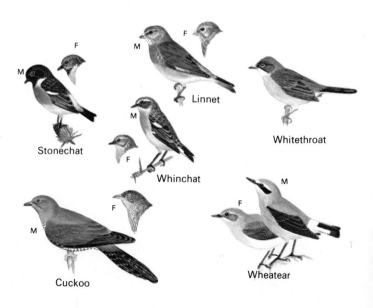

Linnet

Stonechat

Whitethroat

Whinchat

Cuckoo

Wheatear

390

Woodland

In spring and summer, broad-leaved woodland offers birds many hidden nesting places. Various species choose different levels to feed or nest. On the ground, birds such as the chiffchaff and the wood warbler build their domed nests while, a few feet above, the nuthatch cracks open nuts with blows from its 'hatchet' bill, and higher again the woodpecker probes for insects. Coniferous woods, however, are poorer feeding places and the few birds there are usually small insect and seed-eaters or predators feeding on small birds and mammals.

Greater spotted woodpecker

Nuthatch

GREATER SPOTTED WOODPECKER 9 in. Widespread resident which feeds on insects.

NUTHATCH 6 in. This resident nests in tree holes. It cracks nuts which it wedges in the bark.

Jay

Long-tailed tit

Treecreeper

Marsh tit

Wood warbler

Chiffchaff

Green woodpecker

Redstart

Blackcap

JAY 14 in. Nesting in bushes, the jay helps to spread woodland by burying acorns.

LONG-TAILED TIT 6 in. Builds a domed moss and cobweb nest in trees or bushes. Feeds on insects.

TREECREEPER 5 in. Resident that nests in crevices behind loose bark. It feeds on insects.

GREEN WOODPECKER 13 in. Resident with a laughing call. It probes the ground for ants.

MARSH TIT 5 in. Uses ready-made hole in tree for nest. Feeds on insects, seeds and wild fruit.

WOOD WARBLER 5 in. Summer visitor with a shrill song. It stays high in trees and feeds on insects.

REDSTART 6 in. This summer visitor nests in holes in trees, and feeds on insects.

BLACKCAP 6 in. Summer visitor with a melodious song. It feeds on flies, insects and berries.

CHIFFCHAFF 4 in. A ground-nesting visitor feeding on insects, it sings high in the trees.

Coniferous woodland

CROSSBILL 7 in. A resident and visitor which takes seeds from pine cones with its bill-tip.

COAL TIT 5 in. Nests in holes in trees or walls. Lives on insects, seeds and wild nuts.

SISKIN 5 in. This finch nests in conifer trees and is fond of alder cones and birch catkins in winter.

GOLDCREST 4 in. This insect-eater slings its mossy nest below a pine branch. It has a shrill call.

REDPOLL 5 in. This stubby-billed finch nests in trees and feeds mainly on conifer seeds.

LONG-EARED OWL 14 in. Usually hiding in dark places, this owl preys on mice and small birds.

Crossbill

Coal tit

Siskin

Goldcrest

Redpoll

another form of same species

Long-eared owl

Farmland

Cultivated ground offers birds a gamble in which sudden death could be the penalty for rich living. As the seasons change they can feed on insects in newly tilled land, on seeds, foliage and fruit. But man constantly disturbs them and nesting sites are vulnerable in areas where farmers have demolished hedges. Predatory birds hover overhead to snatch them, while the increased use of chemical pesticides and weed sprays make their life even more hazardous.

ROOK 18 in. The only communal-nesting crow. Gregarious and noisy, it feeds in open fields.

MAGPIE 18 in. Wily, weak-flying resident of hedges and copses; it has a domed stick nest.

YELLOWHAMMER 7 in. A hedgerow resident with a monotonous song. It nests low in lush herbage.

SWALLOW 7 in. An insect-eating summer visitor which builds a mud nest in barns and sheds.

SKYLARK 7 in. Vigorous, soaring songster of bare, open fields. A ground-nesting resident.

FIELDFARE 10 in. Visitor which arrives in autumn from its breeding grounds in northern Europe.

CORN BUNTING 7 in. A resident, sluggish bird of open places, with a repetitive song.

KESTREL 12 in. Small, hovering hawk which pounces on mice and insects. Nests in trees.

LITTLE OWL 9 in. A resident of hedgerows which hunts by day and night for insects and mice.

BARN OWL 14 in. A nocturnal hunter of fields and hedgerows. It nests in a barn or tree-hole.

CARRION CROW 18 in. A wary resident that scavenges and raids nests to eat the eggs and young.

WOOD PIGEON 16 in. Soft-cooing, tree-nesting pigeon that wreaks havoc on crops.

COMMON PARTRIDGE 12 in. Quiet, ground-nesting gamebird which lives in crops and grassland.

JACKDAW 13 in. Small, grey-naped crow which nests in holes in trees or buildings.

PHEASANT 30 in. A gamebird, breeding on heaths and commons. It often hides in woods.

RED-LEGGED PARTRIDGE 14 in. An introduced gamebird on drier soils. It nests in hedgerows.

LAPWING 12 in. A pied bird which lives in meadows and ploughed land and nests on bare ground.

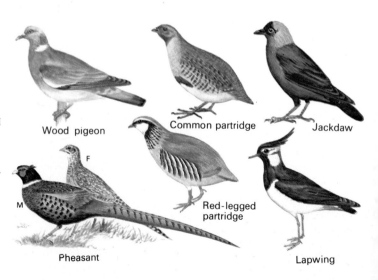

Parks and gardens

Birds such as the black-headed gull and feral pigeon, that once roosted on cliffs and ledges, have readily adapted to life on the crevices and window-ledges of city office blocks. Natural food is scarce, however, and these town birds have to rely on foraging for waste or gathering scraps given to them by people. Garden birds, such as the blackbird and thrush, once lived on woodland fringes, and they fare better on readily available berries, seeds and insects.

Great tit

Blackbird

Robin

GREAT TIT 6 in. A resident with a repetitive see-saw song; it nests in holes or nest-boxes.

BLACKBIRD 10 in. This tuneful songster finds food and sites for its nest in most gardens.

ROBIN 6 in. A silvery-voiced resident which proudly defends the territory it occupies.

Blue tit

Dunnock

Wren

Spotted flycatcher

Greenfinch

Chaffinch

Pied wagtail   immature

BLUE TIT 5 in. Tiny, inquisitive resident. It is a frequent visitor to bird tables and uses nest-boxes.

DUNNOCK 6 in. A resident, also called the hedge sparrow; it hops on the ground feeding on insects.

WREN 4 in. A resident and second to the goldcrest as the smallest of our breeding birds.

SPOTTED FLYCATCHER 6 in. This summer visitor perches silently until it pounces on passing flies.

GREENFINCH 6 in. Frequent visitor to bird tables for food. Best known for twittering song.

CHAFFINCH 6 in. This resident is Britain's most common bird. It nests in trees and bushes.

PIED WAGTAIL 7 in. A specialist in catching winged insects, it nests in holes or crevices.

Towns

SONG THRUSH 9 in. A loud-voiced resident which builds a mud-lined nest in trees or bushes.

MISTLE THRUSH 11 in. The largest of our native thrushes, it has a harsh song and nests in high trees.

COLLARED DOVE 11 in. The first pair nested in Norfolk in 1955, but now this dove is widespread.

Song thrush

Mistle thrush

Collared dove

House sparrow

Starling

Swift

Feral pigeon

Black-headed gull

HOUSE SPARROW 6 in. A noisy resident of towns and villages that nests mainly in holes.

STARLING 9 in. These noisy birds nest in holes and feed on insects and fruit in gardens or parks.

SWIFT 7 in. A summer visitor that spends most of its time on the wing, landing only to nest.

FERAL PIGEON 13 in. A resident and descendant of domestic pigeons that have become wild.

BLACK-HEADED GULL 14 in. This gull feeds on scraps in towns. Also common in marshes.

BUTTERFLIES AND MOTHS

The colourful wings of summer

About 60 types of butterfly and more than 2000 types of moth breed in Britain or arrive in early summer from as far as Southern Europe and North Africa. They are the most colourful part of our insect life, but to observe and identify them is not always easy. Moths fly mostly at night and some butterflies are seen only if the weather is fine. Often it is easier to find the caterpillar than the butterfly or moth. The caterpillars illustrated are chosen because they can be identified from their spectacular colouring or strange shape. A quick way to tell a butterfly from a moth is to look at the insect at rest. A butterfly closes its wings leaving the underside visible, while the moth folds the wings down by its body with the upperside visible.

Meadows and fields

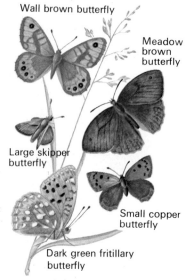

Wall brown butterfly

Meadow brown butterfly

Large skipper butterfly

Small copper butterfly

Dark green fritillary butterfly

WALL BROWN Found in open, sunny countryside in England and Wales from May to August. The caterpillars feed on grasses.

MEADOW BROWN Common on rough grassland and open woods from June to September.

LARGE SKIPPER Suns itself in open fields in England and Wales. Caterpillars hibernate in tubes that they make from grass.

SMALL COPPER Found from April to October everywhere except the north of Scotland. Caterpillars eat sorrel or dock.

DARK GREEN FRITILLARY Flies over downs and cliffs in July and August. The purple-black caterpillar feeds on violet leaves.

Small heath butterfly

Drinker moth caterpillar

SMALL HEATH Profuse all summer in rough grassland at a wide range of altitudes. Caterpillars eat grass.

DRINKER MOTH Found in damp meadows and among reeds. It gets its name because the caterpillar drinks dew and raindrops.

Six-spot burnet moth

Common blue butterfly

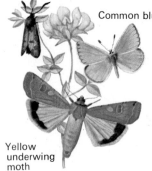

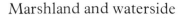

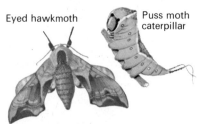

Yellow underwing moth

SIX-SPOT BURNET MOTH Found mainly in southern England from June to August. Caterpillars feed on bird's-foot trefoil.

COMMON BLUE Found in grassy places all over the British Isles. Caterpillars eat bird's-foot trefoil.

YELLOW UNDERWING MOTH Appears almost everywhere in late summer, flying by day only if disturbed. Caterpillar winters on grasses.

Emperor moth

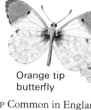

EMPEROR MOTH A silk moth. The chrysalis winters in a brown silk cocoon on heather and low-growing blackthorn bushes.

Marshland and waterside

Eyed hawkmoth

Puss moth caterpillar

Ringlet butterfly

Orange tip butterfly

ORANGE TIP Common in England and Wales. The caterpillars eat the seed pods of hedge garlic.

RINGLET Found in lush grassland in July and August everywhere except north Scotland.

GREEN-VEINED WHITE Seen all summer in damp grassland and roadsides. Caterpillars feed on hedge mustard.

EYED HAWKMOTH If disturbed while resting, the moth suddenly reveals the 'eyes' on its hind wings.

PUSS MOTH CATERPILLAR Its strange shape helps to scare predators as it feeds on poplar and willow.

Green-veined white butterfly

Woodland glades

PEARL-BORDERED FRITILLARY
Common in early summer. The
caterpillars winter on violet leaves.

BRIMSTONE Seen from February
to October. Caterpillars eat
buckthorn; butterflies hibernate
among ivy leaves.

BUFF-TIP MOTH A night flyer,
it looks like a broken twig as it
rests in trees during the day.

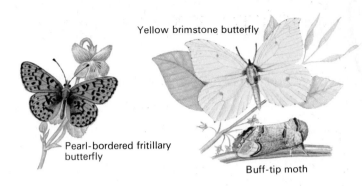

Yellow brimstone butterfly

Pearl-bordered fritillary
butterfly

Buff-tip moth

Hedges and roadsides

CINNABAR MOTH Common in
summer. Caterpillars feed on
groundsel and ragwort.

ELEPHANT HAWKMOTH A pink moth
found on willow-herb. The
caterpillar enlarges its four
eyespots to scare predators.

WHITE ERMINE MOTH Seen in late
summer in gardens and lanes.
Caterpillars eat low-growing plants.

VAPOURER MOTH Seen April to
June. Caterpillars feed on oak and
hawthorn. Their hairy coats may
irritate sensitive human skin.

YELLOWTAIL MOTH Seen April to
June. Caterpillars hatch on
hawthorn leaves and hibernate.

LACKEY MOTH Caterpillars live in
webs on hawthorn and fruit trees.

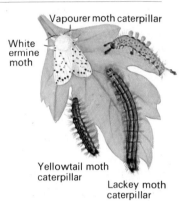

Vapourer moth caterpillar

White
ermine
moth

Yellowtail moth
caterpillar

Lackey moth
caterpillar

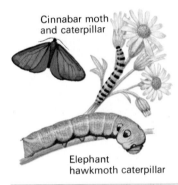

Cinnabar moth
and caterpillar

Elephant
hawkmoth caterpillar

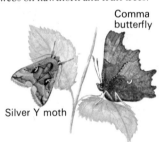

Comma
butterfly

Silver Y moth

COMMA Common in the south.
Resembles a leaf as it hibernates
on branches. Caterpillars eat nettles.

SILVER Y MOTH Common from
May to October. Caterpillars eat a
variety of plants.

Gardens and lanes

Peacock
butterfly
and caterpillar

Red admiral
butterfly

RED ADMIRAL Immigrant from
Europe found mostly in the south
from May to November.
Caterpillars feed on nettles.

PEACOCK Found from March to
October, often near farms and out-
buildings. Caterpillars, living in
colonies, feed on nettles.

GARDEN TIGER MOTH Found July
and August. Caterpillars feed on
nettles, docks and dandelions, and
hibernate in sewn-up leaves.

SMALL TORTOISESHELL Seen from
March to September. Caterpillars
feed on stinging nettles.

MAGPIE MOTH Slow night flyer.
Caterpillars feed on heather, bushes
and fruit trees in late summer.

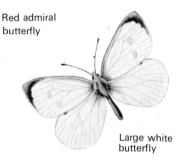

Large white
butterfly

LARGE WHITE Emerges in spring
from its chrysalis. Caterpillars feed
on cabbages and nasturtiums.

Garden tiger moth
and
caterpillar

Humming-bird hawkmoth

Magpie moth
and
caterpillar

Small tortoiseshell
butterfly
and caterpillar

HUMMING-BIRD HAWKMOTH From
June it hovers near flowers.
Caterpillars feed on bedstraw.

395

BRITISH MAMMALS

The teeming wildlife around us

Most wild mammals are secretive, silent creatures, relying for protection on speed or neutral colouring that blends with their surroundings. Nearly half the living land species in Britain are rodents, and another quarter of the remainder are bats – the only flying mammals.

Many are nocturnal and rarely seen. Man is, often unwittingly, their greatest enemy and they tend to avoid him, or move only when they believe they are unobserved. A parked car makes an excellent watching post, but the observer needs to wait patiently and silently.

Rich pickings in the woods

In the woodlands there is an abundance of bark, leaves and seeds for the browsing and gnawing mammals. Numerous flesh-eaters prey on the plant-eaters, or on the host of insects, worms and birds in the ground litter or branches.

Noctule bat

Grey squirrel

Red squirrel

Fallow deer

Roe deer

Badger

Wood mouse

Common shrew

NOCTULE BAT The biggest British bat has a wingspan of 15 in., and it can fly at more than 30 mph. It hunts flying insects and locates its prey by the echo from its own high-pitched squeaks.

RED SQUIRREL Found in coniferous woodland, the 8 in. long red squirrel is often seen in autumn collecting cones to feed on the seeds.

GREY SQUIRREL Introduced from America in 1876, the 10½ in. long grey squirrel is now widespread. It lives mainly in deciduous woodland, and makes nests on branches or in hollow trees.

FALLOW DEER Found in woodland thickets which provide daytime cover, the fallow deer differs from other British deer in that the buck has a broad flattened area on the antlers.

ROE DEER This timid deer usually hides by day in open woods or scrubland. Its presence may be indicated by rings worn in the soil where a buck has chased a doe round a bush or tree during courtship.

BADGER The fastidiously clean badger digs holes to use as latrines and renews its straw bedding annually. A nocturnal creature, up to 3 ft long, it lives by day in a sett, a labyrinth of tunnels and chambers.

WOOD MOUSE The 3½ in. long wood mouse, or long-tailed field mouse, makes kangaroo-like hops of 2–3 ft, and it has the ability to climb with ease.

COMMON SHREW Sometimes confused with mice, this 3 in. long aggressive creature is a voracious feeder which eats its own weight in insects daily.

Feeding by the waterside

Many small mammals are semi-aquatic and search for food, mainly at night, both on land and in water. They generally live near rivers

or ponds – sometimes in elaborate burrows excavated in the banks – or, like Daubenton's bat, they inhabit nearby trees, crevices or caves.

Water vole

Daubenton's bat

Water shrew

Mink

WATER VOLE Sometimes wrongly called a water rat, the harmless 8 in. long water vole feeds on mussels, water snails, worms and various water plants.

WATER SHREW When searching under water for prey, the 4 in. long water shrew looks like an animated bubble because of air trapped in its fur.

DAUBENTON'S BAT This bat, also known as the water bat, flies in slow circles over water soon after sunset, frequently picking insects off the surface.

MINK The 18 in. long mink was introduced into Britain in 1929 for commercial fur farming. Escaped animals now prey on poultry and gamebirds.

Survival in the mountains

The larger mammals living in mountainous country are generally grazers and browsers able to extract a living from the scant vegetation. The most common small animals are rodents, whose habits of burrowing and storing food enable them to withstand the cold and to avoid foraging when snow covers the ground.

Greater horseshoe bat

Red deer

Reindeer

Mountain hare

GREATER HORSESHOE BAT This cave-dwelling bat has a horseshoe-shaped growth around the nose.

REINDEER This deer lives in mountain areas, where it can feed on lichens. It differs from all British deer in that the females also grow antlers.

RED DEER The biggest of the native deer in Britain, the red deer stands about 4 ft high at the shoulder. In summer it lives on upland moors, but descends lower in winter when food is scarce.

BLUE OR MOUNTAIN HARE The dark colouring of this hare's summer coat changes to white in winter, which helps to hide it in the snow from predators.

Living wild on the farmlands

The removal of forests, and the cultivation of crops and grasslands, destroyed many habitats of wild animals; but at the same time new ones have been formed. Plantations, hedgerows and fields provide homes for both agricultural pests and their predators.

Brown hare

Fox

Long-eared bat

Rabbit

Weasel

Stoat

Hedgehog

Mole

LONG-EARED BAT The 1½ in. ears of this insect-eating bat are more than a third as long as its body.

HEDGEHOG The 9 in. long hedgehog is known to kill and eat the venomous viper and other snakes.

MOLE The solitary and nocturnal 6 in. long mole is seldom seen leaving its network of tunnels.

STOAT A bloodthirsty killer, the 11 in. long stoat often preys upon animals several times its own weight. Its white winter coat is ermine.

RABBIT The 16 in. long rabbit lives with as many as 150 other rabbits in an underground warren.

BROWN HARE Normally a timid, shy creature, the brown hare ignores danger in spring and becomes the 'mad March hare' during its courtship antics.

FOX A member of the dog family, the 26 in. long fox lives almost everywhere, even in city suburbs.

WEASEL The 8 in. long weasel looks like a small stoat but it lacks the stoat's black tip to the tail.

Rodents in the towns

Small rodents are voracious eaters. Their curved incisors keep growing so they must keep them trim by constant nibbling.

House mouse

Brown rat

BROWN RAT The 9 in. long brown rat becomes sexually mature at two months. The females produce about six litters of five to eight young each year, but litters of 20 or more have been reported.

HOUSE MOUSE Originally from Central Asia, this 3 in. long rodent has travelled wherever man has spread. In colder places it grows a thicker coat.

The animals we rarely see in the wild

An animal that is rarely seen in the wild is not necessarily rare. It may hibernate, as the dormouse, or spend little time on land, as the grey seal. Some animals, including the wildcat, keep to remote areas, while others have been forced to retreat before advancing urban development. The otter, for example, has been driven by pollution from many rivers. Some animals, however, such as the pine marten, are rarely seen because there are few of them.

WILDCAT Said to be one of the most savage and untamable of animals, the 2 ft long wildcat resembles a big tabby cat with a thick, blunt tail. Unrelated to the domestic cat, it is confined to the Highland moors, where it preys on small mammals.

POLECAT A nocturnal hunter in wooded, rocky parts of Wales, the 18 in. long polecat sometimes makes its den in rabbit burrows, after eating the occupants. Because of the stench it emits when alarmed it is also known as the foul-marten or foumart.

GREY SEAL During autumn these 8 ft long seals assemble in huge colonies on off-shore rocks and rocky beaches to give birth and to mate. The pup enters the sea when it is about a month old and has to learn how to swim and feed itself.

OTTER Shy and nocturnal, the 30 in. long otter is rarely seen, but its piercing whistle when hunting is easily heard. It hunts mainly freshwater fish and eels, moving every few nights to a new stretch of water.

Where to find snakes and lizards

Britain has six species of reptiles—three snakes and three lizards. Of these, only one, the common lizard, is found in Ireland. This is because of the last Ice Age, which drove all reptiles south. As the last ice sheet melted, 10,000 years ago, only the six species returned before the land-bridge which linked Britain with Europe was submerged by the sea. Ireland meanwhile, had already been isolated. Reptiles are mostly found basking on a sunny hillside. Because they are cold-blooded their bodies take on the temperature of their surroundings, to which their behaviour is closely linked: in cool weather they are sluggish; in warm weather they can move about more quickly.

SAND LIZARD Up to 18 in. long, this declining species is now confined mainly to sandy, coastal areas.

COMMON LIZARD 5 in. This lizard is widespread on dry, sunny slopes, heaths and commons.

398

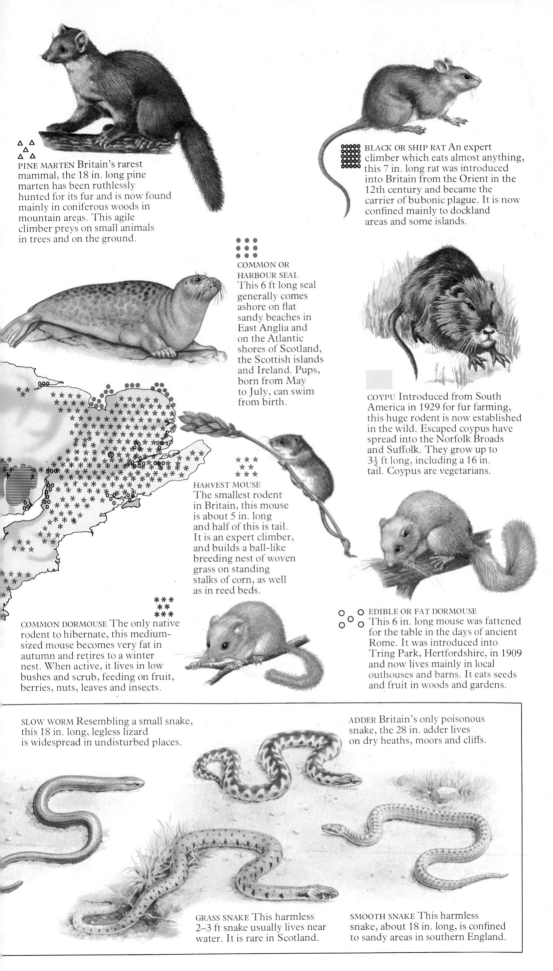

PINE MARTEN Britain's rarest mammal, the 18 in. long pine marten has been ruthlessly hunted for its fur and is now found mainly in coniferous woods in mountain areas. This agile climber preys on small animals in trees and on the ground.

BLACK OR SHIP RAT An expert climber which eats almost anything, this 7 in. long rat was introduced into Britain from the Orient in the 12th century and became the carrier of bubonic plague. It is now confined mainly to dockland areas and some islands.

COMMON OR HARBOUR SEAL This 6 ft long seal generally comes ashore on flat sandy beaches in East Anglia and on the Atlantic shores of Scotland, the Scottish islands and Ireland. Pups, born from May to July, can swim from birth.

COYPU Introduced from South America in 1929 for fur farming, this huge rodent is now established in the wild. Escaped coypus have spread into the Norfolk Broads and Suffolk. They grow up to $3\frac{1}{2}$ ft long, including a 16 in. tail. Coypus are vegetarians.

HARVEST MOUSE The smallest rodent in Britain, this mouse is about 5 in. long and half of this is tail. It is an expert climber, and builds a ball-like breeding nest of woven grass on standing stalks of corn, as well as in reed beds.

COMMON DORMOUSE The only native rodent to hibernate, this medium-sized mouse becomes very fat in autumn and retires to a winter nest. When active, it lives in low bushes and scrub, feeding on fruit, berries, nuts, leaves and insects.

EDIBLE OR FAT DORMOUSE This 6 in. long mouse was fattened for the table in the days of ancient Rome. It was introduced into Tring Park, Hertfordshire, in 1909 and now lives mainly in local outhouses and barns. It eats seeds and fruit in woods and gardens.

SLOW WORM Resembling a small snake, this 18 in. long, legless lizard is widespread in undisturbed places.

ADDER Britain's only poisonous snake, the 28 in. adder lives on dry heaths, moors and cliffs.

GRASS SNAKE This harmless 2–3 ft snake usually lives near water. It is rare in Scotland.

SMOOTH SNAKE This harmless snake, about 18 in. long, is confined to sandy areas in southern England.

FARMING IN BRITAIN

Sheep and cattle on the hills

More than two-thirds of Britain's 63 million acres of land is devoted to farming. This land supports more than 13 million cattle and 29 million sheep, from which we get about 80 per cent of the beef and lamb we consume. The most important breeding areas are in the Pennines, Cumbria, Yorkshire, Scotland, Wales, Dartmoor and Exmoor. In these uplands the sheep, which are able to live off the scanty grazing, are small but they produce good-quality meat. The cattle are mainly stocky and small boned, but they are fattened when taken to the lowlands. Many hill farmers, indeed, keep only a few livestock in winter, selling the young of their stock at autumn fairs for fattening on low-land farms.

Hill sheep

SCOTTISH BLACKFACE This hardy native of Scotland is now abundant in most parts of Britain.

ROUGH FELL Found in the fells of Westmorland, Cumberland, Yorkshire and Lancashire, it produces tough carpet wool.

CHEVIOT Bred for meat and for wool used in tweed. It is found mainly in northern England and southern Scotland.

SWALEDALE Widespread on rough moorland in the north of England. It is cross-bred for early lambs.

HERDWICK A mountain breed found mostly in the Lake District. It produces tough carpet wool.

WELSH MOUNTAIN A hardy, thick-fleeced breed which flourishes on scrubby hillsides in Wales.

Scottish Blackface

Cheviot

Rough Fell

Swaledale

Herdwick

Welsh Mountain

Hill cattle

HIGHLAND The hardiest and shaggiest British breed is found mostly in the Scottish Highlands where it originated. It produces excellent beef.

WELSH BLACK A dual-purpose beef and dairy breed, suited to the wet hillsides of North Wales. It is rarely seen elsewhere.

Highland

Welsh Black

Dairy farming

Britain has about $3\frac{1}{4}$ million dairy cows which produce more than 3300 million gallons of milk a year. Just over one-third of that amount is made into cheese and butter. Other products, such as condensed milk and milk powder, bring the total of milk used in manufacture up to half that of the milk produced. Dairy farming is mainly concentrated in the lowland areas of the Midlands and West of England, Wales, and central and south-west Scotland. Here high rainfall or heavy soil create good grass for grazing. The dairy cows vary in size from the big, heavy Friesians to the lean and dainty Jerseys, which give high quality milk rich in butterfat.

Ayrshire

Kerry

400

Animals and crops in the rich lowlands

On a mixed farm livestock and crops are rotated to rest the soil and improve its fertility. Most herds are composed of dairy cattle, Friesians being the most common, though some of these cows are crossed with beef bulls to produce calves for meat. The sheep on a mixed farm are also cross-bred to provide wool and meat. Many lowland farms have a surplus of fodder crops such as hay, roots, sugar beet and coarse grains, so that in winter, when upland grazing is scarce, they can support additional livestock brought down from hill farms for fattening.

Southdown

Hampshire Down

Leicester

Suffolk

Romney Marsh

Lowland sheep

SOUTHDOWN A breed which has meat of good flavour and fine wool. It is common in the south.

HAMPSHIRE DOWN A breed producing fine quality wool. It grazes on downland and arable land and is found mostly in the south.

LEICESTER This hardy, prolific breed was once widespread but is now found mostly in Yorkshire. It produces heavy-quality wool.

SUFFOLK The most widespread breed in Britain. It produces good meat and fine wool.

ROMNEY MARSH OR KENT A sturdy breed producing fine wool and early lambs. Common in Kent and Sussex.

Beef stock

HEREFORD A beef breed which originated in the Welsh border counties and is now widespread.

CHAROLAIS Originating from France, the bulls are used for crossing with dairy cows to produce beef calves.

ABERDEEN ANGUS Hardy cattle which produce quick-maturing, high-quality beef, the Angus originated in Scotland and is widespread.

SOUTH DEVON A heavily built, dual-purpose breed, producing good beef and an abundance of rich milk. It originated in Devon and is now becoming widespread.

Hereford

Charolais

Aberdeen Angus

South Devon

Jersey

Guernsey

Friesian

AYRSHIRE A hardy breed with rich milk especially suitable for cheese. It is widespread in Britain.

FRIESIAN The most numerous breed in Britain. Primarily dairy cattle but also kept for beef.

KERRY A native of South-west Ireland and rare elsewhere. Hardy and economical to feed.

JERSEY Widespread in Britain and the only permitted breed in its native Jersey. It has rich milk.

GUERNSEY An exclusively dairy breed which originated in Guernsey and is now widespread in Britain. Its milk is rich.

Machines on the land

Farm machinery has made it possible for one man to do as much work as a team of men a century ago. A combine-harvester, for example, reaps and threshes 2 acres of corn an hour, whereas a man took a day to reap an acre with a scythe. Mechanisation is also changing the landscape as farmers demolish hedges to create larger fields for the efficient use of machines.

HAY TEDDER Circular sets of tines are mounted behind a tractor to toss and turn grass cut for hay. This ensures quick drying by increasing the circulation of air.

REVERSIBLE PLOUGH This double-sided plough is reversed at the end of each row so that furrows are evenly spaced by being turned one way.

COMBINE-DRILL In one operation, this drill cuts furrows into which seed is funnelled, fed with fertiliser and buried by harrows at the rear.

FORAGE HARVESTER Green crops, cut and chopped for silage by a tractor-drawn mower, are blown through a tube into a trailer.

Springtime blossom routes

Some of England's finest scenic routes run through orchards which in spring are smothered with the blossom of the pear, plum, apple and cherry. The AA signposts orchard routes in Kent and advises when best to see the blossom there and in the Vale of Evesham.

The Vale of Evesham

The plum was a staple fruit in England from the last century until the Second World War. In the last few years it has lost popularity and many orchards have been turned over to growing other crops. Although this has happened in the Vale of Evesham, in Hereford and Worcester, blossom time there is still spectacular. Sweeping stretches of white blossom are seen for about ten days, usually from late April to early May; but owing to variations in the seasons it is advisable to consult the AA about the best time to see the blossom each year. The AA has suggested a 27 mile circular tour that can be joined at any convenient point. It is mostly along unclassified roads and passes through some charming villages on the lower Avon.

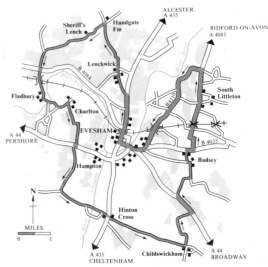

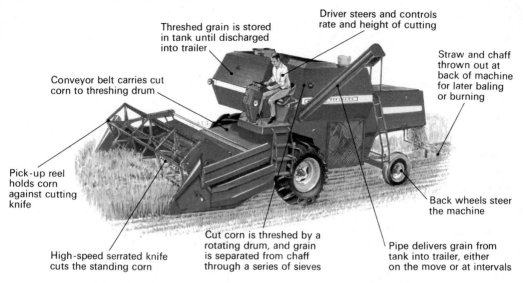

COMBINE-HARVESTER A combine cuts and threshes corn, then holds the grain in a storage tank and deposits the straw behind to be picked up by a baler.

Threshed grain is stored in tank until discharged into trailer

Driver steers and controls rate and height of cutting

Conveyor belt carries cut corn to threshing drum

Straw and chaff thrown out at back of machine for later baling or burning

Pick-up reel holds corn against cutting knife

Back wheels steer the machine

High-speed serrated knife cuts the standing corn

Cut corn is threshed by a rotating drum, and grain is separated from chaff through a series of sieves

Pipe delivers grain from tank into trailer, either on the move or at intervals

Farmland crops

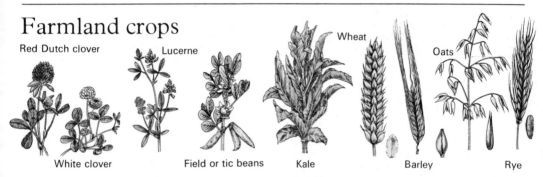

Red Dutch clover

Lucerne

Wheat

Oats

White clover

Field or tic beans

Kale

Barley

Rye

Winter dictates the kind of crops a livestock farmer is to grow. From late autumn, cattle must be fed on vegetables, such as the protein-rich field or tic bean, which grows in summer, or hardy kale, which is cut fresh. Red Dutch clover is sown with grass for making silage, while white clover is sown for grazing. Lucerne is grown for green-feed, for hay or for silage. Wheat is grown for making into flour and for feeding poultry. Barley is grown mainly for livestock, but the best grain is used for brewing. Oats are grown for human consumption and feeding livestock but rye is mainly given to animals.

The orchards of Kent

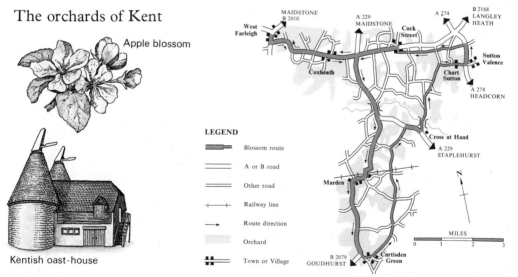

Apple blossom

Kentish oast-house

LEGEND

Blossom route

A or B road

Other road

Railway line

Route direction

Orchard

Town or Village

Apples, pears, plums, cherries and other fruit are grown in 60,000 acres of orchards in Kent. Motorists following a 48 mile route signposted by the AA may see cherry blossom from early April and apple and pear blossom in mid-May.

Along these routes and in many other parts of Kent hops are grown for the brewing of beer. The vines grow up strings set between posts and the hops are picked in August, then dried in oast-houses, or oil-fired sheds.

403

OUR BUILDING HERITAGE

Castles and fortifications

In their heyday between the 11th and 14th centuries castles were almost impregnable, and defenders were mostly defeated by starvation or treachery. The Normans built castles to consolidate their conquest and in the 13th century Edward I built more in his wars against the Welsh and Scots. But the day of the castle was over with the invention of gunpowder.

IRON AGE: *Maiden Castle, Dorset, 4th–1st centuries BC*. A tribal fortified settlement consisting of concentric earth dykes built as a defence against other tribes and later the Romans, who captured it in AD 43.

ROMAN: *Burgh Castle, Norfolk, AD 200–300*. One of a number of rectangular forts built by the Romans to defend the East coast against Saxon attacks. Burgh, called Gariannonum by the Romans, has 8 ft thick walls of brick and flint.

MOTTE AND BAILEY: *Windsor Castle*. The Normans introduced this type of fort in the 11th century. The motte was a hill, and the bailey the living area defended by a ditch and palisade, at first made of wood but later of stone.

Town houses

The design of a town house has always been governed by the expensive piece of land beneath it. In the Middle Ages the first floors of clustering houses were cantilevered out to save space at ground level. As timber gave way to brick or stone, narrow terraced houses were built higher – to be followed in the concrete age by high-rise blocks.

TUDOR *Old Wool Hall, Lavenham, Suffolk, 15th century*. A half-timbered building, with the timber frame filled with wattle and daub. The first floor is cantilevered out to gain space.

MEDIEVAL *The Jew's House, Lincoln, c. 1180*. A stone-built house with a hall on the upper floor. The large windows are in the round-arched style of Norman abbeys and cathedrals.

QUEEN ANNE *Queen Anne's Gate, London, early 18th century*. A graceful terrace with delicately balanced proportions of glass and wall, while the rich red brick is set off by white string courses—horizontal bands.

STUART *Lindsey House, Lincoln's Inn, London, 1640*. Perhaps a work of Inigo Jones. The proportion and details of the façade are Italian. Only the brick under the later stucco is a local feature.

NORMAN: *Hedingham Castle, Essex, early 12th century.* To make attack difficult the entrance to the keep was on the first floor, which led to the living quarters.

CURTAIN WALL: *Harlech Castle, 13th century.* This was one of eight castles built by Edward I in his campaign to subjugate the Welsh. The outer curtain wall and a wide moat were added to prevent invaders from mining the main wall. The towers gave each other covering fire.

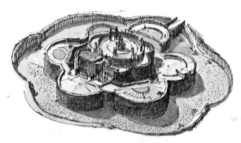

TUDOR FORT: *Deal Castle, Kent, 1540.* This was one of a number built by Henry VIII against possible French invasion. They were little more than gun emplacements, with a clover-leaf design to give a maximum field of fire.

MARTELLO TOWERS: *Pevensey Bay, E. Sussex, 1805–10.* Seventy-four of these were built from Folkestone, Kent, to Seaford, Sussex, because of the possibility of French invasion in the Napoleonic Wars. They were named after a French tower at Cap Martello, Corsica.

GEORGIAN *Queen's Square, Bath, 1729–36.* An example, by John Wood, of the town house as part of a grand design, producing a magnificent sweep. The emphasis in each individual house is to build upwards to save valuable space.

REGENCY *Park Crescent, Regent's Park, London, 1812.* John Nash's powerful façade in a parkland setting gives the impression that a great country mansion has moved to the city.

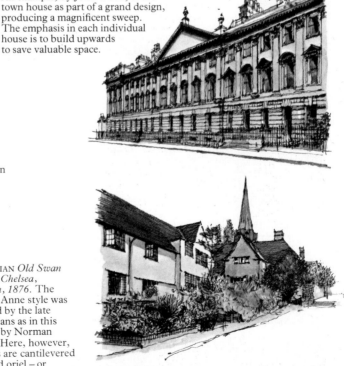

VICTORIAN *Old Swan House, Chelsea, London, 1876.* The Queen Anne style was revived by the late Victorians as in this design by Norman Shaw. Here, however, storeys are cantilevered out and oriel – or projecting – windows are used as in medieval buildings.

EDWARDIAN *Hampstead Garden Suburb, London, begun 1907.* As with Regency developments in Bath and in Regent's Park, this was an attempt to marry town and country, but here buildings are less grand and the atmosphere is that of a village.

405

Country houses

Most of Britain's grand country houses were intended more as symbols of success rather than as comfortable homes. From the late 15th century, when the country settled down after the Wars of the Roses, they replaced castles and fortified manors. Great houses were built as late as the last century, but taxes and running costs made them too expensive even for the wealthiest.

NORMAN *Boothby Pagnell, Lincolnshire, 12th century.* A manor unfortified except that the door was on the first floor to make entry difficult for any attacker. This entrance led to the first-floor hall which was a communal living area.

GOTHIC *Little Wenham Hall, Suffolk, late 13th century.* A fortified house with a first-floor entrance and vaulted ground-floor store as in a castle keep. Part of the first-floor hall was, however, divided by screens from the pantry, buttery and kitchen.

TUDOR *Compton Wynyates, Warwickshire, early 16th century.* When the Wars of the Roses ended in 1485 the need to fortify houses disappeared, but battlements remained as decoration. Many comfortable rooms make up the rambling layout.

ELIZABETHAN *Wollaton Hall, Nottinghamshire, 1580.* A hybrid, forward-looking in its symmetry and use of many features from the Renaissance such as pilasters, or vertical columns; but the curved gables are from Holland and the mixture fails to blend. The large panelled windows contribute most to its late medieval or Tudor flavour.

STUART *Wilton House, Wiltshire, c. 1570.* The house was extensively renovated in the 17th, 18th and 19th centuries. The Stuart part is the South Face built in the manner of Inigo Jones in 1647. Although the exterior is severe, the state rooms have lightness and elegance.

QUEEN ANNE *Blenheim Palace, Oxfordshire, 1705.*
Built by Sir John Vanbrugh for the Duke of Marlborough, Blenheim Palace is one of the most extreme examples of Baroque, the florid style popular in the 18th century. A sense of power and movement is achieved only because of the huge scale of the 850 ft long building.

GEORGIAN *Holkham Hall, Norfolk, 1734.* William Kent's design is more restrained than that of Vanbrugh's at Blenheim, and is almost a return to the style of Inigo Jones, who had been greatly influenced by the Italian Palladio. Holkham is on an H plan with four wings and a central portico. The interior gives long vistas of connecting rooms.

REGENCY *Royal Pavilion, Brighton, 1783.* Built as a home for the Prince Regent, it was turned into an extravaganza with Indian domes and Muslim fretwork by John Nash in 1815 – but it was never lived in again.

VICTORIAN *Scarisbrick Hall, Lancashire, 1837.* Victorians reacted against the classical symmetry of the architecture of the previous two centuries, and returned to the Gothic flamboyance of the 14th century. Augustus Welby Pugin, designer of churches and of the decorative details in the Houses of Parliament, was a leader of the Gothic revival. At Scarisbrick he applied church design to a house.

EDWARDIAN *Pasture House, North Luffenham, Leics., 1901.* Designed by Charles Voysey, this is a balance between the highly decorative side of the Victorians' medieval revival and the uncompromising simplicity and rejection of ornament of the modern movement. It was a forerunner of today's house design.

The inspiration of the Cross

Irish missionaries are believed to have inspired the erection of the first crosses in Wales and the West of England in the 6th century. More elaborate crosses, such as this at Carew, Pembroke, were sculpted and erected between the 9th and 12th centuries.

Market crosses at Swaffham, Norfolk, and Chichester, W. Sussex

Before the Norman Conquest village crosses had already become centres for a weekly market. By the 13th century some of these crosses were covered by weather-proof canopies – the forerunners of the elaborate market crosses which were built from about the 16th century.

The Great Cross of Conbelin at Margam, West Glamorgan, is one of the finest examples of a 'wheel' cross. The central column is missing.

Cathedrals and churches

For more than a thousand years the building of a church has given each age the opportunity to express its art, craftsmanship and deepest spiritual feeling. Soaring columns, sky-reaching spires and simple stone fonts are all monuments to the aspirations of our ancestors. The exuberance of one age and the simplicity of another are found in cathedrals and parish churches.

SAXON *Sompting, W. Sussex, 11th century.* Rough stone, small windows and a 'German helm' roof – a pyramid cap to the tower – typify Saxon churches.

NORMAN *Blyth, Nottinghamshire, 1088.* Normans used cut stone for their massive pillars, which carried round arches between the nave and the aisles. The tops of doorways and windows were also rounded.

EARLY ENGLISH GOTHIC *Salisbury Cathedral, 1220–58.* Narrow lancet windows, pinnacles and pointed arches all combine to give the effect of the building soaring upwards. The spire is 14th century.

DECORATED GOTHIC *Heckington, Lincolnshire, c. 1330.* Similar in style to Salisbury Cathedral, except that the windows are wider to take in tracery – elaborate patterns in stone.

PERPENDICULAR GOTHIC *Lavenham, Suffolk, 1486–1525.* Wealth from the wool trade helped to build lavish churches, like this. The squared-off top to the tower is a 15th-century style.

STUART *St Mary-le-Bow, London, 1670.* Few churches were built between the Reformation in the 16th century and the Great Fire of London in 1666. Sir Christopher Wren then designed a large number of churches for the City of London, including St Mary-le-Bow. The naves were large to accommodate the huge congregations, who regarded sermons as a form of intellectual entertainment.

Clues that help to date a church

Norman, 11th–12th c

Tudor fan vaulting, 15th c

Early English, 13th c

The type of vaulting, the shape of doors and windows and the design of a pulpit or a font all help to give clues to the age of a church and to changes and additions made over the centuries.

QUEEN ANNE *St Philip's Cathedral, Birmingham, 1709–25*. An example of the Baroque, a florid style popular in the 18th century, which included scrolls, oriel windows, domes and columns.

GEORGIAN *Blandford, Dorset, 1730*. The design in Georgian churches is more restrained than that of Queen Anne's time. Classical columns and balustrades are typical of the period.

REGENCY *St Pancras Church, London, 1819*. Ideas from ancient Greece and the Gothic period were introduced in the early 19th century. Galleries were a feature of the interior, and cast iron was sometimes used for patterned window tracery.

VICTORIAN *Keble College Chapel, Oxford, 1873–6*. Victorian architects turned to Italian, French and English Gothic and to Byzantine styles for their churches. William Butterfield mingled the features of English stone buildings with Italian red-brick patterns in his design of this chapel.

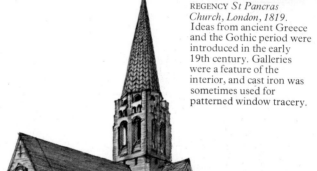

EDWARDIAN *St Jude's, Hampstead Garden Suburb, 1908*. One of Sir Edwin Lutyens' forward-looking buildings, with clean unbroken lines. Only a curved gable and mouldings recall elaborate details of the past.

SAXON 7TH–10TH CENTURY. The stone was roughly cut and the windows were narrow.

NORMAN 11TH–12TH CENTURY. Arches were rounded and stone was trimmed.

PERPENDICULAR 14TH–16TH CENTURY. The motif on the column of the font echoes the style of the church windows and arches.

MODERN *Coventry Cathedral, 1951–62*. Sir Basil Spence rejects superfluous decoration and exploits the use of concrete, sandstone, steel and huge vertical sheets of clear glass.

Bridges and viaducts

The main purpose of a bridge is to allow people to cross a river or chasm – but bridges have played a larger role than that in man's development. They have often given birth to towns. Settlements grew round early bridges, and garrisons had to defend them. Their story is still unfolding, since with new materials and techniques they grow ever longer and wider.

MEDIEVAL *Staverton, Devon, 1413.* Carts were unreliable on bad medieval roads, so horses carried goods. Packhorse bridges such as this had recesses for pedestrians when the horses passed.

GEORGIAN *Wilton House, Wiltshire, 1736.* Three stout arches support this bridge, but the elaborate ornamentation, in the manner of the Italian architect Palladio, was added only to complement the design of the house.

IRON BRIDGE *Coalbrookdale, Shropshire, 1779.* New casting and engineering techniques enabled the world's first iron bridge to be built, but the design was still that of a stone bridge.

SUSPENSION *Clifton Bridge, Bristol, 1836.* Isambard Kingdom Brunel drew the original design, which showed a revolutionary change. Visually, Brunel had turned the conventional arch upside-down.

RAILWAY VIADUCT *Digswell, Hertfordshire, 1850.* Designed by Lewis Cubitt to carry the Great Northern Railway over the Mimram Valley, it is of the same form and material – brick – as Roman aqueducts.

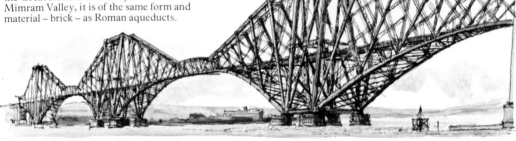

CANTILEVER *Forth Railway Bridge, 1883–90.* In a cantilever bridge the main support is in the centre of the span, whereas with a true arch the two halves get support by leaning against each other.

MODERN SUSPENSION *Severn Bridge, 1965.* The principle is the same as for the Clifton Bridge, but this central span is 3240 ft. That of the Humber Bridge, completed in 1980, is 3464 ft and is the longest in the world.

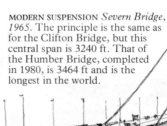

BASCULE *Tower Bridge, London, 1894.* The bascules, carrying a road, can be raised like a draw-bridge to allow ships to pass.

INN SIGNS

The stories behind their names

Inns signs are an illustrated guide to the history of Britain. In the early Middle Ages, when few people could read, an ale-house keeper put up a distinctive symbol – a stag, a white hart or some other animal, for instance. Often the name of the inn advertised entertainment found there, such as cockfighting. Others were named after great events or eminent people. Kings and outlaws, courtiers and courtesans, bishops and Puritans therefore take their place on the signs outside Britain's 70,000 public houses. Here too is a pageant of social history from the Thatchers' Arms and Barley Mow of pastoral England, to the Miners' Arms and Furnace of the Industrial Revolution and on to the Air Hostess and the Propeller of today.

The First Sign

The trading sign for a wine bar in ancient Rome was a bunch of vine leaves. The Romans brought the custom to Britain and hung a bush outside 'inns'. The names Bush, and Bull and Bush, survive.

Mitre

HEREFORD BULL

The religious influence in the first residential inns

Religious houses opened the first residential inns as hostels for pilgrims in the 12th century. After the Dissolution of the Monasteries in the 16th century some religious names of these hostelries, such as the Mitre, survived. A sign of the Ship denotes the Ark, while the Anchor refers to the Christian faith. The Bull may be derived from bulla, the Latin for a monastery seal.

SARACEN'S HEAD

Echoes of the Crusades

At the end of the 12th century inns were built for a new kind of traveller – the knight on his way to fight under Richard I in the Third Crusade. Echoes of the campaign to free the Holy Land from Islam are found in signs such as the Trip to Jerusalem, the Saracen's Head, the Turk's Head, the Blackamoor's Head and the Lamb and Flag. The lamb represented Christ and the flag the cross of the Crusaders. The Gentil Knyght and the White Knight, which is sometimes illustrated as a chess piece, are also inn names dating back to the Crusades.

THE LAMB & FLAG

I Rule For ALL   I Pray For ALL   I Plead For ALL   I Fight For ALL   I Work For ALL

I Govern All   I Fight for All

I Pray for All   I Pay for All

The five alls and four alls

The signs of the Five Alls or Four Alls have both the themes of monarchy (the king who rules all) and religion (the parson who prays for all). Various characters are added such as John Bull who pays for all, the lawyer who pleads for all, the labourer who works for all and the Devil who takes all.

Kings and their battles

After the Dissolution of the Monasteries, the hostelries belonging to religious houses became secular houses. Many changed their titles, adopting names such as the Crown or using a royal device such as the Rising Sun, taken from the badge of Edward III. Inns called the Pope's Head were rapidly changed to the King's Head. Henry VIII, who ordered the Dissolution, is the monarch most frequently shown on inn signs. The next most popular is Elizabeth I. The many Royal Oak signs recall an incident after the Battle of Worcester in 1651, when Charles II escaped by hiding in an oak. Among battles giving their names to inns is Sedgemoor, where James II's army crushed a rebellion by the Duke of Monmouth in 1685.

Heraldic birds and animals

While some inns took the names of monarchs others, such as the Royal Standard, used either all or part of the royal coat of arms. Black, blue, red, green, golden and white lions have appeared on royal badges since the Conquest. A greyhound was on the arms of the Tudors. A unicorn, which figured on the arms of Scottish Kings, was introduced after the union between England and Scotland, and a white horse was on the coat of arms of the Hanoverians. The arms of great families were also used on signs. Sometimes the inns were on their land or old retainers would open an inn and name it after them. In the north are many signs of the Eagle and Child (right), which comes from the crest of the Earls of Derby. The Talbot, a breed of hound now extinct, usually derives from the arms of the Earls of Shrewsbury. The Bear and Staff, Bear and Ragged Staff or Bear and Baculus, all come from the crest of the Earls of Warwick.

Tributes to the famous and infamous

Many inns are named after personalities who have caught the public imagination. Some have been heroes such as Nelson, highwaymen like Dick Turpin or courtesans like Nell Gwynn, a mistress of Charles II. But of all the heroes the Marquis of Granby takes a special place. At the Battle of Warburg in 1760 he was leading a bravely impetuous cavalry charge against the French when his wig blew off – an incident from which comes the saying 'going for it bald-headed'. After the war he set up his disabled non-commissioned officers as publicans in inns from Surrey to Derbyshire. They gratefully named these inns after him – but the gesture ruined the marquis and he died leaving debts of £37,000.

High on the gallows

In the 17th and 18th centuries signs became more elaborate, and some even stretched across the street. One carved from wood and erected outside The White Hart, at Scole, Norfolk (illustrated right) cost £1000. Early in the 18th century a gallows sign in London pulled down the front of a building killing two people. In 1795 a law ordered that dangerous signs be dismantled, leaving only lightweight signs as at The Magpie, at Stoneham, Suffolk (below).

From the stagecoach to a moon rocket

In the 18th century many signs indicated the form of transport travellers could take from the inn, such as the Coach and Horses and the Chaise and Pair, or showed that there was stabling, such as the Horse and Groom. Other inns were named after stagecoach services that stopped there – services romantically named the Glocester Flying Machine, Dairymaid and Flying Bull. When the railways arrived the names given to the inns were less inspired. Many were called the Station or the Railway. It was not until the steam age was ending that inn signs nostalgically recalled names of famous engines such as the Puffing Billy, and Royal Scot. Now signwriters are looking to the Space Age. One of their first: Man on the Moon.

Signs of a trade

The cordwainers, the whitesmiths and the flintknappers all had their favourite local inns. Now these craft names are recalled only on inn signs. Cordwainers were shoe-makers, whitesmiths were tin-smiths, while flintknappers pre-pared flint for muzzle-loading guns. Their arms and those of other craftsmen such as saddlers and plaisterers (or plasterers) appeared either because their society met at the inn, or because a landlord was trying to attract their custom.

Inns for the sportsman

In the past an inn sign often advertised the kind of savage 'sport' that could be found there. The Bear recalls bear-baiting, in which dogs were set on a tethered bear. Near inns called the Dog and Duck, dogs raced across a pond to be first to reach a pinioned duck. Cockfighting took place at any inn called the Cock, and falconry was a favourite sport at the Bird in Hand. Signs depicting ball games came later. An early one was the Mall, in London, where Charles II played Pall Mall, a form of croquet.

Odd names and touches of rustic humour

Some inns have names that are not what they seem. The Pig and Whistle, for example, is believed to have been adapted from the Saxon 'piggen' (pail) and 'wassail' (be in good health). When the ale was served in the pails, drinkers dipped in their mugs and gave the wassail toast. Another sign which means more than it says is the Intrepid Fox. Although a fox is often illustrated on the sign this refers to the nickname of the 18th-century politician Charles James Fox. In Steven-age, Hertfordshire, The Twin Foxes recall two local twins, Ebenezer Albert Fox and Albert Ebenezer Fox, who were notorious poachers at the beginning of the century. Often punsters have also left their villages with such signs as the Drop Inn, the Nog Inn and the Wych Way Inn. Macabre signs include the Quiet Woman or the Good Woman, who is always headless.

AIRPORTS AND AIRCRAFT

Watching jet airliners come and go

Any of Britain's major airports is worth a visit for the excitement that is a built-in part of air travel. Each airport has car parks, restaurants and a place where spectators can watch planes land and take off.

London's Heathrow has been taken as a typical example of a major airport on these pages, because any type of large civil aircraft likely to be seen anywhere in Britain will pass through Heathrow at some time.

It is used by more passengers than the rest of

Britain's airports put together. On it converge 73 airlines from almost as many countries, carrying nearly 24 million passengers and 418,000 tons of freight a year. The airport employs more than 52,000 people.

Accommodation is provided in the Queen's Building between Terminals 1 and 2 for people interested only in watching the hustle and bustle of the airport. A roof garden overlooks the main runways, and there are bars, refreshment rooms, a restaurant and shops.

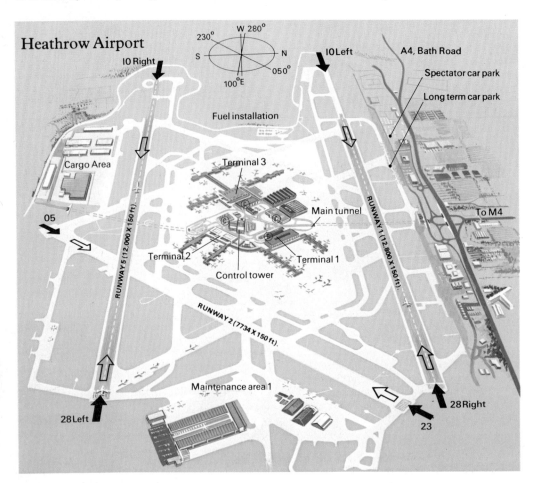

TERMINAL 1 houses UK domestic services, short-haul international services of British airlines, and Aer Lingus. It is designed to handle 5000 passengers an hour.

TERMINAL 2 handles passengers of foreign airlines on short-haul (up to about 1500 miles), and is used by 28 European and Middle Eastern airlines.

TERMINAL 3 is the base for long-haul inter-continental flights to India, Africa, North and South America and the Far East, and is used by 39 airlines.

 Direction of landing  Direction of take-off   Ⓒ Car parks

The runway chosen for take-offs and landings is governed by the direction of the wind and the need to give people living on the flight paths a rest from the noise. Aircraft must land and take off into the wind. If the wind is westerly at Heathrow they will be instructed to land on Runway 28 Left or take off on a parallel runway known as 28 Right. After a few hours this sequence is reversed so that planes approaching

and landing change flight paths. In an easterly wind aircraft land and take off from the opposite ends of the same runways which are then named 10 Right and 10 Left. The runway numbers are abbreviations of the compass bearings—Runway 28 for 280 degrees and Runway 10 for 100 degrees (see diagram above). A third Runway 23 is used into a south-westerly wind and the reverse Runway 05 into a north-easterly.

Some aircraft to be seen at a big airport

More than 30 different types of aircraft use London Airport. A number of the most common are shown below in the colours of the major airlines which use them. The world's largest aircraft—the Boeing Jumbo jet—has two versions, the 747A and 747B. Both are 231 ft long with a wingspan of 195 ft—the difference is mainly in the interior design. The planes can be identified by the number of windows behind the flight deck. The 747A has three on each side, and the 747B eight.

HS 125 British-made light executive plane, carrying up to 14 passengers. Its twin Rolls Royce Viper turbojet engines produce cruising speeds of 450–510 mph.

FALCON 10 French-made twin-engined light executive plane, carrying up to 9 passengers with a cruising speed of 527 mph.

BAC ONE-ELEVEN British-made, short-to-medium-range plane, carrying up to 89 passengers. Its two Rolls Royce Spey engines give cruising speeds of 507–548 mph.

BAC SUPER VC10 (in East African Airways colours). British-made long-range aircraft carrying up to 126 passengers. With four Rolls Royce Conway engines it cruises at 550 mph.

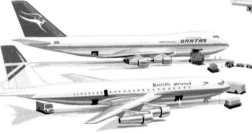

BOEING 707 American-made long-range (5000 miles) aircraft carrying up to 162 passengers. Normal cruising speed 540 mph. Behind, to emphasise the difference in size, is its big brother, the Boeing 747 Jumbo jet which carries up to 490 passengers.

DOUGLAS DC 10 A three-engined, American-made, short-to-medium-range plane carrying up to 332 passengers. Cruising speed 520–540 mph.

AIRBUS Twin-engined, made by a consortium of five European countries, short-to-medium range, 200 to 300 passengers. Cruising speed 582 mph.

HS TRIDENT British-made, triple-engined short-to-medium-range plane, carrying up to 152 passengers. Cruising speed 600 mph.

LOCKHEED TRISTAR American-made, short-to-medium-range plane, with three Rolls Royce engines, carrying up to 400 passengers. Cruising speed 590 mph.

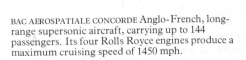

BOEING 747 American-made, long-range plane, carrying 374 to 490 passengers. The 340 ton Jumbo jet is the biggest passenger plane in the world, cruising at up to 608 mph.

BAC AEROSPATIALE CONCORDE Anglo-French, long-range supersonic aircraft, carrying up to 144 passengers. Its four Rolls Royce engines produce a maximum cruising speed of 1450 mph.

ACKNOWLEDGMENTS

The publishers express their gratitude for major contributions from the following:

AUTHORS

Kenneth Beckett Dr George P. Black C. D. Brandreth
Professor T. J. Chandler, MSC, PHD John Clark David Corke, BSC
Andrew Dalby Eric R. Delderfield Roger Dixon F. W. Dunning, BSC, FGS
Edward Fletcher Eric Fernie Jennifer J. George Christopher Hall
Dr Colin Harrison Harry Heywood B. J. Hurren William Inglis Reginald Lester
Alfred Leutscher, BSC Stephen Lock, MA, MB, MRCP Alan Mattingley
Dr Michael Max John Miles Franklyn Perring, MA, PHD, FLS
Julian Plowright Dr A. L. Rice Dr Roger Snook Dr John Taylor
Mrs K. Way Ralph Whitlock

ARTISTS

Norman Barber Broadway Arts Ltd David Carl Forbes Patricia Casey
Roy Castle Michael Davidson Richard Downer, MSIA, MSTD Ian Garrard
Robin Harris, LSIA, FRSA Derek Hogg Norman Lacey, MISTC
Peter McGinn, DA(EDIN.) Cecil Misstear Associates David Nockels Richard Orr
Pat Oxenham Gillian Platt Adrian Purkis, LSIA Brian Watson

Many other people, organisations and firms assisted in the preparation of this book, and the publishers acknowledge the help of the following:

Amateur Athletic Assoc.
British Airports Authority
British Gliding Assoc.
British Horse Society
British Inland Waterways
British Leyland
British Rail
British Tourist Authority
British Waterways Board
Bruton Photography Ltd
Civil Aviation Authority
Countryside Commission
Department of Transport
Derbyshire County Council
Gaelic Athletic Assoc.
The Garden Studio
Rev R. G. Hall
Harrogate Public Library
Highland and Islands Development Board
Hurlingham Polo Assoc.
Institute of Geological Sciences
Irish Tourist Board
Irish Youth Hostel Assoc.
Lawn Tennis Assoc.
Linden Artists
Joseph Lucas Ltd
Lutra Consultants Ltd

Neil MacGregor
Fiona McKenzie
Massey Ferguson (United Kingdom)
National Air Traffic Services
National Farmers' Union
National Greyhound Racing Club Ltd
Natural History Museum
National Trust
Norfolk Lavender Ltd
Norfolk Naturalists Trust
Norwich Museum
Charles A. Oxley
Racecourse Assoc.
Royal Society for the Protection of Birds
Royal Yachting Assoc.
Prof. R. Scorer
Scottish Nature Conservancy
Scottish Tourist Board
Scottish Wildlife Trust
Scottish Youth Hostels Assoc.
Spalding Farmers' Union
Summit Art Studios Ltd
The Golfer's Handbook
Whitbread Flowers Ltd
Wisden
Youth Hostel Assoc.

Cartographers: Clyde Surveys Ltd, Maidenhead

Edited and designed by The Reader's Digest Association Limited, 25 Berkeley Square, London W1X 6AB
Published in collaboration with The Automobile Association, Fanum House, Basingstoke, Hants RG21 2EA

Third Edition Copyright © 1980 The Reader's Digest Association Limited

Reprinted with amendments, 1981

® READER'S DIGEST is a registered trademark of The Reader's Digest Association, Inc.
of Pleasantville, New York, U.S.A.

Printed in Great Britain

Paper, printing and binding by:
Balamundi Nederland NV, Holland; C. R. Barber & Partners, London; John Bartholomew & Son Ltd, Edinburgh;
Brown Knight & Truscott Ltd, Tonbridge; Sir Joseph Causton & Sons Ltd, Eastleigh; Hazell Watson & Viney Ltd, Aylesbury;
Ben Johnson & Co. Ltd, York; Litra Machine Plates Ltd, Edenbridge; Typesetting Services Ltd, Glasgow;
Yates Duxbury & Sons Ltd, Bury

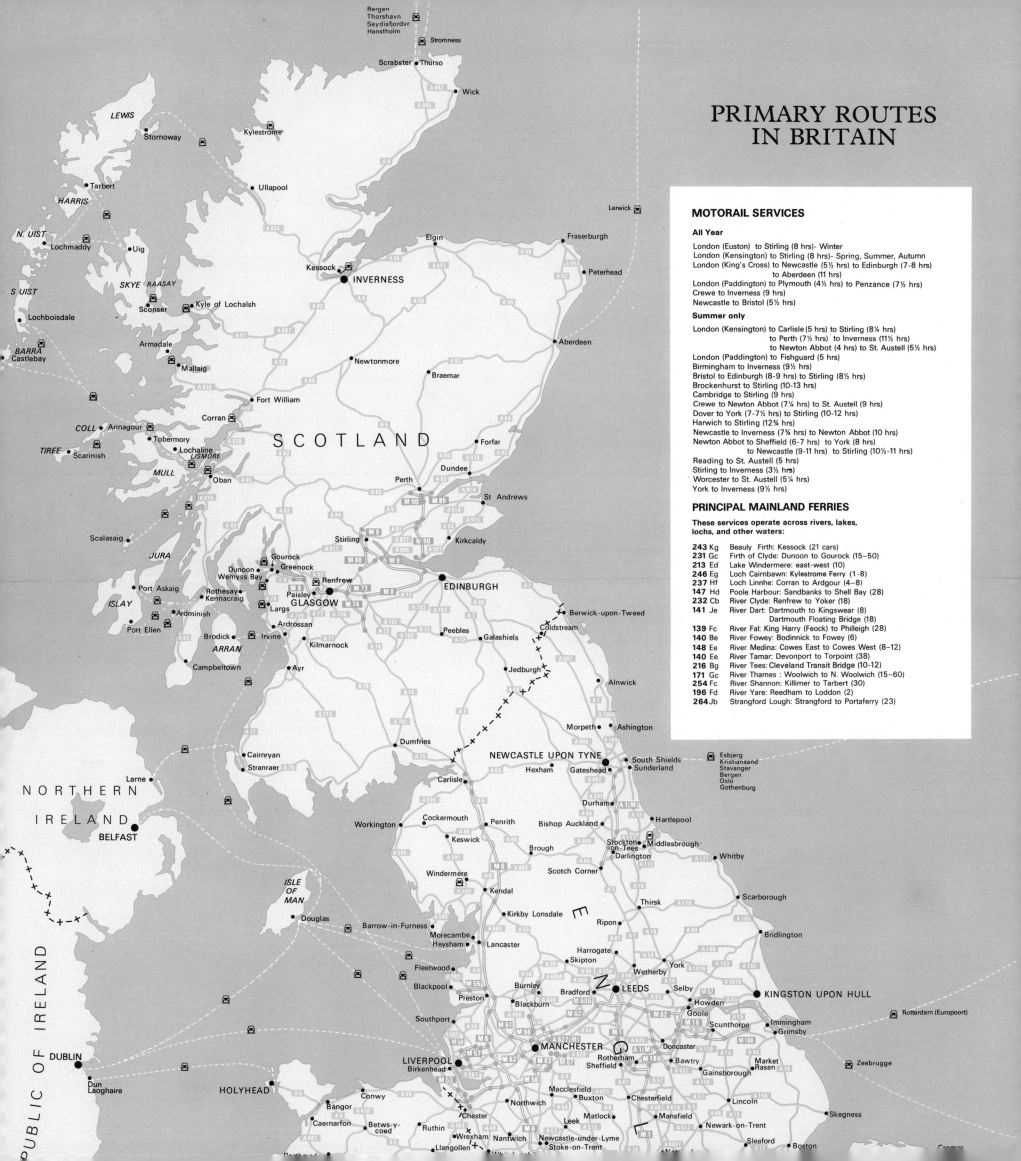

MAJOR ROUTES IN IRELAND

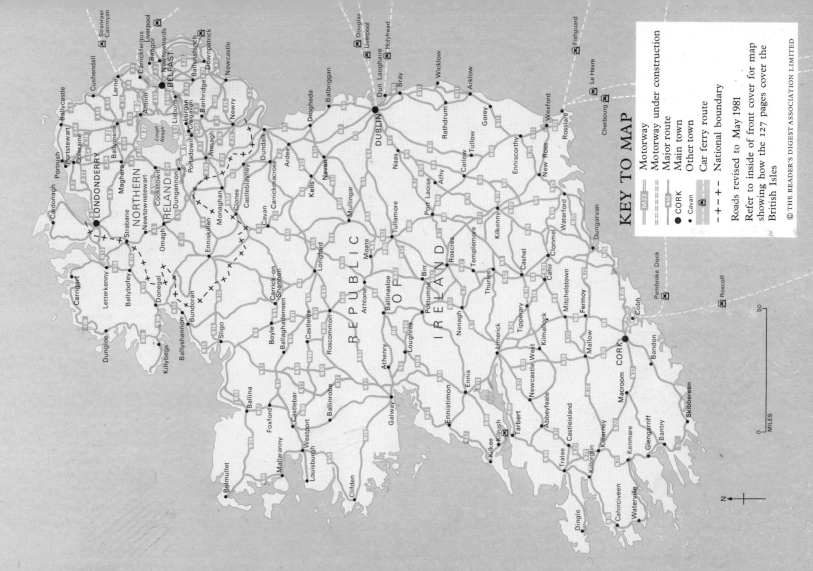

DISTANCES IN BRITAIN AND IRELAND

The mileage charts for Britain and Ireland can be used to calculate the shortest distance on main routes between the selected towns. The towns have been chosen on the basis of their key position in the overall route network and have all been shown on the adjacent route planning maps. Distances between other towns can be calculated from the maps on pages 137–264

KEY TO MAP

- Motorway
- Motorway under construction
- Major route
- Main town
- Other town
- National boundary
- CORK
- Cavan
- Car ferry route

Roads revised to May 1981
Refer to inside of front cover for map showing how the 127 pages cover the British Isles

MILES

N